Why do larger areas have more spec. sity so high near the Equator? Has the number of species grown during the past 600 million years? Does habitat diversity support species diversity, or is it the other way around? What reduces diversity in ecologically productive places? At what scales of space and time do diversity patterns hold? Do the mechanisms that produce them vary with scale?

Species diversity in space and time examines these questions and many others, the author employing both theory and data in his search for answers. Perhaps surprisingly, many of the questions have reasonably likely answers. By identifying these, attention can be turned towards life's many, still unexplained diversity patterns.

As evolutionary ecologists race to understand biodiversity before it is too late, this book will help set the agenda for diversity research into the next century.

Species diversity in space and time

Species diversity in space and time

Michael L. Rosenzweig

Professor
Department of Ecology and Evolutionary Biology
University of Arizona

&

Brittingham Fellow
Department of Zoology
University of Wisconsin

Published by the Press Syndicate of the University of Cambridge
The Pitt Building, Trumpington Street, Cambridge CB2 1RP
40 West 20th Street, New York, NY 10011-4211, USA
10 Stamford Road, Oakleigh, Melbourne 3166, Australia

First published 1995

Printed in Great Britain at the University Press, Cambridge

A catalogue record for this book is available from the British Library

Library of Congress cataloguing in publication data

Rosenzweig, Michael L.
Species diversity in space and time/Michael L. Rosenzweig.
p.   cm.
Includes bibliographical references and index.
ISBN 0 521 49618 7 (hc). – ISBN 0 521 49952 6 (pb)
1. Species diversity.   2. Biogeography.   I. Title.
QH541.15.S64R67 1995
574.5′24–dc20   94–43750   CIP

ISBN 0 521 49618 7 hardback
      0 521 49952 6 paperback

To the memory of my teacher,

ROBERT H. MACARTHUR

Hic situs est Phaëton
  currus auriga paterni
Quem si non tenuit
  magnis tamen excidit ausis.

                                    Ovid

Contents

Preface

People love a good dinosaur story. Surely, after all these years, the ecological question of the number of species ought to qualify as a dinosaur. Yet, no one has ever taken the trouble to write up the glory days of species diversity work, the era of the 1960s and 1970s.

It was a time of great excitement, of elegant theories and huge promise. Modern graduate students must be curious about it. Having played a small role in it myself, I decided to have a go at it. At least, I thought, I won't have to nag my graduate students to read **that** primary literature anymore; I'll give them a little map of it.

I'm not sure when I realized the dinosaur was still alive. There had been a stirring here and there as I poked over the old bones and fitted a few together into an occasional new sub-assembly. But then I heard a roaring. As if attracted by an improved portrait of its progenitors, a living being reared up and spat challenges. By the time I finished this book, the dinosaur was breathing honest fire. At first, only I could hear it; after you read the book, I hope you can too.

Having a living dinosaur to contend with, I had to change my original plan for the book. What I had envisioned as a six-month sabbatical diversion, became a four-year obsession. The book took on a combination of duties.

- Its first function – no, its primary function – remains to tell today's students the story of species diversity in the voices that so delighted ecology in the 1960s and 1970s. Since I have students uppermost in my mind, I mention things, define things and explain things that established ecologists take for granted. I hope those of you who do not require discussion of such basic ideas as negative feedback will forgive me for taking the time to go over them in a book on species diversity.
- Its second is to bring out some things that have been locked up in the data all along, things that help us understand the diversity patterns around us.
- Its third points out the reasons for the successes of a quarter century ago, and thus encourages new students to emulate the kind

of thinking and analysis that led to them. Here again, I beg the indulgence of established ecologists.

- Its fourth is to present some novel analyses. These practically insisted to me that I do them when, to make text figures, I was loading old data into a modern, flexible computer graphics program (all credit to AXUM by Trimetrix, Seattle, Washington).

Thus, the book runs the gamut from history to textbook to monograph. Most of the work is not mine and not new, but some is both.

I will devote some of the text itself to the third function of the book – how to do diversity work. Look for it especially in the first and last chapters. However, I do want to mention five of the book's novelties here. That way you may be especially alert and critical when you notice them.

1. I have tried to combine scales of space and time. The most important consequence of that is the work on the species–area curve. From already published data, I was able to discern a set of nested relationships that carry this curve from scales of a hectare (and less) to those of the whole biosphere.

2. Until working on this book, I thought that Frank Preston's canonical log-normal analyses of species abundances gave us a solid understanding of species–area curves. Now, I believe that Preston's work explains only a fraction of what we see in nature. By the time you finish Chapter 9, I hope you agree with me that Preston just opened the door.

3. Looking at large spatio-temporal scales brought out a surprising conclusion. At the province-wide scale, the scale of evolutionary time, habitats are not causes, but effects. The more species, the more habitats. I've tried especially hard to make the reasons for that proposition clear. I think I did so because I myself was surprised by it and wanted to gain more confidence in it.

4. I also believe that area's effects at large scales are strong enough to cause latitudinal gradients, and I do not hedge in saying so. That does not mean they act alone in all cases. In fact, I suspect that variation in average productivity from latitude to latitude is another important part of the story. But I do not have enough evidence for that conclusion.

5. Wherever possible, I tried to investigate diversity with data from the fossil record. These data constitute a prime source of tests for our hypotheses, but neontological ecologists keep themselves too

distant from them. You will notice that there is no chapter headed
'Information from Paleobiology.' If there were, you might skip it.
Besides, that would not make my point. We need to learn about,
understand and integrate the information that comes from fossils.
We must use it side by side with modern data to help form our
hypotheses and test them.

Like most scientists, I write with difficulty or even pain. Audubon apparently was like the rest of us. He wrote the following gem to fellow ornithol-
ogist, J. Bachman, in 1834 (quoted by Alice Ford, 1957, *The Bird
Biographies of John James Audubon*, Macmillan, NY, pp. vii, viii):

> God...save you the trouble of ever publishing books on
> natural science... I would rather go without a
> shirt...through the whole of the Florida swamps in
> mosquito time than labor as I have...with the pen.

Today, however, we know that writing, at least science writing, is partly a
skill. And skills can be improved. The pain can be reduced.

If you have read anything I wrote more than a few years ago, you will
notice a marked change in my style. My writing talent still lies at the
abysmal end of the scale, but I did deliberately change my style. It may
startle you. It may even repel you. It will sound – if I have learned my
lessons – offhand, conversational, light and unstudied. You may marvel at
my gall in simply dictating a first draft and than abandoning it to the
printer.

The paragraphs are shorter. The sentences are shorter.

And the sentences sometimes start with 'but'. Paragraphs, too.

You will rarely find the passive voice. Short, common, even coarse
Germanic verbs abound at the expense of more delicate, refined Romance
verbs.

Except for the verb 'to be'. My masters have taught me to hate that verb
and to view it as an enemy of comprehension.

Though you may disapprove, you will understand what I write with less
trouble than before. This book presents enough difficulties. I did not want
to make it even harder to understand by using standard, 19th century, scientific, Prusso-Victorian prose. You would not have been amused.

In addition to hoping that you will get excited about the science in this
book, I hope you will enjoy reading it. We enjoy doing science; why should-
n't we enjoy reading it? Reading about the work we love ought not be an
unpleasant chore. If you want to write in simple prose yourself, you can.

Get a copy of a standard modern style book. I use Flesch (1974) and Gowers (1977) and Bernstein (1971). Many computer-based style-checking programs use these authorities too.

But be warned. Writing more clearly takes hard work. The more effortless it seems, the more effort it took. It all depends on whether you have something you want to say. If you do, you'll care to work hard to get it across.

Here's another warning. Clear writing brings a grave danger: **People may begin to understand you**! Then they will probably disagree with you. For example, if I have done my job, you will probably not agree with everything I wrote in this book. I am prepared for that. Not happy, but resigned. Science works that way. I'll give you ten years to change your mind. But then, I may have changed mine.

Meanwhile, I've signed the book. So, you know just where to take any disagreements. Fuzzing up my conclusions in hedge words would obfuscate them. Hedges are for hiding things. I want to be exposed. I want you to argue about and improve my conclusions. I don't want you to wonder what they are.

Papers about species diversity – particularly most of those from the 1980s and 1990s – rarely reach conclusions. They perpetuate controversies. They list as many published hypotheses as they can find, and generally conclude with a call for more research. Hang on, folks! Do you believe that science boils down to a continual poll on an ever-lengthening questionnaire? I have tried to include various sides of controversies if I believe they should still be mined. But there's no sense perpetuating old, well-investigated controversies when we've plenty of new ones. There's plenty of reason to call for more research without insisting we've learned nothing so far.

Besides, why would anybody want to give us more support if we never reach any conclusions? Published papers count as end products only in academia, not the real world. The real world wants conclusions from us, even if they are provisional. Nevertheless, I feel certain the book will be criticized for omitting some hypotheses. I just hope that few are ones I am ignorant of.

I honestly do believe the study of species diversity overflows with results. Not trivial ones, either. We must learn to admit it. Our science has produced fundamental conclusions that bear on great issues of environmental quality and conservation. Please don't think that if we admit it, the world will decide our work is done, and cut us off. On the contrary, it will say hurrah and onward!

Yet, 'life speaks with a voice ... that brings you answers to the questions you continually ask of it (Adams, 1985, p. 98).' Ecological research, in particular, takes patience. Consider the long, multi-laboratory investigations that this book summarizes. They bear witness that good ecology takes a long time. Lots of clues suggest that ecologists know that. For one thing, they say it a lot. Also, they establish long-term ecological research programs. Nevertheless, we ecologists can be terribly faddish.

A typical fad seems to follow a five to ten year course. First, someone comes up with a novel and attractive way to organize a variety of research projects. That someone may be a theoretician, as in the case of optimal foraging. Or the someone may be an empiricist, as in plant–animal interactions. The idea smolders for a year or two and then bursts into flame. Proposals get written, and a few get funded. The fire becomes a conflagration. Almost nothing else gets talked about. Projects generate some data and statistical analyses. Then it is over. We go on to the next hot question and pretend either that the old one got settled, or failed to help us enough.

I have seen that scenario in action many times during the past three decades. For instance, ten years ago, plant–animal interactions got declared passé. Yes. And that, despite the potential invigoration of a stimulating paper by one of its originators (Rhoades, 1985). I guess everyone had expected all the original hypotheses to be either perfectly right or totally wrong. Of course, the initial results disappointed them. And then they showed their real interest in the question by abandoning it at the first sign of scientific reality.

Optimal foraging fared no better. Here is a fundamental research program (Mitchell and Valone, 1990) originally suggested by no less than Charles Elton (1927). It is linking up behavior, natural selection and ecology. Yet, its critics, taking no time to understand its mathematical substance, and confusing 'optimal' with 'perfect', consider it dead because ... Well, I really don't know why they think it is dead. Students of optimality know that 'constraints' prevent perfect outcomes in the real world. But 'constraints' are not foreign to optimality theory. They form one of its central features. Optimalists know that, work with it, and have produced some of the most exciting ecology of the 1980s by sticking to their rusty old guns. I depend heavily on their results in Chapter 7.

Yes, ecology really does take a long time to do. Discerning the patterns takes a long time. Testing hypotheses takes a long time. And going through the process repeatedly takes a long time. But if the question is weighty, like 'How many species should there be?', the time will be well spent. And if it is not, perhaps we should just ignore it in the first place.

I wish I could start the acknowledgements now. If I could, I would begin by thanking my teacher, the late Robert H. MacArthur. This book is an extension of his work. That's the meaning of the dedication: 'Here lies Phaeton, driver of his father's chariot. If he did not handle it, at least he fell in a great enterprise.' This book is *MacArthur's Chariot*. If it were a novel, that's what I would have called it.

Two friends, respected reviewers of the manuscript, wondered about the dedication and my obvious admiration for the work that Robert MacArthur did. I am sorry I made them uncomfortable, but I have not diluted my praise. He earned the praise. And I believe I have earned the right to praise him. I am his student, for one thing, and I come from a culture in which students praise their teachers. In addition, I am hardly the apostle type. When it needed it, I have criticized his work (Schroder and Rosenzweig, 1975). And I did it when others were scraping and bowing. MacArthur set the course for much of what good ecologists still do, and the time has come to admit it.

But MacArthur knew that he was part of a cooperating army, and I do not want to leave you with the impression that we should all have retired when he stopped working. Most of the work reported in this book came after his death. In particular, many scientists helped me in my efforts. Quite a few let me use their valuable data. These include Ian Abbott, Sara and Peter Bretsky, Richard Cowling, Bill Mitchell, Jim Owen, Kasimir Patalas, Carsten Rahbek, Konstantin Rogovin, Jeffery A. Smallwood, Max Specht, Elizabeth Sandlin and David Western. Paul A. Johnson, Laurie Oksanen, Tom Nudds, Wayte Thomas, Bruce Walsh and Tom Whitham showed me crucial unpublished works and let me incorporate them.

The work with Colin Clark was done especially for the book, and I was lost before he showed me the way. Phil Rutter took a valuable day and spent it giving me a field seminar on the American Chestnut. Ian Abbott and Norm McKenzie guided my wanderings in Western Australia and saw to it – though it was mid-winter – that I learned something about that special corner of a spectacular continent. Verne Grant helped me get the polyploid data for Chapters 2 and 11. Bill Heed discussed some of the recent papers on Hawaiian *Drosophila* with me. Peter Yodzis and John Moore led me to understand and appreciate their views of food webs. Greg Adler sorted through his work on birds of tropical archipelagos and gave me an unbiased, informed opinion on which species are endemics. Bert Leigh rescued me from some of my mistakes about tropical plant productivity. Rich Strauss gave me a copy of a digitization program he had written, and taught me how to use it. Rob Robichaux tutored me in the fundamentals of how plant cells respond to variation in light regimes; I hope my rendition in Chapter 7 does not embarrass him. Suggestions from Bob Baker, Ted Fleming, Paul Hebert, Len Milich, Jane Lubchenco, Bob Ricklefs, Bill Schaffer, Don Thomson, Larry Venable, Geraat Vermeij and Pat Webber all added immensely to the book. Michael Canning helped with technical support.

Three hapless groups of guinea pigs (two at Arizona and one at Wisconsin) suffered through trial runs of the course that tested material for this book. One even had to beta-test a flawed preliminary version. They were brave and mostly uncomplaining. I hope their experiences had a positive side.

But Carole Rosenzweig had more to complain about than anyone else. Oy vey, it's not always a joy being married to a zealot. I'll try to find ways to make it up.

Others who suffered include my coauthors on several hibernating papers: Zvika Abramsky, Dick Braithwaite, Goggy Davidowitz, Wade Leitner, Marc Mangel, Debby Rosko, Gareth Russell, Elizabeth Sandlin, Moshe Shahak, Susan Wethington. Please excuse me. I have always been too single-minded.

Stuart Pimm deserves some of the credit for the very existence of this book. Talk about single-minded! After I edited his first book, he spent eight years telling me that now it was my turn to write one. OK, already.

The friends who did me the signal honor of actually reading and commenting on the manuscript have my sincerest gratitude. I know they aren't likely to have the stomach to reread the book and see how much I valued and used their advice. But they were the key. I could not have completed the project without their help and encouragement. Ian Abbott, Zvika Abramsky, Eric Charnov, Andy Cohen, Alan Crowden, Mike Kaspari, Mark Lomolino, Stuart Pimm, Art Shapiro, Larry Slobodkin and Yaron Ziv, I love you all. You straightened me up with deep and fair criticism. You picked my nits. You bucked me up when I felt I'd failed. I tried my best to learn from what you said. Please forgive my obstinacy and pity my denseness.

Mrs Jane Bulleid did an extraordinary job editing the ms. for Cambridge University Press. She was quick, and unbelievably perceptive. And she brought her knowledge of the biology to help me correct some of my mistakes. The ones that remain are just more examples of my obstinacy.

Chapter 12 and some of Chapter 2 was written for this book, but also contributed to Schluter and Ricklefs (1993) with the understanding that it would appear here. I thank the editors for their willingness to follow that plan and for the great work they themselves accomplished in their own book. For a similar courtesy, I also thank the *Journal of Mammalogy*, in particular, Bob Baker, Mike Mares and Jim Brown. A preview of part of Chapters 7 and 9 appeared in their pages (Rosenzweig, 1992).

Owing to a production oversight, the first printing of Schluter and Ricklefs (1993) did not contain its acknowledgements section. Here are mine and Zvika Abramsky's (they will also appear in future reprintings of Schluter and Ricklefs):

We thank Bob Ricklefs, Dolph Schluter and David Wright for their careful and valuable comments. David Jablonski encouraged us to dig out the fossil patterns, and Martin Lockley helped us interpret his important paper. Jim Brown, Mike Mares, Peter Meserve and Bruce Patterson all helped with the New World mammal patterns. Dick Braithwaite, Carsten Rahbeck and Avi Shmida were generous in allowing us to use their data.

NSF grant BSR-8905728, a Brittingham Fellowship in zoology at the University of Wisconsin–Madison, and Warren Porter's DOE grant DE-FG02-88ER60633 thru OHER supported the research and writing. I am particularly grateful for the sabbatical hospitality of Warren Porter and the Zoology Department of the University of Wisconsin–Madison.

To a mouse

On turning her up in her nest with the plough, November 1785

1

Wee, sleekit, cowrin, tim'rous beastie
O, what a panic's in thy breastie!
Thou need na start awa sae hasty,
Wi' bickering brattle!
I wad be laith to rin an' chase thee,
Wi' murd'ring pattle!

2

I'm truly sorry man's dominion,
Has broken nature's social union,
An' justifies that ill opinion,
Which makes thee startle
At me, thy poor, earth-born companion,
An' fellow-mortal!

3

I doubt na, whiles, but thou may thieve;
What then? poor beastie, thou maun live!
A daimen icker in a thrave
'S a sma' request;
I'll get a blessin' wi' the lave,
An' never miss't!

4

Thy wee bit housie, too, in ruin!
It's silly wa's the win's are strewin!
An' naething, now, to big a new ane,
O' foggage green!
An' bleak December's winds ensuin,
Baith snell an' keen!

5

Thou saw the fields laid bare an' waste,
An' weary winter comin fast,
An' cozie here, beneath the blast,
Thou thought to dwell —
Till crash! the cruel coulter past
Out thro' thy cell.

6

That wee bit heap o' leaves an' stibble,
Has cost thee many a weary nibble!
Now thou's turn'd out for a' thy trouble,
But house or hald,
To thole the winter's sleety dribble,
An' cranreuch cauld!

7

But Mousie, thou art no thy lane,
In proving foresight may be vain;
The best-laid schemes o' mice an' men
Gang aft agley,
An' lea'e us nought but grief an' pain
For promis'd joy!

8

Still thou art blest, compar'd wi' me:
The present only toucheth thee:
But och! I backward cast my e'e,
On prospects drear,
An' forward, tho' I canna see,
I guess an' fear!

Robert Burns

Glossary: *agley:* askew; *bicker:* move with a rapidly repeated noise; *brattle:* noisy rush; *coulter:* plow; *cranreuch:* hoarfrost; *daimen:* occasional: *foggage:* pasture; *icker:* ear of grain; *lave:* remainder; *maun:* must; *pattle:* spade; *snell:* fast; *thole:* endure; *thrave:* bundle; *whiles:* at times.

The scottish spelling and pronunciation I lae'e to thee.

Chapter 1

The road ahead

How many rooms in Noah's Ark?

Noah, the first appointed steward of life on Earth, would have been proud of Robert Burns' passionate concern for a humble harvest mouse. But even Burns, living as he did in the Age of Enlightenment, could not have suspected the ominous truth of his poem's last line. We have indeed done dreary things to our splendid world. And we are coming to understand the future terrible cost of our greed and our selfishness.

I believe that the more reasonable our fears, the more potent our voice will be. So this book explores what we know about the science of species diversity.

Steward or not, no one could spend much time working on the mechanics of diversity without being fascinated by it for its own sake. You are about to invest some of your own time in such an effort, so I guess you share that fascination with me. Welcome.

What is it that concerns us? Just how miraculous (or, if you prefer, incredible) is it that Noah got all the world's species onto one boat?

A famous story circulates among biologists about an encounter between two famous intellectual foes. J.B.S. Haldane – a genius of evolutionary biology and a renowned public atheist – was seated next to the Archbishop of Canterbury at one of those formal British dinners known for their civility and sparkling conversation. God knows who put them together like that.

The archbishop broke the ice with a question. What do your studies tell you, professor, about the nature of the Creator?

Haldane's answer has echoed for decades: 'He must have an inordinate fondness for beetles.'

Indeed, generations of biologists have kept an unlovely little secret. The answer to the question, 'How many species?', is essentially the answer to the question, 'How many insect species?' There are but 4004 species of

mammals and about 9020 species of birds. There are 18 818 fish species
(Nelson, 1984). Roughly 255 000 species belong to the great plant taxon
Embryobionta (bryophytes to angiosperms) (Parker, 1982). And even the
most ardent champion of fungi (Hawksworth, 1991) proposes that we will
one day know of 1.6 million fungus species. (We now know fewer than
70 000.) But there are probably tens of millions of insect species. And a very
large fraction of these are beetles.

Stork (1988), relying on data of Collins, divides the 1.82 million species
named by the beginning of 1988 into a pie chart. At the time, insects comprised about 57% of all named species. Beetles comprised 25%. But, as
Stork points out, even those percentages don't do justice to the dominance
of insects on planet Earth. Most non-insects have probably been discovered
and described. Most insects never will be.

In the late 1970s, entomologists began to use knockdown insecticides to
collect insects from the canopy of tropical rainforests. Previously, we had
thought this layer of the forest to be rich, but we had no way to take reasonably inclusive samples in it. The knockdown methods use a fan to spray
insecticide up into the low canopy, or sideways within a layer of the
canopy. Or else they use the exhaust of a motor to fog it up to the very top.
The insects die and fall into collecting devices (Stork, 1988).

Using the knockdown method, Erwin (1982) electrified the ecological
world with his estimate of just how many insects do live in the tropical rainforest. Working in the Neotropics, Erwin fogged 19 individuals of a leguminous tree, *Luehea seemannii*, at different seasons. He collected 9000 beetles
belonging to more than 1200 beetle species. Let us pause briefly to emphasize that number. The rest of Erwin's estimate extrapolates from it, perhaps
accurately, perhaps not. But that number is data: 1200 species of beetle
from only 19 trees of one species. And, as Stork (1988) points out, Erwin
presents no evidence that his trees were running out of beetle species for
him to find. Even more work might have doubled, tripled or done who-
knows-what to the figure of 1200. But it could not have reduced that number. That's 1200 species of beetle from only 19 trees of one species.

Moreover, we believe such numbers may be ordinary. Stork (1988)
reports 2800 species of arthropods from the canopies of ten trees belonging
to five species in the Bornean rainforest. Kitching (personal communication) sampled the canopies of smaller, liana-free trees of Australia's tropical
Green Mountains; he found 465 beetle species among 2238 individuals.

Now come the extrapolations. Erwin estimates that 13.5% of those
beetles – about 162 species – live only on *Luehea seemannii*. Roughly 50 000

species of tree live in tropical rainforests around the world. So, if *Luehea seemannii* represents an average tropical tree, there must be about 8.1 million beetle species specializing on single species of tree.

Erwin now adds beetles that live on more than one tree species. He believes there are about 2.7 million of them. No one thinks that number will long stand as research information accumulates. Nevertheless, it is as good as any other estimate just now, and Erwin repeated it as recently as a carefully prepared symposium talk to the Sixth International Congress of Ecology (Manchester, August 1994). Thus he estimates about 10.8 million species of canopy beetles.

Now Erwin guesses that such beetles represent about 40% of all tropical arthropod species. This figure may be the most debatable in the string of estimates. Stork says that in Borneo, they make up only 22.9% – less in temperate forests. Yet, Erwin's figure has some merit. Stork's pie chart listed beetles at 25% of species and all insects at 57%. That is 25/57 or 44% of insects. Beetles constitute 36% or 37% of all arthropods in the chart. So Erwin may be close to the mark. In fact, the biggest potential error I can see might lead Erwin to an underestimate of diversity!

If beetles are 40% of tropical arthropod species, then about 27 million arthropod species live in the tropics. Add to that the estimated 3 million temperate species. Then about 30 million arthropod species live in the world today.

Most of the serious problems in Erwin's estimate seem to me to err on the side of caution. By supposing that two thirds of beetle species live in the canopy, Erwin may have produced an estimate that is too small by 10 million. Stork actually guesses the truth may be closer to a 50–50 split, i.e. about the same number of species live in each of the two layers. Then of course, we are talking about 40 million arthropod species. Remember, too, that Erwin shows us no reason to believe that *Luehea seemannii* was running out of beetles when he stopped sampling.

What could make Erwin's estimate too high? Suppose *Luehea seemannii* has an unusually large set of insect specialists. Suppose the average tropical tree has only 10 specialized insects to contribute to the total. Then the proper estimate of global arthropod diversity would drop below 10 million.

So we have to admit we cannot yet be sure how many species live in the world. Not even about the order of magnitude. Yet, 2 million are already in the bag. And even 100 million may not be unrealistic. You can read more about this controversy if it fascinates you (e.g. Gaston, 1991;

Hodkinson and Casson, 1991; Hammond, 1992; May, 1990). But Erwin contributed greatly by bringing it up in the first place. It's really not so important if better estimates show that his estimate of 30 million is off by a factor of five. Noah may have needed to know the exact truth, but the rest of us will simply have to admit, with Stork, that there are more insects than we can keep track of in all the world's museums. And that's assuming we have found them all, named them and properly deposited specimens of them in at least one collection.

One day soon, however, we shall know the order of magnitude – and probably even a significant digit – for the number of living species. Erwin has shown us a way to get those, and his way suggests others.

The structure of this book

Patterns

Although we ecologists cannot yet say how many species inhabit the Earth, we have found various regularities about diversity. These patterns are too common for anyone to say they are accidents. They occur repeatedly in different taxa, on different continents and in different geological eras.

Because the patterns happen again and again, we believe that knowable mechanical processes must control the diversity of species. In fact, by studying the patterns closely, we've made considerable progress in understanding some aspects of this control.

In Chapters 2–4, I am going to lay out some of the best known patterns of species diversity. I cannot cover all diversity patterns, but I want you to see some that I consider fundamental and others that appear often in current journals. We can describe some of these patterns very well. For instance, the latitudinal gradient – the decrease in diversity as we move from the Equator to the poles – recurs in all sorts of taxa and has been a feature of diversity for more than 100 million years (Myr.).

But we are much less sure about other patterns. For instance, how does diversity behave as ecosystem energy flow varies? Many believe diversity and energy flow are directly proportional. But others believe they are inversely proportional. Recently, a lot of evidence has appeared that suggests they may be both: directly proportional over low flow rates and inversely proportional over high rates (Rosenzweig and Abramsky, 1993).

The species–area curve is the pattern longest known to science. The larger the area studied, the more species you find in it. But we shall discover that this pattern consists of four different patterns. Each has its own scale of space and time. But they will grade into one another as we begin to understand how they come to exist.

Patterns of diversity with time fall along a scale axis that runs from one year to hundreds of millions of years. Nine orders of magnitude! In Chapter 3, I shall treat time patterns in scale order, from longest to shortest.

Chapter 4 treats patterns that you may never have considered in the context of a diversity book. They are dimensionless, involving regularities of diversity not directly connected to space or time. For example, the higher the trophic level, the fewer the species that use it. These patterns are among the least well defined and most controversial in existence.

In this book, I do not discuss the diversity of microorganisms at all. From the point of view of diversity, they are probably the most poorly known of taxa. Perhaps their diversity shows many patterns, but I am unaware of them.

Processes

We find out how many species there are by counting them somehow. That is not a statement to be tested, but to be implemented. Similarly, we can say that the species got there by speciating or immigrating. And that they are lost by extinction. The rates at which speciation, immigration and extinction operate, now and in the past, determine the diversity of species. Any satisfactory explanation of diversity must be rooted in those rates. Chapters 5 and 6 describe the basic processes that add to or subtract from diversity.

But, I do not intend Chapters 5 and 6 to be a textbook on either speciation or extinction. Others have written those. Instead, I intend them as a summary of certain features of these processes, features that you need to have handy in Chapters 8–12. That is when we get down to the business of explaining some of the patterns we saw in Chapters 2–4.

Explanations

I tried to make the explanations of the rest of the book both theoretical and empirical. No doubt this combination has the ultimate power to convince us of scientific reality. Nevertheless, I could not always achieve it.

When only theory is available, I present it. If the theory is a true piece of deductive logic – and not just a guess – then theory in advance of data has the power to help us collect and use data efficiently.

The reverse of this coin? Data are treacherous when offered in support of explanations free of theory. Do not trust such explanations, no matter how much data seems to support them. Without the theory, it is too easy to confuse scales and to be unaware of what variables need to be measured. For example, you will see that theory claims disturbance has a qualitatively different effect on diversity at different scales of space and time. Yet people unabashedly offer data in support of '*the* disturbance hypothesis', whether or not their data come from the same scales as the theory they cite. Because of this, I avoid explanations based solely on data.

You may now flip through Chapters 7–12 expecting the worst – a text dense with equations and subscripts. You will not find it.

When I was a graduate student, my mentor Robert MacArthur rejected a model I worked up because it was too complex. His advice? Don't try to build everything you know into a model. Make it as simple as you can. Find the intensive variables – the ones that really make the system behave. Join them into the simplest of formal structures. Say only what you know about them. Then what you learn will be robust. If you can reach a conclusion from the signs of a few first or second derivatives, you won't have to wonder whether linearity or additivity is responsible for your result. What you have not included cannot be responsible.

Both Levins (1966) and Slobodkin (1965) offer similar sage advice, and we should listen to them. Levins tells us that precision has a cost. Precise models need to be dense with coefficients and their complex relationships. As a result, they make predictions that apply in only very limited circumstances. Or else, some of the relationships get modeled erroneously but the errors hide in the model's thicket of equations. Then the model never makes valid predictions. Slobodkin, on the other hand, warns us not even to seek such precision. In the real ecological world so full of noise and change and chaos, what good would a coefficient with four significant digits do? If we did an experiment and found the second, third and fourth digit wrong, would we reject the principles underlying the theory?

Like all of us, MacArthur did not always follow his own rules. In one case, the result (limiting similarity) was quicksand that trapped the energies of community ecologists for more than ten years and nearly killed the subdiscipline. Maybe MacArthur was teaching us the hard lesson: even he couldn't get away with an over complex model.

Ecological systems do seem thick, however. It may take decades to pare a problem down to its core. Meanwhile, restricted theory is better than none. And theory that comes from the circuits of a microchip will do for a start. At least it sometimes tells you what might be going on. When I cannot find better theory to write about, I do resort to such theories in this book (and in my own research). A prime example is the pioneering computer work done by Pimm and Lawton that attempts to explain food web patterns as the outcome of dynamical stability filters (Chapter 11). Nevertheless, you should always remember that such simulation theories – not the more general theories – are the ones that need expansion and improvement.

Unpacking. That's what general theories do need (Rosenzweig, 1991a). Unpacking means partly decomposing intensive variables to make them easier to measure. It also can mean building specific equations to fit specific instances. Unpacking prepares theories for testing or for specific use. A wildlife manager charged with setting bag limits for a pheasant population needs a detailed equation for its population dynamics. It will look very different from an equation for algal blooms, although both flow from the same general theory. Too few of us appreciate the strategy of unpacking; examples of it rarely occur in the literature (or this book).

The guidelines for the explanation chapters are easy to summarize. Use theory and data to test explanations whenever possible. Make the theory as general and robust as it can be. Avoid explanations based only on data and lacking any theoretical framework.

In Chapters 7–12, we'll not always succeed in explaining the patterns of Chapters 2–4. But often we will. And the very existence of so many patterns tells us that diversity is a predictable variable, susceptible to scientific analysis. We must try to discover scientific explanations for as many diversity patterns as we can.

Chapter 2

Patterns in space

The job of this chapter is to present some spatial diversity patterns. It is not to judge them or explain them. That part of my agenda comes much later in the book, i.e. Chapters 7, 8, 9 and 12. So read this chapter (and the next two also) as if it were merely an attempt to define what it is that needs explaining.

Species–area curves

You will find more species if you sample a larger area. That rule has more evidence to support it than any other about species diversity. Ecologists noticed it before any other diversity pattern. Williams (1964) credits H. C. Watson with its discovery in 1859 (Figure 2.1). Dony (1963) credits him with the discovery in 1835. I have also seen de Candolle cited as its originator a few years before 1859.

But, as Williams (1943) pointed out, it is not one pattern. Williams detected three. There are actually four:

1   Species–area curves among tiny pieces of single biotas.
2   Species–area curves among larger pieces of single biotas.
3   Species–area curves among islands of one archipelago.
4   Species–area curves among areas that have had separate evolutionary histories.

Williams did not distinguish between the second and third patterns. Preston (1962a, b) did. Despite that, Williams led his generation (and most of ours) in recognizing that different processes are responsible for the different curves. I shall describe those processes in Chapters 8 and 9. In fact, to explain the first and fourth patterns I need merely to reiterate Williams' position about them.

But in this chapter I simply want to present the patterns themselves. I

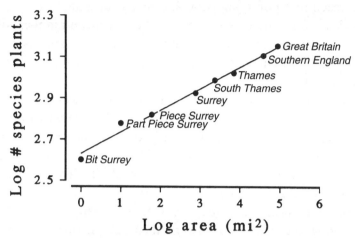

Figure 2.1. This plant species–area curve begins with a bit of Britain's richest county, Surrey, and then builds up to the whole island. It is the world's oldest known empirical example of an ecological pattern.

begin with the two intermediate scale patterns that Williams lumped together. They may already be familiar to you. Then I will describe the smallest and the largest patterns, 1 and 4.

Pattern 2 – among large pieces of a biota

Imagine you know every plant species living on Great Britain and exactly where it lives. Such a degree of comprehensive knowledge comes close to describing what British botanists and plant ecologists know collectively about their flora. The botanical societies of the British Isles work continually to refine their knowledge of plant distribution in that country.

Having the benefit of that knowledge, you now divide Britain into ten equal-area segments. Each will have fewer plant species than the entire island. You write down their diversities, perhaps reducing them statistically to a mean and variance.

You repeat the procedure on areas one-tenth as large as before, that is, on areas each 0.01 as large as the entire island. Probably, you do not use all such areas, but sample them in some justifiable way. Again you note your results.

Now you sample areas 0.001 the size of Great Britain. You keep reducing area one order of magnitude at a time until you begin to worry that the area is too small to house enough individuals for an adequate sample. When you reach that point, you stop and plot your data.

The *x*-axis is area. The *y*-axis is the number (or mean number) of species. The result is a species–area scattergram. To make it a species–area curve, you apply some reasonable statistical technique, like regression, to fit a line through the points.

Using data in Dony (1963), I plotted the actual species–area curve for the plants of all the British isles (Figure 2.2). These data begin with the county of Hertfordshire. Curves beginning with other counties such as Surrey (Figure 2.1) differ in their exact slopes. The richer the county, the more gentle its slope. But they do not differ fundamentally. They all show that if area increases, so does diversity.

In determining species–area curves, you must remember to keep your sub-plots contiguous when you group them to measure the diversity of larger areas. This is called the nested design. If you do not keep them contiguous, but amass them from scattered subplots, the result will have a steeper slope. Figure 2.3 presents an example of this effect from the classic work of Gleason, (1922). The species surveyed are plants in 240 m^2 of

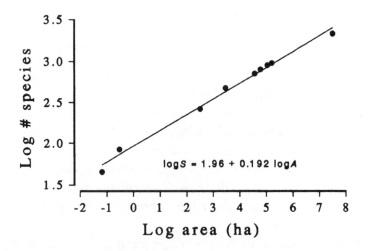

Figure 2.2. A second species–area curve for British plants. This one centers on a county that is not as rich as Surrey. Thus its slope is higher than that of Figure 2.1. Data from Dony (1963).

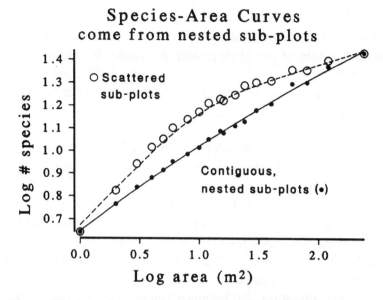

Figure 2.3. A species–area study on some Michigan plants. By definition, a proper species–area curve comes from adding more and more adjacent area to an initial core plot. This is termed a 'nested' design. If area accumulates from tallying the species of scattered plots, diversity will grow faster as in the lefthand part of the curve above. That curve bows over in the example above because of a sampling artifact: there is only one plot of the largest size. So, the nested and the scattered cuves must converge. Data from Gleason (1922).

Michigan aspen forest. Not only does the scattered-plot curve climb too fast, but it also shows too much curvature. That occurs because of the small number of large-area samples. As sample area gets large, those samples get closer and closer together. Finally, at the largest sample area, they all converge because there is only one largest sample area. You can avoid their convergence by having an equal number of samples at each area. But the extra steepness of the scattered curve reflects real biological properties. These include clumping of individuals and of habitats in contiguous sub-plots.

Animal ecologists have settled on a standard way to plot species–area curves for analysis. They transform both area, A, and number of species, S, into logarithms (to the base 10, although I will prove that all bases are equivalent). Usually, the log-log plot aligns the data along a straight line as in Figures 2.1 and 2.2. Plant ecologists have been more likely to use a semi-log plot (log area vs. number of species). I shall return to that difference in both the next section of this chapter and in Chapter 9. Now let us consider the log-log plot.

The straight line in a log-log space has an equation of the form

$$\log S = z \log S + \log c \tag{2.1}$$

In Equation 2.1, z descibes the slope of the log-log relationship and $\log c$ describes its intercept. These parameters will make it easier to talk about the properties of species–area curves.

Equation 2.1 is the standard form of the species–area curve. Frank Preston (1960) called it the Arrhenius equation after the Swedish ecologist who first suggested the equation from which Preston refined it (Arrhenius, 1921). (N.B. I have not seen the 1920 paper in which Arrhenius apparently first published his general equation.)

Ecologists use Equation 2.1 to approximate the line that best fits the species–area curve. If you put your variables in logarithmic form, you can use Equation 2.1 and simple linear regression to come up with estimates of z and c. However, you should be aware that the equation is actually not linear. You can sometimes get better estimates of its parameters by using non-linear regression techniques (Wright, 1981). For example, using true non-linear regression, I estimated the slope of the species–area curve for birds of Pacific archipelagos as $z = 0.669$ ($R^2 = 0.917$). Simple linear regression puts it at $z = 0.54$ ($R^2 = 0.853$) (Adler, 1992; see Figure 8.41).

But most analysts have used the simple linear form. Because relative quantities are most important to this book and consistency is essential, I have used the simple linear form in the book. (There is one exception, but I will mention it in context.)

By going back to non-linear forms of the species–area curve, we can also correct an important misconception (Lomolino, 1989), namely, that $\log c$ is merely an intercept value. Let us transform both sides of Equation 2.1:

$$EXP (\log S) = EXP (z \log A + \log c) \tag{2.2a}$$

$$S = cA^z \tag{2.2b}$$

For decades, ecologists interpreted z as the slope of the species–area curve and $\log c$ as its intercept. This interpretation came from using Equation 2.1 to fit the line. But we are trying to predict S, not $\log S$, so the fundmental equation is (2.2b). It is the one that describes how many species there are. In Equation 2.2b, you see clearly that c helps determine the slope, not an intercept. In fact, c is the slope of a graph whose x-axis is A^z and whose y-axis is S.

An example that helps us appreciate the role of c in setting slopes comes from South American birds. Rahbek has divided the biomes of these birds into four major types: tropical, subtropical, temperate and puna. If we plot the species–area curve of each biome on a log-log space, you will see from their slopes in this space that their z-values are very, very similar (Figure 2.4). This similarity is typical.

But the c values of Rahbek's curves are not so similar. We determine their order by looking at the intercepts in the log-log space (Figure 2.4). That of the subtropics is largest; that of the puna (a high altitude Andean biome) is smallest. Now we replot the data in an arithmetic space (Figure 2.5). Sure enough, in this space, the curve of the subtropical birds – with the largest c – rises fastest, and that of the puna – with the smallest c – rises slowest. We need both parameters, z and c, to describe species–area curves.

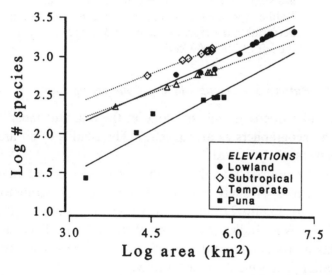

Figure 2.4. Rahbek's species–area curves. The biomes correspond approximately to four different elevations. For a fixed area, diversity of tropical-latitude birds is highest at subtropical elevations where productivity is intermediate. Data from Carsten Rahbek (personal communication). Redrawn from Rosenzweig and Abramsky (1993).

Neotropical Landbirds

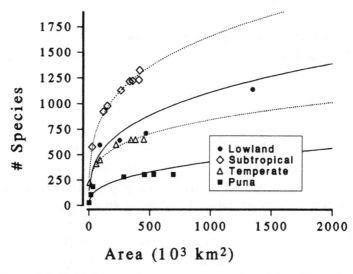

Figure 2.5. Rahbek's species–area curves replotted in arithmetic space. This plot emphasizes that the curves follow an equation of the form $S = cA^z$ in which the coefficient c is a slope, not an intercept. Data from Carsten Rahbek (personal communication). I used all data in performing the regressions, but graph only points to the left of $2\,000\,000$ km^2.

Pattern 3 – among islands of one archipelago

Some islands, like Cocos Island, sit alone in the sea. But most belong to sets defined by geographers as archipelagos. The islands of an archipelago often differ substantially in area.

Biogeographers noticed that the number of species on an island in an archipelago depends strongly on the island's area (Darlington, 1957; Preston, 1962a, b). Figure 2.6 illustrates two classic examples, the reptiles and birds of the West Indies (data from Wright, 1981). Each data set in Figure 2.6 fits a straight line rather well. So, a species–area curve of the form of Equation 2.2b suits them beautifully.

The same is true of most other species–area curves for islands. As an example, Figure 2.7 illustrates a monumental island curve of plant species vs area. It comes mostly from the work of Ian Abbott. He and others have censused the plant species on 144 islands varying in size from mere rocks barely emergent from the sea, to the island State of Tasmania. The graph's areas cover 14 orders of magnitude! Except for the smallest of islands –

Antillean Vertebrates

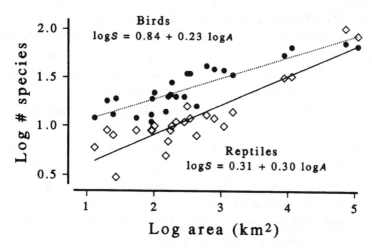

Figure 2.6. Two species–area curves from the Caribbean. Circles: birds. Diamonds: reptiles. Data from Wright (1981).

Australian Islands

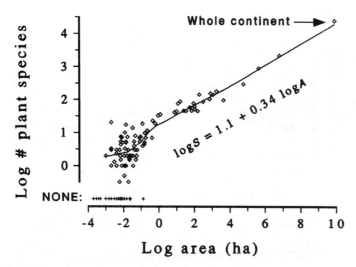

Figure 2.7. A species–area curve for plants of Australian islands. Most of these islands are near Perth, but the largest is the State of Tasmania. The regression is locally weighted. Data courtesy of Ian Abbott. Diversity of Kangaroo Island courtesy of A. Chapman, Australian National Parks & Wildlife Service, Canberra.

those under 1000 m² tend to have 0–12 species almost independent of their area – these islands fit a line of slope about 0.34 in log-log space.

Cody (1975) amassed data to plot the species–area curves of Mediterranean birds on three separate continents (Figure 2.8). They are remarkably similar in both slope and z-value, and their z-values fit right in with those of other taxa. Cody's curves are unsurpassed in quality. He scrupulously followed all the rules of constructing a nested species–area curve, and his work should be viewed as the standard against which to value others.

Since Equation 2.2b suits curves of both Patterns 2 and 3, why claim there are really two patterns as I have? Because, z-values differ systematically between curves reckoned by subdividing an area, compared to curves reckoned by graphing different islands. Interarchipelagic curves are steeper than curves reckoned by subdividing a large area. For example, compare the results for California's mainland and island plants in Figure 2.9

Birds on Three Continents

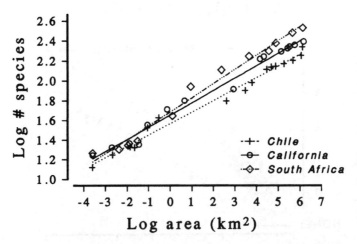

Figure 2.8. These bird species–area curves each begin with tiny patches of Mediterranean chaparral. Cody (1975), who collected them, emphasized their differences. But it is equally valid to note how similar they are. Curves for most other taxa would have intercepts indicating differences of one or more orders of magnitude. And all taxa have similar z-values. In this graph, the z-values are: Chile, 0.116; California, 0.125; South Africa, 0.143.

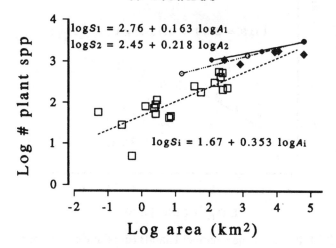

Mainland California (Coast) & Islands

Figure 2.9. Sets of islands have steeper species–area curves than nested areas within a province. I have drawn two nested sets from the California plant data. One (the dots) builds up from San Francisco; it yields a z of 0.163. The other (the circles) builds up from Marin County; it yields a z of 0.218. The diamonds represent other areas in mainland California that lie in neither nested set. The islands (open squares) have a z of 0.353. Notice that the extrapolation of the island curve aims toward the point for the entire coastal flora. Data from Johnson *et al.* (1968).

(Johnson *et al.*, 1968). They typify what we have learned to expect from such comparisons. Values of z among islands range mostly from 0.25 to 0.35. But z-values among subdivisions are less, typically 0.12 to 0.18.

Another example comes from the flowering plants of France and the Channel Islands off its northwest coast (Figure 2.10). The Channel Islands' z is 0.36; the French mainland's is 0.23.

We know of values somewhat outside these ranges too. But invariably, the archipelagic z exceeds the mainland z. I graphed a classic example in Figure 2.11: ponerine and cerapachyine ants on New Guinea and several archipelagos (adapted from Wilson, 1961). The New Guinea mainland curve slopes much more gently than the curve for the separate islands. All island diversities fall below the diversity they would have if they were a piece of New Guinea.

France & Channel Islands

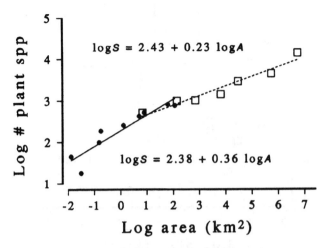

Figure 2.10. Plants of the Channel Islands (dots) have a steeper *z* value than those of mainland France (open squares). Data from Williams (1964).

Ants of Oceania

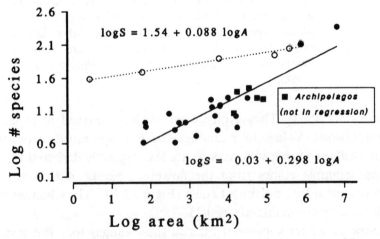

Figure 2.11. Diversity of ponerine and cerapachyine ants on New Guinea, all of southeast Asia and several archipelagos (adapted from Wilson, 1961). Solid dots and line represent all New Guinea, the separate islands (and southeast Asia). Circles are pieces of New Guinea. Dashed line represents them and the whole island. Archipelagos (squares) not included in either regression line.

Begon *et al.* (1990) provide a table of *z*-values from some of the best known studies. Such tables are a hodgepodge of results. People used various methods to get the data. Most mainland curves came from samples that were not carefully nested the way the British plant survey was. There are very few matched pairs of curves such as those from New Guinea ants or California plants. And yet, such tables make their point. Any reduction of island area lowers the diversity more than a similar reduction of mainland area.[1] The closest pair of *z*-values I have seen, applies to flowering plants on Britain (*c.* 0.18) and those on nearby islands (0.21) (Johnson and Simberloff, 1974). But even here, the islands have the higher *z*.

Still, we may have a problem. How do we know that the difference in *z*-values is real? Perhaps it comes about merely because we plot islands differently from mainlands? We plot island species–area curves separately, island by island. We plot mainland species–area curves cumulatively, including in each successive point all the area and all the species of the previous one.

The data suggest that we do not have a problem here. In Figures 2.12 and 2.13, you can see two examples. When island sets are plotted cumulatively, the line does tend to curve. But the slopes of such plots do not change much if we plot the same data using separate island points.

Species–area curves require two parameters, *z* and *c*. A little logic (Box 2.1) will show us that *c* is scale-dependent but *z* is not. By scale-dependent, I mean dependent on the units of area we use to record our data. Thus, when comparing *c* values, we must make sure our curves have all been calculated with the same unit of area.

Do *z*-values vary systematically in some unsuspected way? Does the difference between island and mainland *z*-values exhibit any regular trend? Johnson and Simberloff (1974) suggest that islands isolated only in the past few thousand years and close to a mainland will have *z*-values only a bit larger than their mainland. Schoener (1976) shows that birds of more isolated archipelagos have lower *z*-values. He also claims that the more tropical an archipelago, the larger the *z*-value among its islands. On the other hand, Lomolino (1984) shows that mammalian *z*-values rise in more isolated archipelagos. In Chapters 8 and 9, we will see other patterns in *z*-values and try to sort them out.

[1] The term 'mainland area' may not seem always appropriate. Sometimes mainland areas are defined as portions of islands (like the plants of Great Britain). Furthermore, sometimes island areas are defined as portions of a mainland (like mammal diversity on mountaintops: Brown, 1971a). In Chapter 8, I will be able to define biogeographical islands precisely. Until then, please believe that I have that definition in mind and am trying to use it consistently. Meanwhile, think of an island as a naturally bounded area whose border presents great dispersal difficulties to the taxon being censused. And think of a mainland area as an arbitrarily bounded piece of a larger whole region (which may be a province or an island).

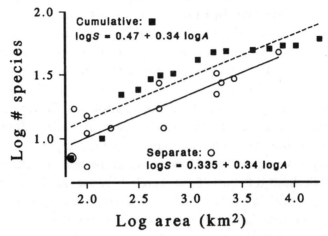

Figure 2.12. Birds of páramos (sky islands in the Northern Andes). Plotting their species–area curve cumulatively (squares) makes it curvilinear. But it has little effect on the slope. Island curves rise more steeply than do mainland curves. Data from Vuilleumier and Simberloff (1980).

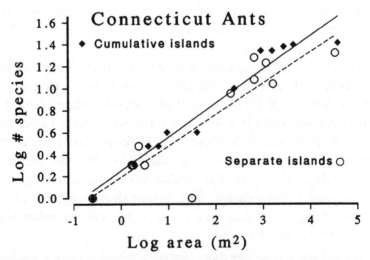

Figure 2.13. The species–area curves of ants on Connecticut islands. The higher one (diamonds and solid line) results when I plot the data cumulatively (as for mainland curves). The other plot (circles and dashed line) represents each island and its ants separately. Data from Goldstein (1975).

Box 2.1 Scale dependence of *z* and *c*

One of the parameters of the species–area equation, z, does not depend on the value of the units used to express the data. But the other one, c, does. So, before comparing the c-values of different places, you must rescale their units to make them the same. In fact, because of the scale-sensitivity of c, you cannot even conclude that an area with higher c has more species than another equal area with lower c, unless both are expressed in the same units and both areas are larger than a fraction of a unit. This box reports an algebraic proof of those conclusions.

Suppose there are two curves, an island and a mainland curve. We will indicate them with subscripts i and m.

$$S_i = c_i A_i^z \text{i} \tag{2.3a}$$

$$S_m = c_m A_m^z \text{m} \tag{2.3b}$$

The whole mainland is also the largest island (as in the case of New Guinea and the ants, Figure 2.11). So the two curves share one point, i.e. the largest area. At that area, namely A_j, $S_i = S_m = S_j$. (The subscript j refers to the joint area shared by both curves, and to its diversity.) Thus,

$$\log c_i + z_i \log A_j = \log c_m + z_m \log A_j \tag{2.4a}$$

$$(z_i - z_m) \log A_j = \log c_m - \log c_i \tag{2.4b}$$

Now we show that z_i and z_m are not scale-dependent. Pick any two areas on a species–area curve, say x km^2 and bx km^2. Suppose their diversities are S and hS respectively. The constant h is larger than 1 because hS is the diversity in the larger area. We solve for z using the logarithmic form of the curve:

$$\begin{aligned}
\log hS &= \log c + z \log bx \\
- (\log S &= \log c + z \log x \,) \\
\hline
\log hS - \log S &= z\, (\log bx - \log x)
\end{aligned} \tag{2.5}$$

Now if we rescale the areas by using different units, the equation for z becomes:

$$\log hS - \log S = z\, (\log abx - \log ax) \tag{2.6}$$

(Suppose, for example, x is in km^2 and the rescaling changes this to mi^2. As 0.3861 mi^2 = 1.00 km^2, we will have chosen $a = 0.3861$.) But $\log(ax) = \log a + \log x$, so we can write:

$$\log hS - \log S = z\, (\log bx - \log x + \log a - \log a) \tag{2.7}$$

The log a terms vanish and the equation for z becomes the same as before rescaling.

Cont. over

Box 2.1 cont.

It also does not matter what logarithmic base you choose. To make your z-values comparable to those of previous work, you do not need common logarithms (i.e. logarithms to the base 10). Recall that the logarithm of any number equals its logarithm to any other base multiplied by a constant:

$$\log_x n = k (\log_y n) \qquad (2.8)$$

Thus, a species–area curve using base 10 can be transformed into any other base with a constant:

$$\log_{10} S = \log c + z (\log 10\ A) \qquad (2.9)$$

becomes

$$k (\log_{10} S) = k (\log c) + zk (\log_{10} A) \qquad (2.10)$$

with no change in z.

Because z-values do not depend on the units of measurement or the logarithmic base, the term $(z_i - z_m)$ in Equation 2.4b does not either. But the term $\log A_j$ most certainly does depend on the units. The larger the unit, the smaller $\log A_j$. Please note that Equation 2.4b always holds; we derived it for all scales and any scale. QED: $(\log c_m - \log c_i)$ also varies with scale.

In fact, if we set A_j at 1 unit so that we measure all areas as fractions of the mainland, then $\log A_j = 0$ and $c_m = c_i$. But if we measure A_j in more conventional units so that $A_j > 1$, then $c_m > c_i$. Finally, if we report A_j as a fraction of the Earth's surface, $\log A_j < 0$ and $c_m < c_i$.

Pattern 1 – among tiny pieces of a biota

Plant ecologists typically census their subjects in 0.1 ha plots (e.g. Naveh and Whittaker, 1979). Nested within these 20 m × 50 m plots are subplots of 100 m^2, 25 m^2, 4 m^2 and 1 m^2 (Shmida, 1984). Species–area curves based on plots so small are not linear in log-log space. They have, instead, a negative second derivative. (They are convex upward.) This is even true of the data in Figure 2.3, which reveals it most clearly by having too steep a z-value – 0.33 – to merge linearly with larger scales. Figure 2.14 shows an example taken from plant censuses in three situations in Broken Hill, New South Wales (Pidgeon and Ashby, 1940). In the figure, the 0.1 ha plots correspond to a log area of 3.

The same shape of species–area curve occurs for animals sampled in tiny plots. Preston (1960) displayed such a plot himself for birds of the northeastern USA (see the left part of Figure 2.15).

Plants at Broken Hill

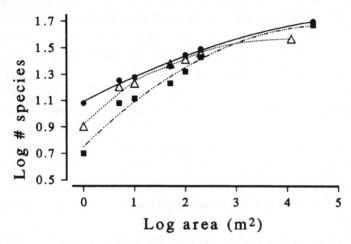

Figure 2.14. Species–area curves in log-log space tend to be convex upward over small areas. Data from Pidgeon and Ashby (1940) in three different areas of their study.

Birds of the World
Over Three Scales

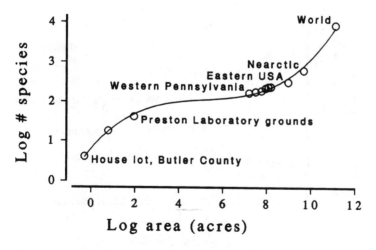

Figure 2.15. Frank Preston's species–area curve for land birds in western Pennsylvania. Notice how steep the curve gets for whole provinces and for tiny parts of one province. Data from Preston (1960).

Pattern 4 – among biotas

Large regions of the Earth have had separate evolutionary histories. If we
graph their diversities, we get *z* values that exceed those of separate islands.
When Williams (1943) first suggested this pattern, he claimed he lacked
more than two points to illustrate it. Actually, he had more. I have taken
these points and added them to the data of Watson (Figure 2.1) for the
British flora. The result is Figure 2.16. The numbers in this graph should
not be taken too seriously as they are old and come from all sorts of biomes. I could have updated them but deliberately did not. (For example,
Williams, 1964, lists the Australian flora at 4200 species, but a more modern estimate is 25 000: Cowling *et al.*, 1989.) I wanted to make the point
that Williams – already in 1943 – had good grounds to believe that the
slope of the species–area curve amongst separate biotas is much steeper
than within biotas.

Preston (1960) agreed and illustrated the pattern within his bird diversity
curve. I have abstracted the data from Preston that accumulates bird diversity from a half acre plot in Beaver County, Pennsylvania, up through the
whole world (Figure 2.1). This figure has all three scales of area that

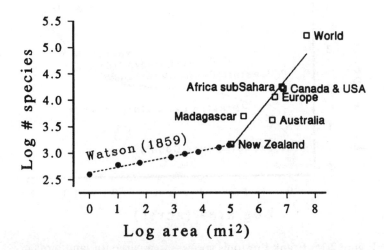

Figure 2.16. The slope of the species–area curve among floras is
much steeper than within a flora. Data from Williams
(1964).

Williams wrote about. In Chapter 9, you will see more examples of species–area curves amongst different biological provinces.

Latitudinal gradients

The species–area curve may be the first diversity pattern described by ecology, but the latitudinal gradient is the most famous. The tropics, if not the seat of life, are the center of its richest display. In general, *the inventory of species declines as you move away from the Equator, north or south.*

Examples of the latitudinal diversity gradient abound (Fischer, 1961). We find it in plants (Figure 2.17) and animals. In vertebrates, aerial and quadrupedal, warm-blooded and cold (Figures 2.18, 2.19 and 2.20). In invertebrates (Figure 2.21). And in aquatic and terrestrial environments (Figure 2.22). Yes, there are exceptions. For instance, marine algae of the Pacific coast of North and Central America (Gaines and Lubchenco, 1982). But exceptions they are.

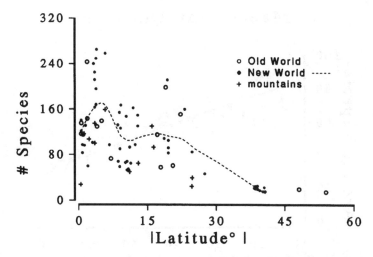

Figure 2.17. The latitudinal gradient in plants. The regression is locally weighted and performed only on New World data. You will learn in Chapters 8 and 9 that 0.1 ha plots – though standard – are usually too small to census large organisms like trees. Small plot size must account for much of the noise in this graph. Data from Gentry (1988a).

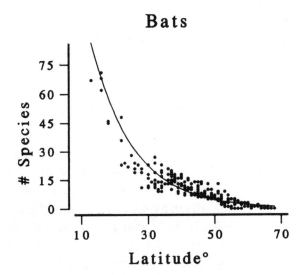

Figure 2.18. The latitudinal gradient among bats of North and
Central America. Each point represents the diversity
of a single square of land about 150 miles (250 km)
on a side. Redrawn from Rosenzweig (1992).

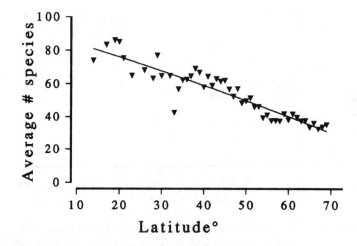

Figure 2.19. The latitudinal gradient among quadrupedal mammals of North and Central America. Each point represents the average diversity of squares of land about
150 miles on a side. Data from Sandlin and
Rosenzweig (unpublished).

Snakes, Frogs & Lizards

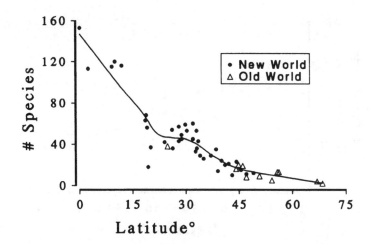

Figure 2.20. The latitudinal gradient among herptiles. The line comes from a lowess regression. Data from Arnold (1972) and Duellman (1990).

Termites

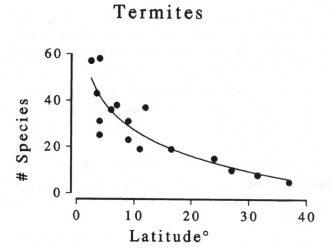

Figure 2.21. The latitudinal gradient in termite species. Data from Collins (1989).

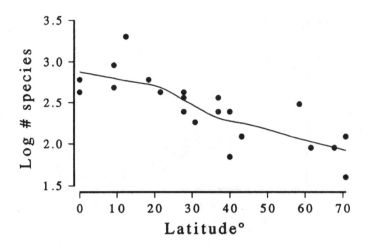

Figure 2.22. The latitudinal gradient in coastal fishes. Data from
Rohde (1992). Each point is actually taken from a
coastline which ranges over a variety of latitudes; I
graph its mid-point above.

The latitudinal gradient is ancient. It is not an historical quirk of an immature post-glacial Earth. It has been around for tens if not hundreds of millions of years.

Geologists can estimate the latitude at which some rocks were born. They do it by looking at fossil traces of magnetic orientation (Allègre, 1988). This locates the latitudes of assemblages of fossil species well enough to examine their latitudinal diversity trend. Stehli *et al.* (1969) were the first to accomplish this. They studied marine Foraminifera, a group with arguably the world's most detailed and reliable fossil record. Their data extend back to the beginning of Cenozoic time some 70 Myr ago. The latitudinal gradient shows up well (Figure 2.23).

Angiosperms also have ancient latitudinal diversity gradients. Crane and Lidgard (1989) trace them back some 110 Myr. If paleobiologists keep measuring the latitudes at which rocks were deposited, I suspect they will bring us many more cases of fossil gradients.

When I was a graduate student, some people wondered about the truth of the latitudinal gradient. They recognized that temperate-zone scientists with temperate-zone experience created ecology. They wondered if perhaps the strangeness and mystery of the tropics misled these ecologists into con-

Fossil Foraminifera

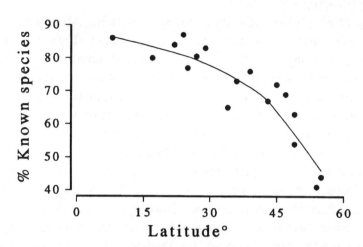

Figure 2.23. The latitudinal gradient among some ancient marine protozoa. The fossil record of this taxon in the ocean is continuous and detailed. Data from Stehli *et al.* (1969). Figure from Rosenzweig (1992).

cluding prematurely that diversity follows a latitudinal trend. But they need not have worried.

Richards (1969), for example, wondered if the rich heathland plant communities of the Cape Peninsula of South Africa (the *fynbos*) and of southern Australia are not the world's richest, even richer than tropical rainforests. But Parsons and Cameron (1974) drew careful species–area curves for these floras. They found that even a tropical island's depauperate rainforest, such as the well studied one on Puerto Rico, has many more species than these heathlands. Two hectares of the Puerto Rican rainforest hold 214 plant species, but the same area of sclerophyll heathland in Victoria has 'only' 138. The heathlands of southwestern Western Austalia (the *kwongan*) are richer than those of Victoria, but even they do not attain the diversities of wet tropical forests in southeast Asia or the Neotropics.

Even if we examine only their trees, we see that mainland tropical rainforests hold huge numbers of species. The champion appears to be a hectare of Atlantic rainforest in Bahia Province, Brazil. It has c. 450 tree species (Thomas and de Carvalho, 1993). More ordinary hectares of tropical forest (in Sarawak) have 233 tree species (alluvial forest); 214 species (dipterocarp forest); 123 species (heath forest); and 73 species (forest over limestone) (Proctor *et al.*, 1983).

Cowling *et al.* (1989) show that amongst southern African biomes, the fynbos' species–area curve has the largest *c* value (Figure 2.24). That demonstrates the superior richness of heathland compared to all other southern African biomes. But what about tropical rainforests? We already know that African tropical rainforest is not as rich as the Malesian[2] or the Neotropical. So let's go right to the places that most would consider the supremely diverse biomes of the world. How does fynbos diversity compare with Malesian or Neotropical rainforest diversities?

The standard way such questions get investigated is wrong. People divide the total diversity by the biome area and report the result as species per unit area. Even such a fine contribution as Cowling *et al.* (1989) uses that technique. Its error lies in not taking account of the non-linearity of the species–area relationship. Suppose, for instance, there are two biomes, *D*

South African Plants

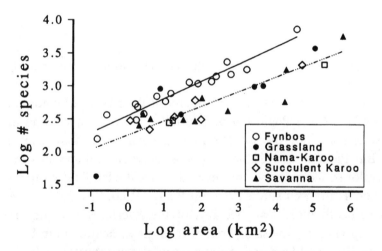

Figure 2.24. Plants of most biomes in South Africa share a single
species–area curve. But those of the fynbos southwest
of the Breede River lie on a parallel line above the
rest. Data from Cowling *et al.* (1989).

[2]Malesia is a biogeographical region that includes Indonesia, the Philippines, Malaysia and part of southeast Asia.

and *F. D* covers $10^5 \, km^2$ and has 500 species. *F* covers $10^6 \, km^2$ and has 757 species. Their values of species/km² are thus: $D = 0.005$; $F = 0.000757$. Is *D* richer than *F*? No. Assuming $z = 0.18$, both biomes fall on exactly the same species–area curve. And of course, $z = 0.18$ is a typical z-value for mainland curves. It is the very value obtained by Cowling *et al.* (1989) for southern African biomes.

We now know enough about z-values of mainland curves to correct for the non-linearity of the species–area relationship. We simply assume that the z-values of two biomes are similar and then we solve for their c-values. (Remember that the c-value is the logarithm of the intercept of the curve in log-log space, but is really much the more important slope parameter in arithmetic space. Remember also that the value of c depends on the units adopted. So make sure all figures are transformed to the same units of area.)

The parameter c is the ratio of diversity to A^z:

$$c = S/A^z \qquad (2.11)$$

So, returning to our hypothetical biomes, *D* and *F*, we substitute their areas and diversities into Equation 2.11:

$$c = 500/10^{5(0.18)} = 757/10^{6(0.18)} = 63$$

Suppose we had used 0.14 as our assumed z-value. It would have made little difference:

$$c = 500/10^{5(0.14)} = 100$$

$$c = 757/10^{6(0.14)} = 109$$

With 0.14 as our assumed z, the area-corrected species densities would have appeared a bit higher in *F*. But the c values of *F* and *D* would have been too similar to mislead us.

Now we are ready to confront real data (from Cowling *et al.*, 1989 and Prance, 1977):

Biome	Fynbos	Neotropical rainforest
Area (km²)	3.66×10^4	5.06×10^6
Species	7316	90000
$c = S/A^{0.18}$	1104	5591

So, the Neotropical rainforest is much richer than the fynbos.

Data from Malesia tell the same story, but I have not found estimates of diversity for just Malesian rainforest. The forest covers $1.88 \times 10^6 \, km^2$ in

Thailand, Malaysia, the Philippines, Indonesia and the nations of the Indochina Peninsula. Altogether about 35 000 species of flowering plants live in the larger region of tropical Asia, Australia and the Pacific (Prance, 1977). So the Malesian forest has 20 000 to 30 000 species. Its c-value must lie between 1485 and 2227, not as large as that of the Neotropics, but larger than that of the fynbos.

To check further on the latitudinal gradient, Terborgh *et al.* (1990) undertook a long and detailed study of the avifauna found in a 97 ha low-land tropical site in Peru. A total of 245 bird species breed in it. An additional 74 species reside in it seasonally or wander through it occasionally.

Terborgh had set out to test MacArthur's conjecture that the same number of bird species breed at any point in a tropical forest as at any point in a temperate forest (see Box 2.2). Everyone agreed that tropical avian gamma diversities (Box 2.2 again) exceed temperate ones. Did alpha (or point) diversities too? Terborgh's data answer the question. Avian alpha diversity in a tropical forest is about 160 species. That is four or five times higher than the alpha diversity in the richest temperate North American forest. Such wealth occurs although the number of individual birds per hectare is quite similar in the two biomes.

Tropical forest life pulses in the canopy, exactly where ecologists have a hard time working. Most of what we know comes from studies conducted in the lowest 2 m of a 50 or 60 m tall ecosystem. Recently investigators have begun probing the canopy with sprays and fogs of knockdown insecticides (see Chapter 1). They find we may have grossly underestimated diversity in the tropics! Where previously we thought 5 million species existed, we now believe there may be 20, 30 or even 40 million. Don't rely on these estimates too much; no one means them to be precise. But they do indicate that the tropics harbor most of the world's species diversity. In part, the doubters were right. We do need to find out a lot more about the tropics. But the more we discover, the more firmly we conclude that species diversity is highest in the tropics for most life forms, and decreases toward either of the poles.

Habitat variety

Conservationists know that each species needs an appropriate habitat or set of habitats to survive. If we know enough about the natural history of a taxon, we can measure the variety of habitats significant to its members. *The greater the habitat variety, the greater the species diversity.*

Box 2.2 Alpha, beta and gamma diversities

Robert Whittaker (1970) named point diversities, 'alpha diversities'. He called another kind of diversity, 'beta diversity'. Beta diversity is the rate at which species accumulate in a census as the census taker moves in a straight line away from a point. Finally, he completed the picture with 'gamma diversity'. Gamma diversity is the number of species in a whole region.

In this book, I avoid the use of these terms. Gamma diversity is no more than the number of species in a region. Having a jargon word for it does nothing to help us pin down the concept of 'region' any more objectively than we already do.

Beta diversity has been the most useful of the trio. But the slope of the mainland species–area curve is one measure of beta diversity. (Caswell and Cohen, 1993, make the same point.) And yet many formulae have served to estimate beta diversity, whereas the species–area curve has standard coefficients. I see a theory of those coefficients just over the horizon. But for beta diversity, I see only a growing thicket of observations.

Robert MacArthur (1964) actually invented point diversities for his work with birds. He observed that birds do a lot of vertical habitat subdivision. He wanted to find out how much of their diversity (in 2 ha plots) they owe to this vertical zonation. Thus, he would separate vertical from horizontal habitat complexity.

Whenever you wish to separate vertical habitat complexity from horizontal complexity, you should use point diversities. But do not expect them to apply in all situations. What, for instance, is the tree diversity of a point on which an oak tree grows? One species? How meaningful is that?

Recognizing such difficulties, plant ecologists have allowed some arbitrary and allegedly tiny area to serve as their point. But in so doing, they have left the notion of a point infinitely behind. And they are no longer studying vertical zonation. They have changed questions. Their new question: 'What is the diversity of a single habitat?' We have better ways to answer that question.

We can actually use a modification of the species–area curve to estimate alpha diversity. We revise Equation 2.2b by adding a new term, q:

$$S = q + cA^z \tag{2.12}$$

The coefficient q is the S-intercept for diversity when area has vanished. Thus, it answers the question, how many species at a point? But q must be estimated with nonlinear regression methods. Appropriate methods having now become available for microcomputers, I expect the emergence of a small industry to address the question of alpha diversity and to look for patterns in the answers we get.

MacArthur (1958) began the job of systematizing this pattern with his work on birds. He perceived that different bird species foraged differently, even within the branches of the same spruce tree. Some feeding went on in the tree tops, some on the ground, etc. Each species seemed to have a characteristic repertoire of feeding behaviors. Without the appropriate habitat in which to use its behaviors, a species would be in trouble.

MacArthur used his knowledge of bird behavior to design an abstract measure of habitat variety relevant to birds. He divided the foliage up by height (usually into three layers corresponding to grassy, shrubby and canopy foliage). Then he measured its density in each layer. A plot with equal amounts of foliage in all layers has the greatest habitat variety. One with all its foliage in one layer has the least. MacArthur used information theory to construct a continuous index of the habitat variety, and to express the number of species on a continuous scale. (You can read about such information indices in Magurran, 1988.)

When bird species diversity of forests and fields of the northeastern USA fit his habitat variety index, MacArthur expected it. But when the birds of Arizona's forests of giant cactus and the birds of its arid mountain slopes also fit the same index, he was astonished. (I was a field assistant in Arizona in 1962 and had the privilege of calculating and plotting the data, and then laying the result in front of his widening smile!) When Recher (1969) found that Australian birds fit exactly the same line, the whole ecological world was astonished (Figure 2.25).

Soon MacArthur's colleagues and students treated other terrestrial vertebrates the same way with similar results (Pianka, 1967; Rosenzweig and Winakur, 1969). In each case, they designed the habitat variety index to suit the natural history of the taxon. These habitat measures are not so robust, however; they resisted transport to other continents (e.g. Pianka, 1986).

Habitat variety indices for many other taxa proved possible. For example, Anderson (1978) defined 24 habitat types in three soil sub-horizons and studied their relationship to the diversity of woodland mites. The more habitats, the more mite species (Figure 2.26). Perhaps the litter level supports more mite species per habitat than the humus level, but the pattern of increase for all levels stands out.

In another case, Harman (1972) studied diversity in freshwater molluscs. He classified the bottoms of freshwater habitats from lakes to ponds to rivers to ditches into 11 substrate types. The number of mollusc species increases as a survey site contains more and more of these substrates.

You will see other examples of the habitat relationship in Chapter 8.

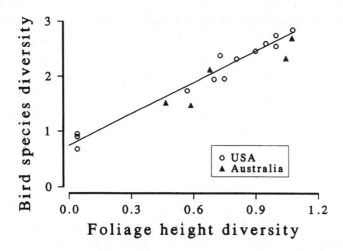

Figure 2.25. Bird species diversity follows the diversity of vegetation layers in North America. Where foliage is more evenly divided among three layers, there are more species of birds. These layers correspond roughly to herb, shrub and tree heights. The birds of Australia fit the same line (Recher, 1969). US data from MacArthur (1964).

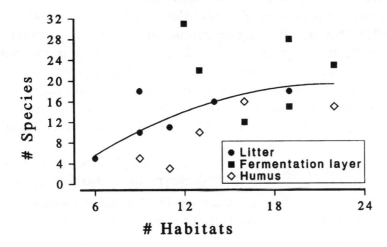

Figure 2.26. Soil mite diversity depends on the number of habitats. Data from Anderson, (1978).

Figure 8.17 shows it for plants and soil types. Figure 8.15 shows it for vertebrates and the plant associations on which they depend. Figure 8.12 shows it for mammals in southeast Australia. I know no one who doubts its importance.

In sum, we begin by understanding something of the natural history of a taxon. Thus we recognize which habitat properties support their species' specializations. Then we can build an index of habitat variety that correlates well with species diversity. You will find other examples of the habitat pattern in Chapters 7 and 9.

Disturbance

The marine–terrestrial interface between highest and lowest tides takes a pounding from the surf. To keep from being washed away, many of its creatures grasp rocks with holdfasts or byssal threads. Occasionally however, a very large wave or a floating log overcomes these defenses and destroys much of the life in a patch of intertidal habitat. Let's call such an event a 'disturbance'.

Some intertidal patches lie on the leeward side of natural breakwaters such as islands. They rarely experience disturbances. Some are more exposed.

We can measure the rate at which disturbances (of any given size) happen to a patch. We also can measure that patch's diversity.

Common sense suggests that the more often a patch is disturbed, the fewer species it will contain. But, said Bertrand Russell (*The Observer*, 24 April 1955), 'Nature, always economical, (has) educated common sense only up to the level of everyday life.' Which, I must add, is not enough – not in this case, nor in many others involving ecological principles.

Actually, patches with very high disturbance rates do have very few species. But so do patches with very low disturbance rates. *Diversity peaks over intermediate disturbance levels.* The curve that results is the disturbance pattern.

Ecologists have spotted the disturbance pattern in other habitats besides the intertidal. One of the first was forests (Eggeling, 1947). Connell (1978) also saw it there, as well as in coral reefs. Osman (1977) noted it in marine epifaunal invertebrates. Consult Petraitis *et al.* (1989) for many other examples.

Many sorts of natural environmental phenomena disturb portions of ecosystems or even whole ecosystems. An unusually powerful wave tears away the residents on a patch of the rocky intertidal zone. A tree falls in a Costa Rican rainforest, exposing a bit of the forest floor to an unusual amount of light. A longtailed weasel moves into a few hectares of prime California chapparal, eats up long-established populations of three species of mice, and moves out two weeks later. (See, for example, McCabe and Blanchard, 1950, if you disbelieve this case.) A cold snap inhibits flowering of a tropical shrub long enough for a nose mite, utterly dependent on its flowers, to become extinct. A mild drought in a semi-arid Arizona grass-land decimates seed production. A meteor strikes the Earth, spewing vast clouds of particles into the atmosphere, reducing solar energy input and causing the extinction of two thirds of the Earth's species – even in the ocean. (And that is the most parsimonious – albeit abbreviated – current account of the Cretaceous–Tertiary mass extinction: Raup, 1992.)

Notice that I deliberately chose disturbances to run the gamut of scale. A scoured rock or a fallen tree seem like small matters compared to a mass extinction. The literature on disturbance ignores the scale issue. I have read articles that lift a disturbance process going on at a scale of hectares (or less), and attribute it without blush to the whole Atlantic continental shelf of North America. The time has come for more care. Extrapolation without logic lacks even the attractiveness of a good party game.

The disturbance–diversity pattern relies on small-scale disturbances. A monumental die-off in one half of a biogeographical province does not count. A mass extinction has nothing to do with the pattern of this section. You may think that the notion of 'small scale' is too fuzzy to be useful, but when we discuss processes in later chapters, we will change from 'scale' to well-defined rate relationships. They are not fuzzy. Whenever these rate relationships hold, we should expect the disturbance pattern (Chapter 11).

Notice also that I chose as examples both abiotic disturbances (e.g. the wave) and biotic ones (e.g. the weasel). Maybe someday we'll recognize that these two sorts of disturbance lead to distinguishable patterns and must be separated (like island and mainland areas). But today, we know of no such distinction. On the contrary, the processes that produce the pattern will work regardless of the source of the disturbance.

Sousa (1979) performed a field experiment on the disturbance pattern. He observed that medium-sized boulders on Ellwood Beach, California, had more species of algae and barnacles growing on them than larger or smaller boulders (Figure 2.27). Sousa suspected that this pattern reflected a distur-bance gradient because when a wave moves a boulder, the motion destroys organisms living on the boulder's surface. Waves can move small boulders

Disturbance

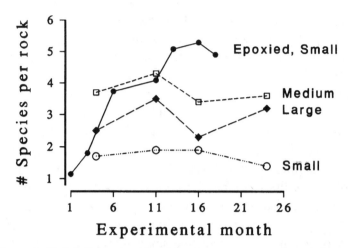

Figure 2.27. Medium-sized boulders have more species of algae
and barnacles growing on them than do other sizes.
But diversity of small rocks climbs past that of even
medium rocks after small rocks are fastened to the
substrate. That experiment eliminates disturbance.
Data from Sousa (1979).

more easily, more often and farther than large boulders. Hence, if diversity
on the boulders follows the disturbance pattern, medium boulders should
have more species than either small ones or large ones.

Sousa tested the importance of disturbance by eliminating it experimentally from several small boulders. He sterilized them with a blowtorch and
glued them to their natural substrate. He followed them, their controls
(sterilized but not glued) and some untreated samples for 18 months. The
results are dramatic (Figure 2.27). The small, fixed boulders rapidly
regained and then surpassed their natural diversities. When the experiment
ended, the small boulders had even exceeded the diversities of the medium
boulders. But other observations indicate that they would soon have diminished.

Sousa's work puts us in an ideal position regarding the disturbance pattern: we know it is real. The ecological world is a tangled plexus of environmental variables. So we always appreciate it when one gets identified for
sure. With correlation, we have only a beginning. Think how many variables must be related to area, for instance. Is area merely a surrogate for
one of them? Thanks to the experiments, we know the answer here. Many

variables may influence species diversity, but disturbance rate surely does. Diversities peak at intermediate rates of small-scale disturbance.

We have learned a lot about the disturbance pattern from Sousa's and other experiments done in the intertidal zone. In fact, intertidal zone ecology, because of the influence of Joseph H. Connell, has led ecology into the realm of field experimentation. You must work harder to perform a field experiment than a laboratory experiment. But the field experiment explores evolved relationships among organisms, whereas the lab experiment's result may derive from the unnatural, 'immature' response of an artificial system. That is why the field experiment is more credible.

Productivity

'Productivity' is the rate at which energy flows in an ecosystem. It isn't a biomass, but a rate, properly expressed as joules per unit time per unit area (or per unit volume).

Productivity gets measured at various ecosystem levels. For example, one could be interested in the rate of energy flow to carnivores. In this book, however, productivity will always mean *gross primary productivity*, i.e. the rate of energy flow through all the plants in the ecosystem. Often, researchers do not measure this productivity directly. Instead they estimate it from some well-known index like rainfall in a desert or depth in an ocean.

At first, ecologists believed that more productivity ought always to raise diversity. But it doesn't. Increasing productivity can depress diversity.

The small-scale pattern

The story begins at immature and tiny scales. Most of the time, adding fertilizer to the soil depresses plant diversity in small experimental plots. Such experiments have a long and distinguished history (Swingle, 1946; Yount, 1956; Patrick, 1963; Kirchner, 1977; Silvertown, 1980; Tilman, 1987; Schindler, 1990; Goldberg and Miller, 1990). Huston (1979) traced them back to 1882. He, and Goldberg and Miller, cite numerous other examples in plants.

The experiments of Goldberg and Miller (1990) support Tilman's refinement of this pattern. He suggests that not extra productivity *per se*, but extra productivity *brought about by adding nutrients* causes the decline in diversity. They found that adding water greatly increased productivity, but did not change diversity. On the other hand, adding nitrogen caused only a small increase in productivity, but greatly depressed the diversity. Much the same phenomenon appears in aquatic systems polluted by adding nutrients (Pearson and Rosenberg, 1978; Wu, 1982).

All these experiments involved increasing productivity. Occasionally diversity did not respond to the change. But far more often it decreased dramatically. Only one experiment (Abramsky, 1978) reported an increase. Thus, these experiments establish the first pattern of diversity with productivity. *In plots of about 1 m² to about 1 ha, experimental increases of nutrients tend to increase productivity and decrease diversity.*

The regional pattern

Ecologists hoped that experimental results on a small scale did not matter at larger scales. They expected that at larger scales of space and time, diversity would grow with productivity. And they trusted that data taken at such larger scales would justify their biases.

Indeed, the natural pattern of small mammal diversity in the deserts of both Chile and the USA did bolster their hope (Brown, 1975; Meserve and Glanz, 1978). In these relatively undisturbed regions, higher diversities do accompany higher productivities (Figure 2.28a).

Then, Abramsky and I (Abramsky and Rosenzweig, 1984) got some unsettling data on Israel's small mammals. Whether we looked at sandy or rocky communities, diversity declined after productivity grew beyond a certain point. The pattern was unimodal or 'hump-shaped'. It was not monotonically increasing.

Other mammalian examples turned up. Australian tropical mammals fit the pattern (Rosenzweig and Abramsky, 1993). Owen (1988) showed that Texas carnivores do too (but not Texas bats). But most important, Owen showed that in Texas, rodent diversities *decline* as productivity goes up (Figure 2.28b). Since USA desert data end at about the productivities where Owen's start, we can conclude that the desert data and the Texas data reveal opposite ends of the same camel. The whole pattern for USA rodents is hump-shaped!

Other biomes, besides terrestrial ones, conform to the unimodal productivity pattern. For example, zooplankton of freshwater Canadian lakes do (Figure 2.29). This observation is something of a breakthrough because well-known data from Danish lakes show a negative correlation (Whiteside and Harmsworth, 1967) and were the earliest serious contradiction of the hypothesis that diversity always grows with productivity.

Rodents

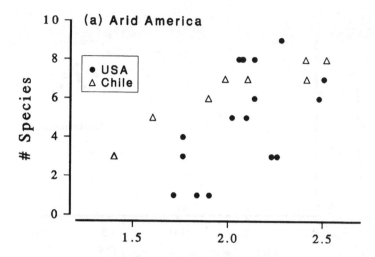

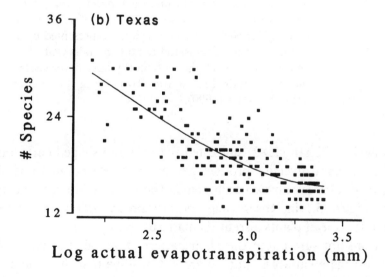

Log actual evapotranspiration (mm)

Figure 2.28. (a) Rodent diversities rise with productivity in arid
and semi-arid environments. Data from Brown
(1975) and Meserve and Glanz (1978).
(b) Rodent diversities decline as productivity
increases in more mesic environments across Texas.
Data from Owen (1988).

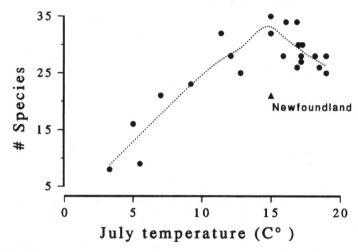

Figure 2.29. Among Canadian zooplankton, diversity peaks in
lakes of intermediate productivity. Productivity scales
with July water temperature. Each point is the total
number of species in all surveyed lakes of a Canadian
region. The Newfoundland region – represented by a
triangle – is the only island region and falls well
beneath the trend. Islands typically have fewer species
than mainlands. Figure from Rosenzweig (1992) after
data of Patalas (1990).

Meanwhile, Tilman (1982) suggested that a hump-shaped curve ought to
characterize plant diversity–productivity patterns. He pointed out the pattern in tropical trees on two continents. The data of Shmida and his colleagues (Figure 5.1 in Rosenzweig and Abramsky, 1993) appear to show
that Mediterranean plants also fit the pattern.

Yet, I am not sure about the plant pattern. Like all examples, Tilman's
rely on surrogate variables. But we are not positive that those he used correlate well with productivity (Rosenzweig, 1992). For his example, Shmida
censused plants in equal-area 0.1 ha plots, a crucial methodological detail.
In Chapter 9 we will see that such small plots may provide inadequate sample sizes to compare diversity accurately between biomes.

Adding to my uncertainty about the pattern among plants, Currie and
Paquin (1987) found that trees in the USA do not lose diversity in regions
of higher productivity. But their survey ends at the southern political bor-

der of the country. What would happen if it were extended into Mexico? In fact, Scheiner and Rey-Benayas (1994) looked at plant diversity in every latitudinal region all over the world. They find no evidence that plant diversity declines over higher productivities.

The best plant examples of the unimodal pattern come from tropical mountainsides. Productivity declines as elevation increases in the tropics (because temperature declines) (Lonsdale, 1988). Bryophytes reach peak diversities at mid-elevation (Figure 2.30). So do ferns (Figure 2.31). The tropical mid-elevation diversity bulge is known for some animal taxa too (Janzen *et al.*, 1976; Terborgh, 1977; Heaney and Rickart, 1990; see also Figure 2.4 and its treatment in Chapter 12).

At first, it seemed that marine benthic (i.e. bottom-dwelling) animals did not fit the pattern. Williams (1964, pp. 173, 174, 181) claimed that data collected by the research vessel Challenger in the 19th century indicated a monotonic decrease in species diversity as deeper marine stations were sampled. Ocean depth is a good inverse index of productivity. The deeper the ocean, the farther the sea floor is from the photic zone at the surface (where production occurs). The rain of organic material from the photic zone to

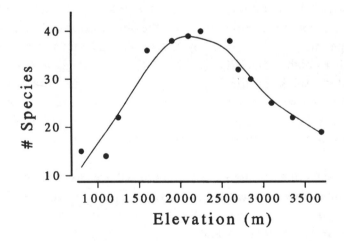

Figure 2.30. Bryophyte diversity on a mountainside in Columbia. Diversity peaks at mid-elevations where productivity is intermediate. Data from Gradstein and Pocs (1989).

Pteridophytes

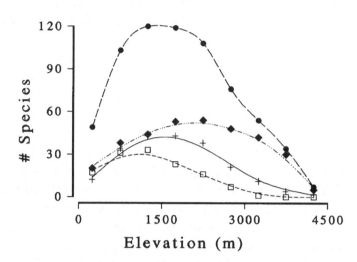

Figure 2.31. Fern diversities peak at mid-elevations in the tropics. Diamonds: *Grammitis* plus Cyathaceae in New Guinea. Plusses: Cyathaceae in Andes. Boxes: *Thelypteris* in Chiapas, Mexico. Circles: sum of the three. Data from Tryon (1989).

the bottom-dwelling community has to travel a longer distance and more of it will be intercepted along the way. So, the ocean floor will be less productive in deeper water. Thus, Challenger's results say that more productivity always leads to higher diversity.

But modern work in the oceans has revealed the unimodal pattern. Marine biologists see it in many animal taxa. Haedrich *et al.* (1980) show it for bottom-dwelling decapods, fishes and echinoderms (Figure 2.32). Rex (1981) also points it out in cumaceans, gastropods, protobranchs and polychaetes.

Measurements of standing crop (i.e. biomass) are easier to find than measurements of energy flow (i.e. productivity). The two often correlate well, although not perfectly. Consequently, some use either one to study the relationship of productivity to diversity.

But the two variables do differ. In fact, sometimes they do not even correlate well. Even when they do, only one of them may be causal. If we are to discover which one, keeping them sorted out seems a minimal strategy.

At least one excellent marine data set (Haedrich *et al.*, 1980) establishes

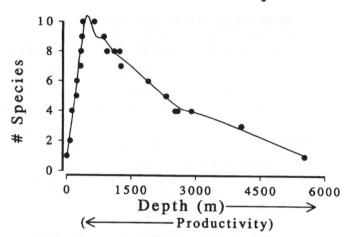

Figure 2.32. Antarctic brachiopods have peak diversities at intermediate productivities. Many other benthic marine
taxa share this pattern. Productivity correlates
inversely with depth. Diversity is the maximum number of species known at a given depth in Antarctic
waters, rather than the number in a collection. Depths
we report in the figure are each the upper or lower-
most depth known for at least one of the species.
Data from Foster (1974). Redrawn from Rosenzweig
and Abramsky (1993).

the problem. It offers separate measures of biomass (grams caught per hour
of sample) and productivity (ocean depth). The authors also separate their
data into fish, echinoderms and decapods. Both fish and echinoderms
clearly show the unimodal productivity pattern. Decapods probably also
show it, though not so clearly. But none of the three taxa's diversities fit
biomass as well as depth. Although larger biomasses are associated with
high diversities, low biomasses are associated with almost any diversity. I
hope to see more such comparisons in future.

Perhaps no diversity pattern is universal. Even the latitudinal gradient
has exceptions. Undoubtedly, the productivity pattern does too. But the
overall trend is clear. *In regions about the size of many nations, animal diversity first increases and then declines as productivity increases.* In Chapter 12,
whose job it is to examine explanations of the pattern, I will show you more
examples of this trend. I hope that soon we will also know whether plants
follow a similar pattern.

Hot spots

Mammals in seismically active regions

Mammal speciation often involves changes in chromosome number. A few places in the world have many such chromosomal variants, all in the same set of sister species. Vorontsov and Lyapunova (1984) discovered *high concentrations of chromosomal variants in places subject to frequent catastrophic earthquakes.*

One such case occurs in members of the superspecies *Elliobus talpinus*, a set of burrowing rodent species. The superspecies lives from the southern Ukraine in the west, to northeast China, and from the Siberian steppes in the north, to the Qara Qum Desert in the south. There are 24 karyomorphs.

Yet in most of its range, there is only one of two karymorphs. *E. tancrei* lives in the east; *E. talpinus sensu stricto* lives in the west. Both have 54 chromosomes, with fundamental number 56 for the eastern and 54 for the western form.

But in the Vakhsh-Surkhob Valley of Tadzhikistan (39° N × 70° E) you see a vast range of karyomorphs. This is a valley in the Pamiro-Alay Mountains about 100 km long. It constitutes a tiny fraction of the overall range of *Elliobus*. In the valley, members of the superspecies have 31 to 54 chromosomes. I don't know exactly how many 'good' species this amounts to. But Vorontsov and Lyapunova suggest that such a concentration is the stuff of prolific mammal speciation.

What is special about the Vakhsh-Surkhob Valley? It contains the Garm (or Vakhsh) Fault where the great Hindustan Plate has collided with the Asian Plate. All of it lies in an area where great earthquakes happen about once in 1000 years. Much of it lies in an area where they happen about once in 500 years (or more). Other regions of the Pamiro-Alay Mountains have similar topography but lack the concentration of chromosomal variants. They also do not share the valley's intense seismic activity. A great earthquake is 16 times more frequent in the Vakhsh-Surkhob Valley than elsewhere in the Pamiro-Alay Mountains.

Not satisfied with that single association, Vorontsov and Lyapunova recount several others, all in rodents. Mole rats in the Balkans and the Middle East fit the pattern, as do pine mice from Europe, and red-backed voles from the Rhine to the Chukchi Peninsula (66° N × 170° E) (Table 2.1).

Table 2.1. *Number of populations of* Ellobius *in regions of different seismic activity*

Seismic zone 9 is the most active and has been subdivided into four parts: a = great earthquake once in 10^4 years; b = once in 2×10^3 years; c = once in 10^3 years; d = once in 5×10^2 years.

	Seismic zone				
Karyotype	8	9a	9b	9c	9d
Normal	2	3	6	2	0
Variant	0	1	1	33	28

Data from Vorontsov and Lyapunova (1984).

Here is the pattern for house mice in Italy, Switzerland, Slovenia and Croatia (Table 2.2). (Because of the small sample sizes for most zones, its overall χ^2 is not significant. But, in zones 7 and 8, we have enough populations to avoid the need for Yates' correction. Here $\chi^2 = 5.49$; $p = 0.02$.)

Table 2.2. *Number of populations of Mus musculus in regions of different seismic activity. Seismic zone 9 is the most active*

	Seismic zone				
Karyotype	5	6	7	8	9
Normal	1	4	11	4	2
Variant	0	3	5	11	6

Data from Vorontsov and Lyapunova (1984).

I will offer no explanation for this pattern, but I find it intriguing and possibly very useful.

Diversity in hybrid zones

Tree species of the same genus often blend in hybrid zones. There we find various intergrades between the two pure forms. Insect diversities in such zones can be unusual.

Whitham *et al.* (1994) have studied the insects and fungi of eucalyptus hybrid zones in Tasmania. They collected 40 species altogether. Five of them lived almost exclusively in the hybrid zones.

Within a hybrid zone, pure parental type eucalyptus trees supported 18 insect and fungal taxa per tree. Hybrid trees supported 28. Outside the hybrid zone, pure trees supported only 15 taxa per tree.

Evidence indicates that the eucalyptus pattern is not unique. On the other hand, some hybrid zones (such as those of oaks: Boecklen and Spellenberg, 1990) seem to support fewer species than their pure counterparts. A nice surprise seems to await whoever can delimit and explain what is going on.

Relative diversity of polyploid species

New species sometimes arise by one of two processes involving an increase in chromosomes. These processes are grouped together as polyploidy. (See Chapter 5.) If the new species has twice the chromosome complement of a single parent species, it is called an autopolyploid. If, rather, it has the chromosomes of both of two parent species, it is called an allopolyploid.

Autopolyploids are rare. But a large fraction of plant species derive from allopolyploidy. Stebbins (1950) thought that perhaps 25% or even more are allopolyploids. The rest of this section deals with this proportion.

Botanists have come to expect polyploidy to be common among plants. So, when Hagerup (1932) looked at the plants of Timbuktu (17° N) and discovered only 37% polyploids, he conjectured that the low proportion might typify tropical floras. Later work confirmed his suspicion. The higher the latitude, the higher the proportion of species formed by polyploidy. Figure 2.33 displays the data I have found in the literature. The points come from Europe, North America, Asia, Africa and New Zealand.

Because many believe that a similar gradient exists for elevation, I have separated data from mountains. But the elevation pattern depends on latitude too (Hanelt, 1966). Tropical mountains do have higher proportions of polyploids than their lowlands. But the pattern becomes insignificant at higher latitudes. Mountain floras in Scandinavia (Sweden and Iceland) certainly do not show it (Gustafsson, 1948; Davidsson, 1946). Their mountains often have smaller proportions of polypoids than their lowlands – although no one has claimed significance for those differences. And the flora of the Caucasus Mountains has only 50% polyploids, a figure typical of lowlands at its latitude.

Because of the obvious parallel of polyploid proportion with overall species diversity, and because islands tend to have fewer species than mainlands, I also separated island points. The island data seem to have greater

Plants

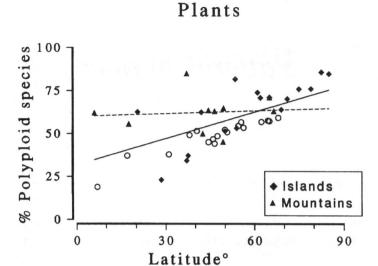

Figure 2.33. Floras at higher latitudes have a greater proportion
of polyploids. Data from several reviews
(Ehrendorfer, 1980; Grant, 1971; Hanelt, 1966; Hair,
1966; Hopper, 1979; Johnson *et al.*, 1965; Knaben,
1961; Löve, 1953; Löve and Löve, 1943, 1957).
Mainland and island points regressed together.
Highland points do not show the trend and are separately regressed.

variance than mainland data, but they fall on virtually the same trend line.
The principal signal – *the rise in polyploidy with latitude* – stands out boldly.

Notice that the polyploid pattern treats the proportion of species instead
of their number. A large proportion of a poor flora may amount to far
fewer species than a small proportion of a rich one. I shall present other
proportional patterns in Chapter 4.

Chapter 3

Patterns in time

Patterns of diversity with time fall along a scale axis that runs from one year to hundreds of millions of years. Nine orders of magnitude! The range makes trivial work of emphasizing how important it is to keep aware of scale. I shall treat scale patterns in order, from longest to shortest.

Evolutionary time

Phanerozoic time

For hundreds of millions of years, life has been leaving abundant testimony to its existence and history. The fossil record teaches us that the number of species has increased over that vast time scale (Sepkoski, 1984). Figure 3.1 shows the number of species of marine invertebrate fossil (per million years) for the ten geological eras preceding ours. (Diversities are divided by the length of the interval to avoid biasing the results. If diversities do not change, then longer intervals will accumulate more species because of turnover, i.e. speciations and extinctions.)

The increase did not proceed without reverses. Several monumental decreases in diversity punctuate the record. (More about these in the section on mass extinctions in Chapter 6.) But, on the whole, life expands.

Perhaps the record deludes us? After all, even rocks are not eternal. The proportion that survive must decline with time, taking their cargo of fossils with them as they erode or are carried down into the molten inner reaches of the earth. We will investigate what is known about this problem in Chapter 10. Yet the overall pattern of increase will never disappear. It is supported on a foundation too solid for debate - the expansion of life into new biomes.

When the Cambrian began, life had not invaded the land. The land was entirely barren, its rocks bare or covered with a layer of sterile, inorganic dust. Today, the land supports between ten and fifty million species. That increase cannot be questioned.

The first vascular plants appeared during the Silurian Period (410 Myr ago). Their record and their subsequent diversification appears as Figure 3.2. As in Figure 3.1, we see a gradual but dramatic increase in diversity

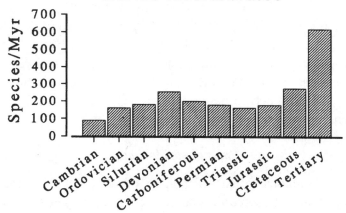

Figure 3.1. Marine invertebrate diversities rise during Phanerozoic time. Geologic Periods are arranged in temporal order, oldest on the left. The periods are similar in duration, but to correct for any differences, diversities are divided by durations. Data from Sepkoski (1984), based on a tabulation by Raup (1976a) of about 70 000 fossil species.

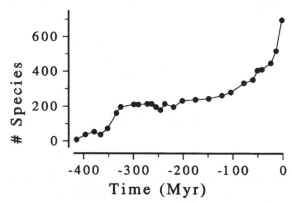

Figure 3.2. The fossil record of vascular plant diversity growth. Redrawn from Knoll (1984).

over the eons. In Chapter 10, you will learn that for most of the time represented as the *x* axis of Figure 3.2, the increase probably is not real. It probably occurred during a much shorter period. But it did occur.

Bambach (1977) pointed out that the oceans too, have seen increases in
diversity. But not many. One of these came when life invaded the muddy
ocean floor toward the end of the Ordovician Period. A fine record of that
expansion is preserved in Quebec. Certainly within 10^6 years (and perhaps
within 10^4), life evolved a special set of species to dwell in and use the
muddy, oxygen-poor ocean floor environment (Figure 3.3).

Taken together, the facts suggest a fitful increase in diversity during
Phanerozoic time. Sometimes there were massive declines, but they were
always repaired. And occasionally there were clear gains as life conquered a
new environment and diversified within it.

Epochal steady-states

For periods of millions to tens of millions of years, diversity changes very
little. Seeing that pattern requires some special techniques because the raw
fossil record is discontinuous and misleading (Rosenzweig and Duek, 1979;

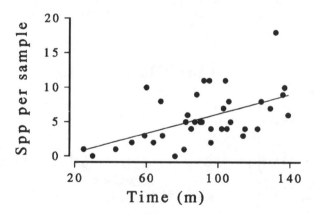

Ordovician Benthos

Figure 3.3. Fossil marine invertebrates from the Nicolet River
Valley, Quebec, reveal the increase in diversity of the
muddy benthos toward the end of the Ordovician
Period. The time interval is roughly 750 000 years.
Data courtesy of Sara and Peter Bretsky. Figure
redrawn from Rosenzweig and Taylor (1980).

Rosenzweig and Taylor, 1980; Nichols and Pollock, 1983; Raup, 1989. See also Chapter 6.) The techniques are familiar to ecologists. They are the ones we use to census populations. My favorite is capture–recapture, because it brings back a pleasant memory.

In October, 1980, I attended a conference on macroevolution at the Field Museum in Chicago. On the first day, a prominent paleobiologist noted that paleobiologists could learn much from ecology, but some methods, like capture–recapture censuses, were never going to work with fossils! A safe bet; or at least one would have thought so.

Next day I presented a study (Rosenzweig and Taylor, 1980) which used capture–recapture on fossils. The idea is to mark species, not individuals. Of course, the datum we then estimate is the number of species.

Imagine a temporal sequence of five fossil-bearing strata. Assume (for now) that during the time of these five strata, no species became extinct and none originated.[1] We identify 15 species in the oldest stratum. We term each of these 'marked'. In the second stratum, we identify 14 species. Seven of these are 'marked', seven are new. So we estimate that we 'marked' half the species when we got 15 in stratum 1. That means there are 30 species (of which we have already seen only 22).

Now we move to stratum 3. There we identify 16 species. Ten of these were seen in stratum 1 or 2. So we estimate that the 22 species marked in stratum 1 and 2 is 10/16 of the total. Hence, our second estimate of the total is 35.2 species. This does not replace our first estimate; it supplements it. We continue with a third and fourth estimate, producing also an estimate of the variance.

Traditional capture–recapture methods assume that all individuals are equally catchable. If instead, they differ, the estimate of population size will probably be too low (Edwards and Eberhardt, 1967). You will agree that species differ greatly in their abundances, distributions and hard parts. So, they must surely differ greatly in their 'catchability', i.e. their probability of being discovered in any particular sample of fossils.

Biometricians have invented special computer-based, capture–recapture analysis techniques for closed populations. These allow capture probabilities to vary among individuals (which in our case are the individual species). In particular, they have worked out ways to deal with a sequence

---

[1] Biometricians – see Nichols, 1992, for a lucid review –call this the assumption of a closed population. Open populations do experience changes in their cast of characters. The assumption of a closed population is a problem, especially if one is measuring diversity during a long period. But it is perfectly good if one has a set of samples from the same stratum and wishes to know how many species are in it.

of samples using a modern technique called 'jack-knifing' (Burnham and Overton, 1979). Hence, Burnham and Overton's jack-knifing technique can produce a much better estimate of diversity in the fossil record than could older methods.

'But wait,' you object. 'Burnham and Overton's method still assumes that populations are closed. Can that assumption also be avoided? Well, the world ain't perfect. Perhaps that is why we call our profession 'science' instead of 'omniscience'. In particular, no one has produced a method that allows for simultaneous relaxation of both the closed-population assumption and the assumption of equal catchability.[2] But if we have a series of samples fairly close together in time, we may expect little turnover. So, we should get a fairly good estimate of diversity with the jack-knife method. If, on the other hand, turnover is great, then our estimates will be rather consistently too high.

Rosenzweig and Taylor (1980) applied the jack-knife method to a fossil assemblage from the Nicolet River Valley, Quebec (amassed by Peter and Sara Bretsky). We previously had estimated its turnover rates (Rosenzweig and Duek, 1979). So we knew they were very low compared to the time between samples. A sequence of 232 fossil-bearing bedding planes represents a period of about 5 Myr. During this time, about 100 species experienced about 40 extinctions. So, the species-players must have been quite stable over the time it took for a few planes to be deposited.

Using a jack-knife window of five bedding planes (c. 10^5 years), we produced a running estimate of diversity for a mixed grill of marine taxa during the 5 Myr record of the Upper Ordovician muddy benthos (Rosenzweig and Taylor, 1980). Using the latest version of the CAPTURE software, Michael Canning and I (unpublished) recently reran these data with a larger window: 10 planes for all intervals except the first and last. (These two used the first and last nine planes respectively.) Figure 3.4 shows these estimates and draws our attention to two things.

- Diversity first increased. That reassured me because we already knew about this increase before we did the analysis (Figure 3.3).
- Second, despite considerable fluctuation, diversity shows no trend except during those first two intervals.

---

[2] Pollock (1982) has come close, and I discuss his technique later. But Pollock's technique requires multiple samples at each time and place. I know of no fossil data where such repeated samples have been taken.

Ordovician Invertebrate Benthos
Closed-model jackknife estimates

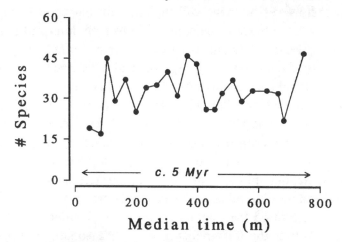

Figure 3.4. Diversity of the muddy benthos during the last
5 Myr of the Ordovician Period. Each point is estimated using a sequence of ten (or nine) fossil-bearing
bedding planes using capture–recapture technology as
explained in the text. Closed models assume no speciation or extinction during the sampling. In reality, that
assumption is only approximately true for these data:
during the roughly 10^5 years of each sequence,
turnover probably averaged about 1–2%. Data courtesy of Sara and Peter Bretsky. Michael Canning
helped with the analysis using the software CAPTURE
(Rexstad and Burnham, 1992).

Yet, this fossil record is dynamic. Many species originate and many
others vanish during the period. During each million years, about 20–25%
of all species get replaced (Rosenzweig and Duek, 1979). But diversity as
a whole goes nowhere. It may rise for awhile or fall for awhile. 'Awhile'
could even amount to 10^6 years. But the overall pattern in the data is flat.

I do not wish to mislead you. Unlike most of the examples in this chapter, the one from the Nicolet River Valley is not typical of others. But its
distinctiveness lies in its transparency to analysis. Most sequences in other
places are continuous, not neatly subdivided into separate layers inter-
spersed with fossil-poor rock. Continuity leaves open the possibility that a
fossil collected at a certain depth actually was first deposited at another

depth and then translocated before rock formation. Such taphonomic problems bedevil other fossil-bearing sites.

I do believe, however, that we will find the diversity conclusion we get from the Bretsky assemblage to be common. Over millions and tens of millions of years, diversity fluctuates within a narrow range. I believe this because theory predicts it (see Chapter 10). I also believe it because other investigations of fossil species show it.

For example, Nichols and Pollock (1983) analyzed Schankler's mammal data from the late Eocene Epoch in Wyoming. They further developed the idea of using capture–recapture tools in paleobiological work. They used the Jolly–Seber estimation technique for open populations. This permits estimates of extinctions and speciations (see Chapters 6, 8 and 10). But it unrealistically assumes that all species have the same capture probability.

In Figure 3.5, I plotted the mammal results for an interval of about 0.5 Myr. (During that time the Jolly–Seber model fits reasonably well.) As in the Ordovician marine invertebrates, diversity is trendless. There are numerous extinctions and speciations. Diversity wobbles a lot. But it does not grow.

I think paleobiologists have been too cautious and slow in applying the

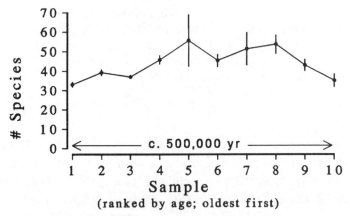

Figure 3.5. Mammal diversity did not tend either to grow or
decline during this 0.5 Myr period of the Cenozoic
Era. Many extinctions and speciations are recorded for
these mammals in this record. Nichols and Pollock
(1983) analyzed the data using a model that allows for
such change, but assumes all species are equally likely
to appear in the record when they exist. Whiskers
show standard errors.

census techniques of ecologists. They are held back by the assumptions of the techniques, and the realization that those assumptions are either difficult to prove for fossil sequences, or else wrong. I have a secret to tell. Those of us who census live animals face exactly the same difficulties. But we work onward. We work onward because the techniques aren't really that fragile. We work onward because we can predict the distortions (and sometimes correct for them). We work onward because often, relative censuses of the same taxa have few of the problems recognized for absolute censuses. And, we work onward because we usually have no better tool than recapture estimation. After all, no science is perfect, but scientists proceed in spite of that, aware that they haven't done too badly with the inexact tools that have been available.

Using techniques more traditional than capture–recapture, Bambach (1977), Van Valkenburgh and Janis (1993) and Webb (1969) also concluded that diversity is trendless. Webb dealt with mammalian genera; Van Valkenburgh and Janis with mammalian species from the past 45 Myr; Bambach with marine invertebrate species throughout Phanerozoic time. Over tens of millions of years, diversity does not often do much more than wobble (Figure 3.6). Allmon *et al.* (1993) reach the same conclusion for the molluscs of the most recent 4 Myr in the tropical western Atlantic.

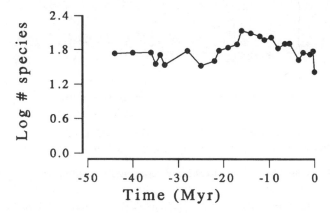

North American Large Mammals

Figure 3.6. Van Valkenburgh and Janis (1993) trace the species diversity of large mammalian herbivores and carnivores in North America during most of the Cenozoic Era. Diversity wobbles along in a trendless series. Data from Van Valkenburgh and Janis (1993).

Benson (1979) provides more evidence. He looked at ostracodes of the shallower parts (<500 m) of the North Atlantic and the deeper parts (>1000 m) of the world-wide ocean. Ostracodes are tiny, heavily armored crustaceans that live on the sea floor. Their bivalved carapaces make excellent fossils, and they leave an unusually good fossil record.

Benson measured ostracode diversities as 'the number of species minus the number of species represented by only one individual'. (Species represented by only one individual are 'contaminants' in his opinion.) Regardless of the particular measure of diversity he used, you can see from Figure 3.7 that diversities at these two depths grow quite differently as sample size increases. The shallower assemblages have about two to three times the number of species as the deeper ones.

Benson then looked at fossil assemblages of these animals in similar samples. The fossils' diversities mimic the modern pattern exactly. There is no hint of any substantive diversity change. And that is true despite the wide ranging ages of the 23 fossil samples (Cretaceous Period to Pleistocene

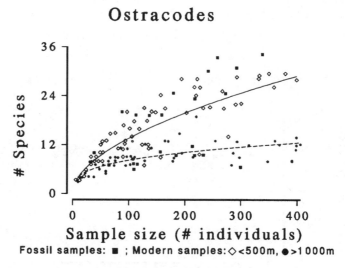

Figure 3.7. Ostracode diversities have remained the same for about 100 Myr. Modern shallow assemblages (diamonds fit by solid line) are usually 2–3 times as diverse as modern deeper assemblages (dots fit by dashed line). 'Shallow' means less than 500 m; 'deep' means more than 1000 m. The boxes come from similar fossil deposits ranging in age from the Cretaceous Period to the Pleistocene Epoch. (Redrawn from Benson, 1979.)

Epoch). As Benson put it, diversity tells you about the environment of the ostracodes but not their geological period.

Watkins and Boucot (1978) were among the first to recognize the pattern in the fossil record. They examined the brachiopods of a 40 Myr stretch of the Paleozoic Era during the Silurian and Devonian Periods (*c.* 400 Myr ago). During the Paleozoic, brachiopods dominated the faunas of the world's oceans. Roughly 80% of species were brachiopods. Proportionally, there were enough brachiopod individuals to stop a filibuster and amend a constitution. It was a world of brachiopods, so, tracing their diversity patterns should tell us what trends characterized their times.

The brachiopods of these times were evolutionarily active. Many species evolved and many became extinct. But their species diversities remained stable all over the world (Figure 3.8).

In Chapter 10, I will review theory that predicts such steady states. We

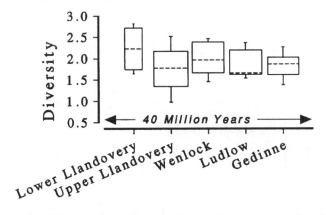

Figure 3.8. The number of species hovered near a set value during this 40 Myr interval of the Paleozoic Era. Diversity was estimated from many fossil assemblages around the world. The box plots show the median and the range; box width is proportional to sample size; each box contains 50% of the samples from its time interval. Diversity was measured with the Shannon–Wiener index; raise *e* to the power of *D* to obtain the number of 'equally common species'. Thus, *D* = 3 means 20 equally common species. Data from Watkins and Boucot (1978).

certainly need more examples of them. But, because this pattern is both supported by data and predicted by theory, I believe we can trust it provisionally.

Host age

Sometimes we can estimate how long particular species of hosts have been accumulating exploiters and other associated species. Then we count the number of such species on each species of host. The result is the host age relationship. Some have suggested a pattern here: the older a host, the more species exploit it. But, as we shall see, that pattern is weak at best.

Southwood (1961) introduced the host age pattern by studying trees of the British Isles. For many years the pattern had its critics. But Birks (1980) reaffirmed it with careful attention to the Pleistocene history of Britain. Birks pointed out that no tree species has lived in Britain longer than 13 000 years. Using radiocarbon pollen profiles, he established an approximate time of post-Pleistocene arrival for each species.

Figure 3.9 gives Birks's result. The regression line in the figure is significant. However, you can see that the scatter tends to fall into a triangle

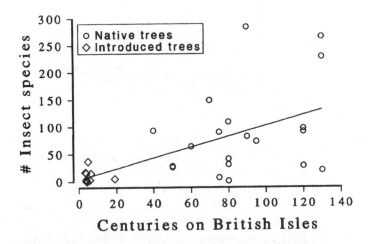

Figure 3.9. Individual species of tree seem to accumulate associated insect species for about 10 000 years. Insect data from Southwood (1961). Time tree species has lived on British Isles from Birks (1980).

rather than along a line. Rather than reaching for a statistical gun and blasting away at the bugbear of heteroscedasticity, let's consider the biology.

Several tree species have few insects despite having lived on Britain most of the time since the glaciers retreated. Thus, some tree species, for reasons unconnected to time, have small insect contingents. Perhaps the entire set of tree species spans the time it takes a tree to collect its contingent of insects. Perhaps, after about 9000 years, all species have about as many insects as they will get, whether this be few or many. This agrees with Goulden (1969) who investigated cladocerans in ancient lacustrine systems. It takes them only 200 to 1000 years to climb to steady levels of diversity. (But it may take somewhat longer for arctic microcrustacea to attain a steady diversity: see Chapter 12, and Hebert and Hann, 1986.)

Strong (1974) suggested the most likely reason for the great scatter on the right side of the figure: The trees have different geographical ranges within Britain. They must act therefore like samples of different area. Tree species that cover large fractions of the island should have many species. But those with restricted distributions should have very few insect associates. Opler (1974) studied leaf miners on California's oaks. All of these leaf miners have lived there at least 18 Myr. He also found a significant effect of a tree's geographical area on its insect diversity.

Kennedy and Southwood (1984) reanalyzed the data of Southwood and Birks with up-to-date estimates of insect diversities. Strong was correct. The main influence on insect diversity is the geographical extent of the trees' range on Britain. Area, by itself, explains almost 60% of the variance.

Does any trace of the host-age pattern remain once we account for the area effect? This is a controversial question. Kennedy and Southwood (1984) say it does. But I was not able to confirm that result using their data. Yet, I believe Birks, and Kennedy and Southwood must be correct to some extent. First, the latter two authors had to exclude two of Birks's points: *Platanus orientalis* and *Abies* spp. Both trees entered Britain artificially within the last half millenium. And both harbor poor diversities of insects. Moreover, no one can doubt that the first contingent of tree colonists of any species will have only a few of the insect species that its mother population has. The other insects will have to arrive over time. Although it disappears for colony ages of more than a few thousand years, the host-age pattern has to exist.

But, investigators who have sought the host-age pattern over grand scales of time have failed to find it. For instance, Bush *et al.* (1990) studied helminth species diversities. They counted only helminths that parasitize the intestines of vertebrates. They compared helminth diversities among major vertebrate groups. Suppose the host-age pattern holds at that scale. Then we expect more parasite species per host among the oldest taxon – fish – and the fewest among the youngest taxa – birds and mammals. Herptiles should harbor intermediate parasite diversities. Instead, Bush *et al.* found that milieu mattered most. Aquatic species, regardless of taxon, have the most helminth parasites. Terrestrial species, the fewest. When taxon did matter, it produced results contrary to the host-age hypothesis. Aquatic mammals and aquatic birds harbored the largest helminth diversities. Among aquatic species, fishes had the smallest helminth diversities. Overall, terrestrial herptiles had the smallest.

Boucot (1983) fairly skewered the host-age pattern at evolutionary scales of time. Moreover, anyone who has read his papers or seen the evidence for long periods of steady diversity in this book will have to agree with him. The host-age pattern operates only over relatively brief periods in rather unnatural circumstances. It depends on introduced species or recent immigrants. Once they have been colonized by their aliquot of pests, the pattern vanishes.

Ecological time

Succession

After a disturbance (such as fire or agriculture), plant species (and animals too) reoccupy the habitat. As they do, they often replace each other in a more or less orderly sequence called succession. Many ecologists have observed such changes and kept track of the diversities during the succession.

In the first few years of succession, plant diversity rises. (Burrows, 1990, reviews the pattern.) But I cannot say much more than that.

Many ecologists have published accounts based on data taken from many types of plant communities. They often did not spend more than a few years looking, although they never claimed to have seen the end of the succession. I guess people need to get interesting results faster than the latter stages of succession can supply them.

Some ecologists cut the Gordian knot by comparing different sites at different stages of succession (these are known as *chronoseres*). We cannot fault that tactic. To it, we owe our very knowledge of succession itself.

Tilman (1988), for instance, compared 22 old fields at Cedar Creek,

Minnesota. They ranged from fields abandoned in the 1920s to those abandoned in the 1980s. Knowing their date of abandonment, he could investigate how their diversity has changed over time. As succession proceeds in this system, plant diversity grows. Bazzaz (1975) got a similar result in Illinois old fields up to 40 years after abandonment.

Nicholson and Monk (1974) supply the longest time horizon I know of. Some of their sites in the Piedmont of Georgia (USA) were undisturbed for 200 years. Like the old fields of Tilman and Bazzaz, Piedmont diversity increases for nearly a century after a disturbance. But then it levels off.

Some studies disagree. Houssard *et al.* (1980) examined diversities in the Montpellierais region of France. After a stand reached the age of 10 years, its plant diversity declined. Whittaker (1970) claimed that plant diversity in the Brookhaven oak-pine forest (New York) peaked after only six years, and then declined by roughly 50% over the next six.

What are we to conclude? In Chapter 9, we will see that many plant surveys are undertaken on 0.1 ha plots and that these are too small. They do not adequately reflect underlying diversities because they include too few individual plants. Usually, succession results in the increase of average plant size (i.e. the individuals in early stages are smaller whether or not they belong to the same species that will inhabit later stages). Thus, we expect fewer individuals per plot as succession replaces herbs with trees.

In Chapter 8, we will learn that diversity does respond to sample size; the more individuals, the higher the diversity. Does that explain why Whittaker saw declining diversity in the Brookhaven forest? I do not know. But in Chapter 8, we shall also learn how to correct for small sample size. We have to ask the plant ecologists to return to their succession data (for surely they have collected enough), and tell us whether a consistent pattern exists in it.

Preston's temporal pattern

If censuses are accumulated year after year in a fixed area, the list of species must increase. But, what about the pattern of increase? Preston (1960) proposed a fascinating answer. Preston conjectured that it would mimic the species–area curve. It would follow a straight line in log-log space and it would have z values like those of species–area curves.

As I will now explain, I do not believe Preston proved his case. Species-time curves may not be straight in log-log space. And even if they are, we have far too few analyses to be confident about their slopes. Let us keep this in mind as we look at the analyses so far accomplished.

Figure 3.10 shows the pattern of increase for one 69 acre (31 ha) area (called Neotoma, Ohio). Data repesent ten censuses conducted during an 18 year interval. I took these data from Preston's paper and plotted them on a Gleason plot (i.e. one that is semi-logarithmic). Yet Preston (1960) insisted that an Arrhenius plot (log-log) does the better job for the species–area curve.

In Preston (1948), we find an astonishing record of moths collected by Seamans at a single light trap in Lethbridge, Alberta, for 22 years (1921–43). Seamans identified 291 species among 303 251 individuals! Yet Preston estimated that only 88% of the species that would eventually be taken had already been caught.

Preston studied the annual rate at which novel species appeared in the trap. I have plotted the actual results on Gleason axes in Figure 3.11. Once again, the Gleason plot works well, as well as the Arrhenius (which I have not shown). Preston too (his Figure 14) used a Gleason plot for these data and similar data from Saskatoon, Saskatchewan.

Williams (1964) also studied the effect of time on diversity. Figure 3.12

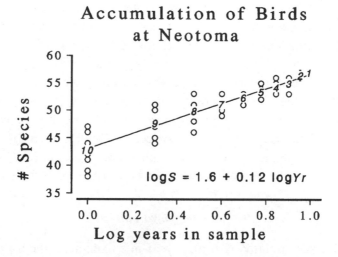

Accumulation of Birds at Neotoma

$$\log S = 1.6 + 0.12 \log Yr$$

Figure 3.10. The number of bird species known from a 69 acre
tract accumulates linearly in a semi-logarithmic space.
Data from Preston (1960), Table II, for 10 years
between 1923 and 1940. The regression goes through
the mean values. These are located by arabic numer-
als, each of which gives the number of estimates for
that length of time. For example, each separate year's
number of species gives an estimate of diversity in a
single year; thus, there are ten such estimates.

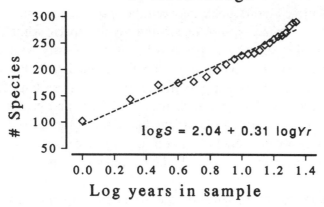

Figure 3.11. Moth diversity grows in a light trap's accumulated collection over 22 years. The data fit a semi-log plot well. Data from Preston (1948), collected by Seamans in Alberta, Canada.

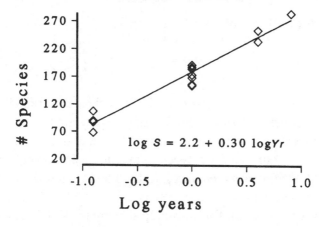

Figure 3.12. Cumulative diversity of Lepidoptera collected in a light trap at Rothamsted Experimental Station, England. Data from Williams (1964).

shows his results for Lepidoptera in a light trap at Rothamsted Experimental Station. Notice that it too fits a Gleason plot extremely well.

Have we identified a difference between the species–area and species–time relationships? Is the first pattern linear in a log-log space, while the second is linear in semi-log space? (Or perhaps keeps its linearity with either axis system?) In the next few paragraphs, I will mimic Frank Preston's own arguments to see if we can support his answer. I will use both the log-log and the semi-log models to estimate the coefficients and errors of prediction. But I shall not be able to favor the log-log plot for species–time data. I will not even be able to conclude that if log-log space is the right space for species–time curves, the slopes of their regressions resemble those of species–area curves.

Let's estimate the coefficients of the Arrhenius equation for Preston's data. We can estimate z as the slope of the line connecting the first census point with the last. At Neotoma, the value of census one averaged 42.8 species. (We get an average because each year provides an independent estimate of the census for a first year.) After nine more spring censuses, there were 57 species. Hence our estimate of z:

$$z = (\log 57 - \log 42.8)/(\log 10 - \log 1) = 0.125 \tag{3.1}$$

which is fairly close to z-values for birds in mainland species-area curves.

Let us now suppose that in about 1000 years, Neotoma will have experienced most or all of its possible successional seres. By our estimate of z, it will have accumulated y species where $\log y$ satisfies

$$(\log y - \log 42.8)/(\log 10^3 - \log 1) = 0.125 \tag{3.2a}$$

So,

$$y = 101 \text{ species} \tag{3.2b}$$

In evolutionary time, all of these 101 will be replaced, so the 69 acres will accumulate 202 species. Preston (1960), using expert advice, estimates this evolutionary replacement requires 4 or 5 Myr. That is 5×10^6. (It won't matter much if it takes half or twice that time.) However, in 5 Myr, Neotoma should accumulate (according to the method and the constants of Equation 3.2a) 295 species. But twice 101 is 202, not 295. So there is a 32% shortfall somewhere. Not bad for an ecologist perhaps. But Gleason's equation does it better, as you will now see.

Gleason's equation for Figure 3.10 is

$$S = 43.07 + 13.61 \log t \tag{3.3}$$

where t is time in years and the initial value of t is 0. With this equation, we predict 83.9 bird species in 1000 years, and 134.2 in five million. Twice 83.9 is 167.8. So our Gleason estimate deviates from the data by only 20%.

Furthermore, the Gleason estimate better withstands the likely prospect that the period '1000 years' overestimates the time for succession. Suppose, for example, that successional processes require only 500 years to accumulate all species. Then the Gleason estimate becomes 79.8 species, whose double – 159.6 – is even closer to the predicted value of 134.2 species. It deviates by only 15.9%. But the Arrhenius estimate becomes 92.8 species. Its double – 185.6 – compares even more poorly to its target, 295 species (error now 37%). So the Gleason estimate produces smaller error, and it is more robust to the probable change that will be required in our estimate of the time of succession.

The moth case is more obviously troubling. The z-value in the Arrhenius analogue to Figure 3.11 is 0.307. That's far too high for a mainland species–area curve.

Preston did not actually use real evolutionary data to test his hypothesis. But I tried just that in Figure 3.13. These data come from the same fossil collections we used above to look at diversity over the scale of 5 Myr (150 m represents roughly 1 Myr). They are a subset of the late Ordovician benthic data from the Nicolet River Valley, Quebec.

Early in this record (i.e. for the first 145 m), diversity was increasing. Thus, for this figure, I did not use the bedding planes of data beneath 145 m. (We want the increase from steady evolution while diversity wobbles within a small range, not the unusual and perhaps rapid rate that would accompany the oldest bedding planes in this sequence.)

The Gleason plot (Figure 3.13) fits quite well. But the regression line is not straight. It is a second order polynomial.

Switching to an Arrhenius plot does straighten the curve (Figure 3.14). For these data, $z = 0.36$. That value resembles the one we got for Figure 3.11 (0.307). But it still exceeds values we expect from mainland species–area curves.

In short, Preston asked a brilliant question but did not entirely resolve it. His data are far too sparse for any firm conclusion. And the data analyses I add here remain inadequate to give us much confidence. But Preston and Williams did show us that species–time curves exist. Perhaps they do not have the same coefficient values as species–area curves. And for some time scales, perhaps they fit the Gleason equation better than the Arrhenius equation. Nevertheless, they exist. We need to focus on Frank Preston's challenge and improve our ability to describe species–time curves.

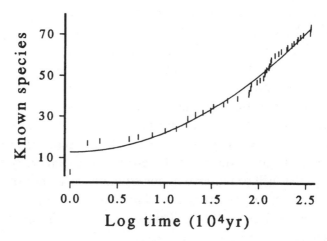

Figure 3.13. The number of species known from the Nicolet River
        Valley, Quebec, accumulates regularly as younger
        bedding planes are examined and added to the
        record. I have not used the first 140 m of bedding
        planes because they record an extraordinarily rapid
        increase in diversity and I wanted to examine more
        usual times. I approximated real time units in years
        by assigning the arbitrary elapsed time of 3 548 100
        years to the period between 145 m and 808 m, and
        then calculating what fraction of that time had passed
        as each lens of fossils was deposited. The figure
        3 548 100 years is not too different from the time that
        must have passed during this period. (The first two
        points on the left side do not indicate an unusually
        high rate of evolution: they are just sampling errors.
        Point 1 had only three species; point 2 had 20. The
        four points immmediately older than these two aver-
        age 10.75 species.)

Seasonal variation

In some regions, like northeastern North America, many species leave during the colder times of the year. Birds are the most noted migrants, but
some species of insects also migrate. An even higher proportion of the biota
vanish physiologically during wintertime. They enter torpor or diapause, or
drop their leaves and send their sap rootward.

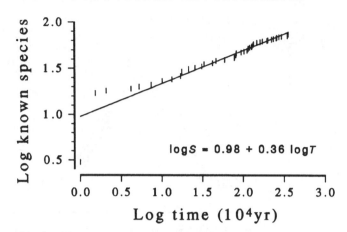

Figure 3.14. The log-log version of Figure 3.14. The z value of
0.36 is within the range of common species–area z-
values.

Britain has 193 species of breeding birds, 117 non-passerine and 76 passerine. Of the non-passerines, 41 (35%) migrate. Of the passerines, 27 (35.5%) migrate. Thus Britain's bird diversity oscillates through the year. In addition to the migratory residents, about 100 other species of migrants pass through on their way elsewhere in spring or autumn, adding further to the annual cycle of bird diversity.

Other taxa also show the annual cycle in diversity. Williams (1964) illustrated the pattern in English Lepidoptera with data of Best (1950). In Figure 3.15, I show that pattern using the numbers of species instead of the diversity index that Williams used.

Of the 57 bird species recorded at Neotoma in south–central Ohio, 36 leave for the winter. That is 63.2%, a proportion typical for the northeastern USA but much higher than that of Britain. Only 11 of the 58 species recorded regularly in a 26.3 ha forest preserve in northeastern Ohio, reside there all year round (Williams, 1936). And many of the individuals belonging to eight of these 11 leave the forest to breed elsewhere. So only three species are altogether sedentary. Figure 3.16 shows the oscillation in diversity among the breeding species.

Pause before you decide this problem isn't very interesting – before you dismiss it with an obvious answer. In particular, do not answer with: 'Of

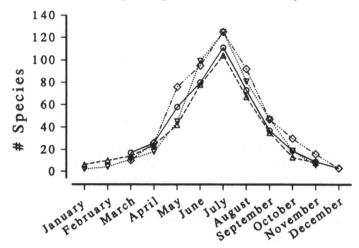

Figure 3.15. Diversities of many taxa oscillate regularly within the
year. These data of Best (1950) come from two light
traps in Woking, Surrey, England. One was 4.5 feet
(1.4 m) above ground; the other 36 feet (11 m) above
ground. Low trap: circles, 1948; inverted triangles,
1949; High trap: diamonds, 1948; triangles, 1949.

course birds fly south; it is warmer there.' I have seen birds of many sizes
coming to our feeders in the frigid cold of a January day in upstate New
York or southern Wisconsin. Are those species evolutionarily stupid? Many
of them are superb fliers and closely related to migratory species. Why
don't they leave too? Eight of the species of that northeastern forest preserve appear there *only* during the winter when so many others have gone
(Williams, 1936). We are a tropical species ourselves. Maybe that is what
makes us so quick to blame everything on harsh winters. Physiology may
play a crucial role. But my guess is that its role will be much more sophisticated than merely informing us that 'Baby, it's cold outside!'

The tropics and subtropics, in fact, have annual cycles, too (see, for
example, Leigh *et al.*, 1982). Wolda (1980, 1982) has examined leafhoppers
(Homoptera) in Panama and documented their seasonality species by
species. A few are active year-round. But most do show seasonality, albeit
not as pronounced as leafhoppers from colder climes. And some tropical
leafhoppers 'have seasons as short, and seasonal peaks as sharp as, species
from northern Finland' (Wolda, 1982, p. 319).

Annual Cycle of Diversity
NE Ohio Breeding Birds

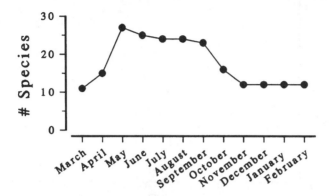

Figure 3.16. Most breeding bird species in a northeastern Ohio
forest preserve migrate elsewhere during the off-
season. Censuses from 1932–35 inclusive (Williams,
1936, Tables 16, 17, 18). Diversities showed no
variance during the winter and little in spring or
summer; maximum: 28 species (1933); minimum:
26 species (1934).

We can even find evidence of annual cycling in tropical aquatic species
diversitites. Figure 3.17 shows the macrobenthic diversity in a subtropical
Australian estuary through the year (Saenger *et al.*, 1988). Why is diversity
about twice as high during the austral winter and spring as during summer
and fall? Is the water too wet in the summer? Is it too cold? Maybe it's too
hot? Oxygen solubility does decrease with temperature, so maybe warm is
harsh! On the other hand, it's not too harsh for about 130 species.

As for birds, many tropical species move up and down mountains
throughout the seasons. Preston (1960) already noted that migrants constitute a small minority of the avifauna in the tropics, even during the winter
– perhaps only 10–20%. So we may expect any seasonal tropical bird pattern to be generated by local species that alter their elevations regularly
during the year.

Subtropical regions often exchange species between summer and winter.
Certain species leave and others move in. Diversity may not change very
much, but the exchange prompts some questions.

Why is Israel such a good idea in winter for a stock dove or a spotted
eagle, while turtle doves and short-toed eagles come only in summer, and

Temporal patterns

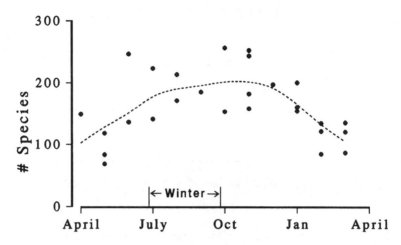

Figure 3.17. Diversity of macrobenthos peaks during the winter in an Australian subtropical estuary followed for several years by Saenger *et al.* (1988).

palm doves and golden eagles stay all year long? What makes it such an ideal wintertime spa for thrushes like the stonechat and European robin, while other thrushes like the black redstart stay all year, and still others like the nightingale and isabelline wheatear use it only for a summer resort? In a country where a persistent and lucky birder can hope to see 11 different species of falcon, why are those 11 species subdivided almost evenly among winter visitors, summer visitors, residents, and passage migrants?

Seasonal patterns of diversity deserve more attention. Merely because we suspect that their explanations are trivial, we have allowed ourselves to be inhibited from even documenting them properly. But the simple explanations may be completely unsatisfactory. And the real explanations may go well beyond helping us understand annual cycles.

Chapter 4

Dimensionless patterns

Not all diversity patterns are rooted in space or time. Some are dimensionless. These show how diversity varies with other properties of organisms. Below, I give four examples. Marzluff and Dial (1991) study others (such as reproductive rate and longevity) connected with life history. You may think of more.

In including such patterns, I have stepped outside the bounds of this book's title. Yet, I believe that their discovery and explanation will occupy some of the most interesting pages of our journals during the next decade.

Body size

G. E. Hutchinson co-authored only one paper with his student R. H. MacArthur. It introduced the world to the body size pattern of species diversity (Hutchinson and MacArthur, 1959). *Within a taxon, there are more intermediate-size species than either very large or very small ones.* Figure 4.1 shows the pattern they found for dragonflies of the northeastern USA.

Hutchinson and MacArthur presented a theoretical explanation of the pattern. The explanation has not lasted because it depends on patch size being the same for all species regardless of body size. But the pattern itself remains fascinating.

May (1978) shows similar patterns among mammals, birds, beetles and butterflies. Also, he develops a reasonable, albeit speculative, overview of the distribution of body size among all species of animals. It, too, appears unimodal.

Others have reorganized this pattern (VanValen, 1973; Kochmer and Wagner, 1988). They ask how many species there are in a taxon (genus, family or order). They find that taxa whose individuals tend to be larger, have fewer species than those with smaller individuals. But their question differs from the one we owe to Hutchinson and MacArthur.

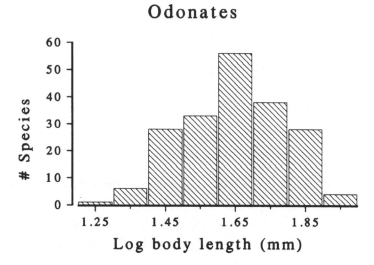

Figure 4.1. More dragonflies have intermediate body sizes than
large or small sizes. Data from northeastern USA.
Redrawn from Hutchinson and MacArthur, (1959).

More puzzling is the result of Lindsey (1966). He looked at non-warm-
blooded vertebrates. In most cases he did find the unimodal relationship.
But not always. Three tropical distributions peak on the small side. This is
true of deep sea fishes, freshwater fishes, and frogs. That is, in the tropics,
there are more small species of these three taxa than of any other size.
Meanwhile, marine fishes of the Arctic peak on the large side. Moreover,
for most taxa, the higher the latitude, the larger the body size that holds the
most species. (Snakes – the exception – peak over large size regardless of
latitude.)

Lindsey's result suggests a pattern to the exceptions. In the tropics, small
body sizes are most common. As we proceed toward a pole, the modal
body size moves higher and higher, passing through intermediate sizes and
coming to rest at the largest size when we examine the taxon at its highest
latitudes. Where Lindsey's pattern applies, the unimodal pattern of
Hutchinson and MacArthur will describe the body size pattern only at
intermediate latitudes.

But Lindsey's result cannot be entirely general. One of May's butterfly
figures comes from Australia and another includes all terrestrial mammals
except bats. Morse *et al.* (1988) revealed the intermediate peak among beetles in the Bornean tropics. In what taxa does Lindsey's pattern hold and

why? We need to improve our description of the pattern, perhaps by tracking it at different scales (Brown and Nicoletto, 1991), different latitudes, or in different taxa. But the job has just begun and as yet we have no answers.

Dial and Marzluff (1988) have begun the work for different taxa. They examined body sizes of species in 40 taxonomic groups of plants and animals. (They also looked at six other groups, but not at the species level.) Within each group they calculated the average size of species in a larger taxonomic unit (genus or family or, in one case each, an order or class). Then they ranked the units from smallest to largest average body size. They identified the most diverse of the units and assigned it a relative body size. If it is the smallest, it gets a score of 0%. If the largest, it gets 100%. The percentage tells what fraction of the rest of the units have smaller average body sizes.[1]

Figure 4.2 shows the results. The most diverse taxon in each group varies from one extreme to another. For instance, *Corvus*, the most diverse genus of Corvidae (jays, crows, ravens), also has the largest body size. But, Viverridae (mongooses and civet cats) is the most diverse family of

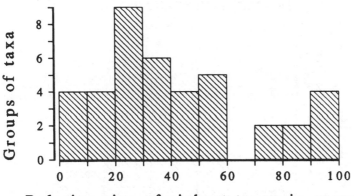

Figure 4.2. The most diverse taxon in a group of closely related taxa tends to be of intermediate average body size. Data from Dial and Marzluff (1988). See text for details of calculating the *x*-axis.

[1] Marzluff and Dial (1991) note that the formula given in the 1988 paper is wrong. John Marzluff sent me the original data so that I could plot the correct values.

Carnivora and has the smallest average body size. Most of the taxa do fall between the extremes, however. Thus the overall pattern supports Hutchinson and MacArthur's observation. The highest diversity in a taxon tends to occur at intermediate body sizes.

Furthermore, grouping species into larger taxonomic units has forced some of the results toward the extremes. Figure 4.3 shows what happens when you plot North American Carnivora as separate species without first grouping them into families. Instead of the most diverse size being the smallest, it lies in the intermediate interval 2.6–2.8. Similarly, when you ask which corvid genus has the most species, the answer is *Corvus*, the one with the largest average body size. Yet, corvid species are most likely to have intermediate body size (Figure 4.4). It's just that ornithologists call all the big black corvids '*Corvus*,' and split up the smaller ones into many genera of jays, etc. I'm not saying that's wrong. I am pointing out that it has no bearing on which body sizes are most common among the species of a taxon. Thus, Dial and Marzluff reached the correct conclusion, in fact, understating their case.

Lawton (1991) connects the body size pattern to another. Species of inter-mediate body size are not only more diverse then others, they are also more

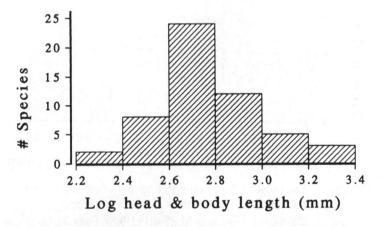

Figure 4.3. Although the most speciose family of North American carnivore (Mustelidae) has the smallest average body size, the body size distribution among carnivore species ungrouped by family has an intermediate mode.

North American Corvids

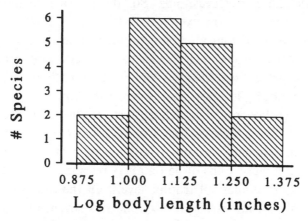

Figure 4.4. Most species of North American corvids are not particularly large-sized or small-sized. They are jay- and magpie-size.

abundant. Lawton suggests that we combine these three axes –abundance, diversity, size – and study the entire problem as a three dimensional pattern. Blackburn *et al.* (1993) have followed that suggestion and emerge with a novel hypothesis for the size–abundance pattern. But it sheds no new light on the size–diversity pattern. So far, we must admit that we cannot explain it.

Patterns in food webs and food chains

A food web is a set of species amongst which energy transfers take place. A food chain is a sequence of such transfers.

Diversity declines at higher trophic levels in a food chain

All species use free energy ('free' in the physical sense, i.e. available for work). Their trophic level is an expression of where they get their energy.

The species that take energy from inorganic sources such as sunlight, are termed autotrophs or primary producers, and constitute the first trophic level.

Those that take it from autotrophs, are primary consumers. Herbivores, folivores, granivores, frugivores, etc. are primary consumers. These constitute the second trophic level.

Those that consume primary consumers, constitute the third level. They are predators and parasitoids. But many third level species have their own predators and hyperparasitoids. So, there is a fourth trophic level. More rarely, we see a fifth and even a sixth (Schoener, 1989).

You may see that no logical reason prevents a seventh, eighth, etc. Big fleas have little fleas upon their backs to bite 'em, and little fleas have smaller fleas. So on, *ad infinitum.* (Apologies to Jonathan Swift and Stuart Pimm.) But of course you know that is not true. Almost no metazoans live beyond level six (Schoener, 1989; Schoenly *et al.*, 1991). Most of the world's known food webs have three or four trophic levels (Figure 4.5). Only three of the 92 webs in Schoener's Figure 5 – all marine pelagic webs – have more than six. Among insects, webs of gall makers resemble pelagic webs in having unusually high numbers of trophic levels. Of the four such community webs in Schoenly *et al.*, two have six, one has seven, and one has eight trophic levels! Only one of the other 57 community webs they analyze has seven. And none has eight (Figure 4.6).

Close inspection of the few pelagic webs with high numbers of trophic levels (Table 4.1) shows that the species that belong to levels eight and nine

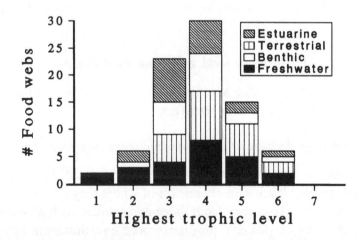

Figure 4.5. Most food chains have three or more levels, but few use trophic level 6. Data on 82 food webs from Tables 1, 2, 3 and Figure 5 of Schoener (1989). Marine pelagic webs not included; they appear in Table 4.1.

Table 4.1. *Pelagic maximum food-chain lengths*

Length	1	2	3	4	5	6	7	8	9
No. Webs	0	0	0	2	4	1	0	2	1

Data from Schoener (1989).

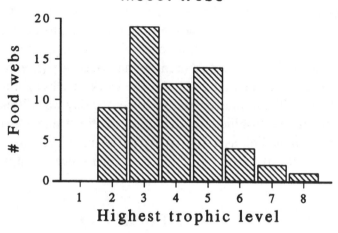

Figure 4.6. Most insect food chains have 3–5 levels. Data from the 61 community webs of Schoenly *et al.*, 1991.

get much or most of their food as members of lower trophic levels. For example, web No. 41 (Cohen *et al.*, 1990) comes from tropical epipelagic seas and has eight trophic levels. But the species at the eighth level is 'large sharks'. The chain that puts them there has them eating 'medium-sized sharks' which eat lancetfish, which eat squid, which eat lanternfish, which eat hyperiid amphipods, which eat copepods, which eat dinoflagellates. But that is probably a very rare pathway for their resources to take. Most pathways to large sharks have them on level 5 or 6. The pathway that puts them on level 4 may be the most common. (They eat tuna, which eat euphausiids, which eat coccolithophores.) And any pathway involving their eating of medium-sized sharks probably has more to do with interference competition than feeding (Rosenzweig, 1966). Schoenley *et al.* (1991) have enumerated the number of insect species feeding at each trophic level in 61 community food webs. In their study, a species counts only once – i.e. at the highest trophic level it uses. I placed their data into Figure 4.7 so that we could actually see, for the first time, the decline in diversity as trophic level increases. Because Schoenly *et al.* (1991) caution that the species at level 1 have been lumped together into internally diverse groups, I did not include that level in the figure. (But you will find it in Chapter 11.)

Yodzis (1989, p. 240) notes that defining 'trophic level' for any particular species has complications not always appreciated. These lead to different definitions among investigators. Yodzis (p. 209) lists six (and these do not include the definition of Oksanen – see Chapter 11). Some investigators favor the maximum length definition as used by Cohen *et al.* (1990). Some, like Yodzis himself, prefer its opposite (minimum length) because the lowest level used probably supplies more energy and resources than any other. Such differences have confused us in more than one case. (See, for example, the section of Chapter 11 that compares the work of Oksanen and his colleagues to that of Pimm and Lawton.) I hope one day we will have enough data to return to the trophic level definition of Pimm and Lawton (1977). They define a trophic link as a flow between a trophic level and a consumer species that carries at least 5% of the consumer's energy input. Trophic

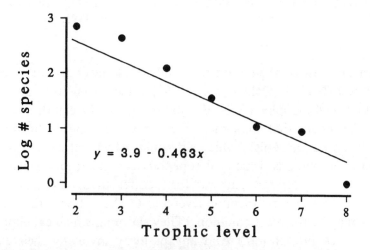

Insect Food Webs

$y = 3.9 - 0.463x$

Figure 4.7. Insect diversity declines with increase in maximum trophic level. The fit is linear in semi-log space. Data come from 61 community food webs collected by Schoenly *et al.* (1991).

level is the average length of these pathways weighted by the proportion of energy they carry. (This is essentially Yodzis' fifth definition.) This definition would get rid of most crypto-competitive links and pay little or no attention to exceedingly rare pathways. Thus it should also agree fairly well with Yodzis' minimum length definition. I believe such a change would show us that the set of chain lengths in use by life is even more restricted than we now believe it to be. It also would allow 'trophic level' – now an integer – to become a continuous variable.

What is the effect of switching definitions from the maximum to the minimum chain length? It is only to reinforce the impression that that there is a sharp limit to the number of trophic levels. Yodzis (1993) examined 507 species of top consumer to see how short a trophic chain they use to get their food. All but two have lengths of two, three or four levels. The two exceptions have lengths of five. Moreover, Yodzis points out that neither of the exceptions is well enough studied, and both will likely be found to use a shorter food chain for most of their food. Recently, my class and I re-examined most of the webs cited by Schoenly *et al.* Of 896 consumer species, only two function at level five. Both are spiders that specialize on wasps. All the rest are on lower levels.

So, even without a unique definition for trophic level, we can recognize that maximum food chain length gives us another dimensionless pattern: *Metazoan diversity declines as trophic level increases and dips to near zero at trophic levels higher than six (maximum length) or four (minimum length).*

Few species are omnivorous

Define an omnivore as a species that takes at least 5% of its energy from a trophic level different from the one it most often feeds from. Suppose, for example, it takes 92% plants and 8% herbivores. In other words, an omnivore commonly takes food from at least two trophic levels.

Pimm and Lawton (1978) defined omnivores that way and looked for them by surveying 23 known data bases of food webs. They found only one omnivore per web.

One omnivore per web seems very few. But how can we be more confident that omnivorous species are unusual? Perhaps, if trophic linkages were assigned randomly, 23 webs would often have only 23 omnivores.

Pimm and Lawton (1978) demonstrated the scarcity of omnivores using a Monte Carlo computer simulation. A Monte Carlo simulation solves a probability problem too difficult for straightforward calculation. The computer is programmed to assign properties according to a set of probabilities, and see what fraction of the results pass a certain test.

In this case, the computer knew the following about each food web: the number of species of primary producers; the number of species of predators (at any level); the number of trophic levels; the number of species being eaten; the number of predators eating other predators; the number of predator–victim links. These numbers came from real food webs.

Randomly, the computer assigned trophic links between species to each web. After each run, the number of omnivores was tallied. The computer ran and reran the simulations thousands of times.

Having specified all those properties from the real systems, you might guess the systems all would be constrained to have no fewer and no more omnivores than they do in real life. But that is not what happened. Very few of the simulations had the same number of omnivores as the real webs they mimicked.

Well then, at least you might expect the *average* number of omnivores to be the same in simulations and real webs. But even that did not happen. If the medians had been the same, then half the simulations would have had more and half would have had fewer omnivores than real life. But 0.747 of the simulations had more omnivores than real webs. Pimm and Lawton (1978) had shown that if omnivory occurs randomly, then omnivores ought to comprise a much larger fraction of the world's species than they actually do. Real webs have few omnivorous species.

Predator-victim ratios

Diversity varies a lot from place to place and time to time. Arnold (1972) introduced the idea that predators merely follow their victims' lead and attain a diversity proportional to that of their victims. Arnold studied reptile and amphibian diversities in various parts of the world. To his collection of data, I added that of Duellman (1990), and produced Figure 4.8. It shows that the predator diversity may not respond much to increases of their prey's diversity beyond those studied by Arnold. (The higher values of diversity, absent from Arnold's sample, are supplied by Duellman.)

Jeffries and Lawton (1985) amassed the records of freshwater invertebrate communities and analyzed their diversities. I plot Jeffries and Lawton's data in Figure 4.9 Again, you see the strong tendency for more predator species when there are more victim species.

Is the ratio of predators to victims a constant? Cohen (1977) studied 14

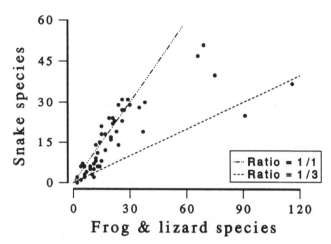

Figure 4.8. At high diversities of lizards and frogs, snakes (their predators) have fewer species per species of prey. Data from Arnold (1972) and Duellman (1990). For reference, I have plotted the lines that correspond to the ratios 1/1 and 1/3.

food webs and classified their predators and victims into 'kinds'. A kind is not a species. It may be a distinctive stage of a species' life cycle. Or it may be a collection of species with very similar morphologies and escape tactics. Schoener (1989) reports about 0.68 trophic kinds per species, so the difference is substantial. Nevertheless, Cohen – and, I guess, every other ecologist – finds it intriguing that the number of kinds of predators corresponds linearly to the number of kinds of victims. Using many more food webs, Schoener (1989) reaffirmed the pattern.

Jeffries and Lawton – working not with kinds but real species – suggest that the ratios in their data set vary systematically with diversity. In fact, they wrote, 'Although numbers of prey species and predator species are highly correlated, the ratio of predators to prey is not constant.' They estimated that in depauperate samples the ratio was about 0.48; in average ones, 0.36; in rich ones, 0.29. Perhaps, but as you see in Figure 4.9, the relationship is fairly weak and insignificant. The solid line that transects the data is actually the second order polynomial regression forced through the origin. It has a tiny squared term (which equals -7×10^5 and has $p = 0.91$). The deviation from linearity is so small that your eye cannot detect it. The dominant trend follows the ratio 1/3.

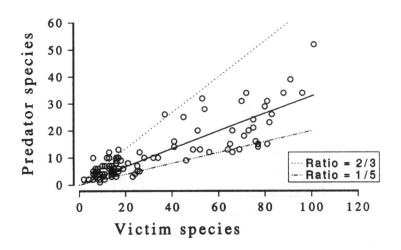

Figure 4.9. Predator–victim ratios in freshwater invertebrates.
Data from Jeffries and Lawton (1985). In contrast to
their log-log plot, I have used an arithmetic plot for
these data. The arithmetic plot shows that the ratio
does not decline monotonically with diversity. The
solid line shows the second order polynomial regression. (Its squared term, although plotted, is insignificant.) The line falls almost precisely on that for a 1/3
ratio. The other two ratios are plotted for reference
only.

But the data of Figure 4.8 clearly deviate from a constant ratio. Once victim diversity reaches fairly high levels, predator diversity does not respond
very much at all. Thus, the ratio of predators to their victims declines as
diversity increases.

A pioneering study of fossil diversities also suggests that decline (Van
Valkenburgh and Janis, 1993). These data come from large mammals. (See
Figure 3.6 for the diversities plotted through time.) The data even suggest
(Figure 4.10) that the decline may be piecewise linear instead of smooth.
From about 50 species up, there is about one species of carnivore for every
four of herbivores. From 20 species to about 50, the ratio falls from about
1/2 to about 1/4.

I turned next to the Schoenly *et al.* (1991) data set. Their results suggest a
constant predator–victim ratio. They have sorted their data in sophisticated
ways and attended to the life history details of each species.

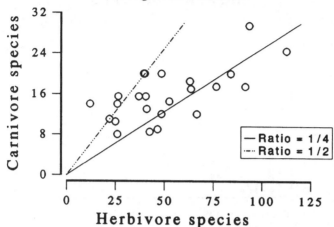

Figure 4.10. The predator–victim diversity ratios among large
herbivorous mammals and their carnivores in the
Cenozoic record of North America. The ratio falls
over increased diversity, although it may reach an
asymptote. For reference, I have plotted the lines that
correspond to the ratios 1/2 and 1/4. Data from Van
Valkenburgh and Janis (1993).

Nevertheless, I cannot claim to understand their result entirely. Where
are its zeros? Several systems have species at levels one and two only. These
should appear on their Figure 2.B as points arrayed along the y-axis – some
possible victims, but zero predators. But no such points are there. So, I
took their data and replotted it in various ways.

I looked at the ratio of third level to second level species (remember
that level one is overlumped). The result is very noisy but a linear signal
explains a significant amount of the variance. Then I repeated the analysis
with level 2 constituting the victims, and levels 3 to 8 (inclusive) as the
predators (Figure 4.11). Again there is a linear signal ($R^2 = 0.29$). I'm not
sure how they got their result, but I had no trouble coming up with the
same conclusion from their data. Cohen's rule does seem to work here.
Predator–victim ratios in insect webs seem constant despite varying diversity.

So, Figures 4.8 and 4.10 lead us to believe that Cohen's rule does not
hold for species diversities (rather than kinds). But, Figures 4.9 and 4.11 tell
us that it does. What are we to conclude? First, there is pattern. The more

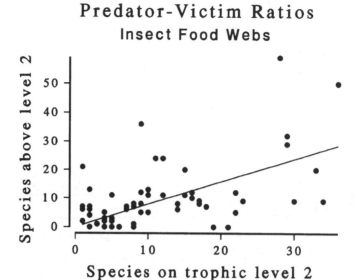

Figure 4.11. The predator–victim ratio among insect webs. The
number of predator species is the sum of the species
in levels 3–8. The number of victim species is the
number of species in level 2. Data from the 61 community webs of Schoenly *et al.* (1991). Neither a polynomial nor any other curvilinear method improves
the fit significantly.

species of victims, the more species of predators. Second, the ratio of predator species to victim species may decline at higher diversities, but we cannot
yet be sure. With only four collections of data, we already see some variation in the pattern. We need many more data to establish whatever regularities these four collections may exemplify.

Chapter 5

Speciation

Whenever a lineage splits into more than one branch, it has undergone speciation. Yet, I should hate to be asked exactly when the time comes to call them 'split'. That is like asking exactly when a child becomes an adult. I am content to know that initially there was one lineage and now there are more.

But I would like also to know what mechanism drives the speciation. Like the maturation process of a human being, that mechanism can be studied and described.

Three basic modes of speciation have given us life's diversity:

- Geographical speciation
- Polyploidy
- Competitive speciation

Geographical speciation is the most orthodox. Polyploidy is the best tested. Competitive speciation is the most controversial. You probably learned other words to describe speciation processes, but I believe they all describe one of these three modes.

Geographical speciation

Here is an outline of the process of geographical (also called allopatric) speciation.

- A geographical barrier restricts gene flow within a sexually reproducing population.
- The isolated subpopulations evolve separately for a time.
- They become unlike enough to be called different species.
- Often the barrier breaks down and the isolates overlap but do not interbreed (or they interbreed with reduced success).

Evolutionists ask many questions of geographical speciation. How long must the barrier remain? How effective must it be in isolating the subpopulations? What drives the evolutionary separation? Is it different environmental pressures or small populations prone to genetic drift or other neutral evolutionary changes? What happens after the populations come back together? Do they then evolve secondary isolating mechanisms such as different reproductive behaviors (that avoid unsuccessful interbreeding)?

As interesting as these questions are, most of them will not be treated here. I will focus on rates, specifically the rates of isolate formation and the rates of formation of new species after isolation. The focus does not mean to say that the other questions are settled. But we need to focus on rates to understand the dynamics of diversity. How should we achieve our focus? We do it by baldly stating our goal: we are trying to explain geographical and temporal diversity patterns.

It follows from that goal that we need to identify variables correlated with space and time that also affect the rate of speciation. If they have no influence on that rate, they will not help. If they vary orthogonally to space and time, they also cannot help explain a temporal or a spatial diversity pattern. The criterion of relatedness to both the dependent and the independent variables seems trivial, but it is not. It is the way to pare down a huge list of factors into a manageable few. Moreover, we lose nothing by doing so. All too often, ecologists try to measure and model everything, when their very questions already eliminate the possible significance of most of their work.

I believe that the strongest space-time influences on geographical speciation rate work through the first step in the process, population isolation. The second and third steps depend on evolution within the populations themselves; if location or time affect these evolutionary rates, they should do so weakly. And the fourth step, the rate of barrier breakdown, seems hardly likely to be influenced by space or time at all.

At least two spatial factors can affect the rate of barrier formation directly: geographical circumstances, and the geographical range of the species. Let us consider these in turn. Then we will consider interesting factors that may have to do with the rate of divergence after isolation.

Geographical circumstances

Populations may inhabit a region that comes ready-made with isolating barriers. Suppose propagules[1] occasionally cross those barriers, but usually

---

[1] Propagules are small populations of colonists sufficient to establish a species in a new place. Sometimes they are called founder populations.

after enough time for speciation has passed. Then the region and its barriers act like a speciation machine, rapidly cranking out new species.

Archipelagos and rugged mountain ranges can constitute such speciation machines. Often they contain many, many closely related species. The species typically are restricted to one or two islands, or to a single mountain valley or peak. Another island or peak has a similar, but different species.

Hawaii, for example, has a total area of only 16 600 km². But it is subdivided into seven principal islands and many smaller ones. It also has significant mountainous relief. You should not be too surprised to learn that it has supported some spectacular radiations (Simon, 1987). The subfamily of birds called honeycreepers (Drepaninae) descended from a single species. But it contained *c.* 43 species when Polynesians colonized the islands about a thousand years ago (Freed *et al.*, 1987). Two genera of land snail have radiated to extraordinary diversities: *Partulina* with 44 species and *Achatinella* with 42. One composite plant species produced a radiation of 28 species (Carr, 1987). Lobeliads also burgeoned; we know six endemic genera, five of which – with 90 species – descended from one colonist (Simon, 1987). Various insect genera have exploded: the moths *Hyposmocoma* (350 species); the wasps *Sierola* (182) and *Odynerus* (105); the beetles *Proterrhinus* (181) and *Plagithmysus* (140). And legion is the number of species of drosophilids (the same family as the all-purpose genetic fly, *Drosophila melanogaster*). More than 700 are known. But at the rate they are being discovered, no one will be surprised if there are 1000 (Carson and Kaneshiro, 1976; Kaneshiro and Boake, 1987; Grimaldi, 1990).

Not everything on Hawaii has speciated as extravagantly. The honey-eaters (also passerines) may all now be extinct in Hawaii. But even at their zenith, they numbered only six species (Freed *et al.*, 1987). In Australia, New Guinea and elsewhere they reach high diversity (at least 120 species in all). And a tree, *Metrosideros polymorpha*, grows profusely in virtually every Hawaiian terrestrial habitat and displays a wide range of morphologies in doing so (Mueller-Dombois, 1987). But it has not speciated at all. Archipelagos are not equal-opportunity speciation machines.

Nonetheless, archipelagos and mountains tend to enhance speciation rates. The Geospizinae force us to make that admission. This subfamily of birds fascinated Charles Darwin and bear his name in English, i.e. Darwin's finches. Darwin's finches live in two places, the Galapagos archipelago and Cocos Island. The former is a desert archipelago, yet it harbors many species of this subfamily. The latter is a tropical forest. It has the kind of habitat we expect to overflow with bird species. Yet, Cocos Island has only one species of Darwin's finch. We think it has only one because Cocos Island sits alone in the Pacific Ocean.

Geographical ranges

As geographical ranges change size, they become easier or more difficult targets for geographical barriers. Usually, small ranges are unlikely to be subdivided by a barrier, because most barriers will miss them (Rosenzweig, 1975, 1978b).

Maybe a species finds ready-made barriers as on an archipelago. Or maybe some geological phenomenon finds the species. In both cases, the greater the range of the species, the greater the number of barriers in its range. You can surely find exceptions (say by comparing a large-range species of zooplankter living in the vast, uniform North Pacific gyre to one living in lakes on the island of Honshu, Japan). But you will probably not wish to doubt the likelihood of the trend.

What does the number of barriers have to do with geographical speciation rate? The more barriers, the more isolates. The more isolates, the more speciation. There is but one caveat. A range can be too large – at least theoretically.

Suppose a range is so large that it engulfs the entire barrier. Then, whether an isolate forms depends upon what kind of barrier we have.

Geographical barriers come in two varieties: knives and moats. A moat surrounds its isolate. It is a closed curve like the water around an island. In contrast, a knife has a beginning and an end, like a mountain range.

If the barrier is a moat (however irregular), it walls off individuals within it and sets them on their own, independent evolutionary pathway. So, to produce an isolate, moat barriers must merely encounter a range. The larger the range of a species, the greater the chance that it will encounter a moat set at random on the Earth's surface.

On the other hand, if the barrier is a knife (however curved and irregular), then it forms no isolate in the population that engulfs it. Genes may flow around an engulfed knife barrier, thus maintaining the integrity of the original gene pool. So, knife barriers set at random on the Earth's surface may fail to produce isolates because they penetrate a range, but do not cut through it. To produce an isolate, a geographical knife must cut entirely through a range from one border point to another. It may take a short cut and not cut the range at its greatest extent, but it must cut entirely through.

The larger the range, the more likely it totally engulfs a knife barrier or fails to be cut asunder by it. However, as you will see, such failures are not likely to influence overall trends. Only immense ranges are harder to cut through than to find.

The probability that a knife barrier will both **encounter** and **cut through** a range is the product of the two separate probabilities. These depend on the shape of the range and on the length of the barrier. We could model shapes in an infinity of ways. We could assume all sorts of frequency distributions for barrier lengths. But I think there is a general conclusion we can count on for all but the most pathological of such assumptions. When a joint probability comes from multiplying a probability rising from zero, times one falling to zero, the maximum will occur at some intermediate point. So, *intermediate size ranges are the most likely to be subdivided by a knife barrier.*

'Intermediate' could be almost anywhere along the spectrum of possible range sizes. Let us try one 'vanilla' model and locate the intermediate point at which knife barriers have greatest effect. For this model, let us assume that range borders are perfect circles. Now let barriers be segments of great circles,[2] and let the segments have random orientation. Further, let us assume that any segment size (from 0 to a whole great circle) has the same probability of occurrence as any other. Given this model, the probability that a segment finds and cuts a range peaks at a range size covering 29.7% of the surface of the Earth (Rosenzweig, 1978b) (Figure 5.1).

Because all the world's land area amounts to only 29% of its surface, all terrestrial ranges lie on the upslope (lefthand) section of Figure 5.1. So all terrestrial species' ranges would probably produce isolates faster if they were larger.

In the sea, ranges may get so large they are unlikely to be cut. But even here this may be rare. Most marine species have ranges along a coastline. Such ranges approximate line ranges. But, as ranges elongate away from circularity, their limit is a line. To be cut, such a line need only be found. Its probability of isolate formation thus increases monotonically with range size. Therefore, the case I worked out for Figure 5.1 may have its peak as far left as possible; real marine ranges may usually become more cuttable if they are larger.

Moreover, the model I graphed in Figure 5.1 covers only geographical knives. Moats, you recall, never need to cut through a range. They produce an isolate by just finding the range. So, reducing a range's size always reduces the chance that a moat will subdivide it, even if that range initially covers all the world's oceans.

---

[2] A great circle (like the Equator) has the same radius as its sphere. A 'segment' means a piece of such a circle ranging from 0% to 100% of its length.

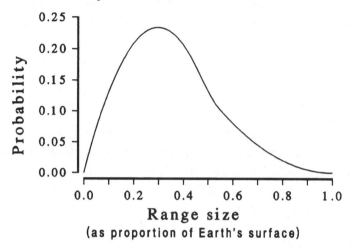

Figure 5.1. The probability that a geographical barrier will enter
and cut through a species range. If the barrier succeeds, a new isolate arises and speciation can start.
Barriers stand the best chance of cutting through a
species range if that range covers about 30% of the
Earth's surface. That is about equal to the proportion
of the Earth that is terrestrial. So most ranges, if they
shrink, will have smaller isolation rates. For this calculation, I assumed that each barrier is open (a 'knife'
barrier), has random length, and is randomly placed
on a great circle of the Earth. I also assumed circular
range borders. But the general result also holds for
much more irregular shapes. Redrawn from
Rosenzweig (1975).

I doubt that any species exists (or ever did) with a range so large that
reducing it would make it an easier target for barriers. But even if there
were such species (say in the open ocean), the predominant range sizes (and
shapes) lead to the opposite relationship: *the smaller the range size, the less
the probability of subdivision.*

Rate of divergence after isolate formation

Once isolates form, they must diverge. People have examined the divergence
process both as a genetic phenomenon and as an ecological one.

The genetic considerations stress non-selective evolution. For example, genetic drift is the evolutionary change caused by statistical accidents of sampling small populations (Wright, 1931). Mayr often draws our attention to the times when a propagule founds a new population in an isolated area. Though both mother and daughter population may be large, the propagule is a genetic bottleneck. The bottleneck can change gene frequencies in the daughter and set it off on a very different evolutionary course. Cohen (1976) emphasizes how permanent such drift can be. Without selective pressure to restore parental frequencies, it should last forever.

There are other genetic considerations. Numerous minor mutations may accumulate steadily and differentiate isolates. Isolates also may diverge if they use different mechanisms to solve similar problems. Suppose they are pressed to get darker, for example. Each may alter the production of melanic pigment at different points along its metabolic pathway. And if they are pressed to become mottled, who knows what degree of infinity describes the scope of their evolutionary solutions?

Ecological considerations begin with the realization that no two areas on Earth are exactly alike. So, surely, natural selection will mold isolates differently. The more dissimilar the environments of the isolates, the faster they should diverge.

Mayr (1954) noticed a systematic way environments of isolates may differ. A population covering a large geographical range has diverse selective pressures. It constitutes a kind of compromise among them. Now imagine a small isolate split off at the range periphery. It should be free of most of those conflicting demands. It can adapt more precisely to its local environment. According to Mayr, that explains why certain kingfishers living on nearby offshore islands of New Guinea evolved to be so different from their probable progenitors on the nearby mainland. The island environment differs little from the nearby mainland, but the kingfishers of the mainland are part of a gene pool that also adapts kingfishers to distant, dissimilar environments.

Both ecological and genetic considerations suggest the same conclusion. Divergence should develop fastest in a small isolate that buds off a large one. The small isolate may experience a founder-effect bottleneck. The large isolate, particularly if it has a large range, should embody compromises that the small one can rid itself of.

Yet, some evidence supports the opposite hypothesis, i.e. the large isolate evolves quickly and the small one is conservative. Much of the evidence depends on the chromosomes of mice in the genus *Peromyscus*. *P. manicu-*

latus has a huge range that covers most of North America. On the periphery of that range, it has produced several new species with very small ranges (Blair, 1950). Examples include *P. polionotus* and *P. melanotis*. But the karyotypes of these two species closely resemble the common ancestor of all three. The karyotype of the large-range species, *P. maniculatus*, has changed much (Greenbaum *et al.*, 1978). Moreover, *P. melanotis* sometimes finds itself isolated on mountaintops in southeastern Arizona. These tiny isolates do not appear to have diverged from each other in 10 000 years (Bowers *et al.*, 1973). Their karyotypes and their alleles match. They can interbreed amongst themselves and with other populations of *P. melanotis* from three Mexican populations. They have changed very little while their large-range parent has evolved a lot.

Brown (1957) proposes a model of geographical speciation called 'centrifugal speciation'. He predicts that most change will occur in the large-range isolate because most favorable mutations will occur within its larger population. Responding to barriers, it will bud off new species from time to time, but these will be conservative. Their features will change very little while their larger sister (or mother, depending on your perspective) will zip off on an evolutionary fast track. Brown supports his model with diverse phenotypic data taken from many taxa. We shall want to recall these data and Brown's idea when we consider the effect of area on speciation rate.

Frey (1993, 1994) is developing cladistic methods to determine whether variation within species tends to agree with the centrifugal model or some other pathway of geographical speciation. She has applied these to three species of rodents (*Microtus montanus, Tamias minimus* and *Zapus hudsonius*). Tamias variation matched the predictions of centrifugal speciation well, although Zapus variation did not and the *Microtus* results have no unambiguous interpretation.

Walsh (1994) has modeled an important genetic process which I believe has much to do with centrifugal speciation. He points out that since Haldane (1932), evolutionists have viewed gene duplication as the principal first step in the evolution of new genes. After duplication, natural selection moves the new copy in one of two directions. Some new copies are inactivated. Some new copies get a new function. We expect that new functions will be most likely to promote speciation. Walsh asks how likely is the evolution of the new function.

Walsh's variables come from the traditional set used by population geneticists since the 1930s. He gives the inactivation process a mutation rate. He does the same for mutation to a new function. He stipulates a population size for the species. He also allows alleles for the new function to have a selective advantage. In one model, the advantage is fixed; in another, it comes from a distribution of values. As the results are qualitatively similar for these models, I will examine only the one with a fixed selective advantage.

Walsh uses the following standard symbols. Let $\theta = 4N_e s$, where s is the selective advantage and N_e is the effective population size. He also introduces a new symbol, ρ, which is a ratio, i.e. the mutation rate to a new function divided by the mutation rate to an inactivated allele. Then he delineates three extreme cases (others will lie somewhere in between these).

- Case 1: $\theta <\!< 1$
  Approximate probability of a new gene function : ρ
- Case 2: $\theta >\!> 1$ and $\theta\rho <\!< 1$
  Approximate probability of a new gene function : $\theta\rho$
- Case 3: $\theta >\!> 1$ and $\theta\rho >\!> 1$
  Approximate probability of a new gene function : $1 - (\theta\rho)^{-1}$

Walsh assumes that ρ is very tiny, perhaps on the order of 10^{-5} or 10^{-6}; it is conventional to assume that beneficial mutations are especially rare. Of course θ will be small (Case 1) when population size is small or selective advantage is small. So, small populations have only a tiny chance of developing a new gene function. But θ will be large when both population size and selective advantage are large. Even then, unless it is so large that $\theta\rho$ also greatly exceeds unity, populations still have only a tiny chance of developing a new gene function (Case 2). But what happens if population size is quite large (Case 3) so that $4N_e \rho > s^{-1}$? Then a new gene function probably will develop.

How large is 'quite large?' Suppose the selective advantage is only 1%. Then, if $\rho \approx 10^{-5}$, population size needs to be 2.5×10^6 to reach Case 3. At twice that population, the new gene function probability is 0.5; at four times, it is 0.75. Of course, if $\rho \approx 10^{-6}$, all the population sizes must be one order larger. Walsh points out that these estimates are conservative; somewhat smaller populations may also be capable of generating new gene functions by intercepting the silencing process with a beneficial mutant before the inactivated allele fully takes over. But the basic message remains clear: populations much less than 10^5 or 10^6 may have a hard time evolving new genes. Their evolution is likely to be limited to reshuffling their gene frequencies or producing a rare new beneficial allele at an old locus. Perhaps that tells us why some small isolated populations appear to have such relictual gene pools, while their widespread, common sisters – which have had no more time to evolve – have diverged at a rapid rate.

Besides population size, generation time looms largest among the many other influences on the rate of divergence. Suppose selection proceeds at a certain rate per generation, and one taxon has ten times as many generations per century as another. Then, divergence should go ten times faster in the first taxon. Martin and Palumbi (1993) review the evidence that confirms the effect of generation time on nucleotide substitution rates. Marzluff and Dial (1991) collect data from 33 taxa and find that short generation time is indeed associated with higher diversity. We need to pay more attention to such associations.

Polyploidy

Meiotic irregularities can produce diploid gametes. If two of these combine, the result is a new species with more chromosomes than either of its parents. Each chromosome of the new species has a meiotic partner. These can pair during meiosis. So the new species should undergo normal gamete formation. (See Jackson, 1976, for a review of details.)

Compared to geographical speciation, polyploidy is fast. It has even been termed 'instantaneous', although you will recognize that as hyperbole. (Even meiosis takes some time.) Nevertheless, it is blazing fast compared to all other kinds of speciation. It is so fast, it has happened in the laboratory.

When both the diploid gametes come from the same parent species, the process is called autopolyploidy. When they come from different species, it is called allopolyploidy. An autopolyploid is tetraploid (or even more if the gametes themselves came from a polyploid). An allopolyploid is diploid – you would not know it started with four sets of chromosomes unless you found its ancestors and their karyotypes.

If an autopolyploid produces a tetraploid gamete, and its parent species a diploid gamete, and the two combine, the result is a new hexaploid species. Such hexaploids exist. But don't ask me whether to call them allopolyploids or autopolyploids. That is a topic for a debating society. They are genetically like an autopolyploid. But, after all, they do come from separate species.

The rate of polyploidy ought to be sensitive to two variables, the taxon speciating and the number of species itself. Some taxa must make ideal candidates for polyploidy. Plant taxa, for instance, often contain species with the capacity for self-fertilization. That saves the first individual of the new species from having to find a mate like itself. It looks in the mirror. In addition, Charnov (1979) points out that plant pollen cannot simply land on a stigma of the wrong species then choose to leave so as to look for another female of the right one. Pollen must be selected to attempt the fertilization 'even if the resulting hybrids would be of low vigor.' On the other hand, I know of no polyploid mammal or bird. Many features of a taxon may promote or discourage its polyploidy.

Unlike any other kind of speciation, polyploidy leaves plain tracks. You might call them 'karyotracks'. They tell us that plants do commonly form polyploids. They also tell us that allopolyploids are more common than autopolyploids, and that some taxa form polyploids much more often than others. Grant (1971) devotes an entire chapter to discussing the factors that promote polyploidy.

The more species there are, the more kinds of polyploids can be formed. Thus, polyploidy may have significant positive feedback: the more product, the faster it is produced. Considering the speed of polyploidy, you may wonder why this process hasn't produced a different species out of every individual! What keeps polyploidy under control?

We don't really know the answer to that, but we can guess. The rate of meiotic anomaly in a species depends on its population size. The more meioses per unit time, the more diploid gametes per unit time. But, as diversity grows, species must subdivide the same ecological resource base into smaller shares. Their consequent rarity makes some (most?) polyploid combinations unrealistically improbable.

In addition, polyploids themselves may not make such great sources for new polyploids. How many chromosomal sets can co-occur in a cell and still leave it functioning well? Thus, higher order polyploids (hexaploids, octaploids, etc.) are much rarer than tetraploids. Figure 5.2 shows the data for all species of the genus *Atriplex* whose karyotypes are known. Figure 11.5 shows the same phenomenon for a large sample of the flowering plants of New Zealand. I will return to this phenomenon in Chapter 11. It helps in a new explanation for the rise in polyploid proportion with latitude (i.e. Figure 2.33).

Competitive speciation

Polyploidy does not require isolated populations. So it is a kind of sympatric speciation – speciation without geographical separation. But many evolutionists have believed that polyploidy is not the only form of sym-

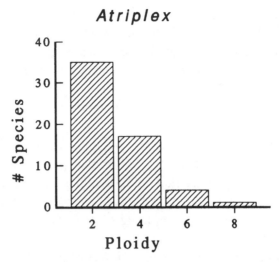

Figure 5.2. A substantial fraction – 39% – of *Atriplex* species are
polyploids. But most of the polyploids are first order,
i.e., tetraploids. Data from Osmond *et al.*, 1980,
pp. 66–71.

patric speciation. They have described many phenomena and suggested
many terms to try to convince each other that some other form of sympatric speciation is abroad in the land (and the water). These include 'host
race formation', 'stasipatric speciation', 'speciation by disruptive selection',
etc. They are not all equivalent, but many evolutionists recognize their similarity and use one term, 'sympatric speciation' to refer to them all. But, I
contend that these phenomena exemplify a mode of speciation I call 'competitive'.

What is competitive speciation? It is the expansion of a species from a
single ecological opportunity to an unexploited ecological opportunity, followed by that species' sympatric breakup into two daughters, one using the
original opportunity, the other the newly exploited one. Both the expansion
and the breakup come about because of competition. The expansion happens because of lack of competition to use the unexploited ecological
opportunity. The breakup happens because of too much competitive pressure on phenotypes in between those best able to exploit the old and the
new opportunities.

Certainly, competitive speciation involves disruptive selection, i.e. the
separation of a unimodal phenotypic distribution into a bimodal one
because the mode becomes unfit. Yet competitive speciation is more. What

is its key feature, the feature that makes me reluctant to call it merely sympatric speciation? To answer that, I must introduce two concepts and two assumptions:

- Concept 1: *Density-dependent fitness.* This simply means that the fitness of a phenotype changes according to the density of other individuals. Usually the relationship is negative (more individuals cause lower fitness). But it could be positive.
- Concept 2: *Frequency-dependent fitness.* The fitness of a phenotype depends on the proportions of all phenotypes in the population.
- Assumption 1: each phenotype can use a variety of habitats, but that variety is limited. Individuals that tolerate a wide variety of habitats are called *eurytopic*. Individuals that do well on only a small set of habitats are *stenotopic*. (This assumption and the next can apply to resources as well as habitats.)
- Assumption 2: the more similar are two phenotypes, the more they overlap in their abilities to use habitats. The more they overlap, the more they can depress each other's fitnesses by competition.

We can certainly find exceptions to the two assumptions, but most ecologists would expect them to be statistically valid. In addition, I am not concerned with cases that deviate from the assumptions, but with the likelihood that they are often true. What happens when they are?

Imagine an array of habitats much bigger than the variety usable by any single phenotype. Perhaps these habitats vary in salinity or soil nitrogen or light intensities or elevations. For each value of the variable measuring the array (say, light intensity), the biologist can imagine a most suitable phenotype. This will be that value's specialist. Although the specialist is the phenotype with maximum ability at that habitat value, it probably can and does use habitats with similar values also. Specialists change as we move from one end of the array to the other. (The change does not need to be continuous.)

Now assume that the frequency distribution of habitats does not fit any unimodal curve. Instead, let the distribution be rugose (or multimodal). Each peak in this rugged distribution has its specialist.

Suppose there are two peaks, *A* and *B*. Now we perform what the physicists call a 'thought experiment,' that is, a laborious experiment we do not really expect anyone to do because we think we already know the answer. One by one, in a long series of trials, we introduce infinitesimal homogeneous populations of the various specialists at each value along the array.

We then measure fitness in each of these infinitesimal populations. The result is an adaptive landscape (Figure 5.3).

Now comes the density dependence. The resources of a habitat run out as the population of its specialist grows. At carrying capacity, the average fitness in the population is unity – one-for-one replacement, generation after generation. Yet, because each phenotype can profit from only a limited range of habitats, some habitats will be empty. These offer opportunity – ecological and evolutionary – to other phenotypes.

Let us now introduce a small, realistically diverse population whose modal phenotype specializes on peak *A*. As before, the population grows,

Wrightian Surface

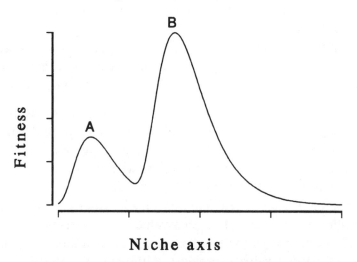

Figure 5.3. A hypothetical empty adaptive landscape with two adaptive peaks, *A* and *B*. Fitnesses are really ecological opportunities because they are measured with infinitesimal homogeneous populations that span the set of possible phenotypes. Once an actual phenotype invades, it increases in population and depresses the fitnesses in the part of the landscape to which it is best suited. That sets up pressure for the phenotypic variance to expand into unused parts of the landscape. As the array of real phenotypes grows, joint competitive pressure from more common phenotypes adapted best to the peaks builds. It may get so large that it causes disruptive selection by undermining the chances for the midrange phenotypes to reproduce successfully.

using up the opportunity afforded by the peak habitat and those similar to it. Eventually it reaches carrying capacity.

Assume that the phenotypic variance in such a population is small compared to the habitat variance. (This should be true at least when new regions of the array are born.) In particular, assume that this variance leaves peak *B* entirely unexploited. That is the key to competitive speciation – unexploited ecological opportunity. Other models begin by assuming a wide range of phenotypes exploiting everything available. This one begins with a narrow range of phenotypes that cannot profitably exploit some habitats.

The next step is disruptive selection. Disruptive selection takes place when the midrange of a phenotypic array lacks fitness. Laboratory experiments to demonstrate it begin with a single species whose phenotypes range from one extreme to another. Laboratory technicians keep midrange phenotypes from reproducing by killing them all. I will mention some of these experiments soon, but they all present a paradox. How could both extreme phenotypes ever have evolved if the midrange phenotypes are so poor? Wouldn't one extreme have had to evolve continuously, first to the intermediates, then to the second extreme? But, disruptive selection assumes that the midrange phenotypes are disastrous. So, how could natural selection ever have favored them?

Here is the answer of competitive speciation: the midrange phenotypes lose their fitness only **after** they evolve. In fact, because of competition, that loss is almost predictable. A phenotype at peak *A* (say) does well and increases to a steady-state population size. Natural selection then forces it to expand its variance to exploit the unused ecological opportunity. It produces midrange individuals, and they produce individuals specialized on peak *B*. Then the combination of peak *A* and peak *B* phenotypes exerts competitive pressure on the sparse resources of the middle habitats of the niche axis. Then and only then do the midrange individuals become unfit no matter how few there are.

So, competitive speciation begins with the expansion of a species' phenotypic variance to make use of unexploited ecological opportunity. But this first step is not trivial. Under conditions of random mating, phenotypic variance barely responds to even the most intense selective pressure (Slatkin, 1970). 'Notoriously conservative' describes it well. Can natural selection change the mode of a phenotypic distribution? Sure. But change its variance? That variance is determined by the genetic and reproductive structure of the population. There is very little room for change.

Random mating is the lynchpin in the argument that conserves phenotypic variance. Without random mating, variance **can** increase. But, do we expect random mating in a habitat selector? That depends. If there are genes that specify which habitat to choose, then yes, we can expect random mating. And, as Rice (1987) points out, such a habitat selection system makes it even more difficult to increase the variance. Phenotypes with the ability to exploit lightly used habitats will rarely have the genes to choose those habitats. So, they have no way of passing on the gene combination to their progeny. Even if they do have those genes, most of their mates in the lightly used habitats will be ordinary phenotypes.

On the other hand, suppose the habitat selection genes encourage habitat searching until the organism achieves a certain physiological state. 'Keep moving until you feel safe and well fed', they might order (figuratively, of course). Then, individuals with a special ability to exploit a habitat are likely to meet similar individuals in it. If they also mate therein, their mating is not random, but homogametic. In sum, if the phenotypes find good habitats by using a flexible system, then natural selection does have the power to expand the range of habitat specializations (Rosenzweig, 1978a).

So, suppose we observe a species that satisfies our criteria. It faces a two-peak adaptive landscape. One peak is fully used, and the phenotypic variance of the species is expanding outward toward the other peak. What happens next?

There are three outcomes (Rosenzweig, 1978a):

- The population may expand until scarcity of an intermediate habitat removes the selective pressure for further expansion. In that case, the second peak stays empty.
- The population may expand until it uses all habitats. But then, having expanded,
  - it may split into two reproductively independent units.
  - or it may not split.

If it splits, then and only then may we say that competitive speciation has occurred. Here is what could cause the split. Imagine that the variance expands to encompass both peaks, and that the population has grown close to its carrying capacity. Recall that each phenotype uses a range of habitats. So, individuals adapted primarily to a peak also may exploit the valley's habitats. If they exploit them at all successfully, no opportunity may remain for valley phenotypes.

If valley phenotypes have only negative logarithmic fitnesses (i.e. arithmetic fitnesses less than unity), natural selection will favor peak phenotypes that do not interbreed across peaks. Thus, they will avoid producing valley phenotypes as progeny. That process is the disruptive selection step (Thoday, 1972). Maynard Smith (1966) was first to recognize that it could play a role in sympatric speciation.

My model of competitive speciation has a lot of good company. Some of these companions tackle the problem with genetically explicit models. For example, using a simple computer model, Pimm (1979) showed that the genetics of competitive speciation pose no problem. Rice's (1984) more complex simulation had the same outcome. Other companions provide geographically explicit features. Endler (1977), for instance, imagined the habitats spread out along a geographical gradient and showed how speciation could occur without geographical barriers. Stasipatric speciation (White, 1978) gives us a second geographic example (see next section).

I believe Felsenstein (1981) offered the greatest challenge to competitive speciation. He demonstrated that the scenario of disruptive selection is preposterous under certain conditions. Suppose a gene for preventing interpeak matings works by causing a preference for a mate with a particular phenotype. Then, it's too difficult to combine the mating preference genes with the phenotype genes. A phenotype adapted to peak A may find itself preferring to mate with a phenotype adapted to peak B! It will have less fitness than if there were no mating preference genes at all. So, the species will need – in addition to mating preference genes – a system for linking the preference loci to the phenotypic loci.

Rice (1984, 1985, 1987) resolved this problem with exactly the same tactics as I used to allow the phenotypic variance to expand in the first place. Instead of genes to prefer, say, red-haired mates, he imagines genes to prefer whatever potential mates an individual finds in its own preferred habitat. Some homogamy gets established automatically and simultaneously with habitat selection. Natural selection intensifies it and the population splits into two species. Possibly, some specific mating-preference genes need to evolve to finish the process off, but that point is emphasized only by Johnson *et al.* (1995).

Johnson *et al.* elaborated a model very like Felsenstein's but got an answer like Rice's, i.e. competitive speciation can occur given reasonable values of the parameters in their model. They assume three sorts of genes. Some genes code for a specific habitat preference, some for a specific mate type, and some for fitness in two different habitat types. No one previously used all three types in a model with habitat-specific preference genes. Their model has more than one locus for each type of gene.

Johnson *et al.* model gene penetrance explicitly. Each preference allele has an effect on its target character. The combined effect of the set of alleles determines the probability that the genotype will chose this or that mate, or this or that habitat. Once the combined effect of a set of alleles has produced 100% choice of a habitat or a mate, further addition of similar alleles to a genotype can happen but does not change the phenotype. Johnson *et al* (in press) suggest we call this 'excess penetrance.' Progeny are more likely to make the same choices as their parents if their parents have more than enough alleles to make a 100% choice of either mate type or habitat.

The model of Johnson *et al.* has other, more ordinary features too. For example, mating always occurs within the exploited habitat. But the two novel features – excess penetrance and three types of alleles – work together to produce a new result for models with fixed habitat-preference genes: sympatric speciation can occur.

The simulations performed by Johnson *et al.* resulted in a real surprise. The speciation took a long time. Hundreds to thousands of generations. Moreover, its first steps – formation of some weak host races – were hardly noticible. Then, in a 'short, dramatic process' after hundreds or thousands of generations of quasi-equilibrium, the host races separated into two non-interbreeding species. Separation itself took between 50 and 100 generations with the parameter values they did the most work on.

Johnson *et al.* have discovered that excess penetrance is implicit in other models, such as those of Rice and perhaps those of Kondrashov (1983a, b). They believe that excess penetrance may be essential to all forms of competitive speciation. That is a very interesting hypothesis. But we will need to check it either with other simulation models or with a general analytical one.

Should we take the trouble? Perhaps you think all competitive speciation is too improbable to warrant much more effort. The array of habitats has to be broad. The degree of specialization must be narrow – but not too narrow or else valley phenotypes will remain good strategies even after the peaks are fully utilized. The supply of habitats must be rugose, but not too rugged or the competitive pressure from the individuals under the first peak will prevent expanding to the second. Individuals must choose habitats, but in one kind of model not very precisely and not by having genes for particular habitat types. And in another kind of model (with preference genes for particular habitats), they must also have mating preference genes with strong enough effects of their alleles to produce excess penetrance. And, in both models, individuals must mate in the habitats they exploit. It all seems so restrictive as to be improbable.

But, when did improbability dishearten an evolutionist? In truth, all life is somewhat improbable. And, as the astronomers say, it depends on the Earth winning a Goldilocks contest – not too hot and not too cold; not too wet and not too dry ... Competitive speciation is just another Goldilocks contest. Besides, evidence backs it up as you will see in the next part of the chapter.

Evidence for competitive speciation

Many evolutionists have suggested that non-polyploid, sympatric speciation works. They use different terminology, often just calling the process sympatric. But I view their work as encompassed by the process of competitive speciation. Thus, their separate efforts combine to yield a substantial body of evidence. In fact, Bush and Howard (1986) claim that there has been enough convincing evidence for decades, but most evolutionists rejected it for lack of a theory they trusted. Let us briefly review a small part of this evidence.

In the laboratory, Thoday and Gibson (1962) produced two species of *Drosophila* by selecting against flies with intermediate numbers of bristles on the thorax. Paterniani (1969) disrupted field-grown populations of maize into late-blooming and early-blooming populations by selecting against intermediate bloomers. These experiments should have established the efficacy of disruptive selection, but they did not. They inspired criticism.

Scharloo (1971), especially, criticized Thoday and Gibson for collecting their flies from dustbins (garbage cans). Such wild flies have lots of genetic heterogeneity, and it is both uncontrolled and unmeasured. Scharloo could not repeat disruptive selection on more homogeneous laboratory stock. But, we must ask, so what?

Species in nature are not carefully bred laboratory stocks. They do resemble dustbin populations. And homogeneous laboratory populations may lack the very genetic variance on which natural selection depends for its speed and success (Fisher, 1958).

Besides, the subdivision of one panmictic population into two did actually happen. So it can happen. All the world's failures cannot change that fact.

Bruce Wallace once showed me a new species of *Drosophila* that he and his graduate students produced in their lab at Cornell. It fed exclusively on human urine, a previously unexploited ecological opportunity for flies. They forced the speciation with artificial disruptive selection.

Unfortunately, the species is now extinct. The demigods at Cornell tired of the novelty and the fly lost its niche.

Guided by his computer simulations (Rice, 1984), Rice was also able to disrupt *Drosophila* in the lab, (Rice, 1985; Rice and Salt, 1988). *D. melanogaster* females eclose from their pupal stage and search for food before they mate. Mating takes place in the food-containing habitat. Rice devised an extraordinary piece of apparatus that forced newly eclosed flies to make three habitat choices in their search for food. They could go up or down, toward darkness or light, and toward the odor of ethanol or acetaldehyde. Altogether that defines eight habitats.

Females that chose any of six of those habitats (as defined by Rice) did not get to reproduce. Females that chose one of the other two did, but only if it was the same one their mother had chosen. (Females displayed their mother's choice in their eye color – brown or yellow – a trait Rice ingeniously rigged to be determined solely by the larval environment.)

Within 25 generations, Rice had produced two species of *Drosophila* where previously only one had existed. In the habitat of the brown-eyed fly, 99% were brown-eyed. In the habitat of the yellow-eyed fly, 98% were yellow-eyed. Since these flies mate where their young eat, their reproductive isolation was virtually as complete as any two natural sister species of *Drosophila*.

Bush (1969) produced the most famous challenge to allopatric orthodoxy. He studied fruit flies of the genus *Rhagoletis*. Before Europeans colonized North America, *R. pomonella* fed exclusively on hawthorn (*Crataegus*) fruit and *R. indifferens* on the native fruit, pin cherry (*Prunus emarginata*). Now each of these species has formed a second 'host race'. The former eats apples (*Malus*); the latter eats domestic cherries. Each of these fruits was introduced by Europeans, and each flowers at a slightly different time from the original hosts. Flies must time their reproduction to coincide with their host. Otherwise their progeny starve.

But the reproductive seasons of the trees vary somewhat, allowing more or less overlap in any given year between *Crataegus* and *Malus,* and between wild and domestic cherries. This variation also encourages a variety of flies because late breeding one year may be right on target the next. It is easy to imagine the new habitat resource 'capturing' a few desperate late breeders one year. Subsequently, natural selection would press their progeny to adapt more precisely to their newly found habitat. Hybrids would tend to breed in the middle when few flowers of either species are usually around.

Tauber and Tauber (1977, 1987) amassed evidence for sympatric speciation in predatory insects. Gibbons (1979) did the same. These are real predatory insects in the real world.

After much painstaking study of morabine grasshopper chromosomes in Australia, White (1978) described a phenomenon called stasipatric speciation. The karyotypes of its groups of species are quite similar. They differ because of chromosomal inversion. One species occupies the core of the range; the others live on its periphery. Hybrids are extremely rare and occupy very narrow zones where species ranges abut. Such karyotypic hybrids (heterokaryotypes) run into meiotic difficulties because their chromosomes cannot pair properly. White attributed their rarity to the resulting loss in fitness. Parents that mate only within their species should have greater fitness than parents that mate with different species.

The usual explanation of stasipatric speciation (Key, 1968) depends upon founder effects. But an alternative explanation relies on competitive speciation and forms a subset of Endler's clinal model. Suppose the heterokaryotype is better than the parent species at dealing with some marginal habitat. Most of its first matings will be with parent karyotypes. So its initial disadvantage in meiosis will be less than that of one of the new homokaryotypes mated with parents. Its ecological advantage may outweigh this disadvantage. If so, it would become more common. Its special chromosome could even accumulate mutations to allow it better to exploit the peripheral habitat. A double dose of the new chromosome would be even better, and as homokaryotypes got common enough, they could develop reproductive isolation and outcompete the heterokaryotypes. This model is wholly speculative, but testable with field experiments on the competitive relationships. These experiments still beg to be done.

There is also fossil evidence for competitive speciation. I shall describe it in the following section.

The relative importance of speciation modes

Different modes of speciation make different predictions about what we should find in nature. These allow us to approach the question of their relative importance. Knowing what modes produce most species will in turn help us to explain the diversity patterns we see. Their speed separates them immediately. Polyploidy is quick. Competitive speciation may occur in as few as ten to one hundred generations based on laboratory evidence. And geographical speciation seems to require thousands or even hundreds of thousands of years.

Geographical speciation rates depend on isolation opportunities. Neither of the other modes does. This means both bigger ranges and subdivided ranges will increase geographical speciation rates.

Competitive speciation rates depend on ecological opportunities. Without a poorly used or unused habitat, natural selection cannot broaden a species' variance. The process of competitive speciation never gets started. Neither of the other two modes have rates that depend on unused opportunities. Polyploidy is entirely independent of ecology. Geographical speciation depends on ecology only after isolates form, and only because their differentiation may speed up if their environments differ.

Because competitive speciation is fueled by ecological opportunity, it should die down as ecological communities accumulate more species. (See Chapter 10, Figure 10.3, for the consequences of realizing that species can be niches for other species.) Speciation rates that decrease as diversity increases? Neither geographical speciation nor polyploidy makes that prediction. Species are factories for other species. Polyploidy and geographical speciation keep those assembly lines rolling. But the competitive speciation departments shut down when demand for the product disappears.

Finally, the most obvious difference. Polyploidy records its history in karyotypes. We can read 'Polyploidy was here!' written plainly in the cells of its products. I guess that were it not for this incontrovertible evidence, polyploidy would be too improbable to believe.

Evidence for polyploidy

Many species of plants are polyploids. Some animals are too, but plant speciation so often operates by polyploidy that it is a dominant mode in some places. Return to Figure 2.33 and notice the high proportion of polyploids at every point. The smallest proportion comes from the flora of the Ivory Coast (18.9%). The largest from the arctic flora of Peary Land in northern Greenland (85.9%).

Geographical speciation

Geographical speciation is the most common mode among most taxa in most places at most times. Standard evolution textbooks (e.g. Futuyma, 1979) do a fine job documenting the importance of geographical speciation. Although I am convinced of the existence and importance of other speciation modes, even I believe that most speciations are allopatric.

Several patterns suggest the dominance of geographical speciation. One is the species–area curve among provinces (Chapter 9). Another is high endemism on islands. A third is the pattern of fish diversity in salt water and fresh. All three of these patterns share one diagnostic attribute: diversity is high where isolation opportunity is high.

Island endemism has attracted the attention of naturalists for centuries (a traditional reference: A.R. Wallace, *The Malay Archipelago*). Spread a species over a continent and it varies but seldom (if ever) forms new species. Follow it after it colonizes a slightly remote island, and presto, a new species. Not always, but often. Of course, no one actually follows the process. We read the results of evolution after colonization only by visiting these islands today. No other mode but geographical speciation predicts that islands should be so dense with endemics. And no other explains why rainforested, isolated Cocos Island has only one species of Darwin's finch while desert islands in the Galapagos Archipelago have many.

The fish pattern is similar. The freshwaters of the Earth cover only about 1% of its area but have 36% of its 18818 fish species (Nelson, 1984; I am indebted to Don Thomson for the idea and the number). Freshwater locales are like fish archipelagos. It's easy to become isolated in one river system. If geographical speciation did not dominate, other modes would overwhelm the effect of isolation opportunity.

Competitive speciation – is it the engine of adaptive radiation?

At least one invasion of a new habitat has left a detailed fossil record. Toward the end of the Ordovician Period, muddy benthic habitats around the world experienced an influx of invertebrate species. These rapidly evolved into forms specific to the muddy benthos. Species diversity increased about one order of magnitude.

In at least one place, the Nicolet River Valley in Quebec, these species left a remarkable fossil record. Thin lenses of fossil-rich rock punctuate thick beds of fossil-poor rock. The result is like a sequence of 218 snapshots of the invertebrate fauna during some 5 Myr.

This series of samples permits us to use ecological census techniques to estimate the number of species. We can even estimate the number of species that we will yet discover (using the same set of fossil recovery methods that have given us what we know so far).

In Chapter 3, I have already discussed the use of capture–recapture techniques on this record. During much of the record, as you have seen, there was no trend in diversity (Figure 3.4). But at the beginning, diversity rose steadily (Figure 3.3).

During the increase, diversity grew at 0.105 species per meter (1 m represents roughly 6250 years). Assuming no extinctions, that was also the speciation rate. Then the speciation rate declined sharply, reaching about 0.034 species per meter at the end of the Ordovician. Figure 5.4 shows the trend for the whole period. The legend explains how I drew the figure.

Because competitive speciation proceeds at a rate that depends on ecological opportunity, Figure 5.4 fulfills the prediction of competitive speciation. Speciation rate falls after the steady state is achieved. Neither geographical speciation nor polyploidy predict that decline.

A similar decline in speciation rate occurred as marine foraminifera recovered from the Cretaceous–Tertiary mass extinction (see Chapter 6). It also occurred to new biotic forms as they radiated to replace old ones in biotic revolutions (Miller and Sepkoski, 1988).

Paleontologists observe two sorts of speciation episodes (Stanley, 1979). Most of the time, speciation putters along unspectacularly. But sometimes it occurs in creative bursts called quantum speciation. We see just such a burst on the left side of Figure 5.4. So, competitive speciation, though usually rare, may be the engine of quantum speciation, engaged only when new forms enjoy unusual opportunity.

I am not saying that competitive speciation produces the key adaptations on which such new forms are founded. Most of the time speciation works with more traditional modes. So most evolutionary breakthroughs ought to come from these modes. But when a new habitat becomes colonizable, or when a key adaptation becomes available, then competitive speciation can go to work to proliferate the novelty (Rosenzweig and McCord, 1991).

Thus, all three modes of speciation play noteworthy roles. Competitive speciation responds to short-term, relatively uncommon episodes of ecological opportunity. Polyploidy is a major force in plant speciation, especially outside the tropics. And geographical speciation is the workhorse supplying most new species most of the time.

Immigration

Depending on the scale, new species may appear in a system without speciating in it. They simply move in from somewhere else.

At the grandest scale, that of the whole planet, origination by immigration may never have happened. (I'll let the proponents of an extraterrestrial origin for life battle it out in another arena.) At the scale of a patch of rocky intertidal seashore, all species originate by immigration. Scales in

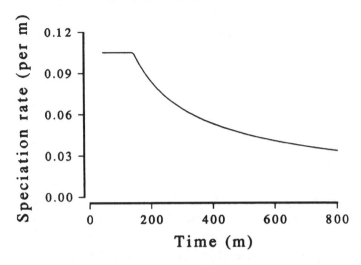

Figure 5.4. The trends in total speciation rate among the Upper
Ordovician invertebrates from the Nicolet River
Valley. Early in the record, species diversity increased
rapidly at a fixed rate of approximately 0.105 species
per meter of rock. (The 800 m total spans about 5
Myr.) We learn that it is linear from Figure 3.3, and
estimate the rate from the species diversities given by
the capture–recapture method. Above 140 m, species
accumulate according to the equation $\ln S = 2.1 + 0.34$
$\ln m$ (Figure 3.14 is a real time plot). The concave segment of the curve is the derivative of that equation:
$2.7765/m^{0.66}$. For two reasons, rates in this figure probably err on the low side: I have not estimated extinctions during the early period, because they were probably rare and there are not yet enough data. But to the
extent they occurred, they do reduce the apparent rate
of speciation. Similarly, I have not included the phantom species discovered statistically by Rosenzweig and
Duek (1979). Some 15 or 20 of these became extinct so
soon after they evolved that we have not yet found
their fossil remains. Including them would raise speciation rates by about 20%.

between have proportions in between. Many of the explanations for diversity patterns in Chapters 8 and 11 rely on immigration as a principal (or
sole) source of origination.

Chapter 6

Extinction

In the year 1865, Père Armand David, a French Catholic missionary to China and a naturalist, caught sight of a strange-looking herd of deer with mulish faces and long tufted tails. Once, such deer must have been common in forests all over China. But mankind cleared the forests for farms. So, Père David found every remaining member of the species living within the walls of the Imperial Chinese Hunting Park near Peking. He described the species for science and somehow got living specimens back to European zoos. During a war, soldiers ate the last Père David deer living in China. Zoos had the survivors. But for all practical purposes, the species was extinct.

By the early 19th century, geologists had unearthed so many extinct fossil species that 82% of all species known to science were extinct (Lyell, 1833, p. 54). By the mid-20th century, so many more fossils had been discovered that Romer (1949) offered the following shocking estimate: probably, more than 99% of known tetrapods from the mid-Mesozoic became extinct without leaving any descendants in our age. Simpson (1953, p. 281) called the Earth 'a charnel house for species'.

Extinction is not extraordinary. It is as certain as gravity. What forms does it take? What mechanisms power it? What wards it off? What are its rates?

Basic causes

Although a welter of specific problems can extinguish a species, I find it useful to group them into two categories, accidents and population interactions.

Accidents

Species may disappear for no predictable reason. Their whole population may be drowned by a rise in sea level. Or buried in a volcanic explosion. Or frozen by an unseasonal ice storm. They might even get trampled by a herd of wildebeest.

Their gene pool might drift to a set of maladaptive gene frequencies and combinations. Or a whole generation might grow up sterile.

Who knows?

Moreover, every species has a bounded set of environmental circumstances within which the species can support itself. If that set of conditions – their niche – disappears... *Voilà!* The species, too, departs. Niches can disappear accidentally, just as species do.

Population interactions

Both predation and competition sometimes subject species to reduced growth rates. They can even make those rates negative. No wonder they can lead to extinction.

Laboratory evidence leaves no doubt. Put some *Paramecium* in a bottle with some yeast. The predators eat the victims, and then go extinct themselves. Put some oranges, some fruit-eating mites, and some mite-eating mites together on a tray. You have to be as clever as Huffaker (1958) to get them to last for awhile. Or, if they are flies and wasps, as clever as Pimentel *et al.* (1963). Or, if wasps and weevils, as clever as Utida (1957).

Both laboratory and field evidence suggest that competition can cause extinctions. Thomas Park, inordinately fond of flour beetles, often put more than one species together and worked out the environmental conditions under which one would outcompete (to death) the other (Park, 1962). Paine (1966) removed a starfish species from patches of rocky oceanside and recorded the competitive devastation. Half its species of prey aggressively overgrew and exterminated the other half. If you like stories like that, you should have no trouble finding them in the literature of ecology (Connell, 1983; Schoener, 1983).

You also will find them predicted by standard deterministic theories of population interaction. Predatory overkill and competitive exclusion did not surprise those who read mathematical ecology.

Who suffers accidents?

Einstein could not believe that God plays dice with the Universe. But, in fact, God is the house and all species must play too. Moreover, the dice are loaded. All species will eventually suffer a run of bad luck that wipes them off the surface of the Earth.

Such accidents are the work of history. Perhaps ecologists should merely salute in their presence? After all, accidents, by definition, lie beyond the control of ecological systems.

But, though we cannot learn to regulate the frequency and intensity of accidents, we can study the effects of accidents with profit. Why? Because some characteristics of species make them accident prone. If we know what those characteristics are, we may be able to manage the risk of accidents. We may not be able to prevent accidents, but we may be able to diminish their impact.

What makes a species accident prone? Especially, what are the aspects of being accident prone that the ecosystem itself may influence? If we can figure that out, we may be able to minimize the Earth's losses.

Extinction and population size

Stanley (1979, p. 197) quips: 'Extinction is simply limitation of population density carried to the extreme.' In fact, ecologists, long aware of the apparent continuum between scarcity and oblivion, have always suspected that scarcity itself must be a prime contributing factor to the risk of accidental extinction.

The principle of the pyramid of numbers suggests that Charles Elton himself already recognized that scarcity threatens existence. Otherwise, we could not even suspect that food chains would ever end. (But see Chapter 11 for a surprising alternative hypothesis on the length of food chains.)

Frank Preston (1962b, p. 411) linked diversity explicitly to abundance: 'Since an island can hold only a limited number of individuals, the number of species will be very small.' Preston thought the idea so important that he estimated the size of the smallest bird population in Finland (one breeding pair) and in England and Wales (three breeding pairs). Preston is really the father of this most fundamental principle of extinction risk.

Ecologists have confidence in the notion that small populations lead to extinction. Conservation biologists (Soulé, 1980; Shaffer, 1981, 1987; Gilpin and Soulé, 1986; etc.) adopted the idea almost automatically, and began writing about 'minimum viable population size'. How many spotted owls need there be before we can stop worrying about their future? How many desert tortoises? How many grizzly bears?

The basic idea could not be simpler. If each individual might die of an accident in one unit of time with probability p, then a species whose total population at one time is N, will vanish in that unit of time with a probability proportional to p^N. Thus, the larger N, the less likely the whole species is to go extinct.

Unfortunately, this idea is a bit too simple. It ignores density dependence. An individual with poor food or shelter probably has a greater chance of accidental death than one in better circumstances. Yet, before extinction succeeds, it has to eliminate even the individuals with good resources and living conditions. Once we restrict our thinking to them, it still seems reasonable that a species with more well-provisioned individuals should last longer than one with fewer. The several widely accepted theories of extinction are grounded in the assumption that rarity matters (Richter-Dyn and Goel, 1972; Leigh, 1981; Goodman, 1987).

Similarly well-founded arguments support the danger of genetic drift. Sewell Wright (1931) invented the concept that stochasticity by itself can alter gene frequencies from generation to generation. Simultaneously, he pointed out that population size determines the severity of drift. The smaller the breeding population, the greater the chance of serious genetic sampling accidents. But it is only in recent papers that conservationists have concerned themselves with genetic drift as a threat to species' survival (for example, see Lande and Barrowclough, 1987).

Rarity begets ultimate rarity. The proposition is so appealing that it sounds like a fundamental truth. Is there evidence to support it? In fact, good evidence for the importance of population size comes from both paleobiology and island biogeography. Let's begin with the recent past.

A set of 16 British islands attracts enough birders to have their breeding birds censused year after year (Diamond, 1984). Of course, birds can't breed unless there is some appropriate habitat. So each island on which a species was recorded must have at least some appropriate habitat available for it. Mere absence of habitat cannot account for an extinction.

Using data from three of the islands (reported by Diamond and May, 1977; Diamond, 1984; and Williamson, 1983), Rosenzweig and Clark (1994) calculated the extinction probabilities for 39 of the species–island combinations. (The data for the other 45 combinations are inadequate for such an estimate.) Figure 6.1 shows how important population size is to extinction rate.

Pimm *et al.* (1988) report that no species whose population exceeded 18 pairs ever disappeared from any of the whole set of 16 bird islands. No disappearances (or only one) from an island was the chief reason a species–island combination failed to yield an extinction rate estimate for Figure 6.1. Of the 45 omitted combinations, 32 fell into that category. We

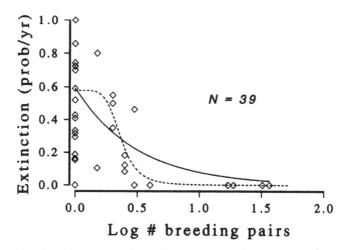

Figure 6.1. Larger population size reduces the extinction rate of a
bird species on an island. Data are fitted by both an
inverse sigmoid function and an exponential. There is
little difference in the goodness of fit. Figure redrawn
from Rosenzweig and Clark (1994).

may at least suspect that a low disappearance rate means a low extinction
rate (although no one can honestly be sure that low disappearance doesn't
mean a very high immigration rate instead). Figure 6.2 shows the considerable difference in population size between the 39 species-island combinations with measurable turnover and the 32 without. Higher population size
is significantly associated with no discernable turnover.

Further evidence comes from orb-web spiders on small Bahamian islands
(Toft and Schoener, 1983; Schoener and Spiller, 1987, 1992). Seven species
occurred on 108 islets. The 1992 paper shows data from the four commonest species. Each had been censused enough on so many islands that
Schoener and Spiller could estimate its extinction rate on many individual
islands. As each one's population size also varied from island to island,
they could also examine whether its extinction rate on an island varied with
its average abundance on that island. All four species showed strong negative relationships.

In some ways, the 1987 paper shows an even more interesting result.
Species that were relatively common during one year tended to stay so. The
rarer ones became extinct and recolonized repeatedly.

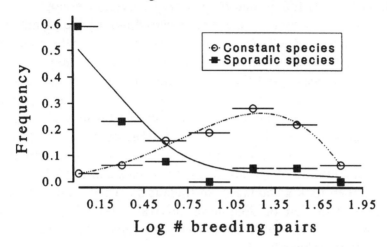

Figure 6.2. Bird species that have never disappeared from an island tend to have larger populations than those that occur sporadically. Sporadic species are the same as in Figure 6.1. Constant species do not appear in that figure. Data from Diamond and May, (1977); Diamond, (1984); and Williamson, (1983).

That is a remarkable pattern: the world of islands seems divided into high-risk species and stable ones. The high-risk species – those with extremely tiny populations – disappear frequently and require restoration from other places.

Is this island pattern relevant to entire species over their whole range? Curiously, it is. Paleobiologists see exactly the same pattern among fossil species. Boucot (1979, pp. 565, 590–4) remarks that collections of marine invertebrate fossils tend to contain two sorts of items: common, long-lived taxa and rare, short-lived ones. Taxa of intermediate abundance and duration are scarcely to be found.

Adequate examination of the evidence from fossils requires us first to take account of a pervasive correlation. The geographic ranges and abundances of species are positively correlated (Hanski, 1982; Bock and Ricklefs, 1983; Brown, 1984; and others). Much of the fossil evidence occurs in terms of geographic range rather than abundance.

Extinction and geographic range

Marine gastropods follow one of two very different developmental pathways. The larvae of some species are dispersed among the plankton where they feed and grow. The larvae of the others do not enter the plankton, but develop close to where their parents conceived them. Plankton, of course, live in the open ocean, and their inhabitants consequently get carried over vast areas. Fortunately, the protoconch of a juvenile gastropod reveals whether its bearer was planktotrophic or not. Fortunately also, the protoconch, being part of the shell, often gets well preserved. That allows paleobiobiologists to determine the larval ecology and thus the relative geographical distribution of species long extinct. A group of biologists discovered – and then took advantage – of these facts. They studied the effect of gastropod distribution on long-term survival rates of species (Jackson, 1974; Hansen, 1978, 1980; Jablonski and Lutz, 1980; Jablonski and Valentine, 1981; Jablonski, 1982).

Both Cretaceous and Quaternary gastropods exhibit the pattern: widespread species have lower extinction rates. For example, Table 6.1 shows the results from Jablonski (1982).

Jablonski (1986) extended these results by working with gastropod and bivalve fossils recovered from some 16 Myr of Late Cretaceous deposits. These deposits extend about 4500 km along the Atlantic and the Gulf coastal plains of the USA. We need not guess their geographical ranges. Jablonski checked them directly. The results appear in Figure 6.3. Species with smaller geographical ranges vanish much more rapidly than those with broader distributions. Jablonski and Valentine (1990) also determined from modern bivalves that their geographical ranges within a region mirror their worldwide ranges.

As before, what we learn from fossils parallels what we learn from islands. Hanski (1982) re-examined the invertebrate data that Dan Simberloff took from small islands in Florida. The more widespread a species, the less likely it was to go extinct on an island. He found the same pattern in Boycott's study of small ponds in England. The more ponds a species of mollusc lived in, the less likely it was to go extinct in any one. And he saw the result again in Kontkanen's leafhopper data from meadows in Finland.

A scale-independent syndrome is trying to attract our attention. A large proportion of species are either abundant, widespread and long-lived or else uncommon, narrowly distributed and short-lived.

Table 6.1. *Extinct gastropods lasted longer if they were widespread*

	Duration (10^6 years)		Range (km)	
	Mean	Median	Mean	Median
Planktotrophs	6	4	1500	1600
Non-planktotrophs	3	2	610	250

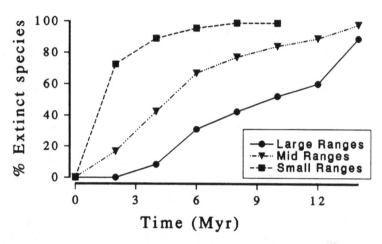

Figure 6.3. Species with larger geographical ranges have lower extinction rates. These Late Cretaceous marine species come from three classes of range: squares <1000 km; triangles, 1000–2500 km; dots, >2500 km. Jablonski (1986) measured the ranges as linear extents along the Atlantic and the Gulf coastal plains of the USA.

Do abundance and distribution both affect extinction probability? We already know that abundance protects from extinction. We should like to know if wide distribution also does. Maybe the apparent effect of distribution derives entirely from its close correlation with abundance? Frankly, I think that is unbelievable.

First, I know of one test using statistics that tries to disentangle abundance and distribution. Levings (unpublished data) sampled ants on six sites of Barro Colorado Island (Panama) from 1976 to 1978 (three years).

Then, Levings and Wheeler (unpublished data) resampled one site on the island at the end of 1983, just following an El Niño drought. Michael Kaspari (personal communication) used these data to analyze the survival rates of 66 species at the site. He found that both abundance ($p < 0.0001$) and ubiquity ($0.024 < p < 0.028$) independently helped an ant species to survive the El Niño. Again we see that abundance reduces the chance of extinction. But, in addition, occurrence at many sites went together with low probabilities of local extinction.

Occurrence at many sites on only one 1500 ha island! We cannot confidently declare that such a property means that a species has a large geographical range too. But I do believe that ubiquity reflects wide tolerance of habitat differences (Rosenzweig, 1989, 1991b). That should mean larger geographical range too. If so, Kaspari's analysis has separately identified both abundance and geographical range as factors that depress extinction rates.

Kaspari's test holds promise. Simultaneous examination of these two extinction factors deserves to be repeated on other taxa and in other places. Possibly, fossil data on abundance and distribution can be carefully processed to add weight to the conclusion that both scarcity and narrow distribution make a species extinction prone.

Meanwhile, logic demands that we accept the importance of geographical distribution on its own. Just as we can make sense of the process relating abundance to extinction, so we think it makes sense that geographic range should exert its own independent effect. The key is niche disappearance.

Every environmental change or perturbation is finite in space. Suppose one such change visits the Earth. The more widely distributed a species, the greater the chance that at least some pockets of its range will remain. If its niche survives somewhere, the species can too. A species may be uncommon wherever it lives. But if it is cosmopolitan, it has a good chance to live on.

Coope (1987) has actually followed some beetle species through Pleistocene time. He observed their ranges expanding and contracting – just as one expects of a period during which, time and again, glacial ice expanded and contracted.

Scientists have seen the losing side of the issue too: the destructive consequences of niche disappearance even for locally common species. Rob Colwell (1985) actually observed the local extinction of a restricted species, a hummingbird flower mite.

Colwell (1973) pithily summarized the natural history of hummingbird flower mites (genus *Rhinoseius*). A flower mite boards a hummingbird's beak and crawls up into its nostril for the ride to a flower. There it gets off, takes nectar and looks for a mate. But the flower must belong to one of the species used by that species of flower mite. Otherwise the mite will not disembark. And if you make it get off, an incumbent of a different flower mite species will force it away or kill it.

It is all very arbitrary. Colwell showed that individuals forced to feed and breed on the wrong flower (and protected from other species) did as well as individuals on the right flower.

During Colwell's studies in Trinidad, an unusually rainy dry season stopped the flowering of *Costus scaber* for ten days. *Rhinoseius bisacculatus*, restricted to that flower species, vanished. It does live in other places however, including the island of Tobago not far away. Four years later, it reappeared in the Arima Valley where Colwell worked.

Carlton *et al.* (1991) reconstructed another case of niche disappearance, this one leading to the only known extinction of a marine invertebrate from an entire ocean basin. The limpet, *Lottia alveus*, lived in the western Atlantic Ocean from Egg Harbor, Labrador to Long Island Sound, New York. It ate only eelgrass, *Zostera marina*, and lived only in fully marine salinities (not estuaries). Despite its high degree of specialization, it was abundant where found.

In 1930 to 1933, *Zostera marina* suddenly vanished from vast areas of the North Atlantic. It survived only in water of low salinity. The decimation of eelgrass – probably because of a slime mold disease – had many severe effects. But one species, *Lottia alveus*, actually vanished forever; its niche, the combination of marine salinity and eelgrass, had been obliterated from its geographical range.

I am handling niche disappearance as a category of accident. But many might prefer it be kept under its own heading. They have a good reason. Before Technological Man, no form of life could control niche disappearance. Any niche disappearance lay wholly outside the processes that regulate natural systems. Now, Mankind moves and the rest of life shakes.

On a small scale, we log a few forests in Mexico, and the overwintering ground of the monarch butterfly vanishes. On a terrifying scale, we warm our globe a degree or three and displace the essential climates of the world's nature reserves so that they can no longer preserve anything.

Events such as these are hardly accidents. We plan them. Carefully. Patiently. Granted, we do not desire nor plan their consequences. But those consequences are not always so difficult to predict.

Variation in abundance

Pimm *et al.* (1988) hypothesize that the more variable a population, the more likely it is to go extinct. They claim support in the data of the British birds (discussed above). Tracy and George (1992), looking at the same data, do not agree. Nevertheless, we can all agree that the question is interesting. In fact, Pimm (1993) notes that we need not stop at two moments of the population distribution. We could also investigate the effects of skewness and kurtosis on extinction rate.

Schoener and Spiller (1992) look at the variation question in their orb-weaving spiders. For the most part, they get the inverse answer: the more variable the population size, the less likely it is to go extinct. Pimm (1993) understands this result in the following way. He recalls that spider populations on these islands fall into two groups: ephemeral and long-lived (Schoener and Spiller, 1987). Small populations (for spiders, those less than eight individuals) immigrate and rapidly go extinct. Because they are always scarce, they have low variability. Because they do most of the disappearing, they cause the negative correlation between extinction and variation. On the other hand, birth and death rates govern the dynamics of the larger populations. It is these that Pimm *et al.* hypothesized would show the positive correlation between extinction and variation. Sure enough, when Schoener and Spiller analyzed only these larger populations, they found a positive correlation.

I do not mean to conclude that the issue of variation and extinction rate has been settled. Although the proposed relationship satisfies common sense, I am sure all participants in its examination would agree that the issue calls for much more study.

Even abundant, widespread species go extinct

R.I.P.: *Ectopistes migratorius* In the year 1813, in the autumn, John James Audubon was travelling to Louisville, Kentucky, from his home in Henderson. A multitude of passenger pigeons appeared from the north and 'the light of the noonday was obscured as by an eclipse'. Audubon paused in his journey for 21 minutes to view the spectacle. During that time he counted 160 flocks (Audubon, 1843, Vol. 5, p. 27). He resumed his journey and stopped for a meal, but the birds kept coming. The pigeon migration did not end for three days.

Audubon ingeniously estimated the speed of the migrating pigeons from his knowledge of their food and digestion. He knew of some pigeons caught near New York with undigested rice in their crops. The rice could have grown no closer than Georgia or Carolina, about 300 or 400 miles from New York. It takes a pigeon 12 hours to digest its food. So, he reasoned, they must have traveled no more than six hours making an average speed of about one mile a minute (100 kph). (This estimate was confirmed in Michigan when pigeons were timed flying over a known distance: Schorger, 1955, pp. 56, 57.) Using other similarly clever estimates, Audubon (1831, p. 322) figured the size of that pigeon army at 1 115 136 000 birds.

Schorger (1955, pp. 200–4) discusses several other careful estimates of other flocks. The father of American ornithology, Alexander Wilson, figured a group at 2 230 272 000 individuals. Based on observations in Ontario, Schorger calculates another at 3 717 120 000 pigeons. Schorger estimates the total population of passenger pigeons when the USA was young at three to five billion. That is much more likely to be an underestimate than an exaggeration.

Several years ago, Ronald Reagan pointed out that people find it difficult to comprehend a billion of anything. But I know two ways you can grasp the concept of five billion passenger pigeons. One is to note that the approximate thickness of an adult passenger pigeon at the breast was 6 cm. Hence, a stack of 1000 adult pigeons would form a column 60 m high and a stack of one billion would form a column 60 000 km high. Five billion would be enough to encompass the Earth at its Equator 7½ times.

A second way is to recognize that at present, all other species of breeding birds in the USA put together have about 5.7 billion individuals. Thus, two centuries ago, every other bird in the USA was a passenger pigeon.

The abundance of the passenger pigeon shows, in the words of Audubon (1843), 'the astonishing bounty of the great Author of Nature in providing for the wants of his creatures'. Can you believe that we could have the power to make such a species extinct?

Yet, in the year 1914, at 12.45 p.m. on 1 September at the Cincinnati Zoo, Martha, the last living passenger pigeon, fell from her perch and lay dead.

A zombie tree: Castanea dentata The American chestnut tree is another remarkably abundant species that has gone extinct. For all practical purposes, that is. To this day, many root crowns of old chestnuts survive and repeatedly send new sprouts into the forest. The sprouts grow until they are a few years old. Then they sicken and die of chestnut blight – *Endothia parasitica* – the disease responsible for the whole problem.

A century ago, chestnuts made up about 25% of all forest trees in their large range (Roane *et al.*, 1986). That range extended from southern Mississippi and Georgia to Maine, and from Delaware to southeastern Michigan and southern Illinois. They were abundant even in forests where they didn't quite belong. For example in a beech–maple forest near Cleveland, Ohio, chestnuts accounted for 14.9% of all trees wherever the land rolled (Williams, 1936).[1]

In the spring of 1991, Phil Rutter led me to a semi-secret spot in western Wisconsin. There, I got to see a hillside covered with American chestnuts, the descendants of nine individuals brought by train in the late 19th century to this place outside their natural geographical range. I saw with my own eyes what had been a commonplace sight to my grandfather's generation. I saw just how successful this species had been. American chestnuts were amazing. They did virtually everything better than other trees.

Chestnuts grew everywhere. They grew in the open alongside the road leading from field to forest. And they grew in the deep shade of their parents. Chestnut seedlings sprout successfully in such shade, and then they enter a resting stage of indeterminate duration. There they form a shrubby understory 2 to 3 feet tall. When an adult dies or is pruned by the weather, a light gap appears. The little shrubby chestnuts change form and function as if they were tadpoles becoming frogs. They adopt the architecture of a single-stemmed tree and quickly head for the sky (Paillet and Rutter, 1989).

While they are small trees (one cannot say young, because who knows how long they have waited in the understory), their bark is smooth and shiny and green and full of chloroplasts. Rutter believes the chloroplasts indicate wintertime photosynthesis and perhaps even wintertime growth. So they are active in all sorts of times as well as spaces. In fact, during better years and in better places, rapid summer growth produces most of the wood. Summer wood has almost no vessels, so it is dense and hard. In poorer situations, spring-grown wood forms a higher proportion of the tree. Spring growth has the vascular system, so it is soft and light. Thus, the chestnut constitutes both the softwoods and hardwoods of its forest.

Softwoods, hardwoods and understory! Evergreen and deciduous! But there is more. They are also the fire-resistant species. Older chestnuts have deeply furrowed, thick bark that resists fire. And they are the predator-resistant species *par excellence*. Their bark and wood have very high concentrations of tannins (so much so, that one use of the species was to tan

[1] Of course, when Williams censused from 1933 to 1935, he found them all dead. He counted their corpses.

leather). Their wood made rot-resistant poles and fences. Their sweet nuts lie virtually impregnable in a strong, spiny pod. Only a species or two of co-evolved weevil can eat chestnuts in the pod. Even soil type seems not to matter. Their soil can range from clay to sand. Yes, their root systems do not protect them from being windthrown; but chestnuts lived a long time anyhow. Zon (1904) surveyed a mature stand of chestnuts and found the average chestnut to be 400 to 500 years old.

American chestnuts were the most formidable competitors in their baili-wick. They grow towards – and through – a canopy of oak (*Quercus*) and big-tooth aspen (*Populus*) as if it were a light gap. Nevertheless, as if they were compulsively collecting competitive tricks, evidence suggests that they also make a pathogenic chemical with which to fight their competitors.

SuperTree incarnate!

Yet, for all practical puposes they are gone. Chestnut blight – a fungus that girdles and destoys its victims – killed about 3.5 billion of them in the 50 years after it was discovered by Merkel (1906). Now, Thanksgiving turkeys must satisfy themselves getting stuffed with chestnuts born to tree species from other continents. Even the isolated stand that I saw has recently been infected with chestnut blight and is doomed. There is no cure. Rutter pursues research that, one day soon, will lead to a resistant American chestnut (Burnham *et al.*, 1986). But without scientific interven-tion we cannot doubt that we would be mourning a magnificent species of unparalleled success, adaptability and abundance.

No species is safe.

The role of population interactions

Many believe that relentless market hunting exterminated the passenger pigeon. Or that it couldn't survive its need to nest in huge colonies. But the basic cause, the underlying signal of doom, was its loss of forest habitat. Man[2] – in need of land for farms – cut down the mast-bearing trees, espe-cially beeches and oaks, that kept pigeon populations so astronomical that no amount of hunting or trapping would have harmed them. The passenger pigeon lost in its competition with man for habitat.

That is not to say we hunted them to no effect. Perhaps they could have survived as a scarcer species had we not seized them and shot them and

---

[2] The common English name of *Homo sapiens*, a large, ubiquitous primate both of whose sexes are remarkably adept at expropriating habitat from other species.

trapped them so relentlessly. We do know their population declined in the hundred years preceding 1870. They stopped nesting in Ohio, for example, by 1838 (Schorger, 1955). Schorger (p. 207) believes, however that the freefall to extinction really took place from 1871 to 1880. The army of market hunters, called pigeoners, grew immensely and found no way to prevent its own demise. Using the latest technology (the telegraph), it followed pigeon flocks for hundreds of miles. 'The fewer the pigeons, the more persistently they were hunted. A flock was reported ... at Racine, Wisconsin, on 11 September 1885 and within an hour 500 men with shotguns were headed for the locality.' (Schorger, 1955, p. 218).

American chestnut, on the other hand, certainly did lose its existence to a predator – a rapacious fungus. In fact, its only known imperfections are chinks in its predatory defenses. Its nuts may be impregnable in the pod, but once the pods dehisce, many species feast on their sweet, tannin-free meat. Individual trees growing in towns did not reproduce because birds and mammals would take all their nuts. The row of nine founders of the Wisconsin patch stood alone for decades before they finally began to spread (Paillet and Rutter, 1989). Rutter (personal communication) guesses that successful chestnut reproduction required a 2 ha stand, thus occasionally to overwhelm seed predators with massive numbers of offspring.

The other problem of the chestnut is its marvelous bark. As this bark transforms itself from smooth to furrowed, it cracks open and becomes subject to infection. That is how the blight works its accursed invasion. But one mustn't think the blight was an avoidable, star-crossed accident. Already in the 19th century another introduced parasite or disease – we don't know exactly – greatly reduced chestnut densities in the Appalachian Piedmont and forewarned us of inevitable trouble.

Most of the 200 species of cichlid fishes in the Lake Victoria species flock have become extremely rare because of a predator. Most may have gone extinct in the last 20 years. The Nile perch, *Lates niloticus*, gets the blame. It is an introduced piscivore that grows to a monumental 2 m in length (Barel *et al.*, 1985; Miller, 1989).

So, population interactions can transform a species from widespread and abundant, to restricted and scarce. Competition and predation can bring a species low.

In many cases, that may be all they actually do. The first theories of these interactions concluded that they could destroy species all by themselves. Competitive exclusion resulted from species sharing the same niche. Predatory extinction from over-competent predators (who themselves would follow their incompetent victims to extinction). But more modern theories suggest that neither predation nor competition need act alone to exterminate a species.

Originally, theories of predation were linear. Even a robust non-linear account of predation (Rosenzweig and MacArthur, 1963) relied on linearized stability analysis. If a linear system is unstable, it is unstable. Regardless of the densities of predators and victims.

But deterministic, two-species predation systems that allow for realistic non-linearity, stay away from extinction. Kolmogoroff (1936) showed theoretically that predation by itself never causes the extinction of either predator or victim. Predation may bring them precariously close, but it will never utterly extinguish either one.

What, then, does exterminate species in a two-species laboratory predation system? A stochastic accident. Densities get so low that a random deviation carries one or both species away.

Similarly, older theories of competition talked of Gause's principle: two competing species couldn't share the same niche and both survive (Hardin, 1960). But MacArthur realized early that since no two individuals will ever be precisely alike, no two species could be either. He proposed that the interesting question was therefore, 'How similar can two competitors' niches be before one must become extinct?' This is the question of 'limiting similarity'.

At first, MacArthur and Levins (1967) proposed deterministic answers to that question. But their theory was wrong. May and MacArthur (1972) showed that limiting similarity is zero in a deterministic system. Competitors can be as similar as you like and not go extinct. The only thing they may not be is identical.

Even if they are identical, Hubbell and Foster (1986) show that extinction may take a very long time. In populations as small as a few thousand, extinction can take as long as speciation. Thus, they conclude that Gause erred in proposing that species with identical niche requirements cannot coexist for long.

Should you re-examine May and MacArthur's paper, you might have trouble finding the conclusion that limiting similarity is zero. It is there. But they embedded it deeply in the very rescue of the question of limiting similarity. They added stochasticity to their model, and showed how similarity influenced extinction in the presence of stochasticity. When stochasticity is zero, so is limiting similarity.

Thus, in the presence of stochasticity, and only in its presence, competing species may be too similar for both to survive. Competition can reduce a species' density to a precarious level, but competition alone may be unable to complete the job of extinction. Although it may take a long time coming, an accident will finish the species off.

By the way, that is about all one can say on the subject of limiting similarity: it exists. Niches that overlap greatly, endanger the competitors that use them. MacArthur hoped we would be able to attach a number to the limit, but Abrams (1983), in a series of papers, showed that limiting similarity changes its value considerably depending on several other environmental and niche properties.

Sometimes predation itself may be the accident that ends a species' existence. One case, usually attributed to predation alone, is the extinction of the Stephen Island wren (*Traversia lyalli*). Stephen Island is a tiny outpost in Cook Strait off New Zealand's South Island. Its wren was unknown to science until, in 1894, a lighthouse keeper's cat brought in a few specimens it had killed (Falla *et al.*, 1970). No scientist ever saw one alive.

But other people did. Subfossil bird remains show that the wren was a common, widespread resident of mainland New Zealand until Polynesians colonized New Zealand in medieval times (Holdaway, 1989). The cat was merely the accidental – but inevitable – *coup de grâce*. It completed an extinction caused by some incompatible use to which the Polynesians had put the wren's habitat, or else by the rats that had accompanied them to New Zealand.

The point is not that population interactions cannot cause extinctions. Many mathematical formulae exist besides those referred to above. And many of these have attractors at or below zero for one of their species. So there is no theoretical reason for us to conclude that interactions on their own cannot ever cause an extinction.

Here's what I hope you will recognize. Interactions may combine with accidents in extirpating species. They probably do so by making widespread, common species into permanently or intermittently rare and narrowly distributed species (Clark *et al.*, 1990). Then, such species get picked off by accidents of all sorts, even something as trivial as a lighthouse keeper's cat.

Extinction rates and diversity

When studying island biotas, MacArthur and Wilson (1963) elucidated the probable relationship between diversity and extinction rate. I see no reason to differentiate the causes and processes of extinction on islands from those on mainlands (Rosenzweig, 1975). So I will review MacArthur and Wilson's theory here in the context of all extinction.

For a null model, let us suppose diversity has no effect on extinction rate per species. Let the (constant) extinction rate per species be μ. Then the total extinction rate in a biota is μS. Of course, that is the equation of a straight line passing through the origin of a graph with abscissa S. So the null model predicts that total extinction rate rises linearly with diversity. But MacArthur and Wilson did not accept that linearity. They predicted the line would be concave upward, not straight.

To deduce the curvature of the extinction rate, MacArthur and Wilson considered the increased interactions on an island with many species. They reasoned that the first few species would enjoy very low extinction rates because they face little competition. Such a soft environment should allow them to spread into all the habitats they can use at all profitably. They should also increase to large population sizes. As more species arrive, competition should become more of a problem. Species should have lower population sizes and also face the possibility of competitive exclusion.

We can add that as new species arrive, some may be predators and increase the predation rates on the island. Toft and Schoener (1983) examined the influence of lizards on population sizes and diversities of the orb-web spiders mentioned above. As you remember, these spiders lived on 108 very small islands in the Bahamas. Some of the islands had lizards and some did not. Those without lizards harbored spider populations ten times as high. Lizards depressed the spider diversity to half what it is on similar-sized lizard-free islands.

Case and Bolger (1991) have shown that the mongoose, which preys upon lizards themselves, depresses the population sizes of lizards on islands. Islands without mongooses have about an order of magnitude more lizard individuals than those with them. Mongooses have certainly caused the extinctions of some lizard species (as has the competition from introduced reptiles). And predators can induce very low swings in population size (periodic or not) which may further increase vulnerability to extinction.

Thus each additional species should tend to add to the extinction rates of those already present. The mathematical result is that total extinction rate should not merely rise but accelerate with increasing diversity.

We can understand the logic of that conclusion by drawing straight lines from the origin of Figure 6.4 to any point on the extinction curve. The slope of these lines is the average per species extinction rate. If this were

Extinction Rate per Species
On Islands

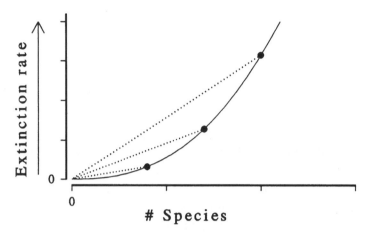

Figure 6.4. Per species extinction rate is the slope of the line connecting the origin with the point representing total
extinction rate and diversity.

constant, the total extinction curve would be a straight line. But we have
argued that it is not constant. It rises with more species as in the figure.
Thus, the curve must be concave upward as drawn: the more species, the
greater the extinction rate per species. Data actually exist to support that
pattern. But we must squeeze the data very hard to get them to do their
work.

The data I will squeeze come from two studies of mammals: Brown
(1971a) and Wilcox (1980). Brown studied the quadrupedal mammals living
in isolated high mountain forests of the southwestern USA. At the end of
the latest glaciation some 10000 years ago, their populations were cut off
from each other by the increasing aridity of the valleys that surround them.
Gradually, they are all becoming extinct.

Wilcox's mammal data come from the Sunda Islands of Indonesia. The
ocean isolated them at the end of the latest glaciation when the glaciers
largely melted and raised the sea level. Biogeographers call such islands
'continental islands' or 'land-bridge islands'. Like mountaintop islands, we
believe that their mammal immigration rates must be very nearly zero. So,
the species we see today on the Sundas are the relicts of the previous connection to mainland Asia.

Notice that the same event isolated both the mountaintops and the Sundas. So they began losing species at the same time. Also, since we are looking at mammal data in both archipelagos, we can expect their extinction rates to be comparable. Any differences we find may be instructive.

We can estimate each island's extinction rate per species. I begin with the Sundas. Assume that the current diversity of mammals on the Malaysian mainland is similar to what it was 10000 years ago. Then, the estimated number of extinctions per species that have taken place on an island *i* which has S_i species remaining is:

$$E_i = (S_m - S_i)/S_m \qquad (6.1)$$

where S_m is the number of species on a mainland area of the same size as the island.

According to Wilcox, the species–area curve on the southeast Asian mainland is

$$S_m = 15.4 \text{ EXP}[0.17 \log A] \qquad (6.2)$$

By substituting that formula for S_m in Equation 6.1, we arrive at our extinction rate estimate.

We now repeat the procedure for the mountaintop islands except that we use the formula of Brown (1971a):

$$S_m = 11.13 \text{ EXP}[0.121 \log A] \qquad (6.3)$$

to estimate the number of species they started with.

Figure 6.5 shows the results of these calculations. In keeping with the equation for E_i above, I fit each set of data with a regression line of the form $y = 1 - k \text{ EXP}[c \log A]$. For the Sundas: $k = 0.122$; $c = 0.130$ ($R^2 = 0.74$). For the mountaintops: $k = 0.079$; $c = 0.326$ ($R^2 = 0.67$).

Two conclusions stand out. First, small islands have lost a larger proportion of their species than have larger ones. Second, a Sunda island tends to have lost a larger proportion of its species compared to a mountaintop of the same size. What can we learn from these conclusions?

You may be tempted to conclude right away that smaller islands have larger extinction probabilities. Don't. You cannot, because smaller islands are smaller areas. And smaller areas start with fewer species than do larger ones. To reach any conclusion, we will need to sort through the alternative hypotheses very carefully.

There are nine hypotheses on two axes of a matrix. The first axis lists the alternate shapes: concave, straight and convex. The second axis lists the

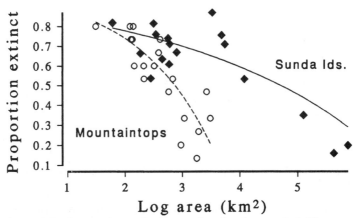

Figure 6.5. Comparison of estimated extinction probability on
Sunda islands (diamonds) and mountaintops of the
southwestern USA (circles). See text for formulae of
estimation and fitted lines. Do not be tempted to conclude from this graph by itself that small islands have
larger extinction probabilities (see text). Data from
Brown (1971a) and Wilcox (1980).

alternate positions: the extinction curve of a small island lies above that of a
larger one; lies beneath it; or is the same. Figure 6.6 displays the possibilities.

Each island provides an estimate of its probability of extinction over the
past 10 000 years. The higher the extinction rate per species, the larger is
this probability. But the extinction rate per species may be estimated as the
arc connecting the island's extinction rate (at its initial diversity) to the origin (Figure 6.4). So, various shapes of extinction curve lead to different predictions about extinction probability per species. For instance, a concave
extinction curve means that at larger diversities, extinction probability per
species is also larger (Figure 6.4).

Because larger islands did produce smaller estimates, four of the nine
hypotheses are eliminated. For example, assume the hypothesis in the upper
right corner of Figure 6.6: extinction curves are concave, and that of larger
islands lies above that of smaller ones. Since larger islands start with more
species, if they lie on a higher curve too, any pair of acceptable beginning
diversities predicts a higher extinction probability for the larger island. But
the data contradict that prediction, so it must be wrong. Similar reasoning
eliminates the other three hypotheses in the upper right of the figure.

Matrix of Extinction Curve Hypotheses

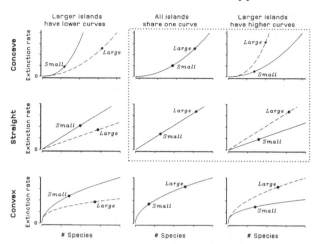

Figure 6.6. The nine geometric hypotheses of extinction and immigration curves on islands. The data of either curve in
Figure 6.5 eliminate only the four hypotheses in the
upper right box. But, if we assume that tropical extinction curves lie at or below temperate ones, then only
the MacArthur–Wilson hypothesis (upper left) allows
the tropical Sunda curve to lie above the mountaintop
curve.

Five hypotheses remain, including one that has extinction rates of small
islands lower than those of large ones, and one that has them the same. But
notice in Figure 6.5 that the Sunda curve lies above the mountaintop curve.
Tropical Sunda islands of medium or large size have had greater extinction
rates per species than temperate mountaintops. As you will now see, this
makes all hypotheses unlikely except one, the one that has concave rate
curves and a lower tropical curve. This lies in the far northwest part of
Figure 6.6 and happens to be MacArthur and Wilson's hypothesis.

Both sets of data come from mammalian extinction over a single 10 000
year period. But because the Sundas are tropical, we estimate that a Sunda
island began at a higher diversity than a temperate mountaintop of equal
area.

Now we make an assumption that is not very controversial, although you
will have to wait for the next chapter to see arguments for it. We assume
that if there are two islands of equal area *and* diversity, one tropical, the
other not, then the tropical island has an extinction rate equal to or less
than that of the other island. (Don't worry. This assumption does not con-

tradict the curves of Figure 6.5. Tropical and temperate islands on that graph may have equal area, but they started with quite different diversities 10 000 years ago.)

If tropical and temperate islands share extinction curves, they must be concave in order for richer islands to exhibit higher extinction rates (Figure 6.7). If instead, tropical curves are lower, they still must be concave (not illustrated). I illustrate the example of them being convex and lower in Figure 6.8. It leads to the prediction that the tropical islands should show lower extinction probabilities. That, you remember, contradicts the data of Figure 6.5. In sum, concave extinction curves that fall as island size increases are the only curves that allow both for larger extinction probabili-

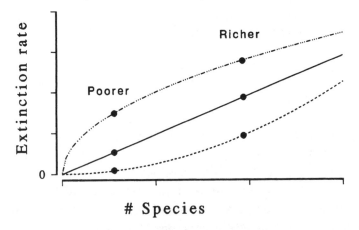

Figure 6.7. Shapes of extinction rate curves determine when tropical islands may exhibit higher per species extinction rates than temperate islands. This figure assumes that tropical and temperate islands share an extinction curve, but begin at different diversities. The diversity of the tropical island is higher. The dots represent the total extinction rates of the two islands at their initial diversities in three cases: concave, convex and straight extinction curves. To assess per species extinction rates, measure the slope of the line connecting a dot to the origin (as in Figure 6.4). When you do, you see that only if the curve is concave will the tropical island's extinction rate per species be higher.

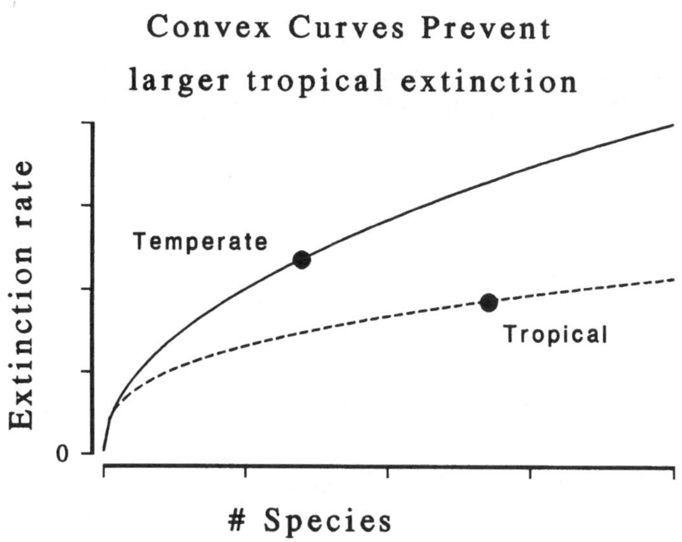

Convex Curves Prevent
larger tropical extinction

Figure 6.8. Assuming a tropical island has more species than a
temperate one, that its extinction curves are convex
and fall below those of the temperate island, the tropical island cannot have the higher per species extinction
rate. The ordinate is total extinction rate. To assess per
species extinction rates, you measure the slope of the
line connecting a dot to the origin (as in Figure 6.4).

ties on smaller islands, and for larger extinction probabilities on tropical
islands.

Look in Chapter 8 for more evidence that interactions raise extinction
rates.

Measuring extinction rates

Extinction is a logarithmic process

Assume all species have and always have had the same rate of extinction.
You may think of this insane assumption as a null model. Surely it is over-
simplified. And yet, it shows that we must deal with even the simplest
extinction process as a logarithmic (i.e. non-linear) function.

Consider a cohort of 100 species sharing an extinction rate of $\mu = 0.2$ per
Myr. After 10^6 years, 80 species remain. After 2×10^6 years, 64 do. In general, after $t \times 10^6$ years, we expect $100 \, \mu^t$ extinctions.

A constant extinction rate is an example of a common differential equation, the decay equation. It is analogous to the exponential equation for population growth. In logarithmic form it is:

$$\ln S(t) = \ln S(0) - \mu t \qquad\qquad (6.4)$$

where $S(0)$ is the number of species in the cohort and $S(t)$ is the number still extant after t units of time.

Because extinction requires logarithmic estimates, we cannot usually measure it linearly. A biota with a constant diversity constitutes the sole exception to that rule. No matter how long the time interval examined, it will generate $\mu t S$ extinctions. So we can recover μ simply if we divide its extinctions by tS. But we will not often want to make the assumption that S is constant. Instead, that will usually be among the properties we want to test for.

Suppose we tried a linear estimate on the example above. After 2×10^6 years the cohort had lost 36 species. So our estimate would have been $36/(100 \times 2)$. That is 0.18 per Myr. But we know the truth to be 0.2. One popular adjustment is to average the diversities at the beginning and end of the sample. In our case, the average is 82 species. That makes the estimate 0.22. Still not right.

Yet, using the logarithmic formula we do no better: $\mu = (\ln 100 - \ln 64)/2 = 0.223$. What happened? We fell into a trap. To estimate extinctions, we applied the extinction rate discontinuously, using a difference equation in two steps. Then we expected to recover the rate with a continuous formula. While the error we caused was not so great, no one can promise it never will matter. We should like to get it right.

To apply the rate continuously, simply use Equation 6.4 as written:

$$\ln S(t) = \ln(100) - (0.2 \times 2) = 4.205$$

Thus, after 2 Myr of an extinction rate of 0.2 per Myr, we expect 67 species (not 64) to remain.

My point? We mustn't wave our arms at the mathematics of extinction rates. Our example seemed trivial, and it was simple. But it also tripped us up repeatedly. Let us therefore consider the problem in some detail.

A simple formula

Equation 6.4 usually will not work on data from the fossil record because both speciations and extinctions occur during evolutionary history.

Equation 6.4 takes only the extinctions into account. Rosenzweig and Vetault (1992) developed a formula to calculate extinction rate despite this.

Let N_L = the number of extant species,
        N_0 = the number of species t years ago,
        N_E = the number that have become extinct in t years,
        t = the time it has taken for these extinctions to occur.

Assume a constant extinction rate, μ, and a constant speciation rate, σ. Now, we can use the logarithmic form of the growth equation (Stanley, 1975, 1979; Sepkoski, 1978) and solve for μ:

$$\sigma - \mu = (\ln N_L - \ln N_0)/t \tag{6.5}$$

$$\mu = [(\sigma - \mu)N_E] / \{N_0[(e^{(\sigma-\mu)t} - 1)]\} \tag{6.6}$$

Vrba (1987) has developed a fascinating set of data on the evolutionary history of large African mammals. Rosenzweig and Vetault (1992) applied Equations 6.5 and 6.6 to the fossil record of these animals. We felt it was worth estimating their extinction and speciation rates as carefully as possible. To give you an idea of speciation and extinction rates in the fossil record, I list them in Table 6.2.

Table 6.2. *Extinction and speciation rates among some clades of large African mammals*

Clade	μ	σ	T
Taurotragus	0.29	0.29	7
Tragelaphos	0.41	0.69	7
Apyceros	0.20	0.20	5
Alcelaphini	1.75	2.14	5
Connechaetus	1.26	1.61	4
Damaliscus	1.66	1.94	4
Syncerus	0.60	0.60	5
Oreotragus	0.33	0.33	3
Kobus	0.73	1.00	6
Anatidorcas	1.00	1.00	3
Phacochoerus	2.30	2.30	3
Giraffa	1.60	1.60	5
Orycteropus	0.33	0.33	15
Loxodonta	0.40	0.40	5
Elephas	2.00	2.00	5

T, age of clade in Myr.

Others have also estimated extinction rates from the fossil record using a logarithmic procedure. Rosenzweig and Duek (1979) studied an assemblage of about 100 species of invertebrates that lived on the muddy sea floor during the late Ordovician Period. They estimated an extinction rate of 0.217–0.235 per Myr during a 3.5 Myr period when species diversity was fairly constant. Other estimates are lower than that from the Ordovician. They are lower quite probably because their authors did not attempt to estimate the number of short-lived species still undiscovered in the record. For example, Stanley (1975) produced an estimate of 0.116 per Myr for marine invertebrates of the more recent past. Valentine and Jablonski (1991) estimate that 13% of mollusc species have become extinct during the past million years.

Nevertheless, all estimates of marine invertebrate extinction rates are lower than those for mammal clades. The difference is probably real. It does not stem from averaging the invertebrates together as a community. If I do that to Vrba's mammals by including three genera with no extinctions, I obtain a community-wide extinction rate of 0.36 per Myr. The usual mammal species is just not as durable as the usual marine invertebrate species.

Plant species become extinct at rates that overlap those of animals (Valentine *et al.*, 1991). For example, conifers have a rate of about 0.2 species per species per Myr; monocots, 0.16 per Myr; and dicots, 0.26 per Myr.

So, all estimates of extinction rate do share an order of magnitude. Their rates are on the order of tenths of a species per species per Myr. That similarity may be more significant than their differences. It gives us an idea of what we mean by the evolutionary time scale.

Maximum likelihood estimation from repeated censuses

Modern data on species diversity sometimes contain repeated censuses. These may be adequate to allow estimation of local extinction rates, i.e. rates of total disappearance from an area smaller than the entire range of a species. Often, we would like such estimates for islands or natural reserves.

The local extinction rate, μ, opposes λ, the immigration rate. The immigration rate is the probability that a species not present in a system will enter it in a given time interval. Clark and Rosenzweig (1994) show that the following procedure yields the maximum likelihood estimates of μ and λ as probabilities in a Markov chain.

Suppose a series of annual censuses of an island show the following sequence of presences P and absences A: $PPPAAPPPPPAAPPPPPAPPAAA$. (This sequence depicts only one species.) Now let δ be the probability that the species becomes locally extinct and does not reimmigrate during one unit of time, and let

k = number of transitions from A to P = 3
l = number of transitions from A to A = 4
m = number of transitions from P to A = 4
n = number of transitions from P to P = 9

The estimated immigration rate is

$$\lambda \approx k/(k+l) = 0.43 \tag{6.7}$$

The estimated local extinction rate is

$$\delta \approx m/(m+n) = 0.31 \tag{6.8}$$

$$\mu \approx \delta/(1-\lambda) = 0.54 \tag{6.9}$$

Sometimes, because of randomness in the data and a small data set, Equations 6.7, 6.8 and 6.9 produce an estimate of extinction probability greater than 1. When that happens, the most likely estimate is $\mu = 1$.

We used Equations 6.7, 6.8 and 6.9 on 39 census sequences of birds from three British islands. (See the section above on Extinction and Population size.) Extinction probabilities ranged from 'too-small-to-discriminate-from-zero' up to 'too-large-to-discriminate-from-unity' (Figure 6.9). In addition, 32 other species-island combinations never disappeared from their census, and so did not allow us to estimate their μ values. These species-island combinations probably have extinction rates one or more orders of magnitude less than those in Figure 6.9.

Often, censuses occur sporadically. Then, you cannot use Equations 6.7, 6.8 or 6.9. Clark and Rosenzweig (1994) report the general formula for likelihood, L, so sporadic censuses also may yield estimates of μ and λ.

Suppose a series of six censuses were taken in years 1, 4, 5, 7, 12 and 20. Suppose their results for a certain species were $APPAAP$. Let t be the interval between two censuses. Thus, in this sequence of censuses, t has the values 3, 1, 2, 5 and 8. Then, introduce the symbol Ω for clarity:

$$\Omega_t = 1 - (1 - \lambda - \delta)^t \tag{6.10}$$

The probability of each of the four possible transitions is:

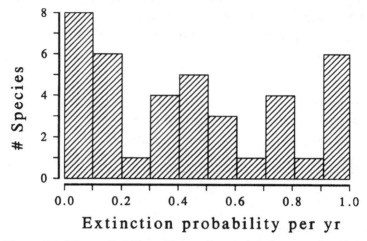

Birds on Islands

Figure 6.9. The probability of becoming extinct (per year) varies widely among British birds whose extinctions have been recorded on three islands.

$$p\{AA\} = 1 - [\Omega_i \lambda/(\lambda + \delta)] \tag{6.11a}$$

$$p\{AP\} = \Omega_i \lambda/(\lambda + \delta) \tag{6.11b}$$

$$p\{PA\} = \Omega_i \delta/(\lambda + \delta) \tag{6.11c}$$

$$p\{PP\} = 1 - [\Omega_i \delta/(\lambda + \delta)] \tag{6.11d}$$

So the likelihood of the particular set of six censuses *APPAAP* is:

$$L = [\Omega_3 \lambda/(\lambda + \delta)][1 - \Omega_1 \delta/(\lambda + \delta)][\Omega_2 \delta/(\lambda + \delta)][1 - \Omega_5 \lambda/(\lambda + \delta)][\Omega_8 \lambda/(\lambda + \delta)] \tag{6.12}$$

We now install Equation 6.12 on a computer and have it substitute various combinations of δ and λ until it finds the maximum value of L numerically. Each combination of δ and λ that is tested, must satisfy the constraint $(\lambda + \delta) \leq 1$.

With only a few censuses, no species can produce reliable estimates of μ and λ. Often, however, we want to characterize an entire set of species. Using Equations 6.11, this is sometimes possible from surprisingly few censuses. Clark and Rosenzweig tried it to good effect on plant data amassed by Abbott and Black (1980) in no more than four censuses. With enough species (about three dozen), the value of L peaked sharply over a small, well-defined set of δ and λ values.

A plant species on these small islands of southwestern Australia goes extinct locally every 10 or 20 years on average. The exact value varies from island to island. Figure 6.10 shows the likelihood surface for Island 88 (Bird Island; 0.89 ha; 36 species recorded in three censuses: 1959, 1975, 1977). It is an example of a modal island. Its likelihood surface peaks sharply at $\delta = 0.05$ and $\lambda = 0.25$. So its extinction rate, $\mu = 0.07$. That is, a species on Bird Island goes extinct about once every 15 years.

Capture–recapture estimation

In Chapter 3, we looked at the use of capture–recapture analyses to count the number of species in the fossil record. The best of these methods (given the nature of the data) assumed closed populations, i.e. no speciation or extinction. However, open models actually produce estimates of the turnover variables. If we could use an open model, we would have statistically reliable and interpretable extinction rates.

Nichols and Pollock (1983) pioneered the use of open models on fossil data. As they produce estimates of diversities and rates, they also produce statistics that warn them of too great a deviation from the assumptions of

Island 88
Likelihood Surface

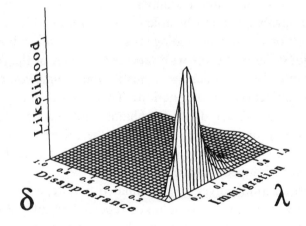

Figure 6.10. A single Bird Island plant species probably becomes extinct on the island about once every 15 years. The vertical axis is dimensionless; it is proportional to the likelihood of a specific combination of immigration and disappearance probability.

the model. We have already seen the results of their diversity estimates for late Eocene mammals (Figure 3.5). This same analysis also yielded extinction rate estimates for nine intervals of 40 000 to 70 000 years. The probability of extinction ranged from 0 during three intervals, up to 0.18, 0.19 and 0.21 for three others. (These estimates are plotted against speciation rates in Figure 10.2)

I wanted to get an idea of how these probabilities compare with the other rates we have so far calculated from the fossil record. An interval of 50 000 years is 0.05×10^6 years. So in 10^6 years (i.e. 20 intervals), a cohort of species at an extinction rate of 0.2 per species per 50 000 years will keep only $EXP(-0.2 \times 20)$ of its species. That is fewer than two species of each hundred! The extinction rate per species per million years is 0.982 – a devastating rate compared to the others. Of course, I selected a rate of 0.2 as my example, and that is higher than the extinction rate during all but one interval. Nevertheless, these mammals did not last long. When I multiplied the actual sequence of nine extinction rates together (covering an interval of close to 500 000 years), the cumulative extinction rate was 0.585. In two such intervals (i.e. 10^6 years), 69% of all species would have vanished.

Pollock (1982) developed a combined method – called Pollock's robust design. It allows capture probabilities to vary among species. And it allows species to come and go. However, only Nichols and Pollock (1983) have used it on fossil data. The trouble lies not in the method, but in the data collection. You must know about Pollock's method before you collect your data or else you probably won't be able to use it. I hope this book serves to flag this method for young paleobiologists so they can take advantage of it.

Pollock's robust design begins with repeated samples of the fossils in one stratum. They must be of similar age to justify the assumption of the closed population (no extinction, no origination). Then their diversity is estimated using a closed model. (Rexstad and Burnham, 1992, have written a manual for their computer program CAPTURE. Together, these bring the technology of jack-knifed capture–recapture to anyone with an IBM-compatible, math-coprocessor-equipped, personal computer.)

After the first stratum's diversity is estimated, you repeat the analysis on the next – from which you also have taken repeated samples. And then you do the third and fourth, etc. When you have finished, you will have unbiased estimates of the diversities of a series of fossil assemblages.

Now you estimate the extinction and origination rates with an open model. Some version of the Cormack method or the Jolly–Seber method is customary. (Again, computer software in the public domain is freely available – e.g. JOLLY91.) Each capture period is the combination of all the repeated samples you took from a stratum. If a species is recovered even once from any of these samples, it gets recorded as present during that time.

I see nothing to stop paleobiologists who want to take advantage of Pollock's robust design.

An unusually fine example: reptiles on islands of known age

Wilcox (1978) surveyed the reptiles on small islands in the Sea of Cortez, Mexico. These islands are just as isolated as the mountaintops of the southwest US. But we know, at least approximately, how old each is. The older they are, the fewer species remain. So, Wilcox could actually measure their rates of extinction.

In model fashion, he began by accounting for two variables that are almost ubiquitous in their effects on diversity: area and latitude. First, he obtained the relationship of lizard diversity to area (Figure 6.11). Then he studied the deviations of the actual diversities from their species-area curve (Figure 6.12). At higher latitudes these deviations tended to fall below the curve; at lower latitudes, they were above it.

The deviations from the line in Figure 6.12 constitute the residual variance left to understand after both area and latitude have been taken into account. Wilcox showed that the age of the island explains a significant part of it. The older the island, the more it tends to fall below the line in Figure 6.12; the younger it is, the more it tends to lie above it (Figure 6.13).

The linear regression in Figure 6.13 provides an estimate of lizard extinc-

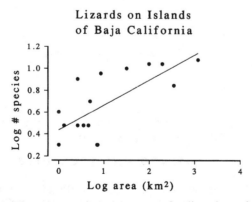

Figure 6.11. The raw species–area curve for lizards on islands in the Sea of Cortez. Data from Wilcox (1978).

Excess Species For Area

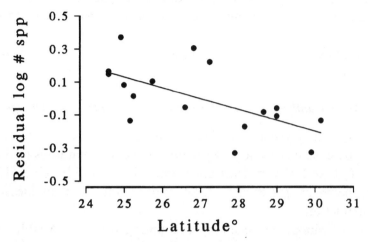

Figure 6.12. Latitude helps to explain the deviations of diversity
from its regression line in Figure 6.11. The higher the
latitude, the smaller the diversity. Data from Wilcox
(1978).

Excess Species
for area and latitude

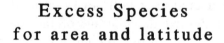
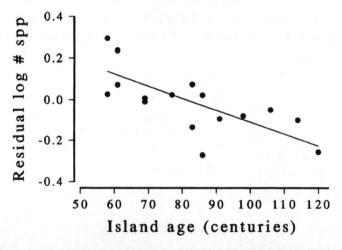

Figure 6.13. Age helps to explain the deviations of diversity from
its regression line in Figure 6.12. The older the island,
the smaller the diversity. Data from Wilcox (1978).

tion rate on these islands. The coefficient of age in a multiple linear regression (where the independent variables are log area, latitude and age in years) is -6.3154×10^{-5}. So, $\log S$ is proportional to [age $\times$ (-6.3154×10^{-5})], and S is proportional to $EXP[(-1.454 \times 10^{-4}) \times$ age]. Thus, the exponential extinction rate of these lizards is 0.1454 per species per 1000 years. That is a very high rate indeed. But the other island rate estimates in this chapter were also very high, the bird rates often three orders of magnitude higher. We shall learn in Chapter 8 to expect such high rates of islands.

(Note that the estimate 0.1454 is not identical to Wilcox's. I used the number of species as the independent variable. He used the Shannon–Weiner index of diversity. It is not clear that any diversity index – all of which take relative abundances into account – ought to be preferred to the simple number of species as the dependent variable for the particular independent variable set we both used. See Chapter 8 for the discussion about such indices.)

Doomed species – extinction may take a long time

Accustomed as most of us are to the time scale of a television program, we sometimes have difficulty conceiving of the enormous amounts of time Nature takes to do her work. But, because many – perhaps even most – extinctions require an accident, we can expect to wait a long time to see the inevitable. Maybe a long, long time. It's not that species are aging. They are merely waiting for a stochastic event.

Consider the island systems studied by Brown, Wilcox and others. These land bridge islands and sky islands formed some 10 000 years ago, but neither their mammals nor their reptiles have fully compensated for their increased isolation. More extinctions are on the way.

Webb (1984) notes the long delay in many extinctions of large mammals that followed the climate change of the Late Miocene Epoch. North America dried out, and its grasslands expanded at the expense of its savannas. Grazers proliferated. Twenty whole genera of browsers disappeared in the first wave of extinctions some 9 Myr ago. But the climate change preceded the largest wave of extinctions by several million years. Between 5.4 and 6 Myr ago (during the Pliocene Epoch), 24 genera suddenly vanished. Altogether, North America lost 62 whole genera of large mammals in about 4.5 Myr. (The average generic diversity during this time: about 25.)

My colleague Paul Martin (1984) has long championed the hypothesis that paleolithic humans, by developing new and devastating hunting skills including deliberately set fires, precipitated the waves of extinction seen in the New World, Australia and Polynesia. Perhaps in Eurasia too. I believe he is correct. But we surely had nothing to do with the Miocene–Pliocene extinctions, the most extensive set of mammalian extinctions in North American history. So I wonder whether, at the end of the Pleistocene Epoch (when we lost 39 genera), we did not merely trigger some long-awaited die-off. Were we the lighthouse keeper's cat?

Sher and his colleagues make this scenario most believable with their studies of woolly mammoth extinction (Vartanyan *et al.*, 1993). *Mammuthus primigenius* grazed on the tundra-steppes of Eurasia from Western Europe to the Pacific in the Pleistocene. By about 12 000 years ago, climatic change virtually eliminated those steppes south of 70° N. The mammoth, its belly full of high Arctic grasses, suffered the same great restriction in distribution. By 9500 years ago, all relics of the once plentiful biome had disappeared from the mainland. So had the mammoth.

But the mammoth survived in the one place its biome did: Wrangel Island, Russia. Wrangel is a large island in the Arctic Ocean. To this very day, you can go there and see, not mammoths, but their habitat, the tundra-steppe. Land to the south of Wrangel is too warm and too wet for this biome.

Mammoths survived on Wrangel Island until only 3700 years ago. In fact, by 7000 years ago they had even evolved a dwarf form. So they must have done well enough to reproduce for many generations. Yet they were not hunted to extinction by *Homo sapiens*; they became extinct before humans ever colonized the island.

What finished them? For now, we can only speculate. But whatever it was, it merely administered the *coup de grâce* to a rare species, a species set up for extinction by the disappearance of its niche over most of its former range. After all, a dwarf elephant is still bigger than your average lemming. There could not have been all that many mammoths on Wrangel Island.

Mass extinctions

The causes and rates of extinction I have so far mentioned, typify the Earth's history. But, occasionally, so occasionally that your fingers and toes – and maybe just your fingers – are enough to keep track of them, real catastrophes have visited the planet.

Table 6.3. *Mass extinction probabilities (approximate likelihood of a species' extinction from Sepkoski, 1989; Jablonski, 1991)*

Time	Age (in 10^6 years)	Probability (%)
Middle Miocene	11.6	24
Late Eocene	35.4	35
End Cretaceous	65.0	76
Late Cenomanian	90.4	53
Aptian	116.3	41
End Jurassic	145.6	45
Pliensbachian	187.0	53
Late Triassic	208.0	76
Late Permian	245.0	96
Late Devonian	367.0	82
Late Ordovician	439.0	85

Toward the end of the Permian Period, diversity began to plummet. Before the catastrophe ended, about 96% of all species became extinct. At the end of the Cretaceous Period, a similar mass extinction cost the Earth about 76% of all its species (Table 6.3). In producing these estimates, Sepkoski (1989) also produced a daunting set of arguments that such declines in diversity occur periodically (Figure 6.14).

Sepkoski calculated the interval between mass extinctions. It is about 26 Myr. The data fit this period rather well, especially the six mass extinctions since the end of the Jurassic. That is one indication of their periodicity.

Many methods exist for objectively analyzing time series to determine whether they are periodic. Most cannot be used for Sepkoski's work because, despite the length of the fossil record, there are not enough data. However, one that he could and did use, combines power with simplicity.

Imagine a sequence of 49 extinction rates. (Sepkoski's actually has 49 rate estimates.) If we order them randomly, we will still see peaks and valleys. In between will be the intervals (i.e. line segments connecting data) where the randomized data just happen to continue upward (or downward). We know there is no significance to such continuations, because we ordered the numbers randomly. We can expect such pseudo-trends to last

Extinction per Genus per Myr

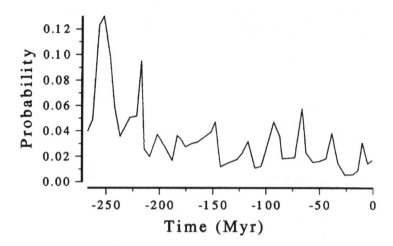

Figure 6.14. The probability of a marine animal genus becoming
extinct in 1 Myr has varied considerably through
time. Data come from 17 500 genera of which 13 000
are extinct. Data for species extinction rates are not
as complete, but probably show the same variation.
Peaks are mass extinctions. But the method of graphing greatly underestimates their rate because mass
extinctions occur in much less than 1 Myr (Kerr,
1991). (Redrawn from Sepkoski, 1989.)

for only a few intervals because no mechanism maintains their momentum;
they are just accidents of sampling.

Now imagine a sequence derived from a cyclic process. It will have
longer intervals between peaks and valleys (and fewer of them) because
those intervals are part of some deterministic process. If we compare the
size of the actual intervals with those predicted by the random model, we
can estimate the probability that the sequence actually came from a series
of random values.

Table 6.4 shows Sepkoski's result. Intervals of only one line segment are
much rarer than expected. Those of three or more are much more common.
The set does not fit the null hypothesis. The pattern seems real. Coupling
this result with the good fit of the 26 Myr period to the data, we must
acknowledge the pattern. Better data may even extend it backwards in time.

Table 6.4. *Number of intervals between local minimum and local maximum extinction rates (genera per Myr). The data intervals are too long to be random* ($\chi^2 = 19.9; p < 0.001$)

Interval size	Frequencies	
	Observed	Expected
1	5	19.17
2	6	8.25
≥3	8	2.92

I do not know what causes mass extinctions. Fischer (1984) believes that some of them have occurred about every 150 Myr as the Earth changes abruptly from an 'icehouse' to a 'greenhouse' or vice versa. Quite possibly, extraterrestrial objects or massive volcanoes sometimes change the Earth's climate briefly, and greatly upset the distribution and availability of appropriate habitats causing many species to suffer intolerable losses. Meteorite impacts could do the job. Interested readers should consult Van Valen (1984), Jablonski (1984), Raup (1992) and others.

Mass extinctions constitute severe disruptions to the usual regime of slow background extinction. They affect many taxa in many environments, but they do not (by definition) last very long. They are like the perturbations a scientist imposes on an experimental system to study how it regulates itself. Valentine *et al.* (1978) estimated that only 2% of all extinctions occurred during the five main mass extinction events (End Cretaceous, Late Triassic, Late Permian, Late Devonian, Late Ordovician). Improved data over the last decade have not changed that estimate much. In a recent letter (11 Feb 1993), Valentine allows the possibility that as many as 4% of extinctions took place during these mass extinction events.

Hansen (1988), studied the recuperation of marine molluscs on the US Gulf coast in the early Tertiary Period. In the late Cretaceous, this region held more than 500 species. But in the wake of the Maastrichtian mass extinction, it held only a bit more than 100. By the middle of the Eocene Epoch, some 25 Myr later, a diversity of about 400 had built back. Hansen interprets this to mean that marine molluscs are constantly recovering from the previous mass extinction. But a close look at the data in his Figure 6 leads to another interpretation.

The time after the mass extinction is marked by a low level of diversity (perhaps because of a decrease in sustainable diversity, but more likely just because Paleocene and early Eocene rocks are scarce – see Chapter 10). This low level lasted some 20 Myr. It did not exhibit steady growth in diversity, but seesawed about during that time. Then in the mid-Eocene, mollusc diversity exploded, rapidly reaching the 400 species level. Finally, in the late Eocene, it crashed again and returned to the low levels of the previous 25 Myr. That is very much what the graph looks like to me, at least. If I am correct, the explosion of the mid-Eocene would appear to have nothing to do with the Maastrichtian mass extinction at all. The gastropods would appear instead to have recovered their diversities very, very rapidly (during the earliest Paleocene) by the radiations of several families whose unusually high speciation rates Hansen both demonstrates and emphasizes. But the diversities that could be sustained in the Paleocene and early Eocene were either just low, or else poorly preserved.

In sum, I believe that mass extinctions, however dramatic, leave diversity wounded only for geological instants. The longest term graphs (e.g. Figures 3.1 and 3.2) show them as brief depressions in the trend. Diversity seems to recuperate quickly enough so that mass extinctions rarely need to be reckoned with as one of diversity's molding forces. Even workers who stress and study the interesting consequences of mass extinctions (e.g. Kauffman and Fagerstrom, 1993) admit that recuperation takes only 1 Myr to 8 Myr. Thus, the Earth spends about 90% of its time with diversities unaffected by mass extinctions. For this book, then, we need to recognize the existence of mass extinctions but need not know their cause.

Chapter 7

Coevolution of habitat diversity and species diversity

Why should species be ecologically restricted? Why doesn't one omni-talented species evolve and put all the others out of business? When we can answer that question, we will clearly know the explanation of the habitat pattern. We shall know why we see more diversity in places with a greater variety of physical and chemical conditions. But, it turns out, we will also be well on our way to understanding most other diversity patterns too.

The seeds of our answer lie in the very mechanisms of speciation. None of the mechanisms, however, will help without the basic assumption of evolutionary ecology, the tradeoff principle. So, I begin there.

The tradeoff principle

Suppose one single phenotype – call it the super-hero phenotype – could do everything better than any other. Natural selection would discover it and promote it. All other phenotypes would disappear. Only one homogeneous super-hero species would remain.

The tradeoff principle asserts that a super-hero species does not exist and has never existed. (I omit saying 'will never exist' because I fear that the onslaught of the human species against all others has not finished.) It says that phenotypes excel at most functions by losing the ability to perform other functions well. Tongue-in-cheek, the humorist Ephraim Kishon put the point perfectly: 'If only they'd manufacture pins with heads on both ends, nobody would prick himself.'

At one time, there may have been ecologists who thought all functions must be subject to the tradeoff principle. Today, we realize that only some need to be. Those that are not will not figure in supporting species diversity.

We know many examples of tradeoffs, some directly relating to habitat

differences. One example is barnacle growth rate and resistance to desicca-
tion. Connell (1961), in a well known series of experiments, showed that
because of their faster growth, *Balanus balanoides* could overgrow and
smother *Chthamalus stellatus*. But fast growth requires more food, and so,
more time spent under water filter-feeding nutritious bits. The high intertidal zone is usually above water. There, *Balanus* dries out and dies, leaving
its precious space to the *Chthamalus*.

A similar tradeoff involves freshwater ostracodes. McLay (1978a) studied
four species in a 31.1 m rut left by a military truck in a Vancouver suburb.
The ostracodes feed on the detritus of grasses washed into the rut.

The rut was 0.34 m wide and filled with water to a depth of 1 cm – except
during the summer when it was dry. Its southern end filled first, dried out
last, and was the warmest point. Its northern end not only dried out for
more of the year, it also tended to freeze up during the winter (which kills
the ostracodes). Thus, the rut contained a linear gradient of habitat quality
from its wetter, warmer end to its drier, colder end.

Each of the four species found its place along the rut gradient. Each was
the most abundant at some distance from the southern end. McLay (1978b)
brought individuals of the two most common species into the laboratory to
study their growth and survival. He found that larger ostracodes, even
larger members of the same species, withstood starvation longer than
smaller ones. The pressure of population density itself would cause such
starvation as ostracode numbers grow during wet periods.

On the other hand, smaller ostracodes develop faster. Thus they are
favored in the parts of the rut that fill later, dry out sooner and get interrupted by freezing in midwinter (McLay, 1978c).

We meet a second example among dabbling ducks of the genus *Anas*
(mallard, teal, shoveler, gadwall, etc.). These ducks filter invertebrates from
water by means of a sieve. Lamellae – fine projections growing at the base
of their bill – form the sieve and determine the size of the food it will trap.
The denser the lamellae, the smaller the food (Nudds and Bowlby, 1984).

Duck species vary considerably in lamellar density (Nudds *et al.*, 1994).
Anas clypeata, northern shoveler, has the densest sieve: 21–25 lamellae per
cm^2. *Anas platyrhynchos*, mallard, has the coarsest sieve: 8 lamellae per cm^2.
Coarser sieves will miss some smaller invertebrates. So, why shouldn't all
species have the dense sieve of the shoveler?

The answer appears to be connected with habitat. Shovelers forage
mostly in clear water, far from shore and free of vegetation (T.D. Nudds,
personal communication). There, the densest sieve is an advantage. But

where much vegetation grows in a pond, debris and grit can clog the sieve and interfere with feeding (Tolkamp, 1993; Mott, 1994). It is in such well-vegetated microhabitats that the tradeoff occurs. Coarser sieves get only larger invertebrates, but do so efficiently and support the largest body sizes. Finer sieves get a much broader range of prey sizes, but at the cost of efficiency (Figure 7.1)

Among plant species, fast growth may be traded for the ability to withstand poorer or harsher conditions. Mulkey (1986) provided a good tropical example. He studied three species of bamboo on Barro Colorado Island, Panama. All three grow in the forest understory. When trees fall, a light gap is created. Such a gap allows more sunlight to reach the understory plants, but it also subjects them to higher temperatures and lower humidities.

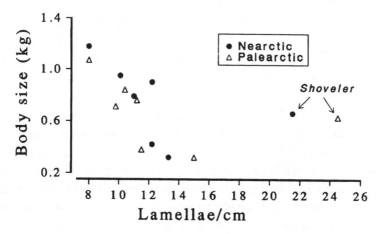

Figure 7.1. Ducks of the genus *Anas* filter invertebrates through lamellae in their beaks. In clear water, this lamellar sieve does not clog up; the duck that uses it (i.e. shoveler) can have a very fine sieve. But in well-vegetated water, many suspended particles can clog up the sieve. Thus, ducks that use such habitats have coarser sieves. The particles also cause a tradeoff: finer sieves take a broader variety of invertebrate sizes but clog up more easily. Ducks with such finer sieves forage less efficiently and are smaller. Most of the species in the figure live in both the Nearctic and the Palearctic, and are represented by two points. Data from Nudds *et al.* (1994).

Only one of the bamboo species, *Pharus latifolius*, increases its photosynthetic capacity in the presence of full sun. But it has a lower photosynthetic efficiency in the shade compared to *Streptochaeta sodiroana*, the species that cannot adapt at all to the treefall. *S. sodiroana* showed a very high mortality when exposed to full sun. The third species has intermediate properties. But none of the three showed the range of adaptability Mulkey expected. None could both increase its photosynthetic capacity in full sun and reduce its respiration in the shade.

Björkman (1981) fully explained the physiological basis of the tradeoff between photosynthetic capacity and photosynthetic efficiency. Having a high capacity requires a high concentration of various enzymes involved in the dark reaction of photosynthesis. Perhaps the most important is ribulose bisphosphate carboxylase. RuBP carboxylase catalyzes the reaction of oxygen and RuPB, a rate limiting step in the dark reaction. Plants with little RuBP carboxylase cannot photosynthesize very rapidly even in the presence of high light levels.

On the other hand, RuBP carboxylase and other proteins involved in the dark reaction require maintenance. They turn over rapidly. Therefore, plants with a lot of RuBP carboxylase have high respiration rates. When there is very little light, they use much more energy than they store. But plants with low amounts of RuBP carboxylase can profit at very low light levels. They don't need much RuBP carboxylase to use such light, and they aren't saddled with the costs of having a lot of RuBP carboxylase to maintain.

Björkman *et al.* (1972) provided some classic comparisons among species. They studied two rainforest understory plants in Queensland, *Alocasia macrorrhiza* and *Cordyline rubra*. These two species live in the darkest part of the forest where light levels average only 22 μE per cm^2 per day (Björkman and Ludlow, 1972; μE is a microEinstein of light energy). In comparison, the canopy receives 5010 μE per cm^2 per day. Thus, the vegetation of the understory gets less than 0.5% of the light that falls on the forest. These are about the lowest light levels of any habitat occupied by vascular plants.

One day during the study, the sky turned deeply overcast. That day, only 14.9 μE/cm^2 reached *Alocasia*. Yet, the plant made net energy gains on it. It fixed energy at an efficiency of 16%, the highest ever measured for any plant anywhere.

The two shade lovers could make a profit as long as light fell on them at a rate greater than 0.2 nanoE per cm^2 per second (0.17 in the case of *Alocasia*). A sun loving plant like *Atriplex patula* requires 6.3 – more than

30 times as much! The reason is that the *Atriplex* must consume 2.09 μmol of CO_2 per minute per dm^2 just to keep its engines ready. But the dark respiration rate of *Alocasia* is only 0.05 μmol of CO_2 per minute per dm^2, and that of *Cordyline* is only 0.06.

Atriplex gets its reward in the sun. Its abundance of RuBP carboxylase allows it to fix 20.3 μmol CO_2 per minute per dm^2. The two shade lovers can fix only 1.95 (*Cordyline*) and 1.90 (*Alocasia*). In fact, put out in full sun too long they actually die (from inhibition of their photosynthetic processes, etc.).

Insects also trade advantages in shade and sun. Shelly (1984) studied 15 species of robberfly (Asilidae) in Barro Colorado. Robberflies ambush their insect prey in mid-air. So they must be able to zip out from their ambush site and outfly their victims. The warmer their body temperature (within tolerable limits), the faster they can go. On the other hand, it usually costs more energy to keep a body warmer.

Shelly found that each species of robberfly belonged to one of two groups: ten were shade-seekers; five were light-seekers. The light-seekers had higher body temperatures (average, 9.2 °C greater than ambient vs 1.3 °C greater than ambient for the shade-seekers). Shelly examined many aspects of robberfly behavior to see what each group might be missing because it was not a member of the other. But the main point is the very existence of the two groups. Most light-seeking robberflies have thoracic temperatures about 10 °C greater than their shade-seeking counterparts. That is a large difference to which a fly's whole enzyme chemistry must be adapted (Somero, 1978). Whether prey are more or less abundant in shade, shade does have some. To catch them you must be able to operate at sustainable temperatures in their environment. The same can be said for prey in light-filled spots.

Body size sometimes causes an elegantly simple tradeoff. Large size costs more to maintain but can provide an advantage in aggressive encounters. Small size is cheap, but must be satisfied with what larger animals cannot care to exploit. Thus antbirds subdivide the marching swarms of army ants (*Eciton burchelli*) into dominance rings (Willis and Oniki, 1978). The largest species – such as *Phaenostictus mcleannani* – dominate the central zone of a swarm. There the ants flush out the richest concentration of arthropods. The medium–sized species – such as *Gymnnopithys bicolor* – get the intermediate zone which is too poor to deserve defense by *P. mcleannani*. And the smallest antbirds – such as *Hylophylax naevioides* – take what gets left, the sparse zone at the periphery of the swarm.

A well-studied case of habitat tradeoff occurs in two species of freshwater crayfish (*Orconectes*) of Minnesota and Iowa (Bovbjerg, 1970). Riffle habitats are rich in oxygen. Muddy ponds are poor. Both species of *Orconectes* prefer riffles. However, *O. virilis* aggressively excludes *O. immunis* from most riffles. Presumably, its more aggressive behavior derives from a higher metabolism; the two species are similar in size and shape. In any event, *O. virilis* has a higher metabolic requirement for oxygen and dies in water like that of ponds. *O. immunis* has a lower requirement for oxygen and lives mostly in oxygen-poor waters.

Someday I hope to see a book devoted exclusively to tradeoffs. But this is not it. I encourage you to think about them as you examine research papers in the future. You will find many, related not only to habitat but also to morphology. Meanwhile I hope these few examples convince you they exist.

Speciation will break up a cartel of phenotypes

Even with no super-hero species, you might imagine a combination or cartel of phenotypes in one species that managed to excel at everything. Speciation, however, would soon break it up.

If ecological opportunities are not smoothly distributed but are rugose or multimodal, then competitive speciation by itself can do the fractionation. In fact, the cartels will break up even as they form. When the species' phenotypic variance grows, disruptive selection should respond to density-dependent and frequency-dependent losses of fitness in formerly fit phenotypes. Breeding that risks producing them should stop. The would-be cartel should radiate.

Recall that competitive speciation uses habitat selectivity both to expand the phenotypic variance and to achieve homogamous matings. So a clade of species wrought by competitive speciation probably contains diverse habitat specializations and preferences. The diversity of the clade in one place should be proportional to the diversity of habitats there.

Other forms of speciation also will break up the cartel. If there were only one species, it might produce an autopolyploid. And it would soon become the target for geographical speciation. An isolate would get cut off and begin to diverge. Even if the isolates were in the same mix of environments, just getting cut off genetically would eventually do the trick. But will these new species differ in the habitats they use?

We can assume the tradeoff principle is operating. That tells us the species probably differ in their abilities from habitat to habitat. Then what happens? Do they keep at it, some more successful here and others there? Or do they become selective? How should their niche breadths coevolve?

The coevolution of niche breadth

The extensive literature on the coevolution of competitors goes back to MacArthur and Levins (1967). But the traditional approach won't do. It gives each species a fixed niche breadth and studies only the coevolution of the modal positions of niches.

To study the evolution of niche breadths, you need to think of life as a game in which every individual tries to win as much as possible. As Darwin taught, ultimate winnings are progeny. That gives evolutionists a great advantage. An economist, say, worrying about maximizing winnings, can't always be sure what is most valuable. Profit? Jobs? Stability? But in life there is just one goal. Keep on playing (Slobodkin and Rapoport, 1974). We accomplish that by leaving descendants.

Knowing what we must monitor brings us a powerful set of theoretical tools that we can use to do it. Most scientists who work with them call them collectively 'optimization theory'. Optimization theory cannot tell you what to optimize. But, if you already know **what**, it can help tell you **how**.

There is one general rule of optimization theory. It is not an axiom, not an assumption. Optimization theory actually produces it. (Notice I wrote 'produce', not 'prove'. I know of no general proof.) Here is the rule:

As much as possible, avoid doing what you do poorly. Play to your strength.

This rule seems commonsensical, if not commonplace. Card players learn it; athletes learn it; negotiators learn it. My experience, however, teaches me that ecologists have not learned it. Most are shocked when optimization directs individuals to emphasize their strong suits. We feel instead that individuals should try to make up for losses by repeating the very activities that caused the losses.

You don't believe me?

OK, does the following 'argument' sound familiar? 'The larvae of a species suffer heavy mortality from predators. So, natural selection forces parents to lay many more eggs to make up for it.' Do you think that argument makes sense?

Optimization theory says the opposite (e.g. Schaffer, 1974). If predators usually zap your zygotes, worry less about zygotes. Enhance your fitness by spending your time doing something else.

But wait, you insist. How can there be any fitness without progeny? Well, sure. You cannot expect any return of fitness if you stop trying to reproduce at all. The point is to ease up, to reduce the time and other resources spent on young. Remember, this started with a feeling that parents ought to increase their rate of producing young if predators were likely to eat those young.

One startling field experiment has actually shown that the principle of optimization correctly predicts behavior, whereas intuition fails (Mitchell *et al.*, 1990). Israel's sandy habitats commonly contain two species of gerbil. The smaller one, *Gerbillus allenbyi*, weighs about 26 g. The larger, *G. pyramidum*, weighs about 42 g. Other rodents, including other gerbils, occur there too, but only the two I mentioned are common enough to investigate intensively. For this purpose, Abramsky built a set of six 1.0 ha, matched enclosures. In this chapter, I will refer to several experiments conducted in these enclosures. The first is Mitchell's.

Imagine a gerbil out of its burrow foraging for seeds. It is exposed to predation from owls and snakes (Kotler *et al.*, 1991, 1993). It may have other responsibilities like burrow maintenance that it cannot fulfill while foraging. The principle of optimization requires that it not spend any more time foraging than needed to maximize its fitness. It ought to cease foraging as soon as its rate of collecting seeds falls to match the sum of its likely loss to predators plus the benefits it could gain from activities besides foraging. Thus, optimization says, the more food there is, the more time a gerbil should spend collecting food.

Now imagine what you might predict without optimization. When seed gets scarcer, each individual will need to work longer to get enough. If that is what they do – i.e. forage to get enough food – then less seed per individual should force each gerbil to spend more time foraging. Mitchell *et al.* develop these models formally, but I believe you can grasp their essence just from this paragraph and the previous one.

To vary the amount of seed per gerbil, Mitchell *et al.* varied gerbil densities in the enclosures. The more gerbils, the less reward per gerbil. Then, by recording the gerbils' tracks in the sand, they looked at how much foraging an individual did every night. Both species reduced their foraging efforts as their own populations were increased (experimentally). *G. allenbyi* also responded to increases of its larger competitor. Figure 7.2 shows how dra-

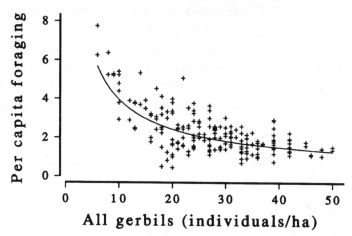

Figure 7.2. The more gerbils there are to compete with, the less each *G. allenbyi* forages. Gerbil totals include both *G. allenbyi* and *G. pyramidum*. Thanks to Bill Mitchell for supplying the data set for the figure. It is based on a figure in Mitchell *et al.*, (1990).

matically and definitely the average *G. allenbyi* cut back its foraging activity as that activity produced less profit.

Let's briefly summarize where we are. We started with one species. Geographical speciation or polyploidy subdivided it. Ruled by the tradeoff principle, the daughter species differ in their abilities to use different habitats. Finally, from optimization theory, we get a sense that each species should evolve to choose the habitats it does best in, thus separating the species by habitat – at least to some degree.

But we can do better than applying an empirically derived, rule-of-thumb generalization to habitat selection. We can let optimization theory operate on the habitat selection problem directly.

Behavioral ecology provides most of the literature on optimal habitat use. There are also some first attempts to investigate how the set of abilities evolves. But they remain preliminary. So I will concentrate on the behavioral aspects in this book. Given varying abilities, how should individuals use habitats?

Ideal free distributions

How should individuals use habitats? Fretwell and Lucas (1970) began by asking this question of individuals in a single homogeneous species. They ranked the habitats and plotted fitness in each as a function of population density in each (Figure 7.3). A single individual must spend all its time in the best habitat type. But as more individuals appear, they use up the resources of that habitat and drive their fitnesses down. If there are enough in the best habitat, an individual moving to the second best habitat actually

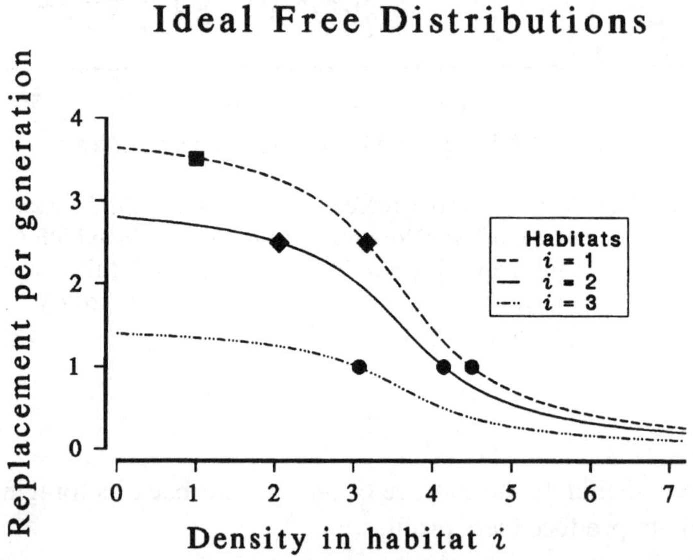

Ideal Free Distributions

Figure 7.3. Three sample ideal free distributions. The sigmoid curves show how, as the population using a habitat grows, the rate of population replacement per generation falls in that habitat. With density at 1.0, all individuals use only habitat 1 (the box on the top curve); they have a replacement rate of 3.5 per generation. With density at 5.22, individuals spread out in habitats 1 and 2. Density is 3.17 in habitat 1, and 2.05 in habitat 2. They have a replacement rate of 2.5 in both habitats (the diamonds on the top two curves). With density at 11.73, individuals spread out in habitats 1, 2 and 3. Density is 4.5 in habitat 1, 4.15 in habitat 2, and 3.08 in habitat 3. They have a replacement rate of 1.0 in all habitats (the circles on the curves). Thus, 11.73 is the carrying capacity of the species.

improves its lot. At higher populations, individuals distribute their activity among habitats, so that the advantage of habitat type disappears. All utilized habitats yield the same average per capita fitness benefit. At carrying capacity, individuals live everywhere they can make a gross profit, and no habitat yields a net profit; population growth rate is zero everywhere.

Fretwell gave a special name to the distribution of individuals that equalizes fitness across habitats. He called it the Ideal Free Distribution. IFD depends on many assumptions. The most important are:

- It costs nothing to select habitats. Possibly, travel between them is free. Otherwise, each individual lives its life in one patch, and the population as a whole arrives at IFD.
- Resource densities adjust instantaneously to an equilibrium determined fully by the density of consumers. That is how the density of consumers can be mapped uniquely into its fitness.
- Despots do not monopolize the better habitats. They do not maintain in them a superior fitness for themselves.

Adding a cost to habitat selection alters the distribution away from IFD. So does adding despots. But neither changes the basic fact of interest to us here: *as their population rises, members of a species must spread out into all sorts of habitats.*

The resource-density assumption may sound preposterous. But if you have ever used a population growth equation like the Pearl–Verhulst or Lotka–Volterra, you have made it too. Even the most modern sorts of nonlinear dynamical equations make it. It may not provide precise accuracy, but what does? And it does often allow us to describe and understand broad trends in population growth rates.

Nevertheless, like Hardy–Weinberg distributions in population genetics, ideal free distributions prove most useful when we use them as starting points for more realistic and interesting situations. For example, Recer *et al.* (1987) extended Fretwell's model in order to compare two sorts of habitats: those in which resource supply varies and those in which it is constant. Then they tested the model on ducks taking bits of bread in a pond. The ducks acted as if the theory mattered.

For this book, the more realistic and interesting situations occur not when ducks confront resource unpredictability, but when species diversity exceeds one. Jeffery A. Smallwood has developed one fascinating way to study that. He looks at a whole guild of species. A guild is a collection of species with a similar ecological function. In his case the guild was foliage gleaning insectivorous birds in a single biome. The biome is the pine–oak woodland of Big Bend National Park, Texas. If IFD has meaning in a multispecies context, these insectivorous birds should distribute their collective foraging activity in accordance with the abundance of their resources.

Smallwood measured the foliage density and the insect density at various heights in 10 ha sample plots. In the same places he also measured the amount of foraging activity exhibited by the guild. Activity tracks opportunity very closely (Figure 7.4).

Smallwood's investigation is not meant to tell us about differences among species however. Do the individuals foraging between 5 m and 8 m come from the same species as those utilizing the interval 10–13 m? Or do different species forage at different heights? Actually we know from very many field studies that bird species do have foraging height preferences. Why? What prevents natural selection from settling on a multispecies IFD with no foraging distinctions between species?

Adding competitor species

Imagine a second species added to the first. Its abilities could differ from those of the first in either of two directions. It may not rank habitat the

Bird Community Foraging

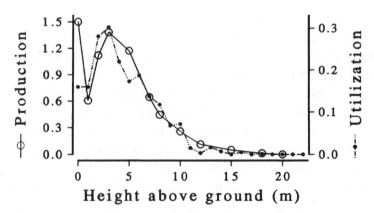

Figure 7.4. The guild of foliage-gleaning insectivorous bird species matches its foraging effort to the opportunity offered at different vegetation heights. Production: foliage density × insect density. Utilization: relative activity density of insectivorous birds. Concept, data and analysis by Jeffery A. Smallwood (UCLA).

same as the first. Or it may be more (or less) tolerant of suboptimal habitats than the first. What do I mean by those differences?

- 'Rank' means 'list in order of ability to use for achieving better fitness.' If a species performs best in a certain habitat, then it ranks that habitat first. The choice must be measured in the limit as population approaches zero. Otherwise you won't know whether the superior performance had to do with population interactions or truly reflects better adaptation.
- Tolerance is invariance in ability. An individual whose fitness is almost the same in all the habitats is tolerant, whereas one that suffers great loss of fitness outside its best habitat is intolerant.

To study how the two species should behave in each other's presence, I invented isoleg theory (Rosenzweig, 1979, 1981). Such theory is useful whether the second species differs in tolerance or in rankings. What is an isoleg theory?

Isoleg theories require a certain kind of graph called a state space (or phase plane). Each axis of a state space measures one of the population sizes. Fitness is not an axis. Time is not an axis. So, if we want to study two species whose population sizes are N_1 and N_2, we need one graph with axes N_1 and N_2.

Now we deduce and plot lines called 'isolegs' onto the state space. Isolegs divide the space into regions of different optimal behavior. Refer to Figure 7.5 as an example. It models the case of two species with access to two habitats, but different rankings. Species 1 ranks habitat A better; Species 2 ranks habitat B better.

Figure 7.5 has three subdivisions (Brown and Rosenzweig, 1986). Through its middle is the region of (N_1, N_2) points at which any individual of either species must choose to use only its better habitat. In the region above this, Species 1 sticks to its better habitat, but Species 2 uses both. In the lower region, Species 2 sticks to its better habitat, but Species 1 uses both. The lines that separate these regions are the isolegs.

Look at the lower isoleg of Figure 7.5. At every point on it, the fitness of the individuals of Species 1 – all of which use only their better habitat (A) –equals the maximum they can ever get from the other habitat (B). How do we know? At any point on the line, they do not use B. But if we increase their population an infinitesimal amount, then they start using B. That scenario implies that after the increase, a patch of habitat B previously unused by them held more reward than they were getting from A. So they had to

Distinct Preference Isolegs

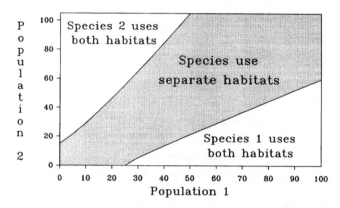

Figure 7.5. A map of optimal behavior for two species that each
prefer a different primary habitat. In the middle band
of the map, that is the only habitat each uses. Thus
they are completely segregated in habitat use. In the
lower triangle, species 1 also invades the best habitat
of species 2. In the upper triangle, species 2 invades the
habitat of 1. The borders between the three regions of
the map are its (two) isolegs.

expand and accept B too. Thus, when they were precisely on the line, the
unused reward available in B must have equalled what they were already
getting from A. The argument is true for Species 1 at every point on the
line. So, an isoleg is a line such that at every one of its points, one of the
species finds itself with essentially the same conditions of habitat opportunity.

Isoleg models frequently result in regions of state space in which species
do not overlap in habitat use. Sometimes we can predict that they do not
overlap even when they have reached their equilibrium population sizes
(Pimm and Rosenzweig, 1981; Brown and Rosenzweig, 1986; Rosenzweig
and Abramsky, 1986). So the salient prediction of isolegs is that competitors can prevent a well-adapted species from occupying all the habitats it
could if it were alone.

We have been testing isloleg models in the field with hummingbirds and
gerbils (Pimm *et al.*, 1985; Rosenzweig, 1986; Abramsky *et al.*, 1990). We
look for situations that allow us to manipulate population sizes experimentally. Then we record the effects of the population sizes on behavior. So far,
the tests have encouraged us to continue to use isoleg theories.

For example, the literature had concluded that a pair of common gerbil species (*Gerbillus allenbyi* and *G. pyramidum*) differ in their abilities to use densely and sparsely vegetated sandy habitat. *G. allenbyi* was thought to prefer stable dunes liberally covered with perennial shrubs. *G. pyramidum* was supposed to prefer more open, mobile dunes.

But isoleg analysis suggested that neither species prefers either of these habitats. It predicted that we would find a third habitat, intermediate in shrub cover, preferred jointly by both species. Our experiments confirmed the existence of this third habitat. They also confirmed the prediction of peculiar non-linear isocline shapes for *G. allenbyi* and *G. pyramidum* (Abramsky *et al.*, 1991, 1992, 1994).

Brown (1988) offers an alternative way to model the effect of a second species. He relaxes the assumption that population densities uniquely determine fitnesses. To accomplish this, he actually models the resource densities too. But he must add another assumption. Brown's individuals must be more perceptive than those in an isoleg model. They must be able to assess the richness of each patch they encounter before they actually exploit it.

Resource patches recuperate after they get used and that may take time. If a patch is found before it returns to its full complement of resources, it may not offer enough to be worth the time it takes to exploit. Brown's individuals know where a patch is on its recovery curve. Thus, they can pass it up if that will help their fitness.

Brown invented a new variable for his studies: giving up density (GUD). The minimum resource density at which a patch should be used is its GUD. Of course, different species still have different abilities. So, a patch type's GUD for one species is likely to be different from its GUD for a second. Having a lower GUD in one habitat means a species is better able to use it and ranks it higher than it does another habitat.

Differences in GUD's promote differences in habitat use. Suppose one species has a lower GUD than a second species in habitat A, but a higher GUD in habitat B. Then species 1 will tend to use some patches of A that species 2 passes up. On the other hand, species 2 will tend to use some patches of B that species 1 passes up. Large populations of a species may revisit patches of their best habitat so often that they keep most below the GUD's of their competitors, and maintain almost exclusive use of them.

Brown and Rosenzweig (1986) joined the GUD and isoleg approaches, emphasizing their complementarity and compatibility. Sometimes either approach will do. Sometimes one is more useful than the other. But they agree in concluding that, although single species must use the widest possible variety of habitats, competitors force each other to withdraw to a more restricted set.

Rosenzweig (1987b) pointed out that once a species is restricted to a subset of available habitats, it is untested (by natural selection) in the habitats it ignores. Let us assume such a species exists and does ignore many habitats. If there is a tradeoff in the use of one habitat compared with another, then such untested individuals cannot afford the cost of the tradeoff. They never use their ability to exploit the untested habitat, and so must relinquish it. Tradeoffs should therefore impel the loss of any physiological or morphological adaptations used solely in the habitats being avoided. Of course, any such loss makes the habitat separation even stricter – because the species that profits from the loss of ability to exploit a habitat, has even less to gain from the habitat after the loss than before it.

'Profits from the loss.' Isn't that a remarkable phrase? It sounds like an oxymoron but it isn't. Just consider all the corporations that divest themselves of complete factories and product lines in order to improve what remains. Now you are beginning to understand the principle of playing to your strength.

Brown (1990) confirmed and extended that result using dynamic game theory. His work also adds a third possible outcome to those I got. I had concluded (Rosenzweig, 1987b) that in the presence of two habitat types, selection produces either two specialists or one generalist. Brown showed that another reasonable result is a generalist and a specialist. His result depends on one of the habitats being scarce compared to the other. The common habitat supports a specialist, but the other habitat does not. Yet, a second species can take advantage of the scarcer habitat. This species depends utterly on the scarcer habitat to keep it from going extinct. Yet because the common habitat is so common, it cannot be ignored. Tested by both habitats, the second species never becomes a specialist.

Plants also restrict themselves to their best habitats

Does the notion of plants selecting habitats sound strange? I am not proposing that they make conscious choices. But they do achieve habitat selection without consciousness. And they are just as subject to the rules of optimality as animals.

Clonal plants can move through their environments exploring them for nutrients or light. Their ramets are the structures that most of us call a plant; they have roots and stems and leaves. Ramets do the feeding and the photosynthesis. But, unseen by most of us, the clone also sends out rhizomes or stolons to take the clone (also known as a genet) into new places. The longer the stolons, the greater the distance between ramets. Watkinson (1988) writes of plant genets expanding and foraging in new areas, discovering and occupying gaps in the vegetation.

When genets encounter better habitat patches, they grow short stolons and send up many ramets to take advantage of the patch. When they encounter poorer patches, they grow long stolons to grow away from those patches as rapidly as possible. For example, Salzman (1985) showed that all but 3% of the ramets of western ragweed (*Ambrosia psilostachya*) grew within 20 cm of their mothers if they were growing in non-saline soil. But in saline soil (which is unfavorable for ragweed growth) 28% grew beyond 20 cm. One ramet was 80 cm away.

Slade and Hutchings (1987) discovered a similar response in a mint native to Britain, *Glechoma hederacea*. This plant responded to high nutrients and light by growing in a compact shape with many ramets crowded together on short stolons. But, as it foraged outward in poorer conditions, it grew its ramets at lower density and elongated its stolons.

Sutherland and Stillman (1988) model plant growth and architecture to investigate optimal plant foraging tactics. Their survey of the plant literature revealed that genets do tend to send out more ramets in good patches than in bad, thus altering their tactics to take better advantage of better places. Another theoretical study (de Kroon and Schieving, 1991) emphasizes the close analogy between foraging studies of plants and animals. These authors add stolon costs to the benefits considered by previous students. Stolon costs force plants to invest little in their stolons not only in rich habitats, but also in the very poorest.

Plants have another way they can vary their phenotype to make good use of their habitat. They can become male or female or even hermaphrodites. Charnov and Bull (1977) point this out and explore its ramifications. Orchids of two genera become female in bright sun, male in the shade. Some plants change their functional sex according to the seasons. Simultaneous hermaphrodites should allocate the resources they put into female or male functions as their environment varies in space or time.

Now consider a dodder. Dodders are a clade of species in the milkweed family. They are vines.

All vines grow cheaply, either up or out, in search of the best local spots. A vine growing up can use the support of a tree to find adequate light. The tree had to pay dearly for the height; the vine does not. A vine growing out-ward may be seeking many other habitat properties as well as light.

Dodder, for example, wants victims. Dodder (*Cuscuta subinclusa*) is para-sitic on other plants. It grows special organs called haustoria which can penetrate the tissues of other plants and sap them of nutrients.

A single dodder individual spreads its stems outward over members of various other species. Upon encountering a new individual, it grows a few haustoria as if to taste it. Most of the time, that's all. The dodder grows on in search of another victim. When it finds one of the 'right' species, it coils profusely, sending out a mass of haustoria into the hapless host (Kelly, 1990). After a while, a dodder becomes a viny maze of its own menu deci-sions. When I see a dodder, I cannot help thinking of the carnivorous plant in *Little Shop of Horrors*: 'Feed me, Seymour!'

Although some adult plants do move through space, we can agree that the root systems of most plants limit their mobility. But environments parade past even those plants in time. Consequently, plants can specialize along two major habitat axes: space and time. Their rootless stages or the ramets of clonal plants can find specialties in space. And they can time their activity differently to specialize temporally. I have room for only a few examples.

Rootless stages

Plants are rootless as seeds. Their gametes are rootless as pollen. Consider the myriad properties of seeds and pollen that enable them to restrict their distribution in space.

Plants may be wind-pollinated or animal-pollinated. I do not know whether the first is as random as it seems. But the second clearly is not ran-dom. Pollination strategies may help to promote homogamy, and homogamy promotes speciation. In that sense, animal pollination promotes habitat differences among species. However, a pollen grain has only one job. So, it makes no sense to attribute any direct ecological significance to its ability to find a stigma of the same species.

Seeds are another story. They come small as a sand grain and large as a coconut. They are smooth as millet, hooked like a devil's claw, and barbed as a cholla fruit. They often come in sweet, nutritious packages like cher-ries, or in armor as hard as a hickory nut or thorny as a chestnut. Some seeds sport aerodynamic appendages like the wing of a maple samara or the feathery achene of a dandelion. Many of these seed variations bias the place where a seed comes to rest in the soil. I assume those biases have had a beneficial effect on the fitness of seeds by steering them to places where they have improved chances of survival and growth. Sometimes, of course, the features of a seed work against mobility and keep progeny near their parent. But that is also a bias.

The night-blooming cereus is my favorite example of a plant carefully restricting its seeds to a single habitat. This scraggly cactus with a massive, starchy underground storage organ grows only in the shade of leguminous shrubs like mesquite and palo verde. The only ones I ever saw, grew in some small semi-desert plots I cleared to do a rodent experiment. As the last few branches of a mesquite would get lopped off, there it would be, unseen before, although I had been working those plots for two years. Not pretty, its branches only a couple of centimeters in diameter, it was most often the last plant found. Yet we did our clearing in midsummer when the night-blooming cereus had big, bright-red fleshy fruits. We began to notice these all around us in adjacent patches of mesquite.

Night-blooming cereus, also called Reina de la noche and Arizona queen of the night, achieves its restricted habitat through its seed distribution. It blossoms in late spring. Its large white flowers emit a perfume that *cognoscenti*, including presumably its pollinators, can smell several km downwind. The flowers open only at night. After pollination, the fruit matures and attracts birds foraging in the mesquite. The birds eat the fruit together with its seeds. They also tend to defecate while roosting in a mesquite or other favorable site. There plops the seed, in a veritable bed of warm nutrients, a perfect canopy over itself. What more could you ask of life?

Dividing time

Plants are adept at restricting their activity to certain times when the habitat is most favorable. Consider seeds again. Seeds have mechanisms that restrict their germination to ecological conditions that give them their best chance to mature and reproduce (Koller, 1955).

Many seeds in arid environments have a biochemical system that triggers their germination only after a favorable series of rainfalls at the right temperature. The result can be a palette of color carpeting the desert. For example, seeds of *Pectis pappoza* require a summer rain of 25 mm (Went, 1957). A series of smaller summer rains (even totaling more than 25 mm) or a 25 mm rain in winter fails completely to stimulate their germination.

Summer 'annuals' (the word 'ephemerals' does a better job of describing
them) need to wait 5 to 20 years for the right summer rain.

   Other seeds germinate after winter rain and require their precipitation at
cooler temperatures. In fact, seeds of desert annuals fall into groups
depending on the circumstances required for their germination. In Western
Australia, there are two distinct floras: a summer-rain flora and a winter-
rain flora (Mott, 1972). In the Colorado and the Mojave deserts of southeastern California, there are four groups (Went, 1953). One germinates
after summer rain, one after winter rain, one after autumn rain, and one
germinates after rain at any time during the year. About 500 species of
ephemerals belong to one of these groups in southeastern California.

   In Morocco there are three groups of annuals, but they are based on the
amount of rain required for germination (Negre, 1953). One group requires
more than 250 mm. A second needs 100 to 250 mm. And the third needs
only 50 to 100 mm. The individuals of these groups develop from seed to
new fruit in a very short time. Moreover, the time it takes depends on the
amount of rain required. Those needing the least rain go through their life
cycle in only 10 to 15 days. Those needing the most take longer than 40
days. Thus even the development time of a desert ephemeral appears to be
adjusted to the length of time its habitat patch is likely to last.

   I want to emphasize the lesson of the three Moroccan plant groups.
Koller (1956) worked with the seeds of a shrub, *Calligonum comosum*. It
grows in coarse sands of the Sahara and the Negev Desert where rainfall
does not exceed 150 mm per year. Its seeds require warmth and a small
amount of moisture to germinate. And they need to be buried in sand (they
fail to germinate in light). But soak them in water for a short while, and
they also fail to germinate (Table 7.1).

Table 7.1. *Germination percentage of* Calligonum comosum

Temp. (°C)	Not washed in H_2O		Minutes washed in H_2O			
	In light	In dark	1	2	5	30
15	0	0	–	–	–	–
20	14.6	71.1	7	–	–	–
26	4.0	59.4	8	0	0	0
30	0.4	12.0	2	–	–	–

Data from Koller (1956).

Another example comes from the California deserts. Soriano (1953) studied three annuals and found that each had its optimum rainstorm size for germination. For *Pectocarya spp., c.* 15 mm. For *Eriophyllum ambiguuum, c.* 10–12 mm. And for *Filago californica, c.* 9 mm. Rains outside each species optimum range (larger or smaller) reduced germination.

Koller and Negbi (1959) demonstrated that seeds, even within a species that grows in different climates, adapt closely to their own particular region. *Oryzopsis miliacea*, a grass, grows in dry climates averaging only 100 mm per year. It also grows successfully in much wetter climates, averaging 600 mm per year. Compared with seeds from the drier region, *O. miliacea* seeds from the wetter region require more simulated rainfall before they will germinate.

So, what's good for germination? 'Warm, moist soil,' we may have answered a few pages back. But that answer comes from our bias as temperate zone farmers and orchardists. We now see that many species tolerate conditions that we might be tempted to call more stressful. Some actually require them! One plant's stress is another plant's seedbed.

We might have absorbed the same lesson from the work on the physiology of photosynthesis. Plants need light to live. But in many species, too much light can actually inhibit photosynthesis. If it continues too long, it can even damage a plant permanently. Organisms need the habitats to which they have adapted.

Biologists like to wade in on the physiological side of arguments about diversity. But, if we argue that good physiological conditions lead to high diversities, we must ignore the ability of plants – animals too – to evolve species that actually find their optima in what we often think of as stressful environments. Br'er Rabbit **needed** to be thrown by Br'er Fox into that briar patch. It was his only hope of survival. But I am an optimist. I think biologists can learn that merely because we humans try to avoid a habitat doesn't mean it is so bad for another species.

Actually, the germination situation is even more complex. Venable (1989) studied two winter annuals that grow near Tucson. Even when it does rain the correct amount in the proper season, only a fraction of the viable seeds 'decide' to germinate: 63% in *Schismus barbatus* and 85% in *Plantago patagonica*. And some germinate early (in October or November) while others germinate late (in December or January). Thus they dilute their risk of germinating at the wrong time. **What has been**, gives only an inexact clue to **what will be**, especially in a desert.

Moreover, as you might expect of well-adapted organisms, the less pre-

dictable the environment, the smaller the proportion of seeds that germinate after any one trigger. New Mexico, for example has regular summer
rainfall but inconsistent winter rains. Most seeds of summer annuals germinate once those rains begin. But a significant fraction of the winter annuals
hold back to germinate in another year (Freas and Kemp, 1983).

Artemisia monosperma is a small shrub that grows in abundance on
dunes in Israel. Shifting sand can bury its seed so deep that if it germinated,
it could not reach the light. Shifting sand can also disinter it. Not surprisingly, *A. monosperma* seeds need light to germinate (Koller *et al.*, 1964). In
artificial light, they germinate best under a thin layer (2 mm) of sand.
Under natural light, they may do best in somewhat deeper sand.

Blue palo verde seed coverings (*Cercidium floridum*) must be impacted or
abraded before the seeds will germinate. Adults grow along arroyos and
drop their hard, flat, 9×7 mm oval seeds in late spring. The seed coverings
are virtually as hard as pebbles. Should summer rains bring a flash flood,
rocks, gravel and sand will race along the arroyo, hammering at the seed
coats and wearing them away. That rain also brings enough moisture to
support the seed's early establishment. Seeds may wait years for the right
rain (Went, 1957).

Some species depend on fire to clear out leaf litter, reduce shade, and
return some nutrients to the soil. We see them germinate in abundance only
after a fire. Jack pine cones hold their seeds until they are heated by a fire.
Bury *Rhus ovata* seeds $1/4$ inch deep in sand. Thirty-eight percent will germinate after a fire burns on the sand's surface. Without the fire only 1%
germinate (Stone and Juhren, 1951).

Many species can wait decades for the right time to germinate. In 1879,
W. J. Beal buried seeds of 20 species of Michigan weeds. He put them in
bottles filled with slightly moist sand and buried the bottles tipped downward but open. The bottles were dug up periodically to test the viability of
the seeds. After 25 years, 11 of the species still had viable seed. Five did
after 80 years, and the seed of three species lasted an entire century. That
should give them a fair look at a wide variety of habitats! (These data and
others are summarized in Fenner, 1985. You will also find Beal's experiment in Kivilaan and Bandurski, 1981.)

In fact, some seeds can wait centuries for the right time. Spira and
Wagner (1983) studied 40 species of seeds extracted from adobe bricks
made in 1769 – 1837. After their extraction, the seeds were stored in glass
vials in a laboratory for 50 years. Then Spira and Wagner placed them in
an environment known to encourage their germination. Despite the cavalier

treatment for such a long time, seeds of seven species germinated! They were between 143 and 200 years old. But the Guinness claim belongs to a seed of *Chenopodium album*. Odum (1965) found one viable after 1700 years.

Germination timing does not end the set of adaptations. For instance, American chestnut can enter a quiescent stage – call it the launching stage – years after germination. American chestnut is a massive tree that used to dominate the forest canopy in much of eastern North America (see Chapter 6). It can germinate and grow in its own shade. When it reaches a height of about 1 m, it looks more like an understory shrub than a tree. It lacks the single, well-defined, vertical stem that it will have later.

Providing there are no light gaps, the chestnut stops growing, maintaining its brushy physiognomy as it maintains its balance between income and expenditure. When a light gap appears, however, it races for the canopy, shooting straight up at a rapid growth rate. It has found its time. Ian Abbott tells me that jarrah, *Eucalyptus marginata*, makes much the same developmental switch in the forests of southwestern Western Australia.

Most plants also time their reproduction. In part, such timing undoubtedly helps them find their pollinators and mates. But sometimes it also must keep them reproducing in appropriate seasons. Summer-flowering perennial grasses in southeastern Arizona undoubtedly benefit from the regular rainfall appearing only during that season.

Growth and metabolic activity may reveal a plant's choice of temporal habitat. Again I turn to my own haunts, the Arizona desert, for a spectacular example. Ocotillo (*Fouqueria splendens*) is a sharply thorned 3 m tall shrub of our rocky hills. Usually it has no leaves. However, within weeks after good rains, no matter what the season, it has leafed out fully. Of course, it is concentrating its photosynthetic activity not so much while the sun shines – for that is rarely a problem – but while the soil is moist – for that often is a problem. Soon after the soil has dried out, the leaves yellow and fall off. Like all optimizers in the game of life, it plays only when rewards are available. It may repeat the cycle of leaves-on-leaves-off several times a year, depending only on that year's rainfall regime (Went, 1953).

Many plants time their growth and reproduction. Plants like the ocotillo, however, maintain an opportunistic flexibility. This teaches us an important lesson. Plants may not move very fast, and they may not be conscious either. But they can and do react to habitat opportunities that present themselves unpredictably in time. Ephemeral desert flowers that germinate only after a once-in-a-decade set of rainfalls; blue palo verde, which germinates only after a significant flood; and many other species. They teach us that ocotillo is not unique. Many species in many taxa share its ability to take advantage of brief, rich interludes. Even animals have it!

A remarkable example of animals that subdivide time comes from Australia's Lake Eyre. Lake Eyre drains a sixth of the continent, but it usually has no water (Bonython, 1955). After two years of exceptional rainfall, it does fill. Forty-eight hours later, eggs of certain species of crustaceans – salt lake slaters and brine shrimps such as members of the genus *Parartemia* – hatch into water saltier than that of the ocean. These eggs may have lain waiting for that water for 25 years!

Why don't all desert species lie low metabolically except at times of abundant rain? Because they have other adaptations, and these help them make a profit during drier times. Some, like cacti and euphorbias, store their water. Some, like mesquite (*Prosopis* spp), have long roots that may reach down 50 m to find permanent water. All are playing their strong suits. The saps and suckers that didn't have been weeded out by natural selection.

Seasonality

Diversity varies regularly within years because some months are better than others for feeding and breeding. So, some species restrict their activities to special seasons. They subdivide temporal habitats according to optimality principles.

To consider seasonality further, we must take account of the two costs of ignoring some temporal habitats.

- You lose what resources you would have collected.
- You must pay to travel.

The first is obvious, but the second demands some expansion.

For migratory species, traveling is not a metaphor. It's what they actually do. The robin wings its way south (or north) at considerable muscular cost. Unfamiliar with the territory it must traverse, it may also not find food as readily. Or it may suffer extra predation. The sooty falcon (*Falco concolor*) actually reproduces on the profit it makes intercepting tired songbirds as they migrate southward in the autumn (Frumkin and Pinshow, 1983). To be optimal, the rewards obtained in the alternative location must more than compensate for such losses.

That tells us why some species migrate from some breeding places, but not from others. Sticking around while the snows blow in Michigan may not pay much at all – you might even freeze to death. But a member of your species in (say) North Carolina can expect more for staying put during the winter.

Instead of migrating, many species merely retreat metabolically. These are the time travellers. They lose the resources they would have collected and those it takes to keep them alive while they idle their way through months of inactivity. But by minimizing their rate of resting metabolism, they increase their net profit through the year.

You can see that hibernating species need not spring into existence fully adapted to retreat. All that natural selection should require is periods – perhaps not even seasonal periods – so dangerous or unprofitable that retreat evolves even at full metabolic cost. That sets up the scenario in which cheaper retreat is better. Once cheaper retreat evolves, the retreat period should expand because time travel has become less expensive.

Some species suffer less than others when living in a suboptimal environment. Being more tolerant of habitat variation (Rosenzweig, 1991a), they are less likely to retreat. They become resident species, because, for them, the cost of migration or retreat exceeds that of remaining and staying active. The difference between them and those that find it optimal to retreat can support coexistence (Brown, 1989b).

The evolution of habitat diversity

Imagine a regional pool of species. Collectively, they will use a much greater variety of places and times than each does by itself. The result shows up as the subject of this chapter – species diversity increases with habitat variation.

Fine so far. But what determines the habitat diversity? Are habitats inelastic and pre-defined? Is habitat diversity simply a function of the range of environmental variation present? Or can two places in different biogeographical realms share all values of environmental means and variation, but have different habitat diversities?

The question is very important, and its answer is incomplete. The answer, in fact, is one of the topics that I hope this book draws attention to. Nevertheless, we do know a bit.

I suspect, from what I am about to show you, that habitat diversity is more than a mere measure of environmental variation at a place. Habitat diversity also depends on the number of species in a biogeographical province. The more species, the more habitats they recognize (Rosenzweig, 1992). Species diversity is the horse; habitat diversity is the cart.

Because this statement seems to turn life upside down, I want to emphasize its scale dependence. What I am suggesting is this: at the very large scale of the province, the number of species sets the number of habitats. At smaller scales, say 1 ha to 10^4 km^2, the number of habitats sets the number of species. At both scales, the correlation is positive. But the larger scale reverses the causal relationship of the smaller one.

What evidence exists to lead me to this provisional conclusion?

Species flocks

Extraordinary species diversity sometimes exists based on very little environmental variation. No places better exemplify this than two particular heathlands in Mediterranean climates: the fynbos of South Africa and the kwongan of southwestern Australia. The South Western Botanical Province of Australia packs about 8000 to 9000 species of flowering plants into approximately 200000 km^2 (Hopper, 1992; Marchant, 1991). About 80% are endemic to the province. The Cape Floristic Region of South Africa has about 8600 in only 90000 km^2 (68% endemic) (Cowling *et al.*, 1992). By comparison, the California Floristic Province (324000 km^2) has some 4500 species (48% endemic) and Great Britain has about 1700 species in 230000 km^2 (1% endemic). Similarly small numbers of species in similar-sized areas occur in the State of Victoria and in New Zealand (although of course, New Zealand, being quite isolated, also has many endemics – 81%). Also by comparison, the angiosperms of the two flocks are the only taxa that show unusually high diversities in the fynbos and the kwongan. Cody (1993), for example, gives us a remarkable picture of the great similarity between southwestern Australian bird diversities and those of California (his Figure 13.3).

Figure 7.6 shows that areas of fynbos east of the Breede River (South Africa) have typical plant diversities. Their samples fall very close to the species–area curve of other types of South African vegetation (Cowling *et al.*, 1992). But areas of fynbos to the west of the Breede lie uniformly above this line. The difference between these lines may not impress you. But remember, this is a log-log graph. An area of southwestern fynbos actually has more than twice as many species as a similar area in the southeast. Southwestern fynbos swarms with plant species.

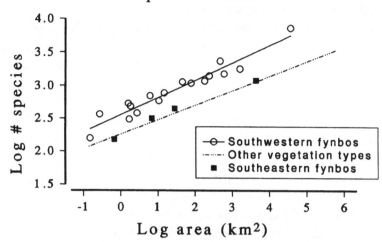

Figure 7.6. The dashed line shows the regression from Figure 2.24 for grassland, Nama-Karoo, succulent Karoo and savanna habitats of South Africa, but not fynbos. Southeastern fynbos fit it well (I did not include these points in Figure 2.24). But southwestern fynbos – areas west of the Breede River – have twice the ordinary diversities for their areas. Data from Cowling *et al.* (1992).

Both fynbos and kwongan heathlands grow on sandy soil that is extremely nutrient poor. Paraphrasing Hopper (1992), we may say that the kwongan's landscape is venerable: typically flat with subdued landforms and highly leached, impoverished soils. The plant cover of both heathlands looks monotonous because there are few growth forms (Adamson, 1927). Neither has a tree stratum or many annuals (Lamont, 1992). But they are among the world's most speciose (Lamont *et al.*, 1977; Hopper, 1979, 1992; Naveh and Whittaker, 1979; Rice and Westoby, 1983). For example, 10 m × 10 m quadrats near Mt Leseur, Western Australia, average about 80 species of vascular plants (Hopper, 1992); one had over 110.

To help account for such spectacular diversity, Groves and Hobbs (1992) emphasize the different adaptations of species to deal with shortages of water and nutrients. But similar adaptive differences exist in many less diverse provinces. Pollinator specializations add to our explanation, since some kwongan species have their own private pollinators. But many more seem to rely on a host of opportunists (Lamont, 1992). Constrained by the range of soils available and the rigors of a hot-summer Mediterranean climate, many species' niches just seem to overlap excessively; many species seem to have duplicate adaptations (Lamont, 1992).

Nevertheless, despite the lack of inherent variety in their soil environment, kwongan plants have subdivided their soils quite finely. Hopper (1979, 1992) recognizes complex local soil mosaics with individual species specialized on certain types of tesserae. The poverty and narrow-ranged continuum of the sandplain and its few hills – no more extensive or discrete in Australia than anywhere – has become a cornucopia of distinct habitats.

Archipelagos like Hawaii afford many other examples of flocks of species (see Chapter 5). Consider the land snails. Solem (1984) estimates that the world has 30 000 or even 35 000 species of land snails. A surprising number, perhaps the majority, live only on islands or only on mountains. Solem lists six islands, plus the island nations of Japan and New Zealand, as having about 10% of worldwide snail diversity all by themselves.

(Of course, we notice immediately that islands and mountains are notoriously depauperate for most taxa. See, for instance, the poor, bracken-eating insect faunas of New Zealand and Hawaii in Figure 9.2 And the small number of vertebrate frugivores and tropical rainforest trees on Madagascar in Figure 9.1 One cannot resist the conjecture that snails are somehow capable of taking advantage of the misfortune of the other taxa. But that conjecture has never even been properly formulated, let alone tested.)

Usually one place, even one on an island or in one of the richer mountain ranges, yields only a few sympatric snail species. Solem reviews the experiences of snail collectors around the world. He concludes that most such areas have a few to perhaps 12 sympatric snails. For instance, Oahu, one of Hawaii's large islands, is rich in snails (395 species; 98% of them endemic), but it harbors only five to eight at any one place.

A few spots have two to four times as many sympatric snails – East African wet forests, western European moist locales, eastern Australian subtropical and temperate rainforests, Jamaican and Hispaniolan forest litter.

And then there is the North Island of New Zealand!

On the Manukau Peninsula near Auckland, you can find 82 species of land snail. Of these, 72 can occur in the same microsite (Solem, 1984). These species come from all the many New Zealand higher taxa of land snail. For unknown reasons, they have accumulated on the Manukau since the Miocene. The rest of New Zealand has fewer sympatric species, and their diversities resemble those found elsewhere in the world.

Some place has to have the highest diversity of land snails. But why that peninsula? And why in particular should its snail diversity be an order of magnitude higher than most snail-rich sites on Earth? Solem makes several suggestions. But none assume that the Manukau Peninsula has extraordinarily high environmental variation.

Surely, the most famous species flocks occur in big, old, freshwater lakes. These include fish, shrimp, copepods, flatworms and gastropods in Lake Baikal, the world's largest body of freshwater. (It holds about 20% of the entire world's supply of freshwater.) And they include several lakes in Africa's Rift Valley, especially Tanganyika and Victoria, where fish, gastropods and ostracodes evolved immense diversities (Table 7.2).

Interested readers should consult some of the many books and monographs about these flocks (e.g. Brooks, 1950; Khozov, 1963; Fryer and Iles, 1972; Boss, 1978; Brichard, 1978; Greenwood, 1982; Echelle and Kornfield, 1984). Note that modern lakes have ancient parallels: big lakes that now are gone. Flocks of fossil species occurred in them too, often in the same taxa (Smith, 1987).

Lake flocks are not merely collections of species. They are separate provinces with extremely high endemism. Their species have accumulated *in situ* by speciation (McCune, 1987; Meyer *et al.*, 1990; Meyer, 1991). Their diversities come from what remains after extinction. It is no surprise that students of these flocks stress finding out how the speciation has proceeded. They want to discover what makes flocking families such rapid speciators.

One factor that often gets mentioned is low dispersal rate (Cohen and Johnston, 1987). The brooding of young, such as occurs among some ostracodes, fishes and gastropods, discourages their dispersal. Gene flow is curtailed and speciation rates enhanced.

Habitat complexity, at least habitat complexity considered independently of life, does not help to explain the phenomenal diversities. How do the rock outcrops and sandy bottoms of Lake Tanganyika foretell the existence of more than 500 species of endemic fishes, crustaceans and molluscs (Cohen, 1992)? Instead, the evidence compels me to conclude that these species are there because allopatric speciation put them there, not because there was some unfilled ecological opportunity waiting to be exploited.

Many of the species of gastropods in Lake Tanganyika have converged so completely that it takes genetic analysis to distinguish them (Michel *et al.*, 1992). Doesn't that make you suspect that such species are ecologically redundant (Rosenzweig, 1991b)? It cannot comfort you if you believe that each species must fill some predictable, distinct niche. Why not try out a

Table 7.2. *Species flocks in old lakes*

Lake	Taxon	Family	Endemic species	
			#	%
Baikal	Amphipoda	Gammaridae	239+	99+
Baikal	Copepoda	Canthocamptidae	35	81
Tanganyika	Ostracoda	Cyprididae	71	94
Baikal	Tricladida	Dendrocoelidae	*c.* 40	100
Ohrid	Gastropoda	Hydrobiidae	39	97
Baikal	Gastropoda	Baikaliidae	33	100
Tanganyika	Gastropoda	Thiaridae	29	90
Malawi	Osteichthyes	Cichlidae	*c.* 500	97
Victoria	Osteichthyes	Cichlidae	200+	98
Tanganyika	Osteichthyes	Cichlidae	171	98
Baikal	Osteichthyes	Cottidae	28	97

Data from Cohen and Johnston, 1987; Miller, 1989; Meyer *et al.*, 1990; Michel *et al.*, 1992.

different hypothesis? Consider the likelihood that they are there merely because their taxon's high rate of speciation has outrun its rate of extinction in that lake. One species lives in an outcrop in one part of the lake; another lives in much the same way in a similar outcrop elsewhere in it.

Of course, should a pair of convergent gastropods from the previous paragraph ever meet in real space, natural selection will force them to subdivide a single outcrop somehow. They will evolve to look different or behave differently. They will also become easy for us to distinguish. When that happens, we will recognize a pair of habitats where previously, we had seen only one.

Island species tend to recognize fewer habitats than mainland species

Island and mainland species come from the same taxa (sometimes even the very same species!). Presumably they are subject to the same tradeoff constraints. Yet, island species tend to recognize fewer habitats than mainland species. Consider the case of the bird diversity of Puerto Rico.

In temperate North America and temperate Australia, the diversity of bird species depends on the number of habitat layers in the foliage (Recher, 1969). The best fit comes from assuming the birds recognize three vegetation layers (Figure 2.6).

But bird diversities in Panama routinely exceed predictions based on a three-layered forest (Figure 7.7). You might think that happens because tropical forests are more complicated and have more habitat layers. However, the tropical forests of Puerto Rico are similar in physiognomy (tree height, leaf density, etc.). Yet, you can also see in Figure 7.7 that they routinely fall short of three-layer predictions.

The trick is to predict the number of birds from the following assumptions (MacArthur *et al.*, 1966).

- In Panama, birds recognize four habitat layers.
- In Puerto Rico, they recognize only two habitat layers.

Then, both the Panamanian and the Puerto Rican results fall into line (Figure 7.8).

Puerto Rico is depauperate because it is an island, not because it lacks richly complex rainforest. Its birds need to recognize only two habitat layers. Panama's birds recognize four, not because the layers exist in some objective sense, but because avian diversity is so high that natural selection forces them to see four.

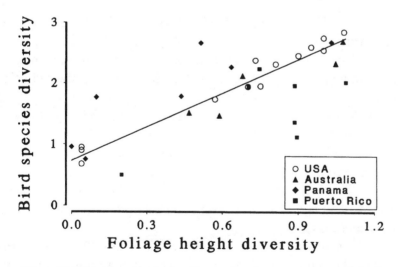

Figure 7.7. Neither tropical avifauna fits the temperate model of three vegetation layers (Figure 2.25). Panamanian samples usually have too many species for their habitat's complexity; Puerto Rican samples have too few. Data from MacArthur *et al.* (1966).

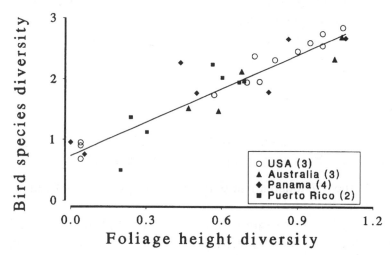

Figure 7.8. Both tropical avifaunas – Panama's and Puerto Rico's
– fit a habitat–complexity model relying on vegetation
layers if we assume that Panama, a mainland tropical
system, has four layers and Puerto Rico, an island
tropical system, has only two. Data from MacArthur
et al. (1966).

Vuilleumier (1972) and Ralph (1985) provide another remarkable exception to the MacArthur–Recher pattern. They claim that in Patagonia, the
forests with the greatest habitat complexity do **not** have the most bird
species. Although this case does not involve islands, now is the right time to
think about it.

Acting on Vuilleumier's suggestion, Ralph censused birds and measured
foliage in 12 plots in northern Patagonia (temperate Argentina). But he
used methods that differed considerably from those of MacArthur, so we
cannot overlay his results on Figure 2.6 for comparison. Unlike
MacArthur's, his plots varied considerably in size. Also, he varied the sampling effort depending on the plot. Nevertheless he provides all the data we
need to consider his claim.

First, we must determine the effect of the sampling differences. In Figure
7.9, I plotted the number of bird species against the number of sampling
stations. The five southern beech (*Nothofagus*) forests give us a good idea of
the effect of the sampling differences alone. I fit a second-order polynomial
regression through them. As we would expect, the three grassland plots fall
below the curve; they have much less foliage diversity and fewer species for

Patagonia Birds

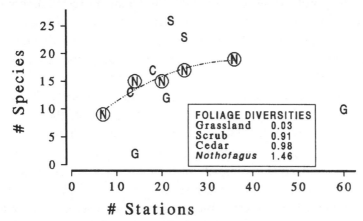

Figure 7.9. Diversities of birds in northern Patagonia. As sampling
   effort increases, more species are found in a plot. The
   trend of the increase is revealed by the second-order
   polynomial regression through the *Nothofagus* forest
   plots (N). But the other habitats depart from the trend.
   Grasslands (G), with less habitat diversity, fall beneath
   it. But scrubland (S) and cedar (C) plots fall on or
   above the trend line despite their lower habitat diversities. See text for interpretation. Data from Ralph
   (1985).

any given amount of sampling. But, the cedar plots fall on the same line as
the *Nothofagus* plots although they also have much less foliage diversity
(0.98 vs 1.46). Thus the birds of *Nothofagus* forests do not make as much
use of the habitat complexity available to them as do the birds of the cedar
habitats. Moreover, the two scrub plots sit far above the line although they
have a bit less foliage diversity than even the cedar plots. Thus birds of the
cedar plots make less use of their habitat complexity than those of the scrub
plots. From scrub to cedar to *Nothofagus*, the pattern of diversity is backwards; the more complex the foliage, the fewer the bird species.

   Ralph explains the reversal thus. Southern beech forests (*Nothofagus*)
supply the most complex plots. But they cover a very small, isolated area
compared with the less complex scrub habitats. Small, isolated areas support only a few species (see Chapter 3 and especially Chapters 8 and 9), and
that relationship dominates and obscures the habitat relationship. Schluter
and Ricklefs (1993) agree and rightly point to the scale difference. The

small scale influence of habitat complexity is superseded by the large-scale effects of area. I will emphasize the role of such scale differences in Chapter 9. But at this point, we need only mark the result. Forested sample plots of equal area with objectively the same habitat complexity in Patagonia, North America and Australia, have different bird species diversities. Given the same environmental opportunities, birds in Patagonia seem to recognize fewer habitats than birds of the other two continents.

We see the same pattern on Australian islands. Abbott (1978), working in 4 ha plots, censused the passerine birds of 20 islands off the coast of south-western Western Australia. He compared his data with those he got from similar plots on the neighboring mainland. The birds of the islands do not fully exploit the absolute complexity of the habitats available to them (Figure 7.10). Precisely as do Puerto Rican birds and birds in *Nothofagus*, they fail to reach the diversities that their habitats support elsewhere. Functionally, they do not recognize the existence of the habitat complexity. It is as if that complexity isn't even present. In a profound sense, the habitat complexity has diminished simply because there are so few species to recognize it.

If that interpretation is right, it leads to a prediction. Suppose we humans define a fixed set of habitats. Then, each species on an island should use more habitats than do species on the mainland.

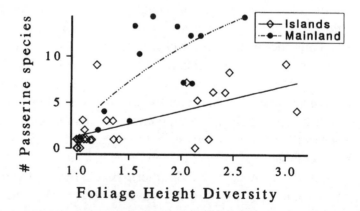

Figure 7.10. Mainland birds of southwestern Australia have more species per unit of habitat diversity than those living on 20 nearby islands. Abbott (1978) took these data from mist net censuses on (*c*.) 4 ha plots.

Gorman (1975) studied the habitats of birds on Viti Levu, the largest of Fiji's islands. Gorman compared the birds there to those on New Guinea, a much larger island with extremely high bird (and other) diversities. In general, the species of Viti Levu each used noticeably more habitats than those of New Guinea.

Some of the species are identical in the two places, allowing for unambiguous, direct comparison. *Halcyon chloris*, a kingfisher, lives in all the habitats of Viti Levu. But in New Guinea, which boasts five other species of *Halcyon*, *H. chloris* lives only in mangroves. The thrush, *Turdus poliocephalus*, occurs from sea level to mountaintops in all sorts of habitats on Viti Levu. On New Guinea it lives only in forest clearings above 3000 m and above timberline. The golden whistler, *Pachycephala pectoralis*, inhabits New Guinea together with several other congeners. But it lives with none on Viti Levu. In New Guinea it lives only in the lowlands, although its genus is much more widespread. But on Viti Levu it uses all the habitats of its genus on New Guinea. The white-breasted woodswallow, *Artamus leucorhynchus*, lives only in dry savanna on New Guinea, but spreads out into many other habitats on Viti Levu. There, it is the only member of its genus. Diamond (1978) documents similar cases for other island birds living both in isolation on small islands and with congeners on New Guinea.

In addition to birds, Gorman (1979) has also studied the perches used by lizards, *Anolis sagrei*, on various islands in the West Indies. The fewer the species of congener on an island, the greater the variety of perch heights used by *A. sagrei*.

Cox and Ricklefs (1977) and Wunderle (1985) observed much the same pattern for the birds of six of the West Indies. They classed habitats into nine categories and studied the number actually used by the various species on each island. The higher the bird diversity, the fewer habitats each species uses (Figure 7.11).

David Lack pioneered studies of niche expansion of birds on islands (Lack and Southern, 1949; Lack, 1969). It is altogether fitting therefore, that he exposed the champion case, the Gough Island bunting, *Rowettia goughensis*.

Gough Island may be the most isolated island in the world. In the South Atlantic, it lies some 350 km from its nearest fellow in the Tristan da Cunha group. The Tristan da Cunha group is itself 2800 km from Africa and 3200 km from South America.

Despite its isolation, Gough rises 910 m above sea level and possesses five distinct terrestrial habitats in addition to its beaches and its tiny human

Caribbean Passerines

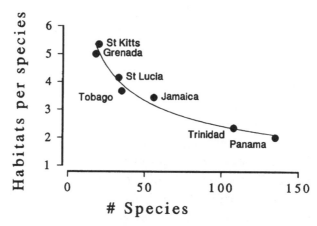

Figure 7.11. The more species of birds, the fewer habitats used by each species. Data from Cox and Ricklefs (1977) and Wunderle (1985).

outpost (Wace, 1961). Tussock grasses grow on the cliffs of its coast. Fern bush covers the sheltered lower elevations up to about 300 m. From that point up to 600 m is a band of wet heathland. And from 600 m up, only montane vegetation grows. Finally, bogs with a deep layer of peat nestle in the upland valleys. That said, we can adequately appreciate our bird.

Rowettia is a finch, the only perching bird of Gough. It uses every habitat on the island. It even feeds in the intertidal. It eats grass seeds, berries and other fruit. It eats flies, moth larvae, spiders and amphipods. It eats vertebrate carrion. And it scavenges in the garbage cans of the few meteorologists who live on Gough. In Lack's own words, *Rowettia* is 'the ultimate, all-purpose bird'.

Species' niches can be arbitrarily close to each other

In a deterministic world, limiting similarity is zero (May and MacArthur, 1972; see Chapter 6). Thus, it may take an accident to consummate the extinction of a species whose niche is very close to another. Meanwhile, if speciation is popping in new species at a high rate, lots of species will accumulate and subdivide habitats quite finely. The point is not that the world is deterministic. It is that limiting similarity has no set value. Species evolve to be as similar to each other as their diversity forces them to be.

Density-dependent habitat selection helps us to understand the cause–effect relationship between diversity and habitats. One species alone spreads out into all sorts of 'habitats' (Fretwell and Lucas, 1970). Add a coexisting competitor, and somebody's niche shrinks (Rosenzweig, 1987a, 1991a).

Lamont *et al.* (1989) give us an exquisitely relevant example because it comes from the species flocks of the kwongan heathlands of Australia. In nature, *Banksia hookeriana* grows only on the crests and slopes of deep sand dunes. Yet it grows well also in at least three other habitats if individuals of three other *Banksia* species are kept out. In the presence of seeds of these three species, those of *B. hookeriana* germinate but do not survive.

The same principle should hold in evolutionary time (Rosenzweig, 1987b; Brown, 1990; Brown and Pavlovic, 1992). Coexisting competitors should restrict each other's niches. Thus, you may imagine a temporal hierarchy. First, on a grand scale, the species evolve. Then, on a somewhat smaller scale, they force each other to become habitat specialists. In the most important sense, the habitats are undifferentiated until there are many competing species to treat them differently.

Hebert and his associates have worked out another fine example among *Daphnia* that live in tundra ponds in the Canadian Arctic. Some of these ponds have clear water; some are clouded with dissolved humics (Hebert, 1982). Though clear water transmits most of the harmful ultraviolet light, *Daphnia* can protect themselves by devoting as little as 0.03% of their body weight to melanin, a black pigment (Hebert and Emery, 1990). Black *Daphnia* manage in either water type.

But they do not live in both water types. Where humics protect *Daphnia*, they do not invest in melanin. Instead, they are unpigmented. This difference is not polymorphism within one species. Different species live in the two pond types.

However, the species are not traditional. They are clones. Many biologists would call them conspecific clones of the same species, *Daphnia pulex*.[1] However, all *Daphnia* at these high latitudes reproduce only parthenogenetically (asexually). So, each new mutation forms a new clone. And such a clone is reproductively isolated from its mother. Speciation is rapid and sympatric.

But how are new clones to coexist? To paraphrase Wilson and Hebert (1992), the sustained coexistence of asexual species requires them to satisfy conditions similar to sexual species. So, they must evolve a specialty. In the

---

[1] Actually, *D. middendorffiana* shows the same clonal pigmentation patterns as *D. pulex* (Hebert, 1982). I could have summarized its story, but that of *D. pulex* is better studied.

case above, that specialty is pigmentation or its absence. The result is two habitats, clear and cloudy ponds.

Predators also exert their influence. Some ponds have the copepod predator, *Hesperodiaptomus arcticus*. Some do not. The diploid clone of *D. pulex* that lives with *H. arcticus* differs from the one that succeeds in its absence, a tetraploid. The predation-resistant clone has smaller sized instars with longer tail spines (Wilson and Hebert, 1993). By the way, *D. middendorffiana* is larger than *D. pulex* and has an even larger tail spine; it lives only in ponds with the copepod predator, *Heterocope septentrionalis*. So, now we have clear and cloudy habitats with no predator, with one predator, and with the other predator. In fact, I admit to simplifying the story: there is acually a third predator, a turbellarian named *Mesostoma lingua*, and yet another clone of *D. pulex* seems to depend on this predator (although sister clones seem insensitive to it) (Wilson and Hebert, 1992).

And there is still more. Weider and Hebert (1987) studied the effect of a moderate salinity gradient on melanic *D. pulex* clones. They sampled 131 ponds on top of three bluffs at the shore of Hudson's Bay near Churchill, Manitoba. Bay water is saline (35 g sea salt per liter). Spray from the bay injects salty water into ponds on the edge of the bluffs, but the further a pond is from the edge, the less salt it gets. The gradient runs over tens of meters from slightly brackish ponds whose water contains about 3 g/l to ponds whose water is almost salt-free (0.05 g/l). Based on their experimental analyses of survivorship for different clones, Weider and Hebert show that melanic *D. pulex* clones subdivide this narrow band of salinities into at least two and perhaps four habitat sub-bands. The clones that live in the freshest water cannot withstand even small amounts of salt. But the clones that live in brackish ponds can survive and reproduce everywhere. Yet they do not. Instead, clones – often distinguishable only after genetic analysis – replace each other in habitats only a few meters apart. Moreover, the distribution of clones in these habitats is stable, at least in the short term; they show the same distribution patterns after 4 years (Wilson and Hebert, 1992).

In sum, one species of *Daphnia pulex* could live in all ponds. It would be a large, melanic clone with a long tail that could live in slightly brackish water. Then we would not distinguish among ponds. We would call them all shallow tundra ponds. But our distinctions are reasonable because there are many species of *D. pulex* and they subdivide the ponds. Moreover, that subdivision leads to their coexistence.

Many of us treat the number of habitats as if it were an inherent, objective, abiotic property of a region. But, in fact, habitat and resource heterogeneity are coevolved responses of organisms. There is no *a priori* reason to expect that life will subdivide any particular variance into more niches than it will a smaller variance. Species discriminate habitats because natural selection forces them to. The more species, the more narrowly they specialize. The more they specialize, the more the ecologist sees different habitats. Remember what Janzen (1967) took for granted in the title of his classic paper: mountain passes **are** higher in the tropics. The same degree of physical change places more of a restriction on tropical species than temperate ones. Physical and chemical heterogeneity is continuous, and, in principle, it is infinitely subdivisible by life.

This will not surprise anyone who has read Williamson and Lawton (1991). They introduce us to the fractal nature of habitats. Viewed from an orbiting satellite, the Earth will seem like a collection of a small number of distinguishable surfaces. You will surely see water, ice and land. You may see desert and forest. You will not see – at least not with the naked eye – that some of the forests are coniferous and some broad-leafed, or that some of the water is salty and some fresh. Those things require you to look at a finer scale.

As Williamson and Lawton have it, you will never lose the power to increase the magnification and see more detail. That is the nature of a fractal landscape. What I here contend is that if we can do that, so can natural selection. As species diversity increases, it can increase the resolution of the landscape, producing significant differences in habitats where none were previously useful to any species. Moreover, I believe not only that it can, but that it does.

Chapter 8

Species–area curves: the classical patterns

Mainland patterns

What could account for larger mainland areas having more species? Three good explanations occur in the literature (Williams, 1964; Connor and McCoy, 1979; Coleman *et al.*, 1982; McGuinness, 1984; Hart and Horwitz, 1991).

- Larger areas have more individuals.
- Larger areas have more habitats.
- Larger areas contain more biogeographical provinces.

I shall briefly describe each of these explanations. Then I shall review the evidence that supports them.

More individuals

It takes more effort to sample a larger area (Usher,1979). Because we spend more time exploring larger areas, we can expect to observe and collect more specimens in the larger area. The more specimens you look at, the more likely you are to see every species in a place. You may eventually work hard enough to see every species. But, until then, the more area, the more specimens; and the more specimens, the more species get recorded (Figure 8.1). Until then, you must take special pains to tell the species–area curve from a mere sampling artifact. Otherwise, you cannot be sure whether diversity truly differs among areas.

More habitats

Area itself is a finite sample of geography. The more area, the more likely it is to include all the available soil conditions, slopes, elevations, salinities,

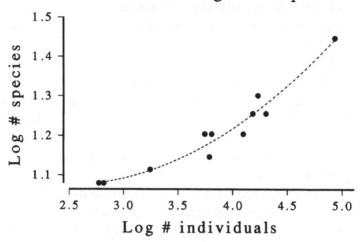

Figure 8.1. More species of mosquito appear at light traps in Iowa
as more individuals get collected. Data from Rowe
quoted in Williams (1964).

turbulences, etc. So, the more area, the more available habitats it incorporates. Notice that no amount of extra work on our part will change the
habitats in an area. In a sense, the area does the sampling for us. And a
1 ha sample cannot be bullied into doing the sampling work of a 1 km^2
sample, no matter how many grant dollars we feed it.

Still, having many habitats is not enough. For this hypothesis to work,
you must assume that extinction, origination and coevolution have done
their work. They must have produced the habitat specializations that allow
habitat variation to support species diversity. Let me reassure you in
advance. That is no problem. As long as species evolve to specialize on
restricted ranges of habitat variables, the habitat hypothesis of species–area
curves will work.

More biogeographical provinces

This hypothesis requires us to consider the machinery of origination. The
first two explanations don't need it. Hypothesis *A*, the sampling artifact,
merely requires that origination and extinction produce a real, positive
number of species. Hypothesis *B*, habitat diversity, requires only that natural selection sometimes produces habitat specialists. But hypothesis *C*
requires us to consider the mechanisms of species origination.

Species first appear in an area either by immigrating to it, or by speciating within it. Hypothesis C needs habitable areas so large and isolated that their speciation rates far exceed their immigration rates. Most of their species must originate internally. Such areas do exist. We call them biogeographical provinces.

Australia and New Guinea – together with a host of smaller, neighboring islands – constitute one such province. Australia's non-marine turtles, for instance, all retract their heads into their 'shells' by swinging them to their side. Such turtles, called pleuroidires, have been radiating in Australia for tens of millions of years. Meanwhile, in North America, all non-marine turtles for the past 50 Myr have retracted their heads by flexing their necks in a vertical plane ('S-necked turtles'). Vertical flexure uses a special set of neck muscle and vertebral adaptations. Side flexure uses a completely different set. Turtles in these two provinces live in similar habitats. But they are isolated from each other, so they cannot compete. Competition never gets the chance to reduce their diversity. George Gaylord Simpson (1950) invented a splendid term for pairs of taxa accomplishing similar ecological functions in similar ways but in separate biogeographical provinces. He called them *ecological vicars*. (The Latin root *vice* means 'in place of' – as in vice-president.)

Although North America has only S-neck turtles, the entire Earth includes both side-necks and S-necks. Large areas will contain more species because they contain more provinces.

Which hypothesis agrees with data?

All three of these hypotheses are correct. But they do not apply equally to all sets of data. I will now argue that most of the species–area curves in the literature arise because larger areas include more habitats.

1. Detecting sampling artifacts. We can easily eliminate the possibility that increases in diversity stem from larger sample sizes. Several statistical measures correct for unequal sample sizes. The best known, called rarefaction (Sanders, 1968), reduces each sample (statistically) to a standard constant size. That size is the number of individuals in the sample with the fewest individuals. Both Freemark and Merriam (1986) and Hart and Horwitz (1991) apply rarefaction to the species–area curve.

But rarefaction makes you eliminate data by reducing all sample sizes to the level of the poorest. No one likes to work hard and then, in effect, throw away a large part of the information. Hart and Horwitz (1991), for example, compare bird diversities of 35 Swedish bogs by reducing all of them to samples of 10 **individuals** (birds); but nine of the bogs have 10 or more **species** of birds and one of them has 22 (Boström and Nilsson, 1983). By discarding all but 10 individuals from each one, we sharply reduce our knowledge of them.

Two straightforward techniques supplant rarefaction. They rely on measures of diversity that do not depend on sample sizes. The older of these is Fisher's α; the younger is Simpson's index. I will now devote a small section to each one.

FISHER'S α: R. A. Fisher deduced his index of diversity based on the assumption that the abundances of species fit a log-series distribution (Fisher *et al.*, 1943). That is, if the total number of individuals is N, and p is a constant proportion, then the most common species has pN individuals; the next most common, $p(1-p)N$; the next, $p(1-p)^2N$; etc. If abundances fit that distribution and you take samples from one set of species, then the number of species you observe will obey this equation:

$$S = -\alpha \ln(1 - x) \qquad (8.1)$$

where α is a constant that depends on diversity alone, and x is a variable that depends on sample size. The variable x satisfies:

$$S/N = [(x - 1)/x] \ln(1 - x) \qquad (8.2)$$

You may use Fisher's α even though the abundances of the species you are sampling do not fit a log-series distribution. Small, incomplete samples of other distributions almost fit the log-series (Boswell and Patil, 1971).

Before computers, it was somewhat tedious to calculate Fisher's α. Perhaps that is why Fisher's α has not been much used to adjust for small sample sizes. Even with the help of Williams's nomograms and Fisher's tables it was much more laborious than other statistics. In the hope that it will become more popular, I have appended some Q-Basic code (Mitchell and Rosenzweig, unpublished) to calculate it (Box 8.1).

Williams (1964) illustrates Fisher's α with Lepidoptera caught in six light traps at Rothamsted, England from 30 June 1949 to 10 July 1949 (Figure 8.2). As data accumulated during this time, the number of species increased steadily. But Fisher's α fluctuated narrowly around 30. So the apparent increase was spurious. Williams also showed that there is no real diversity increase in the mosquito data of Figure 8.1. In that case too, Fisher's α hovers around a constant.

BOX 8.1: QBASIC PROGRAM FOR FISHER'S α

```
'Root finder routine using Newton's method
DECLARE FUNCTION Y! (X!)
DECLARE FUNCTION G! (S.over.N!)
DECLARE FUNCTION DerG! (X!)

DECLARE SUB showresults ()
COMMON SHARED S%, n%, S.over.N!, X!, eps!

DO
INPUT "What is the value of N"; n%
INPUT "What is the value of S"; S%

S.over.N! = S% / n%

X! = .5
eps! = .000001
PRINT
PRINT "RESULTS OF ITERATION"
PRINT
'PRINT "   X     ERROR"
DO
     X! = X! - G!(S.over.N!) / DerG!(X!)
'PRINT X!; G!(S.over.N!)

LOOP UNTIL ABS(G!(S.over.N) < eps!)
showresults
PRINT
INPUT "Do you want to calculate another coefficient (y for yes, n for
no)"; A$
LOOP UNTIL A$ = "n"

END
```

Figure 8.3 shows the result of using Fisher's α on the bird data from Swedish bogs (Boström and Nilsson, 1983). This is the same data Hart and Horwitz treated with rarefaction. Fisher's α also removes the effect of area. Before taking out the influence of small sample sizes, these bogs had a significant and steep species–area slope ($z = 0.46$).

In samples of differing size taken from one set of species that follows a log-series distribution, α does not vary. But, it does increase if the true

Diversity Seems to Grow
With Sample Size

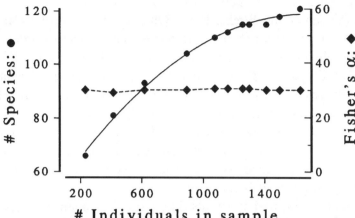

Figure 8.2. Fisher's α, an index of diversity which does not depend
on sample size, shows that diversity does not really
increase in this sampling of Lepidoptera. The apparent
increase is an artifact of sample size. Data from
Williams (1964).

Birds of Peat Bogs

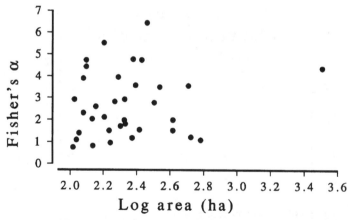

Figure 8.3. Bird species diversity in raised peat bogs of Sweden's
county P. Once we change to an estimator of diversity
which is unbiased by the number of individuals in the
sample (Fisher's α in this case), the species–area relationship vanishes. Data from Boström and Nilsson,
1983). I have followed them in using only bogs whose
area exceeds 100 ha.

number of species rises (Equation 8.1). To illustrate both a steady and a rising α, I calculated another pair of examples from a forest on the island of Mauritius (Vaughan and Wiehe, 1941). On one set of ten 0.1 ha plots, only vegetation > 10 cm dbh (diameter at breast height) was recorded. As you combine the plots of this set into 0.2, 0.5 and 1.0 ha sets, diversity appears to grow. But Fisher's α shows that the increase is illusory; it comes only because of increase in the number of individuals (Figure 8.4). However, there is also a second set of smaller plots. In them, only plants > 1 cm dbh got counted. These plots do show a real diversity increase as you combine them into larger plots. They may even show it at two scales: they appear to plateau over intermediate areas, and then they start to become more diverse again over the larger ones (Figure 8.5).

As an aside, I note that Preston's time pattern also survives the application of Fisher's α. Figure 8.6 shows the data from captures of Lepidoptera at Rothamsted. These are the same data as in Figure 3.12. But Fisher's α (instead of the number of species) forms the y-axis.

A species–area curve generated by the small samples that fit a log-series distribution has another important property. It tends to fit a straight line in semi-logarithmic space (May, 1975):

$$S = k + b \log A \tag{8.3}$$

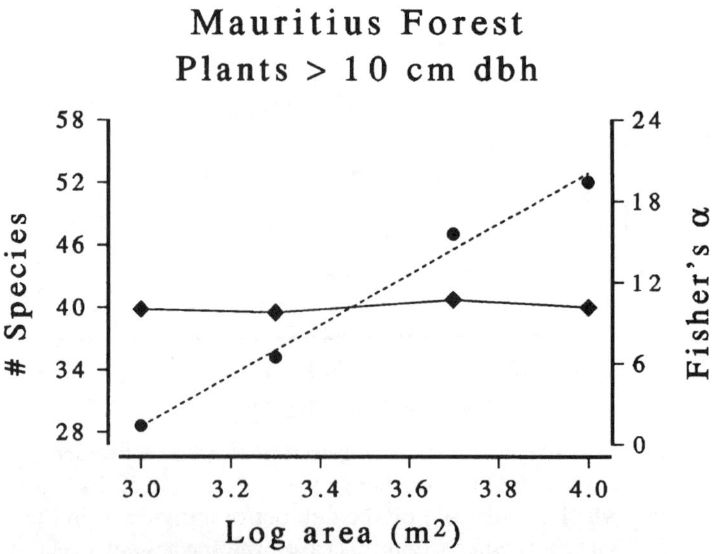

Mauritius Forest
Plants > 10 cm dbh

Figure 8.4. Larger plants show no increase in diversity over a 1 ha scale. Raw numbers are dots; Fisher indices are diamonds. Data from Vaughan and Wiehe (1941).

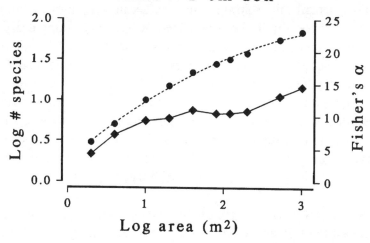

Figure 8.5. Smaller plants do increase over small scales of area. Raw numbers are dots; Fisher indices are diamonds. Data from Vaughan and Wiehe (1941).

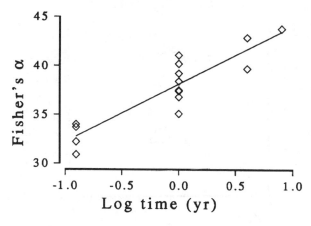

Figure 8.6. Diversity does increase with time, even when Fisher's α is used as the index of diversity. The species are Lepidoptera collected in a light trap at Rothamsted Experimental Station, England. Diversities are cumulative. Data from Williams (1964).

Thus, the log-series appears to explain why plant ecologists prefer Gleason (i.e. semi-logarithmic) plots. Plant surveys, commonly done within 0.1 ha plots, usually fit a straight line better in a semi-logarithmic space because they are too small to have escaped the effects of sample size.

The same is true for very small islands. The 37 small islands of Lake Hjälmaren, Sweden, fit a convex curve in log-log space better than a straight line (Rydin and Borgegård, 1988). In semi-log space the curve is straight (Figure 8.7). The difference isn't much ($R^2 = 0.84$ for a straight line in the semi-log vs $R^2 = 0.78$ for a straight line in log-log space). But such differences occur repeatedly owing to curvilinearity over very small areas. In this case, adding two larger islands reveals that the semi-log relationship does not apply to larger areas (Rydin and Borgegård, 1988).

SIMPSON'S INDEX OF CONCENTRATION: Simpson (1949) proposed another measure of diversity, the index of concentration. Like Fisher's α, it does not grow with sample size. However, unlike Fisher's α, Simpson's index does not depend on the log-series or any other abundance distribution. Instead, to calculate Simpson's index, you must count the number of individuals in each species.

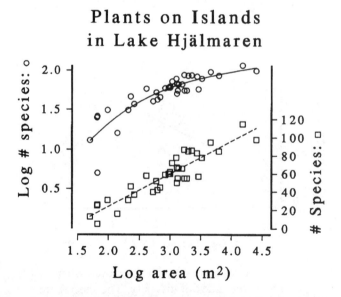

Figure 8.7. These 37 small islands fit a straight line in semi-log space better than in log-log space. Data from Rydin and Borgegård (1988).

Most papers I have seen use a biased form for Simpson's index:

$$SI_b = \sum n^2 / N^2 = \sum p_i^2 \tag{8.4}$$

where n is the number of individuals in a species, $N = \Sigma n$, and p_i is the proportion of individuals in species i.

When Simpson first suggested his measure, he noted the bias of Equation 8.4. But he also presented a corrected formula that made it sample-size independent:

$$SI = \sum ((n^2 - n) / (N^2 - N)) \tag{8.5}$$

Williams (1964) claims that even Equation 8.5 depends on sample size, but it does not. Although Simpson did not prove its independence in his paper, others have. Nei and Roychoudhury (1974) derived it for population genetics. Rosenzweig and Abramsky (1986 and unpublished) deduced it for measuring habitat diversity. (We did not publish our proof because we learned about Nei and Roychoudhury while our paper was in press.)

If you have values of SI_b, you can easily calculate SI with the following:

$$SI = ((N \times SI_b) - 1)/(N - 1) \tag{8.6}$$

Note that SI is not defined at $N = 1$. Since samples of one individual contain absolutely no information about diversity, maybe that's not such an undesirable property.

Similarly, when all species have exactly one individual, SI = 0. That says diversity is infinite. But we know the truth. The sample is still too small to be useful.

SI grows as diversity declines. Its asymptotic upper limit is 1.0 (when all individuals belong to a single species). That is why Simpson preferred to call it a measure of concentration. But Pielou (1974, pp. 297, 298, with credit to C. D. Kemp) shows how easy it is to convert SI to a statistic that grows as the number of species does. Just take its negative logarithm. Thus, when sample size is a problem, $-\ln$ SI can be trusted to reflect underlying diversity in an easily interpreted fashion independently of sample size.

Taylor *et al.* (1976) compared SI to α both theoretically and by applying them to extensive records of insect species. When abundances fit a log-series distribution, of course α worked superbly. But it outperformed SI even when abundances failed to match a log-series. For example, the year-to-year variation in α was slight compared to that in SI (Table 8.1).Those readers interested in other indices of diversity should consult two other works. The monograph of Anne Magurran (1988) discusses the usefulness of Fisher's α

Table 8.1. *Insect diversities estimated by two unbiased indices: Fisher's α and M, an index based on SI that scales like α and was derived by Taylor* et al. *(1976). In Location A, abundances fit a log-series distribution; in B they do not. Despite that, Fisher's α does a more consistent job of estimating diversity because it is less sensitive to the annual fluctuations in the abundance of the commonest species. E is Efficiency*

					Year						σ^2	E
	1	2	3	4	5	6	7	8	9	10		
Location A												
α	49.2	46.6	48.8	45.3	45.3	45.6	44.2	47.0	49.7	51.6	5.7	1.00
M	35.4	31.7	49.2	46.1	36.6	45.8	42.5	50.8	43.0	48.1	41.0	0.14
Location B												
α	33.7	37.3	35.0	31.8	34.3	36.0	35.7	34.5	39.1	36.8	4.2	1.00
M	13.3	11.2	16.5	12.4	9.8	17.0	18.5	19.5	24.2	30.6	40.5	0.10

Data from Taylor *et al.*

and presents clear accounts and examples of Shannon's index, Brioullin's index, and others less well known. The review of Colwell and Coddington (1994) explains how to extrapolate a sequential sample of diversity to an asymptote. It also presents the most useful comparison of capture-recapture estimators (see Chapters 3 and 6 above) that I have ever read.

However, Magurran does not report Kemp's transformation. The commonly used reciprocal, 1/SI, has severe variance problems. And the form preferred by geneticists, 1 − SI, is altogether unsatisfactory for species diversity work. Its maximum value depends on *C*, the number of classes – species, loci, habitats, etc. – in the assemblage you are working on. If you are a geneticist working with a fixed number of loci to compare heterogeneity among populations, you have no problem. But if you are an ecologist working to compare species diversities, then *C* is an important variable. **The important variable.** You don't want to use a measure whose range varies with the property you are studying.

Williams (1964, pp. 148–151) reported that Yule (1944) suggested a sample-size independent measure of diversity:

$$\beta = \sum n(n-1) / N^2 \tag{8.7}$$

Remembering that $N = \Sigma n$,

$$\beta = \sum n^2 / N^2 - 1 / N = \sum p_i^2 - 1 / N \tag{8.8}$$

So, Yule's index is SI_b minus the reciprocal of total sample size.

But Yule's index is not independent of sample size. Suppose, for example, an assemblage has only one species. If you sample five of its individuals, $\beta = 0.8$. But if you sample 100, $\beta = 0.99$. Simpson's index does not have this problem.

Diversity indices do, however, have another problem. They combine the variable we are trying to measure, S, with a second variable often called equitability (Lloyd and Ghelardi, 1964; Hurlbert, 1971). Indices of diversity rise if the number of species goes up or the variation in species abundance goes down. However, I find it better to keep variables separated. That sharpens both questions and analyses. In particular, we have asked no questions of equitability in this book. Our questions concern species diversity.[1]

Even Fisher's α has a subtle problem with equitability. Fisher's α relies on the assumption of a constant equitability, i.e. abundances are always distributed in a log series. But, what if abundances become more and more equitable as they decline? Equivalently, what if we actually have managed a complete listing of all species from sites with very different abundances (or sample sizes)? Then Fisher's α gets into trouble.

Figure 8.8 shows the problem at its most extreme. For each line in the graph, I assumed a fixed number of species. I also assumed that all species were recorded even in the smallest samples. As sample size grows, Fisher's α declines. It is not a trivial decline either. Why?

Suppose there are five species and five are seen in a sample of five individuals. The probable cause of such good luck is extreme evenness of distribution. (Still, even with perfect equitability, fewer than one of 25 samples will have all five species.) But Fisher's α does not adjust for distribution. It always assumes that the log-series holds. From its point of view, a sample of five individuals that contains five species should come from a marvelously rich biota with so many species that we are unlikely to see duplicates in any small sample. Hence, it returns a high diversity estimate.

---

[1] Terminology note: I do not use the term 'species richness' and hope it is abandoned. Hurlbert introduced it to good effect. But I believe the term may now have outlived its usefulness. If we continue to use it, we shall allow ecology to be cheated of a powerful concept. It is time to reclaim our property. Diversity indices were introduced to improve our ability to express the number of species by making it a continuous variable. Hurlbert reminded us that, because they did so by introducing a measure of evenness, they are not pure measures of the number of species. Right. He also pointed out that they cannot be expected to return a consistent ranking among themselves. That is, diversity index 1 may rank Place A the most diverse while, based on precisely the same data, diversity index 2 may rank Place B the most diverse. Indeed. But the solution is not to abandon the term species diversity. Let us reclaim that term from the indices; let us calculate diversity by simply counting the number of species. As Hurlbert makes clear, indices have their uses, but ought to be restricted to them. The use I champion here is estimating the diversity of small samples.

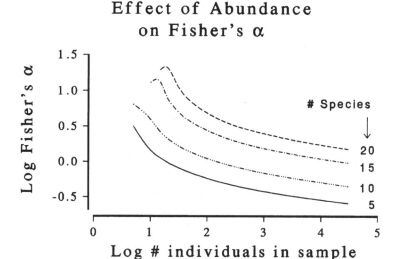

Figure 8.8. Even Fisher's α can have sample-size problems. Once
the real number of species in an area is known,
increasing the sample size drives down Fisher's α. To
calculate the lines in this figure, I assumed that all
species were contained in samples even if they had only
as many individuals as species. Each curve follows α
for the indicated number of species.

Are we damned if we use diversity indices but also damned if we do not?
Not exactly. Ordinarily, samples will be complete enough that the simple
number of species will be the only diversity index you need or should use.
But for small samples, you will want estimates that are free of the influence
of sample size. Then, you will want to use α or SI. I wish I knew a rule to
teach you (and me) when to switch. It's a judgment call. But if you get the
same pattern with and without an index, you should be confident.

Unfortunately, papers on diversity rarely use or report numbers of individuals. So we can only rarely check on diversity patterns by computing
their density-independent diversity indices. I found only a single published
work on the species–area curve that reported the numbers of individuals in
each species at each area (Haila, 1983; Haila *et al.*, 1983).

Fortunately, May (1975) showed us a way to reject the hypothesis that
most species–area curves come from inadequate samples. He determined
the shape of a species–area curve generated by larger and larger samples. It
has much too shallow a slope to be responsible for the data we see. In
Figure 8.9, I calculated the curves for three log-series distributions with one

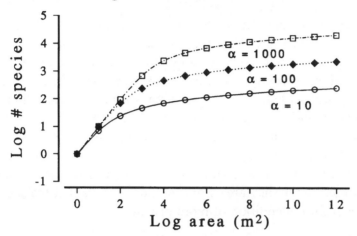

Figure 8.9. Each of these species–area curves comes from a hypothetical system whose true diversity does not vary with
area. Diversity seems to rise because larger areas have
more individuals. But the z-values of these species–area
curves fall below those seen in nature. (See text.)

individual per m^2. They cover a large range of Fisher's α and none are truly
linear. But they all have approximate slopes that are very low:

α	10	100	1000
z	0.0475	0.0550	0.0650

I know of no species–area curve with a slope as low as any of those.

We should have known this all along. Many species–area curves come
from places with long traditions of natural history observation. Who would
have believed me had I concluded that the British plant species–area curve
arises from a lack of sampling effort on the part of British botanists? Even I
would have disowned myself! There are plenty of other species–area cases
(Preston's bird censuses and Abbott's plant censuses, for example) that are
based on a thorough knowledge of what is where.

Yes, we can point to exceptions. There are provisional lists from areas
whose study has only recently begun. There are lists of hyperdiverse taxa
whose species require expert identification. And there are lists from tiny
areas in which only a few individuals can fit. But these are exceptions.

Usually, sampling artifacts have played no role in determining the species–area curves discovered during the past five decades.

2. Provincial effects. No doubt provincial effects exist (see Chapter 9). But many provincial areas have been recognized by biogeographers since Alfred Russell Wallace himself. This is especially true of vertebrate and plant provinces. Most species–area curves are measured within one such province. Preston (1960) for instance kept his bird curve within a single avian province until he had sampled it all. The British plant curve lies entirely within the Eurasian province and the New Guinea ant curve (Figure 2.11) also lies within a single province. In Chapter 9, I shall examine the interprovincial species–area curve. But at the smaller scales commonly used for species–area work, no one believes that the species–area curve arises from the addition of more provinces.

3. The habitat hypothesis. Most (all?) species occur only in the presence of a particular set of habitats. So, as long as our areas are too small to include all habitats, we have to expect more area to contain more species.

If habitat diversity grows as area does, and that is the true explanation of mainland species–area curves, then habitat should be able to replace area as the independent variable. In several cases, it actually does.

Fox (1983) investigated the relationship between species and area in Australian mammals. He classified macrohabitats into seven broad types. Then he showed that larger areas do include more types (Figure 8.10). He also showed that the number of mammal species is even better predicted from the number of habitats than from area (Figure 8.11 and Figure 8.12). Moreover, area does not even help to explain the variance left over after habitat has done its predicting.

Much the same result comes from the work of Tonn and Magnuson (1982). They recorded lake characteristics and fish species from 18 shallow lakes in Vilas County, Wisconsin. The area of a lake predicts its number of species ($R^2 = 0.525$). But so does its habitat diversity ($R^2 = 0.423$) as measured by the variety of its vegetation types (emergent, floating or submergent). Area and habitat correlate so closely that only one variable is useful in predicting diversity.

Kitchener *et al.* (1980a, b, 1982) provide the most detailed investigation of the relationships between species diversity, area and habitat diversity. They studied a system of natural reserves in an intensely farmed portion of Western Australia called the wheatbelt. They measured the diversity of

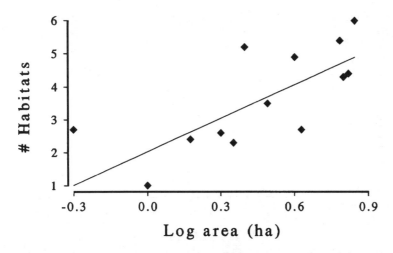

Figure 8.10. Larger areas have more habitats. These are the areas that yielded the mammal samples of Figure 8.11. Redrawn after Fox (1983).

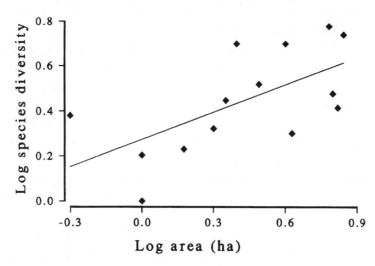

Figure 8.11. Diversity of small mammals in parts of Australia follows a species–area curve. Redrawn after Fox (1983).

Mammals of Southeast Australia

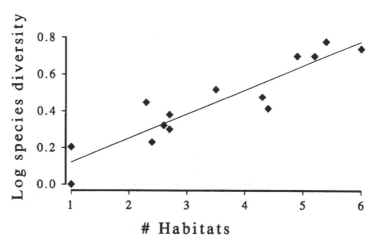

Figure 8.12. The number of mammal species fits the number of habitats better than area. Area explains none of the residual variance. Redrawn after Fox (1983).

plants, lizards, birds and mammals. Using plant associations as a defining variable, they also measured the variety of habitats contained by each reserve.

Figure 8.13 shows the plant species–area curve in the wheatbelt. It is classically linear with a z-value of 0.26. We cannot use habitat variety to explain this curve because the habitat variable relies solely on the plant species associations. But we can use the habitat variable to study the relationship of vertebrate diversity to area. (Note that we **could** use a different habitat variable – one that relied on soil types or exposures or elevations or geological features or some combination of them – to study how plant diversity depended on habitat variety. That is just what Harner and Harper, 1976, have done. See the next example.)

Vertebrate diversity in the wheatland reserves relates well to both area and habitat diversity (Figures 8.14 and 8.15). In both cases we see a slight, but significant curvilinearity caused entirely by a few points on the far left.[2] To emphasize this, I show the species–area curve as a piecewise linear fit, as well as plotting it as a power regression (of the form $\log y = a \log x^b$).

---

[2] The three points on the left are not truly independent. They lie close together in the Shire of Quairading, and have only 4–6 plant associations each. The other reserve in this shire has 12. Kitchener *et al.* show that different habitats carry quite different numbers of vertebrates. So the hyper-impoverishment in the three tiny reserves could reflect merely a bad draw of a small number of habitats, or a few leftover poor spots that the farmers couldn't use. It could also be another instance of very small areas conforming more closely to a semi-logarithmic fit than to a log-log fit – see the section on Gleason plots in Chapter 9.

Wheatbelt Reserves

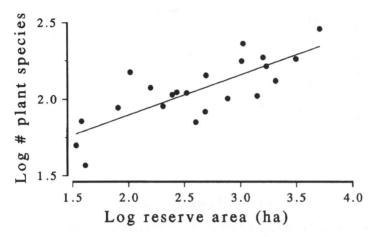

Figure 8.13. The species–area relationship of plants in some Western Australian nature reserves. These reserves are all in a region of farms called the wheatbelt.

Wheatbelt Vertebrates

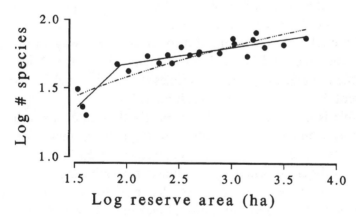

Figure 8.14. The species–area relationship of vertebrates in wheatbelt nature reserves. Vertebrates include resident birds, lizards and mammals. I fitted the points two ways. The curved line is a power regression (see text). The straight lines combine to form a piecewise linear regression. The better fit of the latter emphasizes the linearity of the relationship over most of the range of reserve sizes.

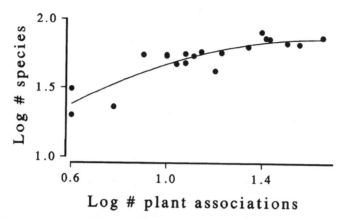

Wheatbelt Vertebrates

Figure 8.15. Vertebrate diversity in wheatbelt reserves also correlates well with the number of plant associations in a
reserve. The relationship is fitted by a polynomial
regression and reflects the underlying dependence of
species diversity on habitat diversity.

The good fit of both area and habitat diversity reflects the action of one
underlying variable. Figure 8.16 shows how closely habitat diversity follows
reserve area. Yet, if we rely entirely on multiple linear regression, the curvilinearity of the relationship springs a trap on us. A two-way linear regession
using both 'log area' and 'log habitat diversity' shows that both variables
determine the number of vertebrate species (for area, $p = 0.03$; for habitat,
$p = 0.04$; joint $R^2 = 0.79$.) But this result misleads us.

The trouble is that the two variables nearly duplicate each other. Thus,
one can act as a surrogate for the other. Multiple linear regression uses one
copy, then uses the second (surrogate) copy to curve the line. We know that
happened here because standard curvilinear regressions, using either variable by itself, produce very similar results. For example, the polynomial
regressions have $R^2 = 0.84$ (for area alone) and $R^2 = 0.79$ (for habitats
alone); the power regressions have $R^2 = 0.78$ (for area alone) and $R^2 = 0.76$
(for habitats alone).

Harner and Harper (1976) pioneered the attempts to separate the
species–area curve into an area effect and a habitat effect. They concluded
that both are significant. But in reality, only one of the variables works. The
second only **seems** to work. That statistical trap I just mentioned is fooling
us; a surrogate variable is improving the fit to a curvilinear relationship.

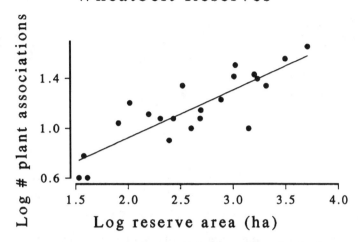

Figure 8.16. Larger areas have more habitats. That is why larger
wheatbelt reserves have more species.

Harner and Harper (1976) studied hectare plots in pinyon–juniper woodland in central Utah and northern New Mexico. They counted the species
of plants in each of the 30 plots. Using a perfect, nested design, they
repeated their censuses in smaller plots of 1000, 100, 10 and 1 m². Then
they performed a multiple linear regression. Both area and habitat are significant. The trouble is that 'area and heterogeneity are tightly intercon-
nected in nature' (Harner and Harper, 1976, p. 1259). So either can serve as
a surrogate for the other. If you look at their Figure 1, you will see what
must have happened. The relationship between 'log area' and 'log species
diversity' is strongly convex,[3] requiring a squared term in a polynomial
regression for adequate fit. But adding a second variable that strongly correlates with area does virtually as good a job.

Harner and Harper (1976) despair of ever teasing area apart from habitat
diversity. But they hint at their belief that habitat diversity is the more
important. Actually, they need not have despaired. Using only whole 1 ha
plots, Harner and Harper regress species diversity against habitat diversity.
Since all plots now have the same size, area cannot be important. But the
regression remains significant (see Figure 8.17). So they actually showed
that habitat must be important. Thus, if only one of the two works, it must

[3] The very small sample sizes afforded by plots only 1 m² or 10 m² probably cause the convexity. See
'Gleason plots' in Chapter 9.)

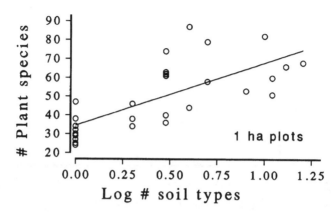

Figure 8.17. Even in equal-area plots, more habitat diversity means more species of plants. Soil type is one of the principal determinants of habitat diversity in pinyon–juniper woodland. Data from Harner and Harper (1976).

be habitat. Many other studies of diversity have also shown that species diversity rises with habitat diversity in equal-area plots (see Chapter 2, the habitat pattern).

A kind of companion study reveals the opposite side of the coin: keep habitat constant and vary area. If habitat alone yields mainland species–area curves then they should disappear when you hold habitat constant. Boström and Nilsson (1983) did hold habitat constant when they censused birds. They worked only in raised Swedish peat bogs. You will recall from Figure 8.3 that indeed, their bird data shows no species–area curve.

Most of the other work that studies the influence of habitat variety on diversity was done on islands. When we consider them (next), we shall see that on islands, habitat diversity only partly explains the species–area curve. We will need at least two other variables to provide a complete explanation of island species–area curves.

Island patterns

What is a biogeographic island?

When I examined island patterns of diversity in Chapter 2, I waffled at the job of defining the word 'island.' But now we need a precise definition, and I must produce it.

Is an island just a 'land mass surrounded by water?' If so, where should we draw the line? Is Madagascar an island? Or is it too large? If it is, how about Australia? How about South America? How about all the Americas? They are all 'surrounded by water.'

Maybe 'inaccessibility' would produce a better definition than 'land surrounded by water?' Ecologists have long recognized that inaccessibility is a fundamental property of an island (Vuilleumier, 1970; Brown, 1971a). A mouse living in a mountaintop forest cannot journey to another mountaintop if, on its way, it must cross hostile habitat. And the reef fish of a coral atoll may have to swim hundreds of kilometers through open ocean to reach another atoll. That atoll is as much an island for the fish as for the insects on its dry sand.

But if inaccessibility defines 'islandness', how much inaccessibility is enough? And what about inaccessible, sub-Saharan Africa (say)? Is it too large to be an island? If it is too large, what makes it so?

If those questions have answers, they must be somewhat arbitrary. I propose we abandon both the watery basis and the inaccessibility basis of islandness. They both lead to arbitrary distinctions. Instead, let's invent a biological definition of islands. We can do it by keeping origination mechanisms uppermost in our minds.

An island is a self-contained region whose species originate entirely by immigration from outside the region. By 'self-contained' I mean that within the region, each of its species has an average net rate of reproduction sufficient to maintain some positive population size, however small. Such species are called 'source' species (Shmida and Ellner, 1984; Pulliam, 1988). The opposite – i.e. net rates are **in**sufficient for maintenance – is 'sink-species'. Islands, by definition, have no sink species.

Keddy (1981) showed us an example. The annual *Cakile edentula* cannot survive on the middle or landward side of dunes without annual replenishment from the seaward population. So, *Cakile* is a sink species on the middle and landward side of dunes, but a source species on their seaward side.

Kadmon and Shmida (1990) showed us another example and a general method for investigating the question in plants. The annual grass, *Stipa capensis*, is three orders of magnitude more common in a wadi than its on adjacent slopes. Its individuals in the wadi also enjoy ten times the reproductive success as those of the slopes. *Stipa capensis* is a source species in the wadi and a sink species on the slopes. (See 'Why are z-values higher on islands?' later in this chapter for more discussion of the importance of sink species.)

The definition of islands completely transforms them from geographical entities to biological ones. Not that the two are unrelated. And not that it will be any easier to draw lines with this definition. But the theory of island biogeography grows naturally out of the definition. Moreover, with this definition, we won't even want to draw lines any more. We will appreciate islands and mainlands as endpoints of a continuum without natural or theoretical discontinuities.

Please notice two things about the island definition. It suggests a parallel definition for mainlands (i.e. *a self-contained region whose species originate entirely by speciation within the region*). And, probably, most real places have some species that immigrated and some that evolved *in situ*. So what's the use? Why bother with definitions that are so extreme?

The definitions of island and mainland set up a continuum whose metric is 'proportion of immigrant species'. At each end of this continuum we can build a dynamic model to explain diversity patterns. Then we can combine the models to generate real world systems.

A word about the importance of the term 'self-contained': The County of Dane, State of Wisconsin, in which I now sit, may never have produced a new species of tree or a new species of mammal. So we might be tempted to call it an island. But that would be a mistake. It is bad enough to admit that I'm going to insist that Hawaii is a mainland. But how can I insist on island status for an arbitrary political subdivision hewn out of the vast sea of similar territory that constitutes southern Wisconsin? You would rebel. And you would be right. Calling Dane County an 'island' would vitiate the usefulness of 'island' as a word. But adding the concept 'self-contained' rescues us. Dane County is completely accessible to constant immigration from its neighbors. So, we can expect many of its species to be maintained by that flow. If we put a barrier around the county, then it would lose those species and become an island.

Theory of island biogeography

MacArthur and Wilson (1963) implied most of the definition of island in their model of island biogeography. They graphed immigration rate against number of species and tacitly assumed no other form of origination. Moreover, they very carefully restricted the definition of immigration. Their definition of immigration is the key to the whole theory. In the theory of island biogeography, immigration is the appearance on an island of a propagule of a species not now on the island. Remember that a propagule is a group of individuals sufficient to get a population started. (It may not survive long, but at least it has the reproductive capacity to grow.) The propagule may belong to a species that became extinct on the island last month. But it does not count as an immigration if the species is already on the island at the time the propagule arrives.

Assume that each species, j, from some mainland pool, sends propagules to the island at a rate i_j. Assume that rate does not depend on which species are already on the island. If there are p species in the pool, then the total rate of propagule arrival (I) is the sum of all the species rates:

$$I = \sum_{j=1}^{p} i_j$$

(8.9)

Now subdivide the species into those on the island, s, and those not, p–s. The propagule arrival rate is

$$I = \sum_{j=1}^{s} i_j + \sum_{j=s+1}^{p} i_j = \sum_{j=1}^{p} i_j$$

(8.10)

Since all elements i_j are positive,

$$I_s = \sum_{j=s+1}^{p} i_j \leq \sum_{j=1}^{p} i_j, \qquad s \geq 0$$

(8.11)

In other words, the immigration rate I_s is smaller than the rate of propagule arrival. In fact, the more species already on the island, the smaller the immigration rate should be, i.e.

$$\frac{\partial I_s}{\partial s} < 0$$

(8.12)

Now we turn to extinction, the negative aspect of the dynamics. By definition, the extinction rate at $s = 0$ is zero; there are no species to become extinct. Assuming no interactions among species, each added species brings along its own specific extinction rate. The total extinction rate on the island rises with s.

So, the total extinction rate rises from zero and the total immigration rate declines to zero. Therefore, the immigration and extinction curves must cross between $s = 0$ and $s = p$. (p is the number in the mainland pool.) Where they cross, input equals output and we have an equilibrium, $\hat{S}$ (Figure 8.18).

The equilibrium should be stable. Extra species beyond equilibrium make

Diversity on Islands:
Non-Interactive Dynamics

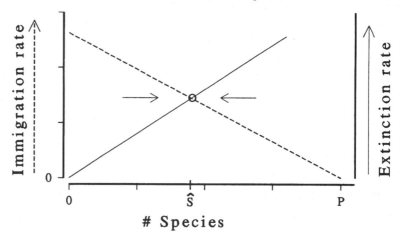

Figure 8.18. Even if species all have the same immigration and extinction rates, and do not affect each other, diversity on an island will tend toward a steady state that is less than the diversity of the source pool.

extinction greater than immigration. Fewer species than equilibrium make immigration greater than extinction. Thus, the system acts to restore its own equilibrium in the face of any perturbation. The figure indicates the system's self-regulatory nature with two arrows pointing toward its equilibrium from diversities that are larger or smaller.

Notice something very important about Figure 8.18 and the arguments that led to it. The prediction of an equilibrium does not depend on competition or any other interaction. Suppose – as we did in building the model – that each species does not influence the extinction rate of any other. If it arrives, it contributes only its own extinction rate to that of the whole assemblage. Suppose that if it becomes extinct, it deletes only its own extinction rate without influencing that of any other. Extinction rate still rises monotonically with diversity. Immigration rate still declines. Equilibrium still occurs where the two rate curves cross.

As you may recall from Chapter 6, MacArthur and Wilson deduced that extinction rate curves rise at accelerating rates in the presence of more species. As you will see in the next paragraph, they deduced the curvature of the immigration rate too (Figure 8.19). But we learned in the previous paragraph that the existence of an equilibrium diversity on an island does

Diversity on Islands:
Interactive Dynamics

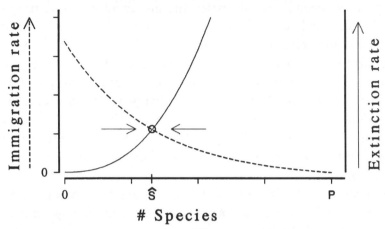

Figure 8.19. MacArthur and Wilson's original model for island biogeography. Its rate curves bend because species add to each other's extinction rates, and because some species immigrate more readily than others. Compare with Figure 8.18.

not depend on whether they were right about the curvatures. Even if they were 100% wrong, their basic argument for an equilibrium still stands.

To deduce the curvature of the immigration rate, MacArthur and Wilson reasoned that species probably have different rates of propagule arrival. Some bird species, the supertramps (Diamond, 1974), arrive at a very high rate; others come at imperceptible rates. Lomolino (1993) shows that mammal species active in winter are much more likely to colonize islands in Lake Huron. MacArthur and Wilson themselves noted that most of the beetle species on the extremely isolated island of St Helena have a great marine-dispersal advantage over other beetles. Most of the beetles found on St Helena bore into wood or cling to bark. So they have a good chance to immigrate over water on floating bits of trees.

On average, the tramps and the supertramps should arrive on an island earliest. Less mobile (or scarcer) species will follow. The least mobile species will tend to arrive last. Thus, the reduction in I_s caused by the arrival of the first few species should be large compared to the reduction from the same number of ordinary species (Figure 8.19). So, the slope of the immigration curve should get less and less steep as diversity rises:

$$\frac{\partial^2 I_s}{\partial s} > 0$$

$$(8.13)$$

The positive second derivatives for the immigration curve, proposed by MacArthur and Wilson, may not lack exceptions. Propagule sizes are context-sensitive numbers. A species' arrival rate may depend on who else is already present. For example, a bird propagule in the presence of a mutualist may be smaller than in its absence. That suggests the possibility that immigration rates could actually rise with diversity. Perhaps some mutualistic interactions are strong enough to accomplish that, but the overall trend cannot rise. Eventually, the disappearance of species from the pool of eligible immigrants must drive down the immigration rate. By definition, it reaches zero when $s = p$.

How does the theory of island biogeography account for island species–area curves? It actually predicts those curves because larger islands should have more habitats and larger populations than do smaller islands. The larger populations reduce the extinction rate curve (Figure 8.20). The increase in habitats may affect both extinction and immigration, lowering the first and raising the second. In any case, larger area leads to larger equilibria.

Diversity on Islands:
Consequences of island size

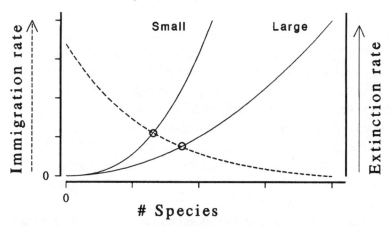

Figure 8.20. Larger islands have more species because their extinction rate curves lie below those of smaller islands. If immigration is measured only by looking at individuals that have germinated or reproduced, then larger islands will also have larger immigration rates (not shown).

I need to add a word about the effect of habitats. I just broke with tradition by declaring that more habitats could lead to more immigration. But finding an appropriate habitat at the end of a long journey must reduce propagule size somewhat. And anything that reduces propagule size increases immigration rates.

Effects of population size and habitat diversity

The theory of island biogeography predicts the species–area curve because larger islands have more habitats **and** more individuals. (It is not accurate to say that the theory depends on only one of these.) However, do both actually matter? The theory could depend on only one. It could generate species–area curves on islands even if more area increased only habitats, or only population size. Thus, we must ask what effect of area actually generates the species–area curve on islands. Is it habitats? Is it population size? Is it both?

Watson (1964) explained the species–area curve for passerine birds on Aegean Islands using habitat diversity. His work deeply influenced MacArthur, who I know saw a copy before 1965. (He told me then how important it was.) But Watson's work has now aquired much good company.

Maly and Doolittle (1977) also found that habitat did most of the work of explaining the species–area curve. Over a 5 year period, they censused the land and freshwater snails of seven Bahama islands ranging from 1 ha to 101 ha. They identified six macrohabitats and found 11 species. (They ignored species so minute that they doubted their ability to find them all with the techniques and resources they had available.) Only the habitat effect is statistically significant. However, species often were absent from islands with habitat that should have supported them. Thus, Maly and Doolittle suggest that habitat does not entirely explain the area effect. Population size also may be involved and its influence could show up with more data.

Levins and Heatwole (1973) attacked the problem experimentally. They introduced species to a cay and found that they usually disappear rapidly unless suitable habitat is present. (But such experiments are rarely ethical, especially with vertebrates.)

Habitat diversity underlies the species–area curve for Galapagos Islands plants too (Hamilton *et al.*, 1963). Taken together, these studies (plus others, e.g. Johnson *et al.*, 1968; Abbott, 1974; Johnson and Simberloff, 1974; Muhlenberg *et al.*, 1977; Abbott and Black, 1987) strongly support the idea that change in habitat diversity causes, to a large extent, the species–area curves of islands.

Haila (1983; Haila *et al.*, 1983) gave us enough data to search simultaneously for the effects of population and habitat. He studied the bird diversity of 44 islands in the Åland Archipelago, Finland. In addition to island area and diversity, Haila reported each species' population size. And he defined, measured and reported ten different habitat types for birds on the islands. I will examine the censuses of 1979 because that was the only year that all 44 islands had their birds censused.

Figure 8.21 displays the strong species–area relationship among these islands. But habitat diversity also predicts bird diversity with considerable accuracy (Figure 8.22). And so does the number of birds counted (Figure 8.23).

One technique often useful for disentangling the effects of many variables is some form of multivariate ANOVA (including multiple linear regression). But we cannot use that here because all three variables are closely correlated (Figures 8.24 and 8.25). Fortunately, we can eliminate the effect of pure sample size by taking advantage of Fisher's α or Simpson's Index.

Figures 8.26 and 8.27 show that neither of these transformations gets rid of the positive correlation between S (diversity) and N (number of individu-

Birds of Åland

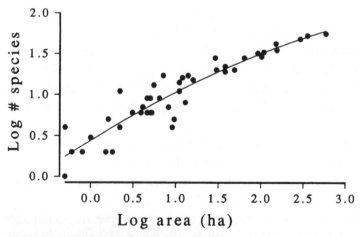

Figure 8.21. The species–area curve for birds of 44 islands in the Åland Archipelago, Finland. Data from 1979 censuses of Haila *et al.* (1983).

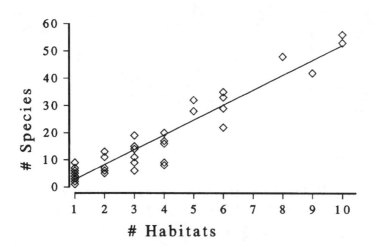

Figure 8.22. Islands with more habitat types also have more bird species. Habitat data from Haila (1983).

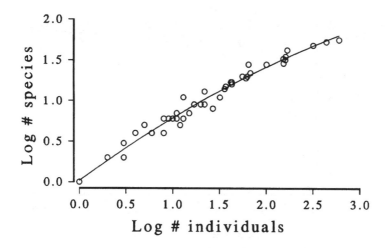

Figure 8.23. Islands with more individuals also have more species. Data from 1979 censuses of Haila *et al.* (1983).

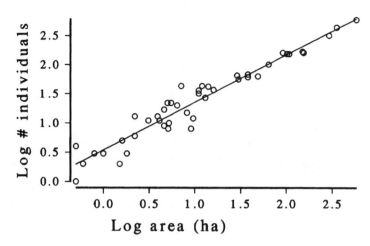

Figure 8.24. The independent variables area and population size are actually not independent at all. Data from Haila *et al.* (1983).

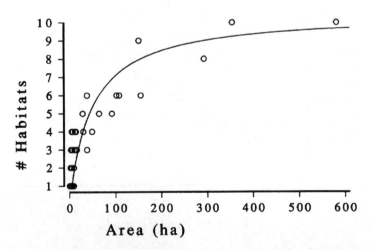

Figure 8.25. The greater the island area, the more habitats it has. Data from Haila (1983).

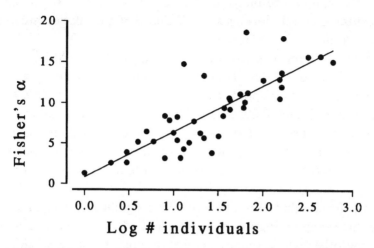

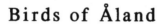

Figure 8.26. Removing diversity's sample-size bias with Fisher's α does not eliminate its relationship to N.

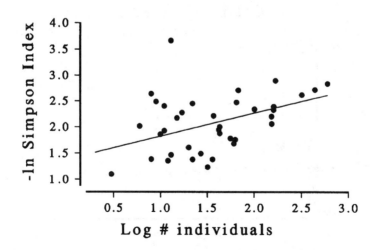

Figure 8.27. Removing diversity's sample-size bias with Simpson's Index also does not eliminate its relationship to N.

als in the sample). Does that mean both α and SI have failed? No. Their job is to take the sample-size bias out of diversity. Once that is accomplished, we still expect a correlation between N and S if the species–area curve is real. Why? Because N correlates with area.

To simplify matters, I now restrict the analysis to α. (Although I could have used SI instead, I follow Taylor *et al.*, 1976, in preferring α.)

The number of habitats predicts α well (Figure 8.28; $R^2 = 0.59$; $p = 10^{-9}$). But so does area (Figure 8.29; $R^2 = 0.59$; $p = 10^{-9}$). Habitat number actually does very slightly better. (The improvement shows in digits of R^2 to the right of those I report, and it lacks statistical significance.) Also, the relationship of N to α has even better statistics (Figure 8.26; $R^2 = 0.68$; $p = 4.3 \times 10^{-12}$).

We can conclude that only one variable is significant here. The residuals from the three graphs (Figures 8.26; 8.28 and 8.29) bear no relationship to either of the other two variables. As an example, Figure 8.30 ($R^2 = 0.016$; $p = 0.42$) shows the scattergram of the residuals of Figure 8.28 against area.

So which variable really matters? To answer that, I think you have to move from statistics to biology. We know α has no sample-size bias. What is left? Either the small islands have fewer habitats or else they have higher extinction rates owing to smaller populations. At this scale, area itself means nothing. It must work through habitats or extinction rates.

Based on the taxon, on the easy accessibility of the islands, and on

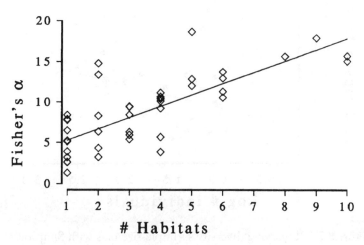

Figure 8.28. Fisher's α also rises with the number of habitats.

Birds of Åland

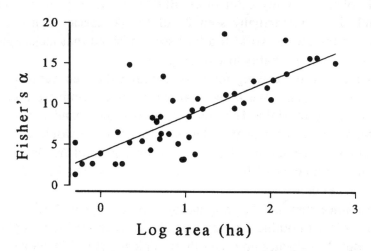

Figure 8.29. Fisher's α also rises with island area.

Birds of Åland

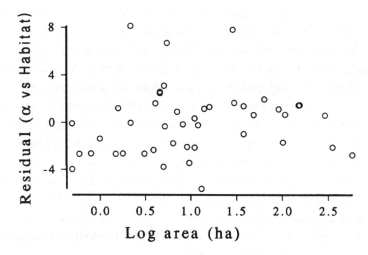

Figure 8.30. Once we use any one of the three variables – population size, area or habitat diversity – to explain Fisher's α, neither of the others is significant. This example shows the failure of area once habitat diversity is accounted for.

Haila's observations, I doubt that extinction rate has much of an effect. Yes, Haila observed many extinctions. But birds fly easily from island to island, and Haila has actually seen 27 of the 80 species flying between islands during the census work! If a bird sees an island that lacks appropriate habitat, it would probably just keep flying.

Habitat must be the driving force determining the true number of bird species on these islands. We know that the birds discriminate among the habitats as defined by Haila. His other censuses show considerable stability in the species lists of most of the islands – not what we would expect of a roiling, random collection of species limited only in total N. On this set of islands, only the number of habitats counts. That number fully determines the species–area curve.

What variance remains for population size to explain? At least with respect to birds, as notable a scholar as David Lack (1969) thought there was none. But the evidence now says there is plenty. Recall (Chapter 6) that birds on British islands and orb-web spiders on the Bahamas provide additional evidence that larger populations have lower extinction rates. In addition, most multiple regression studies of island diversities find that even after habitat variability is accounted for, island size can significantly reduce the unexplained variance. Other things being equal, larger areas mean larger populations.

In one case, the plants of Lake Hjälmaren's islands, one can even conclude that habitat diversity plays no role at all. In Figure 8.31, I show the number of habitats on each island. (Rydin and Borgegård, 1988, identify and determine the areas of ten habitats on these islands.) You can easily see what I found when I analyzed these data. Once an island has two or more habitats, it may have any number of species (among the numbers actually present on these islands). All the islands with only one habitat have few species. That is true. But they also have the smallest areas. Since area does a good job of explaining the entire range of data, we must not introduce a second variable (i.e. habitat diversity) that improves the fit insignificantly. Recall the small size of these islands. Remember too that they fit a line in semi-logarithmic space better than one in log-log space (see early in this chapter). Those facts hint strongly to us that the diversity of these islands depends mostly on their number of individuals.

Nilsson *et al.* (1988) investigate the question elegantly by finding a set of islands for which habitat diversity does not correlate with area, and therefore also not with the number of individuals. On these islands (in Lake Mälaren, Sweden), area correlates significantly with the diversities of

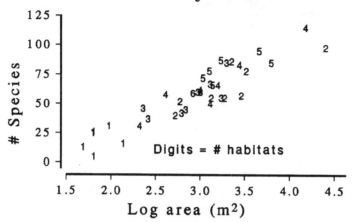

Figure 8.31. Plant diversity on 37 small islands fits island area
well. The numbers show the number of habitats on an
island. Only the islands with 1 habitat have few
species. But these are also the smallest. Data from
Rydin and Borgegård (1988).

plants, land snails, carabid beetles and birds. Habitat diversity does not.
Thus they conclude that area must play an intrinsic role in determining
island diversities.

Although Nilsson *et al.* (1988) are correct for islands in general, we cannot be sure of the importance of area on the islands they studied. Each
island was given a number of sampling sites proportional to its area. In
Figures 8.32 and 8.33 you see the good fit of number of sampling sites to
diversity of snails and carabids respectively. Once I took account of this
relationship, the effect of area disappeared. Nilsson *et al.* provide us with
all the raw data so that we can see the relationship of trap site abundance
to the number of individuals found. Interestingly, although the beetle sample sizes and their number of trap sites correlate well, the same is not true
of the snails. Moreover, in both cases, the abundance of trap sites does the
best job of explaining the variance. Perhaps, after all, these islands do contain some cryptic habitat variability in proportion to their area. As the
authors admit, we ecologists have much to learn about habitat differences
among snails and beetles.

But it's a fine idea to study islands lacking a correlation between area and
habitat diversity. In fact, Simberloff (1976a, b) did just that. But instead of

Lake Mälaren Snails

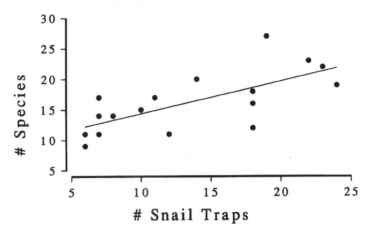

Figure 8.32. The number of species of snails found on islands in Lake Mälaren, Sweden depends on the number of snail trap sites used. $R^2 = 0.49$; $p < 0.002$. Area explains less of the variance and is insignificant as a second variable. Data from Nilsson *et al.* (1988).

Lake Mälaren Carabidae

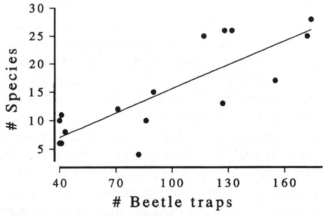

Figure 8.33. The number of species of carabid beetles found on islands in Lake Mälaren, Sweden depends on the number of beetle trap sites used. $R^2 = 0.70$; $p = 3 \times 10^{-5}$. Area explains less of the variance and is insignificant as a second variable. Data from Nilsson *et al.* (1988).

searching for the right archipelago, he made it. Simberloff took a chain saw and actually reduced the size of several mangrove islands by felling trees on the islands' peripheries. Mangrove islands are rather uniform habitats at a scale of many trees. Thus, his treatment did nothing to the habitat diversity of the islands. Nevertheless, the reduction of area resulted in a marked reduction of invertebrate diversity (Figure 8.34). Meanwhile, the control island actually exhibited a small (insignificant) increase in its invertebrate diversity.

Schoener and Schoener (1981) contributed a second experimental demonstration of the importance of area by itself. From a floating dock in Puget Sound, Washington, they suspended formica panels 1 m below the surface of the ocean. The panels had textured undersides allowing many sessile species to colonize them. The panels ranged in size from 6.4 cm² to 6606.4 cm². But they were all made of the same material, so they all had the same habitat diversity.

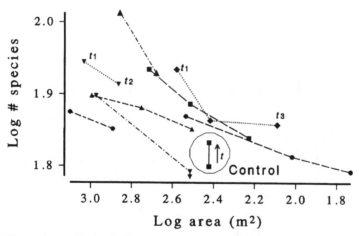

Figure 8.34. Simberloff (1976a, b) showed the effect of island area experimentally. Because these island are mangrove-covered, reducing their areas does not change their habitat diversity. But it does lower their species diversity. In order to parallel time, I reversed the *x*-axis; I included a few *t* values so that you could quickly grasp the flow of time in the graph. The control plot experienced a small increase in diversity between the second and third years. This shows as a vertical line; an arrow to its right points up to indicate the direction of time.

Schoener and Schoener followed the panels for 21 months. A total of about 60 species of sessile invertebrates and one alga settled on them. The fauna included bryozoans, tunicates, sponges, polychaetes, hydroids, molluscs and arthropods. Larger panels usually held more species than smaller ones. I have graphed the average results of weeks 38 and 49 as Figure 8.35. The slope of the regression line through the points from week 49 is 0.215.

Another pattern strongly suggests the importance of population size to island diversity. Remember that Ireland is famous for not having snakes (Jones, 1982). But, tales of St Patrick aside, Ireland is typical. Islands often lack most predators. I can't imagine this comes from lack of suitable habitat. It makes more sense to hypothesize that predator populations, being much smaller than those of their victims, accidentally become extinct with a much higher probability than their victims.

Human diseases supply some of the best evidence that predator population sizes matter. Measles, for example, rarely occurs on islands with fewer than 500 000 people (Bartlett, 1957; Black, 1966). When measles invades such an island population, it wreaks a plague on the people who live there, evokes their immune resistance, and then goes extinct.

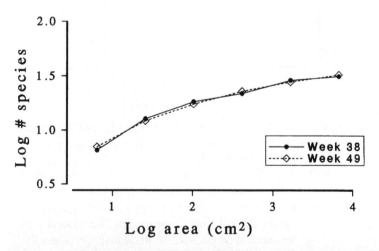

Figure 8.35. Schoener and Schoener (1981) set out formica panels for marine organisms to settle upon. The larger the area of a panel, the more species settled on it.

Population interactions and the chance of extinction

Interactive island biogeography theory claims that extinction rates rise at an accelerating rate when we plot them against diversity. That is, the second derivative of the extinction curve is positive. No 'ifs', 'ands' or 'buts' hedge the reason: more species means a higher rate of competitive extinction. That assertion embroiled island biogeography in more controversy than anyone could have imagined in 1963 (or even 1973).

Today, ecologists know that predation may augment competition in promoting extinctions on islands. Either interaction may increase extinction rates. Let us examine the evidence supporting that statement.

Competition Encouraged by the soundness of the theory and the empirical support it was getting, people began to use it like a forged tool to explain distributions of species on islands. Led intellectually by Jared Diamond, they would point out that the sets of species on islands look as if they have been deterministically filtered by competitive processes. A species of this genus and that, rather than two of one and none of the other. A species of this size and that, rather than two of similar size.

Diamond (1975) proposed the concept of assembly rules. Assembly rules recognize the improbability of finding, on the same depauperate island, species that overlap greatly in their ecological needs. Case (1983) looked at lizards on islands with little or no immigration, and still found evidence of 'assembly'. Lizards with low ecological overlap occurred more often than chance would have predicted. But, other people began asking, where's the null hypothesis, where's the experimental evidence? (Caswell, 1976; Connor and Simberloff, 1979).

The controversy all boils down to the second derivative of the extinction rate curve on islands. Is it zero (i.e. non-interactive)? Or is it positive (i.e. competitive)? But regardless of the way that turns out, the keystone of the theory will remain. The first derivative is positive. The sign of the first derivative does not depend on competition.

Nevertheless, one would like to know **if** competition helps to determine the shape of the extinction rate curve. Are island distributions partly the result of competitive exclusions?

Many thought the easiest way to answer that question was to study island lists of species very carefully. Using a pantheon of computer simulations, Colwell and Winkler (1984) taught us the insurmountable difficulties we could expect if we tried it. Moulton and Pimm (1987) promptly surmounted them. Their success lay in their ability to find a system without the fundamental drawback of all previous work (theoretical and empirical): in their system, all propagules are known.

Moulton and Pimm studied the introduction of foreign bird species to Hawaii. Are you surprised that anybody ever introduced any birds to Hawaii? Is it not paradise already? Woe to us all, few humans can leave well enough alone. From 1860 to 1983, people introduced 49 different bird species. Many of these fly in beauty, but we shall never know the cost to the native avifauna of this unbridled ecological foolishness. Ah well, let us at least learn from our follies.

Moulton and Pimm reasoned thus. If colonists compete seriously, then two species of rather similar size found in the same habitat should be most likely to suffer extinction. Without competitive exclusion, extinct species should be just a random sample of colonists.

They measured many physical properties of the colonists' phenotypes and plotted each species' average in a multidimensional space. Each of its dimensions is a property, so each species occupies one point. If success comes randomly to colonists, then knowing where their point lies should not help us to predict success. But if species that resemble other species have competitive trouble, then the surviving species should be evenly spaced.

Moulton and Pimm measured evenness by connecting the surviving species in the space with a minimum-spanning tree. Such a tree connects all species with a set of lines going from point to point. The lines are never allowed to be redundant. That is, if there are s species, there will be $s - 1$ lines (Figure 8.36). Each is the shortest possible link for a pair of species. The sum of the length of all the lines is the smallest that can link all the points together.

If the species are spaced regularly, then very short branches of the tree will have been rejected by competition. That will have two effects. First, it will make the real trees larger than the random ones. Second, it will reduce the variance of the line lengths. So you should be able to detect evenness. It will produce a larger tree with a smaller variance of line length compared with a random tree.

The mathematics of determining the properties of a random tree are intractable. So, you must use a computer to bootstrap their properties from the actual set of species that have been introduced to an island. For some islands, Pimm and Moulton computed all possible trees of s species selected from the actual set of introductions. (s is the number of surviving species.) For richer islands, where more than 500 trees were possible, they had the computer select 200 at random to represent the properties of a random tree.

Competitive Filtration
of introduced forest birds

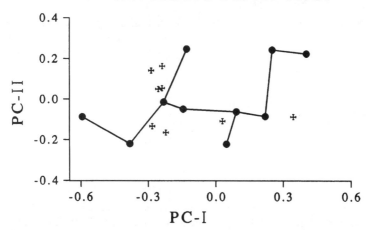

Figure 8.36. The minimum spanning tree for the introduced forest
birds of Oahu. Each point represents a species morphology on two principal component axes. Crosses
are extinct species. Data from Moulton and Pimm
(1987).

On most islands, virtually all the possible least branching trees of forest
birds are smaller and have more variance than the real one (Table 8.2).
Competition had predicted spacing by size and that had happened.
Lockwood *et al.* (1993), and Lockwood and Moulton (1994) got the same
result on the islands of Tahiti and Bermuda.

On the other hand, Moulton and Pimm (1987) also studied the minimum-spanning tree for Hawaiian birds of all habitats combined. The effect
of size sorting disappeared. The minimum-spanning tree has branches of
random length. This, too, competition theory predicts, because birds of
similar size avoid competition if they live in separate habitats.

Predation Exploitative interactions also raise extinction rates. A hint of this
comes from the work of Case and Bolger (1991). They analyzed lizard
population sizes in islands with and without predators (Figure 8.37).
Unquestionably, predators depress those populations. Does this actually
increase extinction rates? From what we know of the effect of small
populations on extinction, I strongly suspect so.

In some cases, we need make no inference. We know with unfortunate
certainty that the brown snake destroyed the avifauna of Guam (Pimm,
1987). Before about 1950, *Boiga irregularis* had not reached Guam. The

Table 8.2. *Minimum-spanning trees based on the morphologies of introduced forest-dwelling passerines are longer and have less variance in branch length than random trees (Moulton and Pimm, 1987)*

Length is measured in arbitrary units in a principal component space. $p\{$Larger$\}$ is the proportion of random trees whose length exceeds that of the real one. $p\{$Smaller$\}$ is the proportion of random trees whose standard deviation is less than that of the real one.

Island	s	Length	$p\{$Larger$\}$	SD	$p\{$Smaller$\}$
Hawaii	5	1.36	7.9×10^{-3}	0.039	3.2×10^{-2}
Kauai	7	1.87	1.5×10^{-2}	0.049	3.0×10^{-3}
Lanai	3	0.95^a	0.5	0.096	0.5
Maui	6	1.50^a	0.14	0.050	0.14
Oahu	10	1.89	3.5×10^{-2}	0.074	0.125

[a] Only a few species have been introduced to Lanai and Maui. So there are very few combinations of species other than the ones actually found on these islands. Lanai has only three others; Maui has six. The tree on Maui has the shortest length of the seven possible.

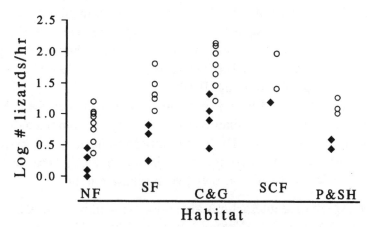

Figure 8.37. Introduced mongoose populations reduce diurnal lizard populations on tropical Pacific islands. Ordinate: lizards seen per hour of census on sunny days by a single investigator. NF, native forest; SF, secondary forest; C&G, clearings and gardens; SCF, sugar cane fields; P&SH, parks and suburban hotels. Redrawn from Case and Bolger (1991).

island had 25 species of birds (7 introduced; 18 native). The snake arrived by accident and began to destoy the avifauna. Species formerly common, disappeared. Seven are extinct and only three – the species that nest away from brown snake habitat – have not declined. Savidge (1987) presents the rest of the evidence that convicts the snake.

It is hard to believe that the Polynesian rat (a climbing nest predator) did not do horrible damage to the avifauna wherever Polynesian man carried it. From New Zealand to Hawaii, roughly half the avifauna disappeared in the wake of Polynesian settlement (Holdaway, 1989; Steadman, 1993); few of these species were hunted by humans.[4]

Direct evidence for the importance of predation comes from experiments performed by Schoener (1986). He introduced spiders (*Metapeira datona*) to some small islands in the Bahamas. Some of these already had lizards, and some did not. The lizards prey on spiders (among other things). Schoener showed that spiders on an island with lizards had much less chance of avoiding extinction.

The combination of interactions and area European rabbits (*Oryctolagus cuniculus*) are often pests on islands. Over 2000 yeas ago, Strabo recorded the plea of Balearic Islanders for help from the Roman army in getting rid of European rabbits (see Flux, 1993, for references). Thus, you may be shocked to discover that people deliberately introduce this misery to island after island around the world; Flux and Fullagar (1992) list 800 such islands.

Usually, almost as soon as the introduction has succeeded, people look for a way to undo it. Flux (1993) found data for 607 islands which he could use to compare the success of various methods to cause the rabbit's extinction. With so many islands involved, he could even partial out the effect of area too.

People use three methods in their usually futile attempts to exterminate rabbits. They try to kill them directly (traps, poison or shooting). They introduce a rabbit exploiter (cats, myxoma virus). They introduce a competitor (hares, *Lepus* spp.). (Actually, the last is rather accidental, and, although it works, only a biologist would have realized what was going on.) Flux had enough data to compare these methods on islands of widely varying area. They all work best on small islands. Table 8.3 shows the data for exploiter and competitor control.

---

[4] My favorite species name attaches to a pile of subfossil parrot remains from the Marquesas Islands: *Vini vidivinci*, the conquered lorikeet (Steadman and Zarrielo, 1987). I propose that the international rules of zoological nomenclature be amended to protect and preserve that name in perpetuity. (Apologies to Latin scholars. The name of the lorikeet genus, *Vini*, antedates by generations its discovery on the Marquesas. So, the species could not, alas, get the genus name *Veni*.)

Table 8.3. *Efficiency of extinction of rabbits from islands by exploiters or competitors. Interactions more readily exterminate this species from smaller islands. Data are percentages extinct (number of islands)*

	Area (ha)			
	$0–10^2$	to 10^3	to 10^4	$>10^4$
Exploiters	36 (39)	15 (41)	2.5 (79)	0 (80)
Competitors	100 (6)	50 (26)	25 (28)	4.4 (45)

Adapted from Flux (1993).

A remarkable set of data confirming the hare effect comes from the Netherlands. Its Wadden Sea Islands, an archipelago of 49 islands, contains but one habitat, sand dunes. Nevertheless the interaction between area and competition remains. Seventeen islands larger than 1000 ha have both hares and rabbits. Only two between 100 and 1000 ha do, and no island less than 100 ha has both species (Flux, 1993). Yet, except for islands less than 50 ha (which lack hares altogether), rabbits and hares occur alone on islands in each size class.

Distance effect

According to MacArthur and Wilson, islands with non-zero immigration rates and varying degrees of isolation should have different immigration rate curves. Less isolated islands should have higher immigration rate curves, and therefore higher diversities (Figure 8.38). MacArthur and Wilson believed that distance from the mainland pool measures isolation well.

Lack (1969) objected, at least for birds. He believed that to know enough to predict bird diversity on an island, you need only determine how many habitats it has. Its degree of isolation does not matter.

But Lack's data themselves suggest he was wrong. For example, he noted that the Madeira Islands cover less area but lie closer to the mainland than the Azores. If area works alone to determine diversity by sampling habitats, then the Azores should have more habitats, and so, more species. Yet the Azores have fewer species of birds, flowering plants, butterflies, beetles, and grasshoppers. Lack even points out that more potential avian immigrants have been seen on the Madeiras (69 species) than on the Azores (50 species). But instead of concluding that distance itself is playing a role, he concluded the opposite. He decided that all those extra plant species and

Diversity on Islands:
Consequences of greater isolation

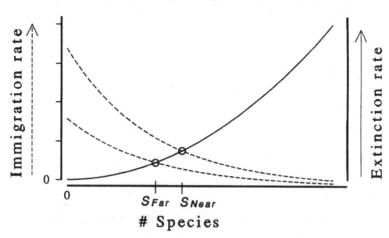

Figure 8.38. Islands farther from the sources of species diversity
have lower immigration rate curves, so they have
fewer species.

invertebrate species on the Madeiras provide more habitat complexity for
birds. He does not address the cause of those richer associations of plants
and invertebrates in the first place.

Lack (1970) himself found the distance effect among hummingbirds in
the West Indies. And both Ricklefs (1977) and Reed (1987) showed that it
exists in the very data sets Lack (1976) had written about, but had
neglected to analyze statistically. Figure 8.39 shows that – after regression
fits island area to the diversity of Bahama's resident birds – distance
explains much of the remaining variance. Reed also points out that in
Lack's earlier work, he had emphasized the importance of isolation to bird
diversity on British islands.

Williamson (1981) synthesized the first sort of evidence brought to bear
on the distance question. The species–area curves of data sets that come
from near islands usually lie above those from far islands. His graph of
these data (from non-marine breeding birds of tropical and subtropical
islands) exhausts the available data and encompasses islands whose areas
range from 5 to 600 000 km². Islands farther than 300 km from any substantial source pool have smaller diversities than islands that are closer.

Even more interesting is an exception (Williamson, 1981). The ferns of
the Azores and the Channel Islands do not fit the rule. The Azores are out

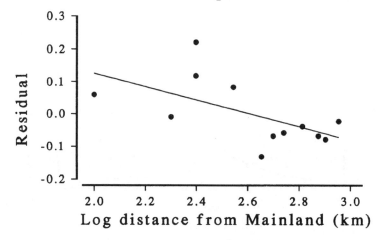

Figure 8.39. Distance explains a significant amount of the variance
remaining after log diversity is fit to log area (p =
0.043). Data from Lack (1976); concept from Reed
(1987).

in the middle of the Atlantic, far from a source of colonists. On the other
hand, the Channel Islands lie just off the coast of France. But the ferns of
the two archipelagos lie on the same species–area curve.

At the same time, the non-marine birds of the Azores and the Channel
Islands follow the rule. The Azores have far fewer species for their areas
than do the Channel Islands.

The key to understanding this exception is simple. Distance *per se* plays
no role in the theory of island biogeography. The real variable is immigration rate. Distance is merely a stand-in, a surrogate variable designed to
quantify isolation and immigration. It does that job well for birds. But
ferns reproduce using light spores capable of being carried over long distances by the wind. Further, those spores pay virtually no metabolic costs.
They are like science-fictional interstellar travelers riding in suspended ani-
mation. So, when they get blown out to sea they have a better chance than
a bird to be healthy if ever they arrive at an island. And spores are tiny,
produced in great abundance compared to baby birds. Thus, the immigration rate of a species of fern is not well measured by distance from the
mainland (Williamson, 1981). Ferns can get everywhere on the face of the
Earth. If you do not immediately agree with that, consider one implication

of the work of Compton *et al.* (1989), Lawton (1984) and Winterbourn (1987) on fern-eating arthropods. They examined those arthropods on one single species of fern (*Pteridium aquilinum*) in Britain, New Guinea, New Mexico, New Zealand, South Africa and Hawaii. People did not introduce this fern to any of these places. It came on its own. (In the next chapter, I discuss the species–area curve that comes from this work.)

Wilcox (1978) provides confirmation that immigration rate depends on the dispersal ability of the taxon and not just the distance from the mainland. He calculated z separately for the birds, bats, reptiles–amphibians and terrestrial mammals in a set of 19 West Indian islands. The birds and bats, superior to the others in dispersal abilities, each had a z-value of 0.24. But the herptiles' z is 0.38 and that of the land mammals is 0.48.

Lomolino (1994) holds the taxon and the species pool nearly constant and studies the effect of passage difficulty. Both the Drummond Archipelago (in Lake Huron) and islands in the middle of Lake Michigan have stable ice bridges to their respective mainlands. They are as far away as 36 km from the mainland. Islands along the coast of Maine and islands in the St Lawrence River look no more isolated on a map. In fact, they are all within 9 km of their coast. But they are separated from their mainland by strong currents and unstable ice bridges. That makes a big difference to non-volant mammals. The islands with strong currents and unreliable ice bridges have fewer mammal species for their area and distance than the others. Their true degree of isolation has more to do with passage difficulty than the distance to the coast.

Diamond (1972) improved upon the idea of separating islands into those nearer and those farther than some *ad hoc* distance from the source. He used a more continous, more analyzable and less arbitrary variable. He tallied the resident, lowland bird species of tropical islands more than 500 km from New Guinea. He then calculated the percentage of such species on the island compared to the number expected from a similar-sized island less than 500 km away. This statistic is the percentage saturation of the island. New Guinea is the main source of colonists for these islands. So, the farther from New Guinea lies the island, the lower should be its immigration rate curve, and the lower also should be its percentage saturation.

Diamond's data unquestionably agree with the prediction. But the percentage saturation statistic is not reliable. It hides a problem that could easily have produced the results even without an isolation effect. I will explain the problem, correct it, and show you that even a good statistic shows that the isolation effect is real.

First we need to be clear about our goal. We want to see whether a series of islands at different distances from the source pool, but of the same size, have diversities inversely related to their distance. But isolated islands tend to be small. And it is hard to find a series of similar-sized islands at varying distances from a mainland. So, to get enough data, we must actually find a way to use islands of many sizes. The trick is to look at their z-values.

Look at Figure 8.40. On it you will see an imaginary series of three islands of the same size but different distances from the source. The closest one is least depressed below the mainland species–area curve. If there were many islands of varying size, we would expect them to fall on a straight line of slope z converging on the source point. So, the line that connects an island to the source point yields that island's estimate of z. Also, the closest island yields the smallest estimate of z because it has the shallowest slope of the three.

Imagine now a series of islands of similar isolation, but different size. We expect them all to fall on a straight line of slope z convergent with the source point. Thus, regardless of their area, they should share a z-value. If we were to measure an island's z, we would therefore have an area-independent measure of its depression below the mainland species–area curve. The

Effect of Island Distance

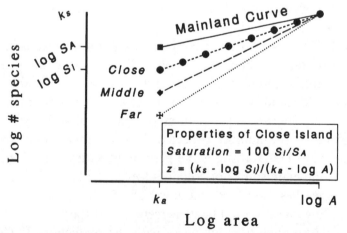

Figure 8.40. An idealized set of island and mainland diversities to explain how z varies with isolation. See text for details. The z value of any single island is estimated by the slope of the line connecting it to its source pool.

larger the z-value, the more rotated-downward is the species–area curve on which the island lies.

On the other hand, percentage saturation does not yield an area-independent measure of depression. For islands on the same species–area curve, percentage saturation declines as area increases. Here is a quick algebraic proof of that statement.

Let there be a source and an island and let

k_s be the log of the number of species in the source pool
k_a be the log of the area of the entire source
z_s be the z-value within the source
z_i be the z-value of the island
$\log A$ be the log of the area of the island
$\log S_i$ be the log of the number of species on the island
$\log S_A$ be the log of the number of species in an area A of the source.

By definition,

$$z_i = (k_s - \log S_i)/(k_a - \log A) \tag{8.14a}$$
$$z_s = (k_s - \log S_A)/(k_a - \log A) \tag{8.14b}$$

I combined the latter two definitions by subtracting (8.14a) from (8.14b). Then I manipulated the combination. This yields

$$\log S_i - \log S_A = (z_s - z_i)(k_a - \log A) \tag{8.15}$$

But,

$$\log S_i - \log S_A = \log (S_i / S_A) \tag{8.16}$$

And,

$$\log (S_i / S_A) = \text{logarithm of the proportional saturation} \tag{8.17}$$

By inspecting Equation 8.17 you will see that saturation does depend on A, the area of the island. As A grows, the distance between S_A and S_i declines and saturation increases. (The log of a proportion is negative.) Precisely the same conclusion results if saturation is computed by comparing far islands with near ones (as Diamond did). This is unacceptable behavior in the parameter, particularly as island size and distance are usually negatively correlated.

Since z is area-insensitive, we can use it without modification to determine if isolation really does reduce diversity. Unfortunately, however, we must first dispose of one more complication.

As soon as an island 'joins' an archipelago, its isolation gets compromised. The archipelago generates its own speciation events, in which the island is bound to participate. And it also gets its share of the speciation events that occur on its sisters. If we got a low z for a small island in a distant archipelago, we couldn't be sure whether the distance hypothesis had erred or the small island's overabundance of species came from interactions with other islands in the archipelago.

Adler (1992) solved this problem by analyzing the birds of tropical Pacific archipelagos, instead of single islands. He summed the areas of all islands in each archipelago to get a joint area for each. He combined the bird lists of each archipelago's separate islands to get its joint diversity. He also measured the distance of each to the nearest larger land and to its nearest mainland source. The set of archipelagos generates a typical species–area curve with the steep z-value of 0.54 (Figure 8.41).

Adler and I restudied his data base to test the distance hypothesis. We calculated the z-value of each archipelago using New Guinea's area and diversity as the standard. (This does not imply that all immigrants to all archipelagos came from New Guinea. It merely assumes that New Guinea has a typical diversity for large tropical land masses in the region.) Figure 8.42 shows the result. The more isolated the archipelago, the larger the z-value. The figure distinguishes between archipelagos with endemics and

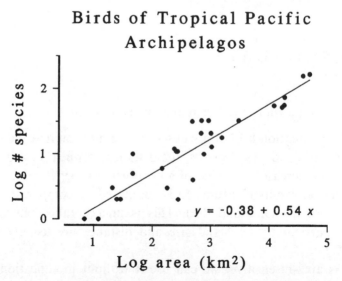

Figure 8.41. The species–area curve for birds of archipelagos in the tropical Pacific. Data from Adler (1992).

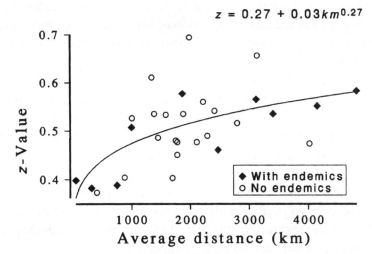

Figure 8.42. Isolated tropical Pacific archipelagos have higher z-values than less remote ones. Data from Adler (1992), and Rosenzweig and Adler (unpublished). The regression line comes from a true non-linear form and is shown as the subtitle.

those without. But the non-linear regression line is calculated from the entire data set. Notice that its intercept, 0.27, is the value we usually associate with island species–area curves. Thus, nearby archipelagos (were any in the sample) would have the 'characteristic' island z-value. But distant archipelagos have higher z-values.

Schoener (1976) studied bird diversity in a set of archipelagos that overlaps considerably with Adler's. Yet he found a strong negative correlation between z and distance. There is no contradiction between Schoener's result and ours. Each of his z's measures the slope of the set of islands within an archipelago. Each of ours ignores the individual islands and measures the z between the entire archipelago and New Guinea. Schoener's result remains an interesting phenomenon that would reward confirmation in other systems, and further study. But it does not contradict ours.

So, Diamond's conclusion was correct after all. Birds of tropical Pacific Islands do lose diversity if their island is far away from its source pool.

Vuilleumier (1970) gives us another case of the importance of isolation to diversity. He examined the birds of the páramo islands of Ecuador, Columbia, Peru and Venezuela. Páramo is a cool, high montane biome that occurs in the Andes surrounded by other biomes. The avifaunas of these islands show a typical species–area relationship. Using the percentage-saturation statistic, Vuilleumier also showed that páramo bird diversity decreased as the páramo found itself farther from the largest, richest source of these birds in Ecuador.

Later, in a reanalysis, Vuilleumier and Simberloff (1980) took all the force out of the earlier paper. They did not say it was wrong, only that other hypotheses existed that were consonant with the results. But that is always true. The point is to make a prediction and test it. MacArthur and Wilson (1963) made the prediction; Vuilleumier tested it.

I believe that the insecurity of Vuilleumier and Simberloff was largely a sign of the times. It had become as fashionable then to doubt MacArthur's work as it had been to praise it a decade earlier. Yet now, we do have good cause to distrust the saturation statistic. Does Vuilleumier's conclusion hold up if we look at z-values instead of saturation?

Vuilleumier and Simberloff also suggested the importance of looking at the size of the páramo islands during the Pleistocene. After all, it's been but a few thousand years since the glaciers retreated. During the Pleistocene, many of today's isolates were joined into larger páramos. And, to this day, these pieces of what were once larger páramos remain poorly isolated from each other.

Using their reconstructions of these prehistoric areas, I graphed the species–area curve of the páramo birds (Figure 8.43). Then, I calculated the z-values. These do increase with distance from the source as predicted (Figure 8.44). So, even with a better data set, and even after we look at z-values instead of percentage saturation, the role of distance remains. The farther away an island from its source of colonization, the fewer species it is likely to hold.

On Figure 8.44, I plotted the areas of the páramos instead of just dots. I fitted the polynomial curve to the large páramos only. (Vuilleumier defines these as islands larger than 200 km^2.) That allows you to see at a glance which islands deviate most from the pattern. Small islands far from Ecuador fall well below the curve. These small páramos are much closer to other large ones than to the Ecuadorian source. Presumably, they can get a few colonists from their closer neighbors, thus reducing their z-values.

Vascular plants on British Islands give us one more example of the growth of z with island isolation. Figure 8.45 shows z for the islands studied by Johnson and Simberloff (1974). Despite the significance of this regression ($p < 0.001$), it is noisy. A good bit of the noise comes from

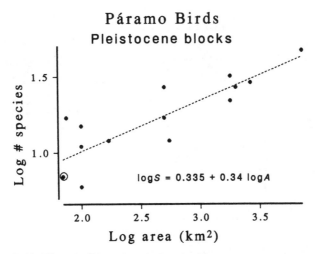

Figure 8.43. The species–area curve for páramo birds. Páramos are
   islands of subalpine vegetation high in the equatorial
   Andes. They have many endemic bird species. In this
   graph, their areas come from reconstructions of the
   extent of the páramo blocks at the end of the
   Pleistocene. Data from Vuilleumier and Simberloff
   (1980).

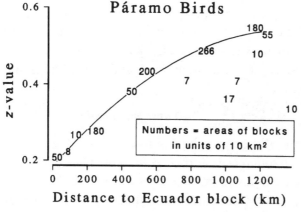

Figure 8.44. The more isolated a páramo block from Ecuador, the
   larger its *z* value. The Ecuador block is the largest
   and the presumed ultimate source for other blocks.
   Some smaller blocks lie close to other larger ones and
   thus show shallower *z* values. They receive some
   species from these nearer blocks, and are not as isolated as they would be without the stepping stones to
   enhance their immigration rates. Data from
   Vuilleumier and Simberloff (1980).

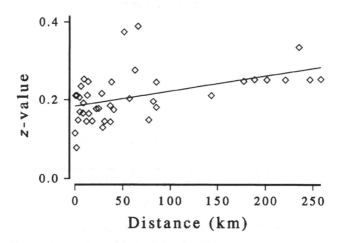

Figure 8.45. The more isolated the island, the larger its *z* value. Data from Johnson and Simberloff (1974) based on plants of British islands.

islands clustered in archipelagos like the Shetlands and especially the Orkneys. Islands in such situations are simply not as isolated as their distance from Great Britain suggests. We need to develop a statistic better than mere distance to summarize the real degree of an island's isolation.

Turnover on islands

MacArthur and Wilson explained different island diversities by understanding what can cause differences in their equilibria. The core of their theory is that island biotas are in a dynamic steady state, held below the diversity of mainland source pools by extinction rates that counterbalance immigration rates. Data from the aftermath of a monumental volcanic eruption support that.

Krakatoa, a volcanic island in Indonesia, literally blew up in 1883. The explosion obliterated its biota. Subsequent censuses tracked its recovery. Immigration, the only source of species, rapidly built back the island's diversity. Within decades, the island returned to a level diversity. But that diversity is less than the source pool's.

Another clue to the validity of island biogeography theory comes from studies of turnover. Island biogeography theory cannot be relevant if species go extinct on a different time scale from that on which they immigrate. How then could the rate processes balance? What we expect instead is some species entering and some leaving an island. And that is what we find. For example, Simberloff (1976a, b) worked with tiny mangrove islands in Florida. He estimated that turnover amounts to about 1.5 species per year.

Other studies confirm the presence of significant turnover. Repeated censuses of both plants (Abbott and Black, 1980) and birds (Diamond and May, 1977) tell us that turnover is quite high. Abbott and Black censused 76 limestone islets near Perth, Australia. Each islet was censused 2, 3 or 4 times in different years. Some of the islands (29 – tending strongly to small area) remained unvegetated throughout the study (see Figure 2.7). But 47 had at least one species. Despite the small number of censuses, the species composition of 34 of these 47 islands varied from year to year. The bird story is similar. But, probably because of a greater number of censuses, it is even more conclusive. Each of the 16 British bird islands were censused at least six and as many as 49 times (Tracy and George, 1992). Every one of them showed some turnover (Pimm *et al.*, 1988).

Moreover, rates of immigration and extinction have the same order of magnitude. Clark and Rosenzweig (1994), and Rosenzweig and Clark (1994) developed maximum-likelihood estimators to measure these rates, even from irregularly spaced censuses. On the plant islets of Australia, the immigration probability of each species tends to exceed its extinction probability. For example on Green Island. (24 species recorded in four censuses), the average plant species immigrates three times in 10 years and becomes extinct once.

The reverse holds for the British bird islands. I could estimate extinction and immigration probabilities for 39 bird species-island combinations on three UK islands. The average bird species immigrates ten times in 77 years and becomes extinct about 34 times.

But the bird calculations almost certainly overestimate extinction because they exclude the most stable species-island combinations. Including these prevents the calculation of separate values for each species. But it results in the following estimates for the 84 species–island combinations: average immigration probability per species per year, 0.0073; average extinction probability, 0.0078. That indicates almost identical immigration and extinction rates, and agrees with the proposition that the rates share their order of magnitude.

Williamson (1983), from whose data I compiled the Skokholm Island. statistics, deems their turnover ecologically trivial, but I respectfully dis-

agree. All but five of the 30 species recorded on Skokholm became extinct
at least once in the sample interval. And one of those five was reduced to a
single breeding pair during one of the census years. He also points out that
many of the changes paralleled population changes on the mainland. But
that doesn't contradict the theory of island biogeography. That theory may
assume the rest of the ecological world holds constant, but no one believes
it. Instead, we introduce the assumption to build an abstraction, a model.
The model contains some variables, but not all real variables. Thus we try
to isolate and assess the influence of the variables dealt with in the model.
Such tactics may not always work, but we do not make simplifying assumptions to claim there are no other variables.

Testing the steady state

The theory makes another prediction: As diversity increases, so does extinction rate, but immigration rate declines. I found enough data in Abbott and
Black (1980) to test that. Twenty-two islands, censused three or four times,
showed some variation in diversity. Of these, 14 had $dE/dS > 0$, and 18 had
$dI/dS < 0$ as predicted (Figure 8.46). Assuming that the random probability
of a positive derivative is 0.5, the joint binomial probability of getting the
two numbers (18, 14) or ones even farther from the numbers (11, 11) is
3.1×10^{-4}. Of course, even longer runs of censuses should show even closer
correspondence to the predictions.

   Using field experiments, Kenneth Crowell (1973, 1986), a student of
MacArthur's, and Daniel Simberloff, a student of Wilson's, set about independently to test the notion of the dynamic steady state. Crowell worked
with small mammals on islands in Jericho Bay, Maine. Simberloff worked
with invertebrates in Florida's Ten Thousand Keys. Otherwise, their strategies were similar. Survey the islands. Then push their biotas away from the
state in which you find them. Then keep watch to see if they return.

   Crowell began first, in the early 1960s. Because he worked with small
mammals, his work took a long time and dealt with very few species. But
he could and did do the experiment of adding missing species to see if they
would become extinct. Levins and Heatwole (1973) did the same with
lizards. Their results were the same. Species not found on an island usually
do not survive there after they are introduced experimentally.

   Crowell also knows more about the ecological details of his subjects than
anyone else does about theirs. He has their breeding records. He watches
their populations ebb and flow. He monitors their habitat distributions.

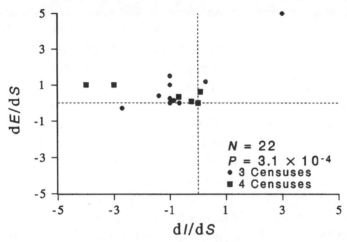

Figure 8.46. The equilibrium theory of island diversity predicts
that data should fall in the upper left quadrant of this
space. There, immigration falls with diversity and
extinction rises. Data from Abbott (1977) and Abbott
and Black (1980). Only 16 points are visible because
some points represent repeated values.

Yet, perhaps because of their large data set and their almost godlike
influence on the fauna – they seemed to me like the incarnation of Noah's
flood – the experiments of Simberloff and Wilson have attracted the most
attention. Careful choice of experimental organisms also allowed them to
start second and report first.

I shall never forget the glee with which Robert MacArthur described the
experimental technique. Whole islands were enveloped in a plastic mem-
brane by a professional exterminator and defaunated with a cloud of insecticide (Simberloff and Wilson, 1969). The dose of insecticide had to be carefully adjusted to avoid harming the plants. The exterminator said he'd
never had so much fun in his life. Crowell had done the same to the mammals on an island in Maine, but accomplished it with mere rat poison.
Low-tech.

Simberloff and Wilson's experiments worked. Islands rapidly regained
their invertebrate diversities. Islands that were richer before the defaunation
returned to a richer state after it. Poorer islands got poor again. Moreover,

the actual lists of species on islands did not recur. The new faunas were about as rich as the old but had different species. That is just what you'd expect of a dynamic process whose state – its diversity – is determined, but whose components – its species – are somewhat unpredictable. When you boil water for a few minutes, you don't expect to be able to predict exactly which molecules will rise from the pot. But you do want to be able to predict how much liquid will be driven off.

On the other hand, we biologists should never forget that we work with complex, evolved, living, adaptable organisms. Not water molecules. Perhaps we cannot predict with certainty exactly which species will remain on an island. But the process is not so random as to keep us from predicting any trends. We know, for example, that predators are more susceptible to elimination. So are rare species. (See previous sections.)

Another of Simberloff and Wilson's observations should now make sense to you. Island faunas tended to overshoot their equilibria. If the theory of island biogeography is the explanation, we must remember that some species – those with higher immigration rates – will tend to arrive first. We also must remember that extinction by interaction takes time. Thus we expect to see an intermediate time when both early arrivers ultimately doomed to extinction and late arrivers marked for interactive success will be present. At this time, the fauna will have overshot its equilibrium. But extinction should bring it back down.

Please remember the idea that, because competition may work slowly compared to immigration, biotas can get more diverse than their equilibrium. This idea will resurface in Chapter 11 and give us part of the explanation for the disturbance pattern.

Lessons from some islands away from equilibrium

MacArthur and Wilson assumed that most island diversities are near equilibrium. Their assumption does not constrain us to the degree some think. You often hear how equilibrium considerations are old-fashioned and silly because few systems are at equilibrium. But we need not assume that systems are at their equilibria. Studying equilibria is worthwhile even if systems are in a dynamic steady state or oscillate regularly.

Two circumstances do attenuate the value of equilibrium studies. The first is strange attractors. Systems governed by strange attractors spend much time far from their equilibria. They may often fluctuate over orders of magnitude in such wild fashion that their dynamics are known as 'chaos'. Equilibria in chaotic systems may not be as useful to study as the rearing of dodos.

Yet island biotas do not seem to fluctuate violently (e.g. Abbott and Black, 1980; Williamson, 1981; Pimm *et al.*, 1988). If chaotic processes influence them, it must be on such a vast time scale that the average island has plenty of time to repair the damage and be governed by gentler and shorter-term processes.

Relying on equilibria causes a second difficulty if a mainland area gets isolated and thus becomes an island. Its new equilibrium will be less than its old, but the island may not achieve that new equilibrium for quite a while. If we predict the island's diversity and visit it soon after it gets isolated, we will find far too many species. For some taxa, the word 'soon' may include 10 000 years!

Brown (1971) examined such a case in the southwestern USA (see Chapter 6). There, small quadrupedal mammals got marooned on isolated mountaintops by the warming and drying that occurred after the retreat of the Wisconsin ice mass (*c.* 10^4 years ago). Immigration of a mammalian propagule practically requires delivery by stork. So we can guess that propagules immigrate to such an island with the same probability as ten square blocks of New York City spontaneously and simultaneously bursting into flame. Don't wait around. (But the probability may actually be greater than zero: Davis and Dunford, 1987.)

With virtually no immigration – and keeping in mind that all species face eventual extinction – the mammals on the mountaintops have an equilibrium diversity very close to zero. But every one of these mountaintops has some species. None of them has had enough time to reach its equilibrium.

Even among these non-equilibrial islands, we observe a species–area curve. And even here we can learn from dynamical biogeography theory how to explain it.

In this case, larger areas do not have more habitats; the areas were all selected to be mesic mountaintops. But larger areas do have larger populations. And larger populations do reduce extinction rates. Hence, smaller areas move more quickly to the near-zero-species equilibrium that all of them share. If we return in 1 Myr (or so), all mountaintops may well have lost all their small mammals. But for now, the different speeds of approach yield a species–area curve.

Please realize that nothing about a mountaintop *per se* keeps its biota away from equilibrium. Mammals on mountaintops have not reached equilibrium because of their low extinction rates and infinitesimal rates of immigration. Plant assemblages on mountaintops, having easier access, do have equilibrial properties (Riebesell, 1982).

Recall that MacArthur and Wilson predicted the shape of extinction curves for island biogeography. They deduced that these curves ought to be concave upward: the more species, the greater the extinction rate per species. We have seen in Chapter 6 that mammal data from non-equilibrium, post-Pleistocene islands in the USA, Indonesia and Malaysia support that prediction. We also recall from the same chapter that the non-equilibrium islands of the Sea of Cortez allowed Wilcox (1978) to calculate extinction rates of lizards.

Some ecologists interpret non-equilibrium archipelagos as evidence against the theory of island biogeography. We now see that the opposite is true. They teach us that the dynamic view of diversity has great power and flexibility. And they also give us a valuable look at extinction rates.

The 'contradictions' in real turnover rates

The theory of island biogeography inspired considerable activity. Not all of the results of that activity claimed to support the theory. In this section, I will re-examine three prominent studies in the light of the previous parts of the book, and ask whether they remain a cause for concern.

1. Plants on islands in Western Australia. Abbott and his colleagues (Abbott, 1977; Abbott and Black, 1980) measured the known plant extinctions and immigrations on 49 islands off the western coast of Australia. The 49 islands were censused repeatedly (two, three, or four times from 1956 to 1978) at sporadic intervals (1–19 years). By comparing lists, they determined all the apparent immigrations and extinctions.

These data afford several opportunities to test the theory of island biogeography. Some of these succeed and some appear to fail.

Abbott used the numbers to estimate extinction and immigration rates. But he warned that an unknown number of species could have become extinct and immigrated repeatedly during intervals longer than a year. Even a species present at two censuses separated by only 1 year could have gone extinct and then reimmigrated. So, Abbott's data reflect minimum rates of turnover. Actual rates may be much, much higher. Diamond and May (1977) make exactly the same point and develop some mathematical machinery to emphasize it. Clark and Rosenzweig (1994) give formulas to estimate the real rates. As we shall see, actual rates probably do not even have the same rankings as measured rates. Those that are relatively high in Abbott's table may be the lowest actual, relative rates.

Abbott's islands follow the usual species–area curve (Figure 2.7; $z \approx 0.34$) albeit over an heroic range of areas. What data do we need from them to test MacArthur and Wilson's theory? We need total instantaneous extinction rate and total instantaneous immigration rate. (Note: Abbott calculated rates per species.) These should match each other.

But recall two other predictions:

- The larger the area of an island, the lower its extinction rate curve in the theory. Hence, turnover at equilibrium diversity should decline with island area (Figure 8.20).
- The larger the pool of species from which an island draws its immigrants, the higher its immigration rate curve. Hence, turnover at equilibrium diversity should increase with pool size (Figure 8.47).

Extinctions and immigrations in the actual data occur during 16 or 19 years, so they do not furnish instantaneous rates. Moreover, island extinctions and immigrations can occur again and again to the same species. So the data are not like data of global extinction taken from the fossil record.

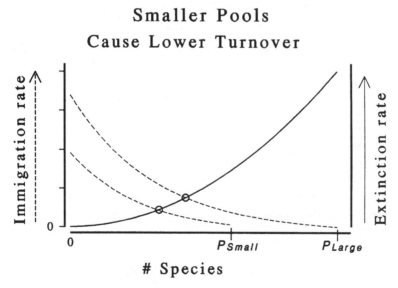

Figure 8.47. Islands drawing immigrants from depauperate source pools have fewer species and lower turnover rates at steady state.

They do not permit a reconstruction of instantaneous rates (as in Rosenzweig and Vetault, 1992). But even net immigration and extinction rates should follow the first prediction of the theory. They should balance.

I calculated net rates simply by dividing the number of extinctions (or immigrations) by the time interval. Sure enough, as Abbott pointed out, these rates tend to match each other (Figure 8.48).

I calculated net turnover rates by taking the average of net extinction and net immigration. Turnover rates show a significantly positive relationship with pool size, as theory predicts (Figure 8.49). However, the greater the area, the higher the net turnover rate (Figure 8.50). This relationship appears to contradict MacArthur and Wilson's theory. Their theory predicts a significant **negative** correlation.

Data that we collect to test a theory sometimes differ subtly but crucially from those we need. That explains the contradiction in the previous paragraph. We used net turnover rates, although the theory predicts gross turnover rates. Net rates differ in a decisive way and mislead us, as we now shall see.

Notice that the relationship of species diversity to net turnover is also significantly positive (Figure 8.51). MacArthur and Wilson's theory does not

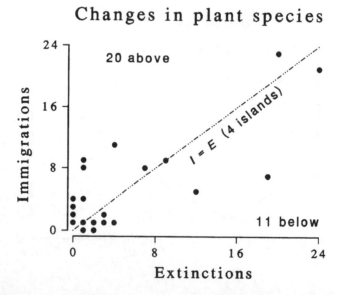

Figure 8.48. Immigration and extinction rates resemble each other for plants of 35 Australian islands. Data from Abbott (1977) and Abbott and Black (1980).

Plant Species

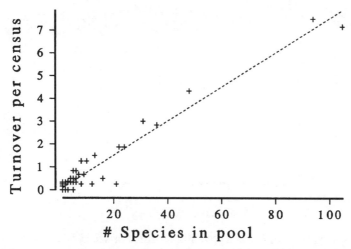

Figure 8.49. Islands on which more species have been recorded at least once have higher rates of net species turnover per census. Data from Abbott (1977) and Abbott and Black (1980).

Plant Species

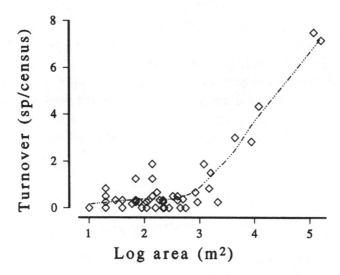

Figure 8.50. Larger islands have higher net turnover – in apparent contradiction to the prediction of MacArthur and Wilson (1967). Data from Abbott (1977) and Abbott and Black (1980). Lowess regression.

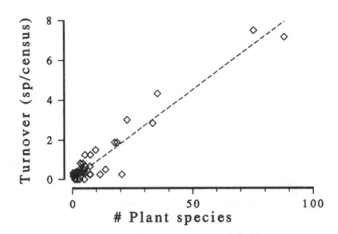

Figure 8.51. Richer islands have higher rates of species turnover.
Data from Abbott (1977) and Abbott and Black
(1980).

predict that either. The culprit is the species–area relationship. Because of
it, area and diversity have the same relationship to net turnover.

Imagine a single island whose diversity is 12 species when first censused.
Its maximum net extinction rate 16 years later (at census 2) is 12/16 = 0.75
species per yr. But there is no such maximum for the instantaneous rate of
extinction! It can be infinite even if equilibrium diversity is only 12 species.
Even the gross rate for annual censuses can be much higher than 0.75. The
12 species may each go extinct and reimmigrate 15 times, yielding a maximum of 180/16 = 11.25. And many other species in the pool may appear on
the island only between censuses, further adding to the true rate.

Let's look at a real case. Island 38 was censused four times:

Year	1956	1975	1977	1978
No. of species	13	19	18	20
No. of extinctions	–	0	2	2
No. of immigrations	–	6	1	4

Altogether, 22 species reproduced on this island at least during one of the
years.

At first glance it looks as if this is a fairly stable island with only four
extinctions in 22 years. Even if we recognize that it is better to treat the
data as covering only three years of potential extinctions (1975, 1976, 1978),

the extinction rate is only 1.33 species per year. Since diversity averages 17.5 species, the rate per species appears to be 0.076 per year. But, once we take hidden turnover into account, we discover that this island is probably in turmoil. The likelihood estimates of its δ (disappearance rate) peak strongly at about 0.10 to 0.15 (Figure 8.52). But there could be many hidden extinctions. So, the data give very little idea of the true immigration rate. In fact, the most likely estimate of the true μ–value is 1!

Island 38 is a small rock in a corner of a sheltered bay of a larger island (Abbott, personal communication). It has an area of only 140 m². Its surface sits above sea level, so it is protected from turbulence. But its summers are long and dry. Perhaps that is why its statistics say that most of its plants vanish annually and have to recolonize the place.

In Figure 8.53, I plotted the net extinction rate curve for a large island and a small one. The large one's net extinction curve is less steep over low diversities. But its asymptote must be higher because its numerator is its higher diversity. That is why large islands with many species have higher net turnover rates compared to small islands with few species.

2. Birds on islands in Panama. Wright (1985) conducted a careful study of bird species on six small islands in Gatun Lake, Panama. The islands

Island 38

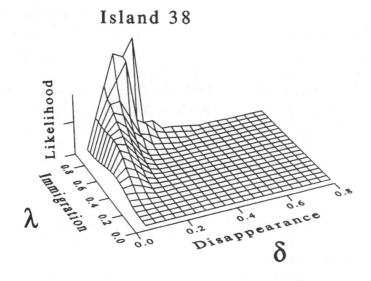

Figure 8.52. Island 38 is a hut-sized rock censused four times in 22 years (data from Abbott and Black, 1980). Although most of its plant species appeared to be stable, they probably go extinct almost annually.

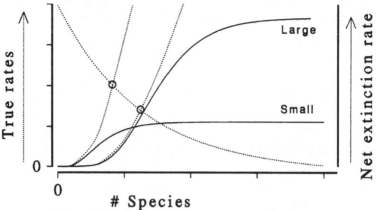

Smaller, Poorer Islands
have lower net extinction

Figure 8.53. Because extinction rates are instantaneous and data
are taken at finite intervals, small, species-poor
islands may appear to have much lower extinction
rates than they really do.

ranged from 7.6 to 76.5 ha. They are not far from the mainland (25 to
3500 m). Wright found that the pattern of their turnover rates disagreed
with island biogeography in two substantive ways. First, their turnover
rates did not decline monotonically with their distance from the mainland.
Instead, turnover rose with distance until it peaked at the island 225 m
away. Only after that distance did it begin to decline. Second, once distance
was accounted for, area played no role in determining turnover. According
to MacArthur and Wilson, turnover should have declined monotonically
with increasing area.

Wright tries to explain the discrepancies with some extensions to the theory. He also points out the narrow range of his sample islands. He might
have added that he had only six islands to work with. Two degrees of freedom are required to fit island distance to turnover, leaving only four for
significance. How can we expect any other variable to reduce the remaining
variance significantly?

I believe that the real answer to Wright's puzzle lies in the nature of the
islands themselves. As in the case of Haila's islands, these geographical
islands – at least for birds – are not biological islands. A distance of 25, 50
or 225 m presents only a small dispersal problem to a bird. Even a distance

of 3.5 km keeps an island in full view of a mainland disperser. Thus, the islands should have sink species and fail the test of 'islandness'.

Another problem Wright encounters relates to the accuracy of turnover estimates. He went to considerable trouble to ensure that pseudo-turnovers did not creep into his data. But he could not address the converse problem. All members of a species on an island may die, yet, if the species gets replaced in the nine months between censuses, it would never be missed. Neither its extinction nor its recolonization would appear in the turnover figures. This problem could make a large difference on small islands near a colonization source. So, it could account for the absence of the area–turnover relationship in Wright's data.

Wright recognizes that immigration to the islands may be so high as to reduce extinction rates. So – he points out – as island distance increases, observed extinction rate should too. This leads him to a perfectly logical explanation of his distance–turnover curve.

I object only to the terminology. MacArthur and Wilson treat the extinction curve as independent of distance. They do so because, for islands, it has to be. Its independence comes with the very definition of an island. A species maintained by regular immigration is a sink species. And islands don't have sink species.

However, we must take special notice of what Wright has accomplished. He built a bridge between island and mainland status. His analyses showed us that as a mainland piece departs from its moorings and its isolation grows, it should gradually lose its sink species. At first that will cause a rise in its turnover. But soon it will be far enough away to be a true island. (It may not even have to get that far, as Wright explains.) Then its turnover will decline with further isolation just as the theory of island biogeography predicts. In the next chapter, we shall see that a similar bridge exists between 'islandness' and 'provincialty'. Those two bridges will join all species–area relationships together into a single space–time continuum.

3. *Mammals of the Sunda islands.* Island biogeography theory unequivocally predicts that *larger areas should have lower extinction rate curves.* But that prediction can be mangled and mistreated. Boecklen and Simberloff (1986, p. 259) claim that 'faunal collapse models predict that extinction coefficients monotonically decrease with area.' They then reanalyze the data of mammals on Sunda islands, find that the coefficient of extinction actually increases with area over small islands (their Figure 4), and conclude (p. 260) that their analyses 'appear to contradict equilibrium theory'. I believe it will help to examine the mistakes that led them to their erroneous conclusion.

First, re-read the initial sentence of the previous paragraph. **Larger areas should have lower extinction rate curves**. That tells exactly what is predicted. Boecklen and Simberloff's restatement differs by speaking of extinction 'coefficients', not 'curves'. What is an extinction coefficient?

It is the logarithmic constant k in an equation of the form:

$$\log S_t - \log S_0 = kt$$

Such forms assume that the logarithmic extinction rate per species is constant. But island biogeography theory argues instead that it decreases as diversity declines. Since diversity is declining on these islands, we must move with utmost care between the 'curve' prediction and the 'coefficient' prediction. They are not interchangeable.

In Chapter 6, I looked at a more complete set of the Sunda mammal data than the one used by Boecklen and Simberloff. (I'm not sure why they did not also use it. They cite Wilcox, 1980, which is the paper with the data.) Figure 6.5 shows that extinction coefficients do in fact decline with increased island area. The data on the left (over small islands) are noisy and decline only very gradually, but they certainly do not increase as claimed by Boecklen and Simberloff.

Nevertheless, we learned in Chapter 6 that these data do **not** necessarily support the theory. We had to work hard comparing them to another data set to realize that the two sets, taken together, do agree with MacArthur and Wilson.

By the way, so do the data on rabbit and hare extinctions from the Wadden Sea Islands of the Netherlands (Flux, 1993). Rabbits have occured on 28 of these islands, hares on 30. So, we could have recorded as many as 58 extinctions. Of these, 14 have actually been observed. But they have been concentrated in the smaller islands. Islands less than 100 ha had a 60% extinction probability ($N = 5$); from 100 to 500 ha, it was 44% ($N = 9$); from 500 to 1000 ha, it was 37.5% ($N = 8$); from 1000 to 5000 ha, it was 14% ($N = 22$); and on islands larger than 5000 ha, it was 7% ($N = 14$).

Why are z-values higher on islands?

We have been careful to separate island from mainland species–area curves. You can now see that was necessary because different mechanisms produce the two. Mainland curves come from the greater number of habitats included in a larger area. Island curves come from that plus the lower extinction curves of larger islands. Moreover, the slope of island curves depends on the rate of resupply by immigration. Mainland areas get resupplied so fast that resupply rates do not determine their diversities.

But island and mainland curves share more features than we once thought. We can even view a mainland patch dynamically. Into the patch come species immigrating from nearby areas. Lost from the patch – albeit temporarily – are species that become locally extinct. Of course, the time scale must be fast compared with that of an island. Immigration rates are probably very high in the absence of barriers like a desert or an ocean. In many cases, they ought to be similar to birth and death rates. Immigration will swamp extinction. Brown and Kodric-Brown (1977) call that the 'rescue effect'. So, virtually all species with habitat in a patch will be found there.

Yet, at least one phenomenon remains to be understood. Before we knew about the differences between islands and mainland immigration and extinction processes, we had separated island from mainland species–area curves. We did so because they differ in z-values. Island curves have z-values of about 0.25–0.33; mainland curves have z-values of about 0.13–0.18. Does the time scale difference explain that? Yes.

The high rate of immigration to a mainland patch means that we can expect some of its species to be constantly on the road to local extinction, but rarely get there. Moreover, they should quickly get rescued even if they do go extinct. Let me explain by stepping down a level, from the dynamics of species diversity to the dynamics of populations.

Every general biology student learns that population growth is 'birth rate' minus 'death rate'. Some ecology students learn that the truth is a bit more sophisticated. Growth is 'births + immigration – deaths – emigration'. A few students then realize that, theoretically, a species can persist in a place although its net rate of change within that place (births – deaths) is negative. Shmida and his colleagues (Shmida and Whittaker, 1981; Shmida and Ellner, 1984; Shmida and Wilson, 1985) identified such persistences as an important component of mainland species diversity. They called that mechanism of contributing to diversity the 'mass effect'.

But how can the mass effect be real? Won't natural selection keep individuals from settling in a place where their prospects are negative?

No. Natural selection often forces individuals to use habitats in which they cannot make a net profit. That happens when trying to find a better habitat would actually cost more than settling for a poor habitat. For example, traveling costs to a better place may be too high (Rosenzweig, 1974). Or, the better place may be rare compared with the poor one (Pulliam, 1988; Pulliam and Danielson, 1991).

Where individuals of a species use a habitat in which their carrying capacity is less than zero, that species is said to be a *sink species* in that habitat (Shmida and Ellner, 1984; Pulliam, 1988). Any area that is part of a larger one may have sink species. A *source species* in an area has a positive birth minus death rate.

Notice the great difference between the extinction of a species on an island, and the processes that promote its local extinction in a patch where it is a sink species. In the latter, its average dynamics are negative; it is steadily disappearing. On an island, however, it will usually do well. What terminates it? The rare event we call an accident.

Hence, a self-contained region, like an island or even a whole biogeographical province, has no sink species. It gets immigrants rarely, and species that become extinct are either lost forever or, in the case of an island, must wait awhile to recolonize it.

Now let us return to New Guinea's list of ant species. There won't be a sink species on it. The same will hold true for a smaller island, say one tenth of the area of New Guinea. But a tenth of New Guinea itself should have some sink species. It will also have some habitats similar to the smaller island. So it should support about the same number of source species. Thus, we expect the total diversity of the piece to exceed that of the smaller island.

Now imagine an even smaller piece of New Guinea and an island of that smaller size. Both should have fewer source species than do the tenth piece and the island of tenth-piece size. But again, the island will lack sink species. The result is clear. As we move from right to left in the species–area graph, each reduction in area costs an island more than the mainland. The mainland can retain some sink species. The island must lose them. Thus, the species–area curve among islands has a steeper slope than that within portions of the mainland.

A paradox: though a whole island has no sink species, a small piece of it probably does. The piece will have species whose presence is maintained by rapid flow from other pieces within the island. Holt (1993) exhibits a graph that independently makes exactly this point. I need not reproduce it here because I will now show you one that comes from data rather than theory.

Knowing that island subdivisions also can contain sink species, we can explain a mysterious result hidden in the literature for more than 30 years.

Wilson (1961) compared the ant diversity of square mile patches on islands of different area. The larger the island, the more species in the square mile (Figure 8.54).

Suppose the same rules governed diversity among islands as those that govern diversity in subdivisions of an island. Then, Wilson would have recorded the same diversities in all the square miles (because their areas were the same). But if subdivisions contain sink species, then the z-values among subdivisions should be smaller than those among islands. The result – in log-log space – will be a set of lines of similar slope but with different intercepts. The larger the island, the higher the intercept, because the total fauna of an island correlates with its area. Thus, a square mile of a large island should have more species than a square mile of a small island. Figure 8.54 shows that indeed they do.

Compton *et al.* (1989) found a similar pattern among the bracken-eating arthropods of Britain and South Africa. Britain has more species altogether and more species in a plot of any fixed area. Yet the species–area curves of the two places are virtually parallel.

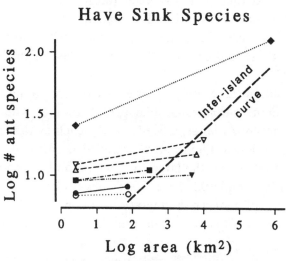

Portions of Islands
Have Sink Species

Figure 8.54. Although separate islands show a typically steep species–area curve, intra-island slopes are much more gentle. Because pieces of an island have sink species and sample them from the total biota of the island, standard-area samples on large islands contain more species. Data from Wilson (1961).

Two other studies tried to find the pattern of Figure 8.54, but did not (Westman, 1983; Kelly *et al.*, 1989). Both looked at plant diversities in equal-area, single-habitat plots of islands. Perhaps something crucial is revealed by these two 'failures' of the theory. But before we know what, we need to be sure the theory did fail. Several attributes of the studies make me wonder if, in fact, it did.

First, the authors use single-habitat plots. Why? According to them, island biogeography predicts that equal-area, **single-habitat** plots of islands should have diversities proportional to the total areas of their islands. But that's not precisely right. Island biogeography theory predicts that equal-area plots of islands should have diversities proportional to the total areas of their islands. I have explained why in the previous paragraphs. There's nothing about single-habitats in that prediction. Yes, the effect of whole-island area ought to remain in single-habitat plots. But, bigger islands have more species in part because they have more habitats. So, if you remove the possibility of sampling more habitats by staying in one, you will attenuate the relationship between whole-island area and diversity in a constant sub-area. You will need many replicates to establish it. Westman studied only four islands, censusing two plots on each of three islands, and four plots on one. Kelly *et al.* studied four plots of beech forest and four of manuka scrub on each of 23 islands. They did find a small effect of area but it was not significant in either case (beech: $R^2 = 0.17$, $p = 0.098$; manuka: $R^2 = 0.10$, $p = 0.134$). Do those numbers signal that more data might have supported the prediction?

Second, small islands in lakes may not be true biogeographical islands for taxa with high immigration rates, like plants. In fact, Quinn *et al.* (1987), working on the same islands as Kelly *et al.*, teach us that they cannot be true biological islands. Quinn *et al.* sampled a patch of mainland about the same size as Pomona, the largest of these islands; it had only 97 species whereas the island had 102. True islands always have fewer species (by definition, because of reduced immigration). Quinn *et al.* concluded that these islands are different sized habitat samples of the mainland, and I agree. The island biogeography of lacustrine islands should be studied with poorly dispersing taxa like land mammals (see the work of Lomolino). Plants on lacustrine islands may vary in diversity because the islands resemble samples of mainland and vary in habitat diversity, or because they are so small, they support only a tiny number of individuals.

Third, sample sizes must be generous. Kelly *et al.* use plots of only 100 m². Westman's are 625 m². That is not enough area to avoid the overwhelming influence of sample size. In the next chapter I will cite evidence that even 1000 m² plots cannot discriminate between the immense differences in plant diversity of African and Neotropical forests. I estimate that we need plots of about a hectare (i.e. 100 times the size of the plots of Kelly *et al.*) to work on tree and shrub diversity.

Summary of island section

The theory of island biogeography holds up well. Island diversities result from the interplay of the rate of immigration of species not on an island, and the rate of extinction of species on the island. Competition probably helps to increase extinction rates as diversity rises. So does predation. On the other hand, as diversity rises on an island, the number of species available for immigration falls and, along with it, so does the immigration rate. On some islands we see evidence that immigration and extinction rates are balanced.

Island diversity is self-regulating. The system that controls it, works by the general principle of negative feedback. In negative feedback, a product depresses its own rate of production. In this case, the product is diversity. It achieves a steady state because low diversities cause diversity to grow, but high diversities cause diversity to fall.

Because larger islands have more habitats and larger total population sizes, their equilibria are higher. The increase in habitats and populations probably reduces extinction rates.

Because more isolated islands have lower diversities, as MacArthur and Wilson predicted, immigration rate curves must also affect equilibria. Good data to test this conclusion are rare and tricky to analyze. But when they do appear, they support the conclusion.

The theory of island biogeography sparked a revolution in ecology. It did so, not because people cared so much to understand the number of species on islands, but precisely because they did not care. With the notable exception of a few forward looking and widely ignored contributions like Mayr (1941), they assumed that because species got to islands by accident, the whole process must be random and capricious. There was no science to discover, only history to recount. So, MacArthur and Wilson tackled the most unlikely of subjects in their attempt to convince us that ecological data emerge, at least in part, from well-defined dynamical processes. Had they picked on something more obvious, I don't think they would have reoriented us quite so thoroughly.

Chapter 9

Species–area curves: large issues

Interprovincial patterns: species–area curves in evolutionary time

We can use the definition of a biological island to define the next larger bio-geographical unit, the biological province. *A biological province is a self-contained region whose species originate entirely by speciation within the region.* Of course, no such region actually exists (except for the whole Earth). But the definition sets up a continuum between islandness and province-ness. As the proportion of originations in a region varies from 100% immigration toward 100% speciation, the region is passing from island to province. The continuum helps us see that we need not create two pigeonholes – island and province – only to battle over the place of one or another region. Instead, for practical purposes, we can say that once a region's species are predominately (60%? 80%?) native, we will group that region with the provinces. Often, that means simply recognizing continents as provinces.

When Williams (1964) extended his plant species–area curve to take in whole continents, he saw a much steeper slope than for the within-province curve. Preston (1960) points out the same phenomenon in his bird curve (Figure 2.15). But neither Williams nor Preston paid much attention to the high between province z-values suggested by their graphs. In the first place, these values had no statistical significance (because of too few data points). Besides, Williams and Preston were more interested in the intraprovincial part of their curves. Today, however, we have enough data to show that z-values between-provinces are indeed steeper. We even have a theoretical understanding of why they should be. In this section, I will show you those data and explain them.

I believe the best data come from wet tropical forests. Findley and Wilson (1983) enumerated the frugivorous bat species of Africa, Malaysia, parts of Indonesia, New Guinea and the Neotropics. They found that the species–area curve for these interprovincial samples is approximately linear. Thus, it has a z-value near unity. Fleming *et al.* (1987) extended these results by adding the frugivorous birds and primates. Still, the result was a *z*-value near unity. There are far more species of birds than frugivorous bats and primates combined, so we can say that both they and the bats have *z* near unity. I have added the numbers for Australia (Figure 9.1), but it makes no difference to the *z*.

Prance (1977) supplies figures for the number of flowering plant species in the world's tropical rainforest provinces. I have included these in Figure 9.1. Their *z*-value too is approximately unity.

Not enough evidence yet supports an interprovincial *z*-value of unity. So we cannot be so sure how closely other examples will conform to that value. In fact, freshwater fish of the Congo and Amazon river basins (Marlier, 1973) suggest a *z* of 2.4. The Congo drains about 3 822 000 km² and has about 500 species of fish. The Amazon drains about 5 620 000 km² and has more than 1300 species. However, having only two points, we cannot have much confidence in the accuracy of the *z* estimate. In addition, the area estimates may be irrelevant except as to rank; fishes use only the one-dimensional stream lengths, not the two-dimensional basin areas.

I know of three other cases that approximate an interprovincial curve. Lawton (1984) looked at diversities of arthropods that specialize on eating

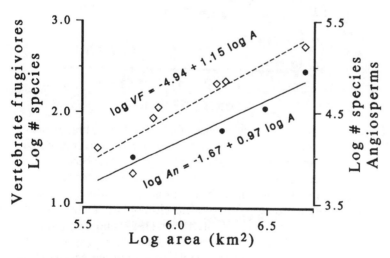

Figure 9.1. The interprovincial species–area curve in tropical rain-forests. Dots: angiosperms. Diamonds: vertebrate frugivores. Madagascar's points have $10^{5.8}$ km². Redrawn from Rosenzweig (1992).

bracken fern (*Pteridium aquilinum*) in four provinces. His data were supplemented with a fifth province by Winterbourn (1987) and a sixth by Compton *et al.* (1989). For these provinces, $z = 0.61$ (Figure 9.2). Contrast that slope with the species–area slope obtained from small patches of bracken on Yorkshire (UK) moors: $z = 0.086$ (Rigby and Lawton, 1981); and from bracken patches in South Africa: $z = 0.083$ (Compton *et al.*, 1989). These two are typical (or even small) mainland values. Yet, the very same organisms that produce these values participate in an interprovincial species–area curve with the very high slope of 0.61. It's not the organisms. It's not the localities. It's not the environment that makes the difference. It's the perspective.

Culver *et al.* (1973) looked at diversities of cave-dwelling species in the Greenbriar Valley system of West Virginia. Caves in cool-temperate places

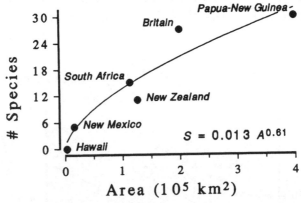

Figure 9.2. The number of species of bracken fern-eating arthropods fits a line with a *z*-value of 0.61. This considerably exceeds island or mainland *z*-values because its component samples come from different biogeographic provinces. The area is that in which bracken fern grows, not that of the entire place. Data from Lawton (1984), Winterbourn (1987) and Compton *et al.* (1989). Note: Because Hawaii has zero species, estimates in the literature rely on adding one species to the total of all places (e.g. Lawton *et al.*, 1993). The result is $z = 0.69$. I did not need this adjustment because I estimated the curve with non-linear regression and plotted it in semi-logarithmic space.

on the margins of what were once the great glaciers of the Pleistocene, promote substantial *in situ* evolution (Barr, 1967). Also, the caves in Greenbriar Valley are divided into sets, with almost no inter-set immigration by terrestrial cavernicoles. Thus, each set of caves is virtually a province unto itself for the terrestrial animals that depend on it. For them, the value of z is 0.72. On the other hand, amongst aquatic cavernicoles in the same cave sets, $z = 0.19$, a value typical of a provincial species–area curve. Aquatic cavernicoles do disperse readily among sets of caves. Other studies of caves dealt with individual caves rather than sets of them. They found z-values more typical of island systems (Vuilleumier, 1973).

Kennnedy and Southwood (1984) studied diversities of insects on British trees. Each tree has its own insects, so each is almost like a separate province. According to Birks (1980), twenty of these tree species are natives. (The others are introduced.) Using the data in Kennnedy and Southwood, I regressed the insect diversities against the geographical ranges of the trees they live on (Figure 9.3). The result ($p = 0.002$) has a z-value of 0.89.

In the fern, cave and tree cases, z was unusually high: 0.60 for the fern eaters; 0.72 for the cave dwellers; 0.89 for the tree associates. But the

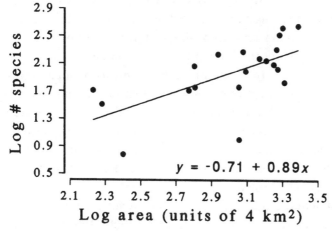

Figure 9.3. Individual species of tree harbor their own faunas of associated insect species. The larger the geographical area of the tree, the more diverse that tree's list of insects. The high z-value (0.89) typifies those that come from separate provinces. Data from Kennedy and Southwood (1984) and Birks (1980).

important point is not the precise value of z in interprovincial cases. It is that all those cases tell us that all interprovincial z-values exceed those among islands or within provinces.

The linearity of species–area curves and their slopes

Species–area curves follow straight lines with characteristic slopes. But nothing we have yet looked at predicts either linearity or z-value. We have understood why diversity increases with area. We know why the slope of that relationship should increase as we proceed from mainland curves to island curves to interprovincial curves. We have also understood the semi-logarithmic form of the curve for very small sample areas. But no theory we have yet reviewed has said, 'Graphed in log-log space the curve should approximate a straight line and z should be about 0.25.' Is there such a theory?

Caswell and Cohen (1993) build a model of disturbance and area that seems to predict quasi-linearity and tolerably realistic z-values. At the end of Chapter 11, I will explain why we cannot use the Caswell and Cohen model for the species–area curves reviewed in Chapters 3, 8 and 9. Basically, the reason is that this model does not incorporate either evolution or habitat differences.

May (1975) argued that both the linearity and the approximate z-values of species–area curves come from the statistical property called the Law of Large Numbers. The body of theory on which May relied is called the theory of the log-normal distribution. But we shall see in this section that this theory has at least one serious problem. Its predictions fail to match the data. It does not predict the known range of z-values or forecast the regular progression of z-values from mainland to island to biological province. So, I believe that the linearity of the species–area curve remains a fascinating mystery. And so does the reason that when different systems are studied at similar scales, their z-values cluster tightly around similar values. This section reviews the principles of the log-normal distribution because I believe that we need to build on them, not reject them. But it also explains my view that we have not yet finished.

Four monumental papers of Frank Preston supply most of the theory of the log-normal distribution (Preston, 1948, 1960, 1962a, b). This is what May relied on and what we must understand. First, Preston determined that species abundance distributions often seem to fit a log-normal curve (Preston, 1948) (Figure 9.4). Such a curve looks like a bell-shaped curve if we plot its x-axis as a logarithm (Figure 9.5). Figure 9.6 shows several examples for plant associations.

Truncated
Lognormal Distribution

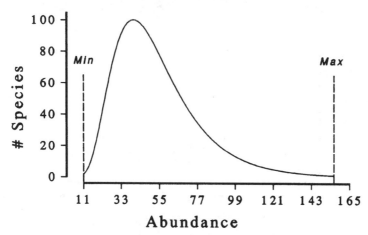

Figure 9.4. A log-normal distribution. Less than one species exists
below the minimum and above the maximum abun-
dance.

Truncated
Lognormal Distribution

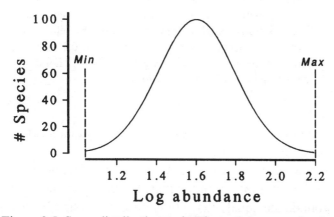

Figure 9.5. Same distribution as in Figure 9.4 except that its
abcissa is a logarithmic scale.

Preston decided that ecological systems must fit log-normal curves
because of all the many multiplicative and independent interactions that go
on in natural communities. But Preston also postulated that a particular
type of log-normal curve seemed the rule in ecology. To understand it, we

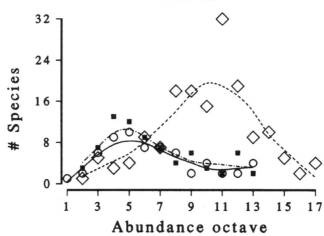

Figure 9.6. Three abundance distributions from Canada. The
species of each successive abundance octave are twice
as abundant as those in the previous one. So the axis
scales as logarithmic abundance using the base 2. Base
two is the convention favored by Preston. Lowess
regressions. Circles: abundance (measured by importance values) of trees in deciduous forests of southern
Ontario. Diamonds: abundance (measured by relative
cover) in arborvitae (*Thuja*) swamp forest in eastern
Ontario. Squares: abundance (measured by relative frequency) of vascular plants in twenty-eight 0.1 m ×
50 m transects in Axel Heiberg Land, NWT. Data
from Beschel and Webber (1963).

need to build another curve. Preston called it the 'individuals curve', and he
called the first curve 'the species curve'.

Figure 9.5 is a species curve. In it, each abundance produces a predicted
number of species. The number of individuals belonging to the set of species
of a particular abundance equals that abundance multiplied by the number
of species that have it. We can thus graph the number of individuals against
log abundance just as we graphed the number of species against log abundance. The latter is the species curve; the former is the individuals curve.

In Figure 9.7 I have graphed the individuals curve on top of the species
curve of Figure 9.5. If it also looks log-normal to you, that is because it is.
Preston (1962a) found a clever way to prove that. But of course, the indi-

Truncated
Lognormal Distribution

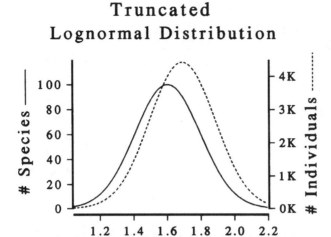

Figure 9.7. The individuals' curve of the log-normal in Figure 9.5
appears as a dashed line. Its *y*-values are the number
of individuals that belong to all species with abundance corresponding to the *x*-value. The solid line is
the species curve of Figure 9.5.

viduals curve is truncated on the right – no individuals can belong to a
hypothetical species so abundant that not even one such species is real!

Because the individuals curve is also log-normal and depends on exactly
the same parameter values as the species curve underlying it, Preston could
calculate the distance between the modes (peaks) of the two curves, R_N. He
standardized the species curve by setting its modal abundance to zero and
calculating each abundance as a deviation from the mode. Deviations are
expressed in terms of the number of doublings of the mode required to
reach the abundance. (To the left of the mode, deviations mean halvings.)
Thus, Preston calculated the abundance of the most abundant real species.
And he calculated the distance, R_{MAX}, from the logarithmic abundance of
the most abundant real species to the logarithmic abundance of the modal
species in the species curve. If $R_{MAX} = R_N$, then Preston termed the log-normal distribution 'canonical'. He meant by this term merely that such a
curve is special because it so often characterizes abundance distributions.

You can see that the log-normal of Figure 9.7 is not canonical. But
Figure 9.8 does show an example of a canonical distribution. In it, I contin-
ued the individuals curve past R_{MAX} as a dotted line. That way, you can see
that both curves are log-normal. But, of course there are no species more

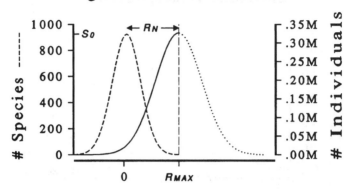

Figure 9.8. A canonical log-normal distribution. The lefthand
curve shows the number of species; its mode is set at
zero. The number of species at the mode is S_0. The
righthand curve shows the number of individuals. The
distance between the modes of the two curves is R_N.
The individuals curve of a canonical lognormal peaks
over the species with the most individuals (R_{MAX}) so
that $R_{MAX} = R_N$. The dotted part of the individuals
curve represents hypothetical species too common to
exist.

common than R_{MAX}. So the actual number of individuals to the left of
R_{MAX} is zero.

May (1975) introduced the statistic $\gamma = R_N/R_{MAX}$ to simplify discussions
of log-normal distributions. If $\gamma = 1$, we have a canonical log-normal. If
$\gamma > 1$, then the individuals curve is still growing over R_{MAX}. If $\gamma < 1$, then
the individuals curve peaks to the left of R_{MAX}.

Why should we concern ourselves with γ? Because, if the abundance
curves of all ecological systems share any constant γ then several interesting
deductions follow. Preston thought that $\gamma = 1$, i.e. that ecological systems
are canonical. But, although the numerical values of the deductions will
change if γ does not equal unity, these deductions can still be made as long
as γ is some constant.

Preston (1948, p. 282) actually offered a flawed proof that real abundance curves have to be canonical. First, he grouped abundances into powers of two; thus his graphs were actually histograms with each higher bar

located at twice the abundance of its predecessor. Then he inspected the largest real bar. He observed that it most often held only one species. If, he pointed out, there would have been a species in the next larger group, it would have been twice as abundant. Thus, the individuals curve would have risen. This shows that the real part of the individuals curve must rise, he concludes. But he merely asserts without proof the conclusion that the individuals curve must be near its peak over R_{MAX}. He never explains why it could not continue to rise well beyond R_{MAX}. And, of course, his proof that the curve cannot fall beyond R_{MAX} depends on his resort to data, i.e. there is usually only one species in the group with the largest real abundance. Without that empirical fact, he has nothing. Suppose, for instance, there were three species in this largest real group. Then suppose you could add a single species to the next larger group. Its abundance would be only $2/3$ as great as the sum of the abundances of the three species in the largest real group. Thus, the individuals curve would fall.

May (1975, p. 93) also tried to demonstrate the necessity of something like a canonical log-normal. He does show that such a curve can be consistent with a wide variety of total diversities and total individuals. But, unfortunately other log-normals with other, quite different values of γ, also can fit a wide variety of total diversities and total individuals.

Sugihara (1980) answered with a proof that explored values of γ as diversity and abundance varied over a more reasonable range of possibilities. In fact, he showed that γ is not mathematically restricted to unity or even to the neighborhood of unity. Sugihara explored the ranges $50 < S < 10^4$ and $10^4 < J < 10^{12}$. (J is an index of abundance equal to the number of individuals in the assemblage divided by the abundance of the rarest species). The values of γ varied from 0.1 to 6.8.

Yet in real systems – especially those with 100 or more species – γ does cluster around 1. Such regularity demands explanation (Sugihara, 1980). Meanwhile, it suggests the key to the actual values of z that we see in nature.

Preston (1962a) deduced the species–area curve for a series of 'isolates' of different areas all having canonical log-normal distributions. By isolates he meant whole ensembles of species, like islands or provinces, rather than samples of ensembles. He discovered that the curve should be nearly a straight line in log-log space with a z of about 0.27.

May (1975) kept the assumption that all γ-values in a single set of ensembles are the same. But he allowed γ to vary among different sets. Thus he tested the robustness of Preston's predictions. They hold up well. The curve maintains its near-linearity at least for $0.6 < \gamma < 1.7$. And for those γ values, z varies between 0.39 and 0.15. (Ugland and Gray, 1982, confirm this result using a different constant which I will not discuss here.)

The range of z suggested by May has been widely quoted and just as widely misunderstood. He never said or implied that this range was stochastic. He never wrote that in the presence of a canonical log-normal, z was going to range between 0.15 and 0.39. Instead he clearly presented this range as the consequence of deterministic differences among the non-canonical distributions, differences that were most likely to exhaust the set of true possibilities in real ensembles. In fact, in his paper, he wonders about the biology that led to the difference between the plant curves of Yorkshire reserves ($z = 0.21$) and California islands ($z = 0.37$).

Now examine Figure 9.9 It shows a series of hypothetical ensembles that I calculated according to the following protocol: I kept the minimum population size in each to the same arbitrary number (11). I began with 10 species (S_0) at the modal abundance, set the modal abundance (N_0) to 30 and the logarithmic width (σ) to 0.50. That provided the lowest curve. Then I increased the parameters, resetting r as needed to keep abundance 11 as the minimum that supported one species.

S_0	10	100	1000	5000
N_0	30	40	50	60
σ	0.5	0.45	0.42	0.415

After calculating and plotting the log-normal distributions of these parameter values, I calculated the number of individuals in each. Preston suggested long ago that this number ought to be more or less linearly proportional to area. And every attempt to determine a species–area curve has relied on his suggestion. So, by calculating the number of individuals, I calculated area. Thus, plotting diversity against the number of individuals gives us the species–area curve.

In Figure 9.10 we see the result for these four distributions. The four points fall almost precisely on a straight line ($R^2 \approx 1.0$). But the slope, z, is 0.912! That is far outside the range suggested by May as reasonable. And one counter-example is all it takes to undermine a quantitative prediction.

What is wrong? The answer is that I selected parameter values far from those of a canonical distribution. The γ-values of the four distributions in Figure 9.9 are (in the same order as above): 0.1615; 0.1028; 0.0783; 0.0697. Yet those values yielded perfectly sane distributions. Is there any biological reason to reject them? None that I know. So island species–area curves

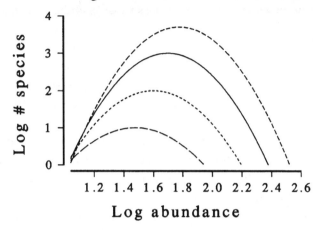

Figure 9.9. Four log-normal distributions with the same minimum abundance, similar variances, but varying modal abundances and numbers of species.

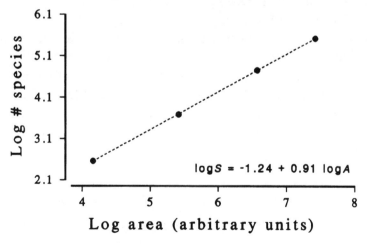

Figure 9.10. The species–area curve for the distributions in Figure 9.9. The curve is linear but its slope is much steeper than that of a typical island or mainland curve.

hover around $z = 0.28$ probably because species' abundance distributions do not stray very far from the canonical log-normal where $\gamma = 1$.

That may explain the z-values of most sets of islands. But the z-values of very isolated islands consistently brush up against and even exceed 0.39, May's upper limit. Take another look at Figures 8.42 and 8.44; they seem to be climbing to 0.55 or even 0.60. We have been able to understand such high z-values as a consequence of reduced immigration rates. Perhaps it also means a low γ, though I'm not sure what we accomplish by noticing that.

Samples of ensembles (i.e. mainland curves) consistently have z-values that come close to or fall below May's lower limit (0.15). But, that does not surprise us because Preston himself expected it and observed it. He wrote of transient species adding to the diversity of a sample. Today we understand that phenomenon as coming from sink species. How does it help us if it also turns out that mainland species–abundance curves have γ somewhat larger than unity? I do not know how.

Finally, we now know that interprovincial species–area curves consistently rise at slopes high above May's range. The smallest we have so far found is 0.61. Those for tropical rainforests appear to average near unity. Such values approximate the 0.912 we saw in the hypothetical case. We know from rate considerations that interprovincial curves have to be steeper than the steepest island curves. And they are. Making a provincial ensemble even partly into an island by increasing immigration to it must result in a higher number of species. And a higher diversity means a reduced z. Can we say anything more than that by guessing that very high z-values may also mean γ-values around 0.1 instead of 1.0? Not yet, anyhow.

It seems to me that log-normal distributions may indeed explain why species–area curves tend to be linear in log-log space. But they do not help us yet in understanding the actual values that the z-values take. And even when we understand z-values, we'll be left with an important puzzle – understanding c-values.

Synthesis: species–area curves at several scales of space and time

What we have learned so far, fits rather neatly onto a single two dimensional species–area graph (Figure 9.11). Let us begin to examine it and understand it by looking at the interprovincial portion.

This curve has the steepest slope. Its elements rarely exchange species. They are thus evolutionarily independent.

Three Scales of Species-Area Curve

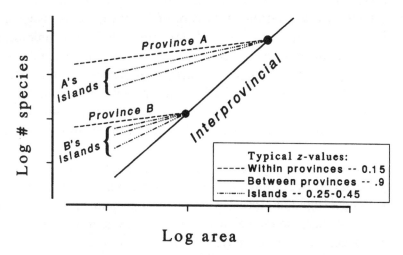

Figure 9.11. Province A is larger than Province B and so has more
species by virtue of evolutionary processes. The
provinces fall on the steepest species–area curve.
Pieces of each province have fewer species than the
whole because they lack all its habitats. They fall on
the gently sloped species–area curves known since the
middle of the last century. Islands fall on intermediate
sloped species–area curves that originate from the
species–area point of their source. The more isolated
they are, the steeper the curve they fall on.

Notice that I used data from similar environments to construct this
curve. The trees and vertebrate frugivores of Figure 9.1 all come from wet
tropical forests. So do the fish of the Amazon and Congo basins. The cave
faunas all come from limestone caverns in West Virginia. And the bracken
eating insects all specialize on one species of fern found in similar environments around the world. Thus, the diversity differences along one of these
curves cannot be traced to any environmental cause other than the differences in area.

In addition, these diversity differences were predicted in advance of the
data being collected. Those predictions came from a model that considered
how area should affect the rate of geographical speciation and the rate of
extinction (Rosenzweig, 1975). Of course, prediction always makes a scien-

tist more convinced that he probably understands the result. History sometimes proves him wrong. But more often, the ability to predict indicates that
the underlying theory is getting at the root of the mechanisms responsible.

The inter-provincial curve comes from the evolutionary time scale. In
contrast, the mainland curve is ecological. It depends upon the presence of
a pool of already-evolved species. Its areas sample the habitats that those
species have already evolved to discriminate. In each habitat, we find all the
species that can live there successfully plus some that cannot (its sink
species). These sink species are constantly, but unsuccessfully, going locally
extinct.

The island curves develop on an intermediate time scale. They depend
not only on larger areas having more habitats, but also on the interplay
between island extinction and island immigration. Sink species never make
it. Other species become extinct from time to time and are replaced either
by new propagules of their own kind, or different species.

Island curves vary systematically in their slope. The lower the immigration curve, the poorer the island. Often, lower immigration rates are caused
by greater distances to the source pool of species. However, immigration
rates can also differ among taxa.

Some taxa, like ferns, seem able to get almost anywhere, no matter how
isolated the island. Others, like terrestrial mammals, almost seem to require
steamship tickets. A splendid analysis of such taxonomic differences comes
from Norfolk Island. Holloway (1977) measured the dispersal ability of
various taxa on the island. He compared the proportion of its members that
had come from Australia (1200 km away) with the proportion that had
come from the smaller, closer source pools of New Caledonia or New
Zealand (each about 700 km away). The higher the proportion from
Australia, the better the taxon must be at colonization. Fifteen taxa of
plants and animals varied over almost two orders of magnitude in their
proportion of Australians.

The slope of the species–area curve reflects the time scale that determines
it. As we proceed from the gentle slopes on mainlands to the steep slopes
among provinces, we are moving from almost daily time scales to the vast
scales of evolutionary time. The Norfolk Island taxa reflect that too. The less
their colonization ability, the more they form endemics (Holloway, 1977).

Some places may be so distant, so isolated, that the ability to colonize
them nearly vanishes. We recognize such places as separate provinces.
Thus, Hawaii – with 81% of its land birds and 92% of its plants endemic
(Bond and Goldblatt, 1984), and with storied radiations of honeycreepers,

lobelias, tarweeds, *Drosophila* and other life forms – is really a province unto itself (see Chapter 5). The same must be said for other isolated archipelagos like New Zealand and the Galapagos, and for old, deep lakes like Baikal. Thus, the dichotomy that I set up in defining islands and provinces is really a continuum. The nature of a place along this continuum is measured by its z-value, which may differ from taxon to taxon.

Figure 9.11 does sweep something under the rug. On the extreme left-hand side of log-log species–area plots, real curves bend into convexity (Chapter 2 and Figure 8.31). I have not shown this in the figure because that part of the curve depends on small numbers of individuals in the sample (Chapter 8). Small-scale curves do not reveal any fundamental diversity properties of the places or the taxa being sampled.

For example, plant species diversities in 0.1 ha plots usually do not give an adequate reflection of the characteristic diversities of larger areas. The 0.1 ha diversities of semi-arid heathlands greatly overlap the diversities of many other types of vegetation (Rice and Westoby, 1983; Rice, 1984; Geldenhuys and MacDevette, 1989). Although the southeastern Australian heathland has much lower diversities than the southwestern, the 0.1 ha plot makes them look the same (Rice and Westoby, 1983). On the other hand, the 0.1 ha scale once led to the astounding and erroneous claim that Australian heathlands were as rich as – or even richer than – tropical rainforests (Richards, 1969).

The 0.1 ha scale does not discriminate well amongst the tropical forests of different continents. At the 0.1 ha scale, African rainforest vegetation closely resembles that of Neotropical rainforests. But Neotropical rainforests have the world's highest total diversities (Whitmore, 1990; Thomas and de Carvalho, 1993), whereas those of Africa have few species by comparison.

I believe that only Abbott's data (Figure 2.7) have so far told the truth about very small scale species–area patterns. They aren't real. Below some threshold area, diversity doesn't change. Of course, that threshold will vary from place to place, from time to time, and from taxon to taxon.

The effect of drifting continents

The Earth's surface has seen many great changes during its history. Sometimes provinces once separate have joined together. Sometimes subdivision has produced new provinces. What have such changes done to global diversity?

Before this book, I would have sought the answer in the work of paleo-biologists. But that work, as you will see, does not look at species diversity. It examines the diversities of families and genera. Usually, we expect the number of species to correlate closely with the number of genera or families. In this case, however, the correlation may not be strong enough.

Because it is intrinsically interesting, I will review the paleobiological work. However, I will then turn to the inter-provincial pattern for additional help. That pattern will not disprove the answer suggested by the fossil record. It will, however, help us to interpret it. At the very least, the interprovincial pattern suggests that drifting continents play no more than a small role in mass extinctions. It also suggests that the number of provinces plays only a secondary role in determining the number of species in the world.

Fossil evidence

George Gaylord Simpson (1950), one of our century's premier paleobiologists, began the investigation of what happens after two provinces join. He studied the land mammals of the Americas. About 2 million years ago, mountain-building events forged a land link between North and South America. (We call it the Isthmus of Panama.) Before then, South America had been entirely isolated from the north. Its quadrupedal mammals were endemic. Twenty-three whole families existed nowhere else. Twenty-five families lived in North America and not in South America. Only two families occurred in both continents.

The Isthmus of Panama removed the provincial barrier and allowed a great transmigration. Northern species immigrated south. Southern species immigrated north. As a result, we got our armadillos and opossums; the south got dogs, cats and camels. Each continent became overstuffed with families and a massive extinction took place. When the bones settled, total familial diversity had declined. The diversity that had been lost, had been supported by provincialization. Webb (1984) counted genera instead of families and got the same answer.

Flessa (1975) quantified the extinction to see how much of an effect provincialization had. He noted that the modern Americas have 15 endemic families in the south; eight in the north; and they share an additional 15. Thus, before the linkage of the two continents, they had a total of 50 families, and today they have only 38. They lost 24% of their total familial diversity.

He then calculated the z-value of the families–area curve for modern mammal families in provinces around the world. It is $z = 0.23$. Owing to the areas of the Americas, that z means the familial diversity should have dropped even more, i.e. to about 29 or 30:

$$4.22^{0.23}/(1.78^{0.23} + 2.44^{0.23}) = 0.588$$

and

$$0.588 \times 50 \text{ families} = 29.4 \text{ families.}$$

So, the reduction in provinciality could have caused the reduction in familial diversity.

Paleobiologists (Valentine, 1971, 1973; Flessa and Imbrie, 1973; Simberloff, 1974; Schopf, 1979) have supplied an even more monumental case involving fossils. Over the course of geological time continental plates have drifted here and there across the Earth's surface. Often they collide and, at least from the point of view of life, they merge. Thus, the effective number of separate biological provinces varies considerably through time.

Pangaea, for example, united all the world's continents into a single super–continent some 200 Myr ago. That coincided with the greatest loss of diversity in the Earth's history (so far) – the Permo–Triassic Catastrophe. These authors (Valentine, Flessa, Imbrie, Simberloff and Schopf) and others believe that the reduction in the number of biological provinces contributed much to that ancient disaster.

Drifting continents also change the number of marine provinces. Those provinces exist because dominant ocean currents keep large segments of oceans separate from each other. For example, the North Pacific Gyre is the world's largest province. But it sits in the middle of the North Pacific Ocean, entirely defined by currents. You can easily travel across its border without knowing it.

Land masses, in part, determine the currents that isolate marine provinces. They do so by deflecting oceanic flow. In fact, we know enough about what sets up the Earth's main oceanic currents to reconstruct them in ancient seas with ancient land masses. The Earth had about 13 marine provinces during the Silurian Period, 14 during the early Permian (before Pangaea), only about eight during the late Permian (when Pangaea existed), and 18 today (Schopf, 1979). The Permian witnessed the most severe mass extinction in the history of life. Today, we would not attribute all these extinctions to loss of provincial isolation. But Schopf may be right to claim that loss of isolation caused some of them.

Schopf's provinces do not reveal the slope of the provincial effect with accuracy because they are very leaky. More than half the species of each also occur in some other province. This led Schopf to the mistaken conclusion that the z-value among separate provinces is similar to that among islands and within provinces. Today we know that interprovincial z ranges between 0.69 and 2.4. How does that change what we can conclude about species diversity and drifting continents?

The lesson of the interprovincial curve.

The interprovincial curve predicts the answer to our question about drifting continents. To begin, let us suppose that interprovincial curves actually have a z-value of exactly one. Thus we may write:

$$S = cA \tag{9.1}$$

In other words, $z = 1$ means the species–area curve is linear in both arithmetic and logrithmic space.

Now suppose the Earth is subdivided into n provinces of various areas. Each province fits Equation 9.1 above. So, total diversity in the world is:

$$c\sum A_i \tag{9.2}$$

where A_i is the set of areas of the world's provinces. Since the surface of the Earth stays the same regardless of how many continents, so does the number of species.

Interprovincial z-values do approach unity. Nevertheless, they ranged down to 0.61. If it turns out that some value slightly less than unity fits them best, subdividing the Earth will enhance its diversity a little. A sample calculation makes this clear.

Suppose

- $z = 0.8$
- The Earth has five continents of equal size.
- $A =$ The total land area of the Earth.

Then terrestrial diversity will be:

$$S_5 = 5c(A/5)^{0.8}$$

With only one continent:

$$S_1 = cA^{0.8}$$

The effect of subdivision:

$$S_5 5/S_1 = 5/5^{0.8} = 1.38$$

Thus, subdivision adds 38% to diversity.

Suppose we change the subdivision to five continents of unequal sizes as follows:

$0.4A$; $0.25A$; $0.2A$; $0.1A$; $0.05A$.

Then diversity will be:

$$S_d = c \sum_i A_i^{0.8}$$

and the effect of subdivision is to add 33.5% to diversity.

I could do a full-scale simulation, but the point is already clear. If z values are close to unity, provincialization has only a small effect on global species diversity.

But what about the two particular fossil cases? The juncture of North and South America cost 'only' 24% of mammal families. Might this have cost a similar proportion of species? The formation of Pangaea at the end of the Permian Period was accompanied by the loss of over 95% of species. Can that loss be accounted for by the drop in marine provinces from 14 to eight?

The mammal case involves terrestrial forms. So we need to use our z estimates from the interprovincial curves. North America's area separated from South America's should hold 14.6% more species if $z = 0.8$. The actual loss of families was 12 of 50. Thus, the indicated excess families supported by the separate continents is 12/38 or 31.6%. Evidently the familial loss was much more severe than the species loss. (And remember, if our estimate of 0.8 is low, the species loss would not even have amounted to 14.6%.)

The other case is marine. Here, we cannot use the interprovincial curves because marine provinces are too leaky. We must use Schopf's estimate instead. Suppose $z = 0.3$ and the world's oceans change from 14 to seven provinces. (That is one less than Schopf's estimate of eight, so it will overestimate the damage Pangea caused to global diversity.)

Without knowing the exact areas of the provinces, we can rank the 14 and then join adjacent provinces (i.e. largest to next largest; third to fourth; etc.). Thus each new province will be about twice the area of the previous ones in its pair. The effect of dividing an area in two equal parts is to add 62% to its diversity (if $z = 0.3$). So, Pangaea could have cost the world

38.5% of its marine species. Yes, that's a massive extinction. But it does not fully account for the losses of the Permo–Triassic Catastrophe.

In sum, loss of provinces does cost many genera and families. But those losses do not appear to translate into similarly severe losses of terrestrial species. And loss of marine provinces has a more severe effect because they are leaky and have smaller z-values. But even in the ocean, loss of provinces can account for only a fraction of the actual species losses of mass extinctions.

Latitudinal gradients

Most ecologists believe we have never met the challenge of the latitudinal diversity gradient (Rohde, 1992). They are mistaken. The literature contains the clues, and identifies a cause that must play a primary role. *Latitudinal gradients must arise because the tropics cover more area than any other zone.* Their greater area stimulates speciation and inhibits extinction. Borrowing liberally from Rosenzweig (1992), I shall now review and explain that answer.

Terborgh's pattern

Pianka (1966) wrote the classic list of hypotheses to explain the latitudinal gradient. He crafted it so beautifully that many still teach from his list today. (See, for example, its treatment in Begon *et al.*, 1990.)

But, when John Terborgh (1973) cut the Gordian knot, his explanation did not come from Pianka's list. Terborgh concluded that the tropics abound with life because they abound with territory. The tropics are richer than any other place because they are more extensive than any other place.

Terborgh noted that those of us who carry around maps of the Earth in our heads, carry something resembling a Mercator projection. This exaggerates the area of terrestrial features in proportion to their distance from the Equator. The farther from the Equator, the larger they appear to loom (Figure 9.12).

Because the Earth is round, the distance between longitudes actually peaks at the Equator. This reduces the apparent overhang of the lands of the Northern Hemisphere, and eliminates it entirely in the seas and the Southern Hemisphere (Figure 9.13).

Terborgh noticed another simple thing. The northern and southern tropics abut. Thus, their area is roughly double that of any other zone.

Apparent Relative Land Area
Mercator projection

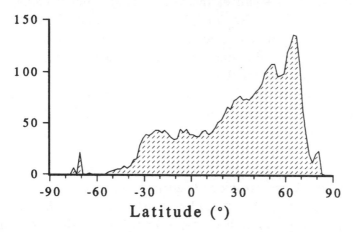

Figure 9.12. The perception of the world's relative land areas that comes from a Mercator projection. From Rosenzweig (1992).

True Relative Land Area
Equal-area projection

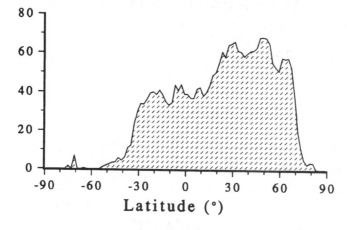

Figure 9.13. The true values of the world's land areas comes from an equal-area projection. The y-axis is linear but its units are only relative. For absolute units, see Figure 9.15. From Rosenzweig (1992).

Finally, Terborgh noted (from data) that a broad belt of homogeneous temperatures, roughly 50 degrees (of latitude) wide, encircles the Earth's midsection. North or south of this belt, average annual temperature falls off linearly (Figure 9.14). So, any place in the belt has the chance of being like any other place. But any place outside it will be more restricted in area. Moreover, it will get more and more restricted as it centers on higher and higher latitudes (because the Earth is round).

Terborgh must be right for the seas and the Southern Hemisphere. But does his general conclusion follow for the vast north? And even if it does, how does having a huge area allow a zone to harbor more species?

I got a simple computer map of the globe that divided it into sea, land and ice. Then, I measured the actual land areas contained in several arbitrarily situated zones: tropics (0–26°); subtropics (26–36°); temperate (36–46°); boreal (46–56°) and tundra (>56°). Sure enough, the tropics are about 3.4 times larger than their nearest competition (the northern tundra). Terborgh was right for northern lands too (Figure 9.15).

Large-scale effects of area

How does a larger area translate into a greater diversity? We must seek the answer by comparing speciation and extinction rates in provinces of different size. We have no alternative, no matter how important are all the stud-

Mean Annual Temperature

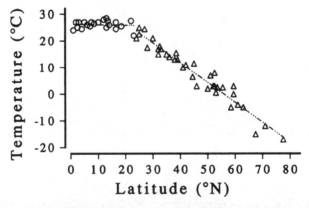

Figure 9.14. Average annual temperature is about the same everywhere within a 50° belt whose center is the Equator. From Rosenzweig (1992).

Land area

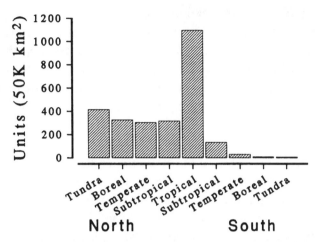

Figure 9.15. The world's tropical lands cover about four times the area as the world's second largest biome, the tundra. Tropical oceans also cover more surface than oceans in other climate zones. From Rosenzweig (1992).

ies of all the other variables. The processes that govern speciation and extinction are the processes that determine standing diversity in a biogeo-graphical province.[1]

Let's imagine a world unlike our own in one detail – a world in which tropics and subtropics have the same diversity. Such a world should not last. We can expect its average tropical species to have a geographical range half an order of magnitude greater than its average subtropical species. Probably, that range difference has four consequences (Rosenzweig, 1975 and Chapter 5).

First, the greater range leads to a larger total population size (assuming densities to be about the same). Larger populations should result in smaller accidental extinction probability (because every individual must die acci-dentally before extinction is complete). No doubt this probability is not lin-ear. Thus, I am not saying that a species with 10^6 individuals has 100 times the chance of accidental extinction as a species with 10^8 individuals. Just that it tends to have a higher probability.

Second, the greater range covers more niche refuges. Any weather distur-

[1] I ignore immigration. For biogeographical provinces, it is a second order process, by definition.

bance or climatic deterioration covers a limited area. Species with big ranges are more likely to have a site or two to tide them over. So, they should again suffer lower extinction rates.

Third, larger ranges are bigger targets for geographical barriers. When a barrier hits a range and produces a population isolate, the process of allopatric speciation can begin. True, some barriers may penetrate a range without producing isolates. But at the size of most (or all) real ranges, the probability of hitting the range dominates the probability of isolate formation. Hence, we expect higher speciation rates where ranges are largest (see also Rosenzweig, 1978b).

Fourth, larger ranges should promote higher speciation rates because the species that have them seem to evolve faster. Recall the model called centrifugal speciation and the evidence in its favor (Chapter 5). The small-range species *Peromyscus melanotis* lives as many isolates, yet they do not diverge. Large-range *P. maniculatus* rapidly spins off species by stranding them as small isolates and then evolving to be something the isolates no longer belong to. From theoretical population genetics we learn to expect such phenomena. A large population's chance to evolve a new gene function far exceeds that of a small population.

In sum, larger ranges should reduce extinction rates on two counts, and increase allopatric speciation rates on two counts. Our tropical regions will diversify faster than our subtropical ones, and leave them relatively poor (Figure 9.16). Given what we know about speciation and extinction, we would have to be astonished if there were no latitudinal diversity gradients.

Terborgh (1973) suggested a powerful way to see if indeed the tropics depend on their large areas for their high diversities. He noted that some tropical biomes are rare on some continents. If area causes the latitudinal gradient, then those biomes on those continents should be impoverished. Africa, for example, is rich in upland tropical grasslands compared with the Neotropics. Sure enough, it also has many more species of vertebrate grazer. The Neotropics, on the other hand, has the world's greatest expanse of tropical rainforest. Sure enough, it also has the greatest diversity of tropical forest trees.

Earlier in this chapter, we examined interprovincial curves of diversity for both trees and vertebrate frugivores (Figure 9.1). Those curves and the fish example from the Congo and Amazon basins (Marlier, 1973), greatly extend Terborgh's observation. There can be no doubt that area, and not just the quality of being a tropical rainforest, produces the wealth of species in the tropics.

Dynamics of Diversity
in Biological Provinces

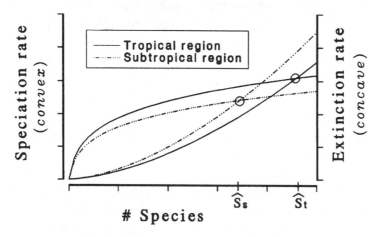

Figure 9.16. Speciation and extinction rate curves for the tropics
should compare with those of the subtropics as in this
figure. Speciation curves are convex upward. The
tropical speciation curve lies above the subtropical; its
extinction curve lies below. The result is a higher
equilibrium in the tropics. Notice that the model also
predicts that the tropics actually should have higher
equilibrial extinction rates. Redrawn from
Rosenzweig (1992).

Moreover, Richards (1973) points out, 'In the forests of tropical Africa ...
a very large proportion of the species have wide, though sometimes discontinuous, ranges. Species of endemic or regionally localized distribution are
relatively few. This is in strong contrast to the situation in South and central America and in Malaya, Borneo, New Guinea and other parts of Indo-
Malaysia where local species are very numerous.' I add that it also con-
trasts with the situation in the Cape flora (fynbos) of Africa itself. There,
the flora is characterized by 'exceptionally high levels of regional and local
endemism' (Cowling *et al.*, 1989, p. 37; see also Cowling *et al.*, 1992). And
the floristic swarm in southwestern Australia also has a high number of
local endemics (Hopper, 1979). It certainly seems that the dearth of tropical
forest species in Africa is connected to relatively slow geographical speciation rates. That is just what we expect to see if the low diversity has come
about according to theory.

Evidence from marine systems supports the conclusion too. The Pacific

Ocean is much larger than the Atlantic although the two contain much the same set of environments. You would expect each type of biome to occur in proportion to the total area of these oceans. Thus, you would expect that Pacific diversities of various taxa will exceed Atlantic diversities. They do. Schopf (1970) noted that Pacific diversities of both ectoprocts and bivalves are twice as high as Atlantic diversities. And Findley and Findley (1985) showed that butterfly fishes (Chaetodontidae) of coral reefs in the Pacific are consistently more diverse than their Atlantic vicars.

McGowan and Walker (1993) review the pattern of diversity among pelagic animals (those living in the upper 200 m of the open ocean). Data are especially good for the Euphausiacea, Chaetognatha, Pteropoda and Copepoda of the Pacific Ocean. Despite the vast areas of their marine provinces, the species of these taxa are not very diverse; the copepods are two orders of magnitude more diverse than the other three, and even they have fewer than 2000 species. Furthermore, these taxa differ from most others in not following a strict latitudinal gradient. Their diversities peak in the temperate and subtropical waters of both North and South Pacific. Tropical diversities are some 15 to 20% less.

We can explain both anomalies in terms of area. First, although the areas of the open ocean are huge, geographical barriers must be quite unusual in them. So, they offer little opportunity for allopatric speciation. Second, the gyres of the North and South Pacific are larger than the area of the tropical Pacific. So, we would expect the former to outrank the latter in diversity.

Mares and Ojeda (1982) discovered another exception. It too obeys unusual patterns of area and latitude. Among the 126 species of hystricognath rodents in South America, diversity peaks in the latitudinal interval from 10° S to 20° S.

Latitude	10°–0° N	0°–10° S	10°–20° S	20°–30° S	30°–40° S	40°–50° S	50°–60°S
No. of species	28	37	61	51	24	9	3

However, South America constricts near the Equator, and Mares and Ojeda found that hystricognath diversities do conform to the areas available within the latitudinal bands they studied (Figure 9.17). Once they reckoned with area, latitude retained no ability to explain these diversities.

Other evidence also suggests that the latitudinal gradient does not require any environmental change other than area. A few perceptive investigators have sought the gradient in equal-area patches of similar environments arrayed along a latitudinal transect. And they have found it.

Specht (1988) presented a most remarkable case of such a latitudinal gra-

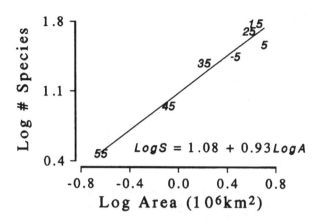

Figure 9.17. Hystricognath rodent diversities follow the area available. Numbers along the line are the midpoints of the
10° bands of latitude studied by Mares and Ojeda
(1982). They do not help explain the residuals from
the species–area regression line. Data from Mares and
Ojeda.

dient. He looked at all the plants in 1 km² patches of sand dunes in
Australia. The samples ranged from about 12° S to about 42° S. Figure
9.18 shows the gradient.

Few studies show a latitudinal gradient independent of both sampling
area and variation of biome type. Most confound the latter variation with
the latitudinal. So I mention three more studies that avoided this trap.

Jeanne (1979) surveyed predaceous ants at five latitudes in the Americas.
Bait, consisting of larval wasps, attracted the ants to collection sites in old
fields and forests. All sites were relatively wet, low in elevation, and near
the eastern coast.

Latitude	45° 55′ N	30° 50′ N	18° 35′ N	10° 26′ N	2° 26′ S
No. of ant species	22	40	66	68	74

Stanton (1979) looked at mites in fields, pine forests and broad-leaved
forests in Wyoming (1300 m elevation) and Costa Rica (2330 m elevation).
In a standard set of samples, she found more species in the tropics, regardless of habitat although she emphasizes in her paper that subsamples
of 600 cm² did not always show the difference.) The following data are
numbers of species:

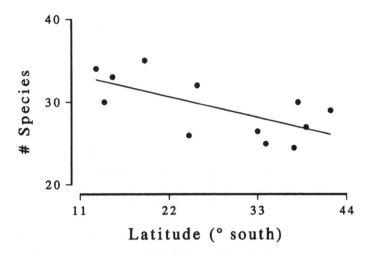

Figure 9.18. Plants of sandy coastal habitats in Australia show a
latitudinal gradient despite their being sampled from
a single uniform biotope. Data from Specht (1988),
with Professor Specht's kind assistance.

	Field	Broad-leaf	Pine
Wyoming	25	55	34
Costa Rica	53	83	108

Recently, Rex *et al.* (1993) have added a similar case from the deep sea
(Atlantic Ocean and Norwegian Sea). Instead of holding the sampling area
constant, however, they rarify the samples to a constant number of individuals. They used Hurlbert's (1971) method. The 97 samples come from soft-
sediment habitats on the ocean floor at depths of 500–4000 m. They extend
from 77° N to 37° S. So far the authors have published the results from
three taxa: bivalves, gastropods and isopods. For gastropods, they rarify
samples to 50 individuals; for bivalves to 75; for isopods to 200. All three
taxa show a significant latitudinal gradient even after Rex *et al.* remove the
effects of different depths and discount the effects of different equitabilities.

   In sum, larger provinces should theoretically have, and do actually have,
greater diversities. Since tropical areas are the world's largest provinces,
they should (and do) have the world's greatest diversities. I think we can
safely say that differences in area must generate at least a substantial part
of the latitudinal gradient. For those who may still balk at admitting this

conclusion, I quote Fay Weldon (*The Cloning of Joanna May*): 'At a certain point, skepticism becomes willful blindness.'

But I am not naive. I know that some of my colleagues pay no attention to Fay Weldon. Nor are they happy with the theory or satisfied with the data. Some of them have suggested a certain kind of comparison to me, or actually performed it and published it (e.g. Anderson and Koopman, 1981; Stevens, 1989). Test the predictions about area and range size by comparing range sizes in temperate and tropics. In one guise, this proposal says diversity is higher in the tropics, so range sizes should be smaller. In its other form, it says the tropics are larger, so range sizes should be larger. What is the correct prediction? Neither.

The area explanation says that speciation **rate curves** are higher in the tropics because the tropics are more extensive. So, we can say that **at similar diversities**, tropical range sizes should be larger. But tropical and temperate zones do not have similar diversities. The equilibrium point of tropical diversity is higher. And, we have no predictions to make comparing tropical with temperate range sizes at unequal tropical and temperate diversities.

The area explanation also says that as the diversity of a province rises, its range sizes should fall. But that cannot be tested in space because it predicts what should happen in a single province over time. *Mea culpa*: I myself am primarily responsible for this miscarriage of science. Rosenzweig (1975) presents two spatial analyses of average range size against diversity. Ranges of both bats and turtles in North America are smaller in places with larger diversities. I stayed within one province to make that test, but never explained why. Even so, I must confess that had the relationship worked out other than the way it did, I would not have believed it: I knew I was testing a temporal prediction on a spatial grid. I guess that makes my mistake even more egregious!

Notice that the area explanation reduces the latitudinal gradient to a type of interprovincial species–area curve. But it is certainly not the same as the interprovincial curve in Figure 9.1. That curve was taken from sets of provinces similar in environment, whereas the environment varies substantially across a latitudinal gradient. Such variation, in productivity and other environmental properties, is bound to influence diversity and thus the latitudinal gradient. Just because Jeanne (1979), Rex *et al.* (1993), Specht (1988) and Stanton (1979) have shown that the gradient does not require environmental variation, does not mean that such variation plays no role. I look forward to the day when we understand how environmental differences combine with area differences to mold the latitudinal diversity gradient.

Though the latitudinal gradient may differ from the interprovincial curve in but subtle and secondary ways, it differs entirely from the other species–area curves. It exists on a far grander scale than either the mainland or island species–area curves. The latitudinal gradient depends on the passage of enough time for speciation. If Amazonia and the temperate forests of North America were to begin today with a few thousand species each, both would exhibit species–area curves. A century or two from now they still would, and they would still have similar diversities. It might take a million years for the area of the Amazon to produce a notably richer province. And it might take 10 million years before the full richness of the Amazon could re-establish itself.

We can confirm that neither mainland nor island species–area curves account for the latitudinal gradient. To do it, we need to show that for a constant area, lower latitudes still have more species. In fact, that is true. For example, recall that in a lowland floodplain forest in the Amazon Basin of Peru, Terborgh *et al.* (1990) counted 319 species of birds in a 97 ha study site. They also found point diversities of more than 160 species. Such point diversities exceed the highest of any uniform habitat in North America by 300% – at least.

Turner and his colleagues measured both bird and lepidopteran diversities in equal-area samples of Britain (Turner *et al.*, 1987, 1988). Even for so small a region, the effect of latitude did not disappear.

Turner reports his results mostly as an effect of temperature. That is, in equal-area samples, warmer places have more species. But, of course, these species did not evolve in Britain. They came from the much larger region of Eurasia. And each 1 km^2 carries the evolutionary mark of its participation in the larger region to which it belongs. Warmer places in Britain will have amassed their species from warmer, lower-latitude biomes. Turner recognizes that the pattern he finds reflects the latitudinal gradient. (I should note that by linking temperature to productivity, he also attributes causality to the relationship between temperature and latitudinal diversity. But there is no justification for this attribution. Moreover, you have seen in Chapter 2 that the statistical relationship between productivity and diversity is unimodal. In Chapter 12 you also will see that no one understands it very well.)

George Gaylord Simpson himself (Simpson, 1964) removed the small-scale area effect from the diversity data of the mammals of North America. Simpson reduced the data to equal-area samples. Afterward, the latitudinal gradient remained. Cook (1969) and Kiester (1971) got the same result when they repeated the exercise for birds and herptiles respectively.

Simpson's analyses were refined by Wilson (1974). Wilson claimed that bats cause the gradient, and that quadrupeds do not show it in equal-area samples. But close reading of his method shows that many of his samples come from incomplete, coastal rectangles containing varying amounts of ocean. With a copy of Wilson (1972), his help and that of Carole Rosenzweig and Elizabeth Sandlin, I reanalyzed his data. The half that comes from full quadrats does show a strong latitudinal gradient among both quadrupeds and bats (Figures 2.18 and 2.19).

Please do not get confused by the two messages about mammal diversities from North and South America. The northern (Figure 2.18 and 2.19) seems to say that area plays no role, the southern (Figure 9.17), that latitude plays no role. But the North American analysis comes from equal-area samples, so we deliberately prevented area from being significant. And the South American analysis concludes that area accounts for the effect of latitude, not that latitude has no effect. A summary sentence consistent with both data sets and with our understanding of the latitudinal gradient would look like this. *Provincial regions of large area – generally, but not necessarily associated with low latitudes – support higher diversities, and equal-area samples of various regions tend to find more species in the richer regions.* If you are having difficulty seeing that these two patterns are consistent, return to Chapter 8, especially to Figure 8.54 and its associated text.

Figure 9.15 shows that northern terrestrial biomes do not show much variation in area. Subtropical, temperate, boreal and tundra all have similar extents. If area is the true basis of latitudinal gradients, then why does the gradient appear within these biomes? You might expect to see a step function: higher diversity in the tropics and lower diversity north of it, but no change north of about 25°. I can think of two reasons to doubt this conclusion.

First, many species have ranges that extend over more than one zone. Many tropical species will reach northward and get counted in northern lists. (The same thing may be going on among species of other zones, but not as often because of the area effect.) The farther north you go, the fewer tropical species remain. The result will be a secondary diversity gradient among zones north of the tropics. This hypothesis predicts that the gradient should disappear if you remove all species with partly tropical ranges from lists of species north of the tropics. (But no one has yet tried this simple statistical experiment.)

Second, primary productivity declines as latitude increases. Perhaps this decline also causes a decline in diversity. Chapter 12 deals entirely with the effects of productivity. It shows that very low productivities do indeed produce very low diversities.

I think both reasons may be valid. The productivity effect and the spillover of tropical ranges into non-tropical zones may combine to produce a gradient outside the tropics in Northern Hemisphere lands. But notice that the spillover effect depends on the area effect: without a tropical bias in the number of species spilling over, spillover effects in different zones would cancel each other out. And, as you will see, no one yet understands the productivity effect. In contrast, we can rely on the area effect. So, the vastness of the tropics gives us a consistent, reasonable and successful primary explanation for their high diversity. And the low productivity of high latitudes suggests a likely, but still unsubstantiated, secondary cause for their low diversity.

Chapter 10

Paleobiological patterns

The epochal steady state

In Chapter 3, we saw that diversity may often – or even usually – wobble around a steady state for millions of years. How can we explain that? We should be able to deduce a theory to do the job. At such long time scales, that theory must center on rates of speciation and extinction.

Many factors influence speciation and extinction rates. But only negative feedback variables can produce a steady state. Recall (Chapter 8) that in negative feedback, a product depresses its own rate of production. Without negative feedback, diversity would go out of control. It would crash to zero or skyrocket to infinity. Thus, we must figure out how higher diversities reduce the rate of change of diversity.

As in all ecological considerations, feedback variables exist because the world is finite. Space is limited. Energy flow is limited. Time is limited. Physics hems life in from all sides. How do these limits translate into diversity's steady states? I begin by considering diversity within one trophic level. Then I show how the steady state changes when other levels get added.

The steady state within one trophic level

Geographical speciation within a trophic level Species restrict each other's niche breadths. We learned this in Chapter 7. Sometimes such restriction also limits geographical ranges. We all know of species not found in this or that country because their habitats aren't.

As their range sizes decline, we expect from Chapter 5 (Figure 5.1), that the rate at which individual species form isolates and new species also will decline. Perhaps also, evolution slows down in smaller ranges. (See the paragraphs on centrifugal speciation in Chapter 5.) So, as diversity grows, the rate of geographical speciation (per species) should fall. Diversity feeds back negatively on itself through the intermediary of range size.

Although the rate of speciation per species should fall as diversity grows, the rate for the whole set of species may not. This rate is the sum of the separate rates:

$$\sum_{i=1}^{s} g_i \qquad\qquad (10.1)$$

where S is the actual number of species and g_i is the rate of the ith species. Each new species may depress the average rate, but it also adds its own rate to the total. That addition may or may not compensate for the rate loss of the others.

Data are not available to determine if Expression 10.1 ever falls as diversity rises. Rosenzweig (1975) suggested that some evidence indicates falling rates may not occur often. The evidence is that even places with high diversity have many species with very large ranges. Thus, adding species may be mostly a process of adding many small ranges rather than reducing all the large ranges. But this evidence is weak. Fortunately, we do not need to evaluate the derivative of Expression 10.1 (with respect to S). We can explain long-term steady states merely from knowing that the speciation rate per species declines as S grows.

Competitive speciation within a trophic level Competitive speciation contains the levers of its own control in its very mechanism. Expansion of a species' variance, which is the first step in the process, requires ecological opportunity. As those opportunities get filled, expansions cease. Thus eventually, as diversity rises, competitive speciation must slow down greatly or stop altogether.

I say 'eventually' because at very low diversities, competitive speciation may also proceed slowly. Species must have phenotypic access to an empty adaptive zone in order to colonize it evolutionarily. In a clade with few species, such access may be limited.

Nevertheless, as in the case of geographical speciation, the per species rate lacks ambiguity. Perhaps a small set of species cannot reach many empty adaptive zones. But each of its species can reach one. And each will speciate fastest when it is unconfined by others nearby (in adaptive – or phenotypic – space). That is, each species will speciate fastest when there are few species.

As the set of species radiates into the space, more and more will lose access to its frontiers. These will thus be cut off from further expansion. Surrounded by their own successful daughter species, they will cease competitive speciation. The average rate per species must decline.

Rates of polyploidy Polyploidy's rates have not been modeled as functions of diversity. However, we can speculate briefly about them. Each new species must add a set of possible polyploids. So, the more species, the more polyploids can form. Is polyploidy therefore a positive feedback process? Does it accelerate and go out of control?

The classic positive feedback process is fire. As the fire heats the air above it, that air rises, drawing in fresh oxygen. The fire burns faster, drawing in oxygen even faster. That's why a good chimney is the key to a good hearth. Yet the whole world does not burn when I strike a match. Why? Because, although it has plenty of oxygen, the fire eventually runs out of wood.

I believe the rate of polyploidy gets controlled like fire. Polyploids form very rapidly when they can. But eventually, all the likely polyploids are formed. Polyploidy must wait for the slower processes of speciation to produce more raw material. That, of course, occurs at the rates of the slower processes. So, in the long term, the rate of polyploidy should be governed by the other rates. Polyploidy is a tiger in a cage – eating ravenously, but only when fed.

Extinction rates We have already figured out how species diversity influences extinction rates. (See the section in Chapter 6.) There you will see that the more species there are, the higher is the rate of extinction per species. We reached that conclusion because more species means both fewer individuals per species and a greater chance of interactive extinction.

Now recall the relationship of geographical range to diversity. As diversity rises, average geographical range declines. Extinction can take place because a species niche disappears for a short time over its entire geographical range. The more restricted the niche and the smaller the geographical range, the more likely such an accident. That reinforces the argument that extinction rates rise with diversity.

Overall dynamics I have not been able to think of other feedback variables that might help regulate diversity. Fortunately, however, what we have learned so far is sufficient. We can already draw a robust outline of the long-term processes that control diversities.

- The rate of speciation per species declines as the number of species grows. Added diversity depresses both geographical and competitive speciation rates (per species).
- The rate of extinction per species grows as the number of species

increases. This sets the trend of extinction against the trend of speciation.

Question: Do speciation rates tend to balance extinction rates? Somehow,
they must.

- If extinction consistently exceeded speciation, we wouldn't be here.
  Neither would anything else. As Déscartes remarked in another
  context, '*Cogito ergo sum.*' I'm here. You're here. So extinction cannot always exceed speciation.
- If speciation consistently exceeded extinction, the Earth would be
  an ever-expanding collection of species. However, the data say otherwise. Rarely does diversity rise permanently. So, rates of origination and rates of extinction must usually resemble each other quite
  closely.

We can now make a graph illustrating the long-term relationship of speciation and extinction rates to diversity (Figure 10.1). Speciation goes

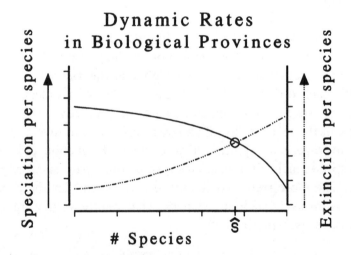

Figure 10.1. Diversity increases extinction rates per species, but
            drives down speciation rates per species. The result
            has to be a steady state diversity, $\hat{S}$. Otherwise we
            would either not be here, or else not see long periods
            of little change in diversity. Notice that in this graph,
            I have plotted rates per species. That is why they
            approach some limit greater than zero at $S = 0$. That
            is also why speciation declines. Figure 9.16 is an
            example of a graph with total rates.

down, extinction goes up, and the two lines cross. The point where they cross is the equilibrium, $\hat{S}$.

The simplest and most robust of stability analyses shows that this equilibrium ought to be stable. Imagine a diversity somewhat greater than the equilibrium. That diversity will cause extinction rates to exceed speciation rates. So, a high diversity undermines itself. Diversity falls toward the equilibrium. Now imagine a diversity lower than the equilibrium. Low diversity causes the speciation rate to exceed the extinction rate. So, low diversity will grow toward equilibrium. Figure 10.1 tells us that diversity is a self-regulating property of natural systems. Erode it and it restores itself. Augment it and it diminishes.

Paleobiologists can test the theory. Does the fossil record show that diversity usually fluctuates within fairly narrow bounds that we can interpret as a steady state? Yes. You will recall what appear to be several examples of this in Chapter 3. Does that moderate fluctuation depend on a balance of extinction and speciation? That is much harder to answer.

So far, few paleobiological examples have surfaced. We need many more, and we probably need to use capture–recapture technology to get them. One example, owing to the analysis of two biometricians (Nichols and Pollock, 1983), comes from mammals of the late Eocene Epoch. Figure 10.2 shows their results. The rate-per-species estimates cover periods varying between about 40 000 and 70 000 years, so they are far from perfect. Moreover, as can be expected, the speciation rates – depending heavily on non-biotic, geological phenomena – are extra-noisy when plotted solely as a function of diversity. Yet, despite the crudeness and the noise, we can see the signal. As diversity increases, extinction rate grows and speciation rate declines. The lines cross at a diversity of 45.8 species. The average diversity during the sampling intervals of these rates was 44.9 species (see Figure 3.5). So, this example reassures us, but only a little. It needs a lot more company before we can lay the issue aside.

Steady states for more than one trophic level

So far, the theory of a steady-state diversity has dealt with species of only one trophic level. Whittaker (1972) believed that additional trophic levels eliminate the steady state. *Species are niches for other species*, he argued. The more kinds of plants there are, the more kinds of herbivores there can be. The more kinds of hosts, the more kinds of parasitoids can coexist. Moreover, the arrow of causality also can point the other way round: suc-

Eocene Mammals

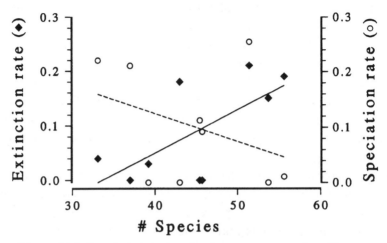

Figure 10.2. Speciation and extinction rates among late Eocene
mammals resemble each other in size. Speciation rates
tend to fall and extinction rates tend to rise as diversity grows. Data from Nichols and Pollock (1983).

cess can come to victims because they specialize on resisting certain species
of predator.

Whittaker's correlation must be true. Every ecologist can spout examples
that support it. Here are some off the top of this ecologist's head.

- Many insect species specialize on plants with obnoxious contents by
  being able to detoxify or sequester their anti-predator compounds
  (Brower *et al.*, 1967).
- The chisel-shaped front teeth of *Dipodomys microps* allow it to strip
  halophytic leaves of their lethal concentrations of salt (Kenagy,
  1972).
- Specialization of predators on limited size ranges of victims has
  long been a fixture of community ecology (Rosenzweig, 1966;
  Storer, 1966; Pearson and Mury, 1979; etc.). We understand it as a
  result of optimal foraging rules.
- Ecologists also know of many cases that support the concept of
  predator-mediated coexistence (e.g. Summerhayes, 1941).
- As you saw in Chapter 4, there is a close correlation between the
  number of predators and the number of victims. Moreover, no one

doubts its causal nature. Predators depend on their victims for existence, and some victims (or potential victims) succeed by avoiding some predators. Thus, predators and victims may act toward each other as evolutionary mutualists.

Whittaker concluded that the mutualistic relationship amongst some species on different trophic levels leads to ceaseless growth in diversity. Indeed, the mutualistic relationship brings a tendency for positive feedback to ensembles of species; the more species, the more opportunities and the lower the extinction rate. But, just because one component of a system exhibits positive feedback does not mean the whole system gets out of control. The negative feedback components also play their roles, and we know these grow out of the competitive aspects of diversity. To determine overall dynamics, we must combine the competitive with the mutualistic aspects. That combination is less difficult to achieve than you might imagine.

Begin with a graph whose axes are the numbers of species on the first and second trophic levels (Figure 10.3). Let P be those on the first and H those on the second. If $H = 0$, we already predict a steady state in P. We mark this steady state as P^* on the P axis. Now we add some species on the second trophic level. We incorporate Whittaker's mutualistic principle by noting that now there must be niches for more than P^* species on the first trophic level. In fact, the more H species we add, the more P species can succeed. Therefore, the mutualism produces a zero isocline in the graph, a zero isocline of positive slope. Inward from the isoclines toward the origin of the graph, diversity will grow.

Whittaker told us nothing about the second derivative of the isoclines in Figure 10.3. Is the isocline concave upward or convex upward? I have argued that it must be concave (Rosenzweig, 1975). As more and more species of P are added, they remain supported by the same resource base. They subdivide the same pool of nutrients, the same area of the Earth, the same energy flow. Each new H adds the possibility of new P species, but at a diminishing return.

The H isocline must be similar. It will differ in that no H species can exist when $P = 0$. So, at $P = 0$, $H^* = 0$. But, starting from its intercept with the origin, the H isocline exhibits Whittaker's principle by having a positive slope. And it also incorporates the diminishing returns accompanying new P species. For the H isocline, diminishing returns mean convexity (rather than concavity).

Mathematically, you can put two curves in a graph like Figure 10.3 with-

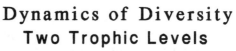

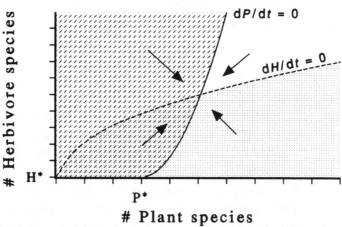

Figure 10.3. Diversity of more than one trophic level can seek an overall steady state even though species on each level add to the sustainable diversity of the other. In the absence of plants, herbivore diversity balances at H^* (i.e. zero). In the absence of herbivores, plant diversity balances at P^*. Herbivores create opportunities for plants to specialize at escaping them. Thus, more and more plant species can exist as herbivore diversity grows. Similarly, more plant species allow more herbivore species. Nevertheless, the zero isoclines of the system should cross because each added species should raise the extinction rates of the assemblage it invades. More species sharing the same resource pie have smaller populations or smaller geographical ranges. (Plant species diversity increases in the diagonally-shaded area; herbivore species diversity increases in the dotted area.)

out having them cross. You allow their slopes to continue changing but make them asymptotic to a pair of divergent straight lines. However, I cannot imagine the biology that could lead to such mathematics. Instead, the isoclines should approach asymptotes that are perpendicular to their axes. (A perpendicular isocline means no further increases in equilibrium owing to increases in the diversity of the other trophic level.) Such isoclines must always intersect.

The point of intersection of the isoclines of Figure 10.3 is a steady state. At it, the diversities of both trophic levels exceed the diversities they would attain without mutualism between the levels. Thus, Whittaker's principle of evolutionary mutualism does not get swamped by competition. We should (and do) find that diversities on one level depend positively on those at another. But mutualism does not cost life its dynamical equilibrium. Logic does not demand that mutualism always forces diversity to grow. Eventually, competition will rule and bring diversity under the control of negative feedback.

Chaos?

The balance between speciation and extinction resembles the balance between the per capita birth rate and death rate in a single population. During the past twenty years, ecologists have been studying single-species dynamics with a new set of tools called non-linear dynamics (Schaffer, 1985). Non-linear dynamics tells us that even in figures as simple as Figure 10.3, we may expect behavior different from a steady state. The state variable (population size or, in our case, number of species) may oscillate in a limit cycle or in an almost-periodic trajectory. Or it may exhibit strange attractor dynamics, including chaos. Such dynamics are very difficult to distinguish from random fluctuations. How do we know that equilibrium diversities don't exhibit such complicated non-linear behaviors? We don't.

However, so far, non-linear studies have not produced any convincing arguments that would cause us to expect non-linearity in the dynamics of diversity. In fact, I do not believe that speciation and extinction contain the properties leading to non-linear dynamics. But my belief will not discourage real research into the question.

We know, for example, of a 26 Myr period in mass extinction events. Does this result from non-linear dynamics? Many paleobiologists (see Chapter 6) believe that the mechanism of the 26 Myr extinction cycle lies outside life – in fact, outside the Earth. I believe they are correct. But I also believe in the need for much more research into the dynamics around diversity equilibria.

Meantime we do have some records indicating steady states. We should accept the likelihood that the reasoning behind Figures 10.1 and 10.3 explains them. Even the most ardent student of non-linear dynamics would admit that some equilibria are steady states. So let's take what we have earned.

Why, over hundreds of millions of years, does diversity rise?

New habitats get colonized

In Chapter 7, I proposed that habitats are coevolved properties of organisms. I also proposed that the fineness of their subdivision depends upon the regional diversity they contain. Nevertheless, some places in the world are non-habitats. They carry environmental properties inimical to all forms of life. Ice-covered wastelands cover much of the Earths' polar regions, and constitute the best, most extensive example. (I excluded them from the calculation of terrestrial areas in Chapter 9.)

Sometimes life evolves to convert a non-habitat into a hospitable environment. Two grand examples show up in the fossil record: the colonizations of 'dry' land and muddy sea bottom.

Terrestrial life does not occur in the fossil record during its earliest hundreds of million years. Plants, invertebrates, and vertebrates all make the transition during the Silurian Period. We see this as a large increase in the diversity of families and genera. Of course, neither families nor genera are species. But when a system goes from zero genera to some, its species diversity must also grow.

Bambach (1977) identified only a few undeniable increases in marine fossil diversity. One of these gives us our second example. Toward the end of the Ordovician Period (*c.* 430 Myr ago), life colonized the muddy ocean bottom and produced a worldwide increase in invertebrate species diversity.

As did the land, the muddy ocean bottom had existed for many millions of years before it was successfully colonized. The fossil record shows life was almost absent for 100 Myr before the Ordovician. One, two or three species perhaps, all rare in the muddy habitat, and all known elsewhere.

Then something happened. We do not know exactly what, but it may not have had anything to do with natural selection. Dissolved oxygen levels may have increased until they exceeded some threshold. Whatever happened, life poured in from clear-water habitats. Evolution *in situ* produced many new species (representing older taxa). Presumably these new species adapted to the muddy water. Within a short time (paleontologically speaking) the process was over and the muddy benthos was 'full'.

You can see the increase in muddy benthic diversity in Figure 3.3. This figure (from Rosenzweig and Taylor, 1980) analyzes the record of the Nicolet River Valley, Quebec, at the precise time of the increase. Recall (Chapter 3) that the Nicolet River Valley exhibits a long-term steady state in diversity. The record of Figure 3.3 occurred immediately before the steady state. In Figure 10.4 I have plotted the entire Bretsky record using the species-per-sample statistic. It allows you to see the increase to an apparent steady state.

The easiest way to detect a trend in diversity is to look at a sequence of individual samples of fossil life collected in about the same way and with about the same amount of effort and technical sophistication. The data of Figure 3.3 satisfy those criteria because Peter and Sara Bretsky (1976) collected them in a short time, and from a series of similar strata in one locale.

Artifacts

More species evolve hard parts You rarely find fossils of guts. Shells, carapaces and bones, on the other hand, make fine fossils. The record we see gets transmitted by this biased filter. If most species have hard parts, we are likely to know about more of them than if most do not.

Paleontologists tell us that the low species diversities characteristic of the pre-Cambrian may reflect a general absence of easily fossilizable hard parts. Perhaps other times and places that we now consider depauperate, also had

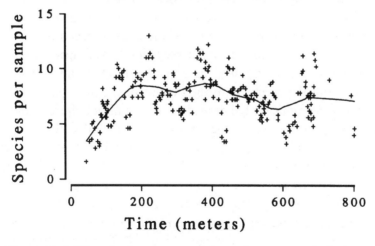

Figure 10.4. Diversity hovers near 6–8 species per sample during the 4 Myr after the evolution of a rich benthic fauna in the late Ordovician. The increase phase shows clearly to the left of 200 m. Data courtesy of Peter and Sara Bretsky. The regression line: lowess with 30% of data per estimate.

rich diversities. Maybe the Cambrian muddy benthos pulsed with life after all. Soft life.

But soft life also leaves fossils, albeit less readily. Thus, the pre-Cambrian is rich in fossil forms. We may be able to trace increases in apparent diversity to increases in fossilizability. But I doubt that qualitative shifts from nearly zero to many species – such as those of the Upper Ordovician's muddy benthos – come about for lack of hard parts. In addition, mud turns into shale, a fine-grained sedimentary rock and the best for soft-part preservation.

Because soft parts also leave fossil records occasionally, one can actually estimate the diversity of soft species using statistical methods. We can assume that species occurrences fit a Poisson distribution, say, and estimate the number of those that have not yet been found. Rosenzweig and Duek (1979) came close to that for the Nicolet River assemblage. Preston (1979) actually did it for bird species unseen in Christmas censuses. You could use other methods as well, such as capture-recapture censuses (Rosenzweig and Taylor, 1980). But I do not know of any case where such statistical tools have been used on the problem of soft species. So, we do not yet know whether some diversity increases are artifacts of more hard parts.

The pull of the recent Geological processes not only preserve the record of life. They also destroy it. Volcanoes can melt sedimentary rock and obliterate most or all the record in it. Whole eons of ocean floor get sucked into the Earth's mantle and melted for recycling. The longer a fossil-bearing stratum is exposed to such risks, the surer its disappearance. So, we know much more about the recent than the distant past.

Raup (1976b) emphasized the need to worry about the completeness of the fossil record. He estimated the amount of rock still surviving from each major geological era (Figure 10.5). Then he calculated the number of species per million years (See Figure 3.1). Figure 10.6 makes it clear that most of the apparent variation in diversity among marine invertebrates during Phanerozoic time comes from variation in sample size. Diversity appears to grow because we have a much larger sample of more recent rock than of older rock. The residuals from Figure 10.6 show no significant tendency to grow with time (Figure 10.7). The clear increase of Figure 3.1 has vanished.

Raup's work proves how treacherous it is to ignore the special characteristics of the fossil record. Removing the bias of the pull-of-the-recent means removing most of the evidence that diversity has grown steadily throughout

Surviving Rock Area

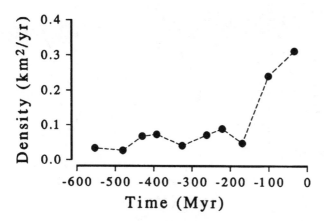

Figure 10.5. The amount of rock of any given age varies greatly
with geological era. However, the two most recent
eras have the most surviving rock. This suggests their
higher diversities may be merely a sampling phenomenon. Data from Raup, (1976b).

Marine Invertebrates
Phanerozoic Time

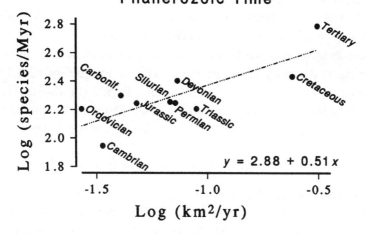

Figure 10.6. The species diversity of marine invertebrates correlates well with the area of rock available for sampling
their fossils (log $S = 2.88 + 0.507$ log A; $R^2 = 0.656$;
$p = 4.5 \times 10^{-3}$). Data from Raup, (1976b); Sepkoski,
(1984).

Marine Invertebrates

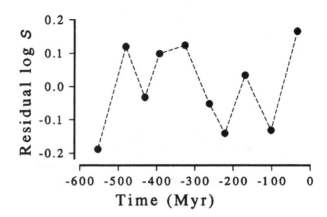

Figure 10.7. Residuals from the regression of Figure 10.6 do not
increase significantly with time. That is what they
would have to do to show that species diversity has
actually grown through the ages. Modified from the
work of Raup, (1976b).

the Earth's history. It explains most of the variation in diversity as an artifact of varying sample sizes. And the rest? Most of it comes from the colonization of new biomes and from mass extinctions.

Indeed, mass extinctions stand out. But those cause declines in diversity,
not increases. And life restores them time after time.

I believe that Raup's work also teaches us that usually, we need to focus
on increases in diversity at a finer scale than 'all marine species'. For example, the increase at the end of the Ordovician Period stands firm. It depends
upon the analysis of similar-aged rocks. And it identifies a particular set of
habitats – the muddy sea floor – in which the increases occurred.

Niche space gets more completely explored

The phenotype of an organism is the set of its measurable non-genetic
properties. These include morphology, physiology and behavior. Organisms
use their phenotypes to establish places for themselves in natural communities. But those places, called niches, do not remove the individuals from the
dynamic interactions they share with other species. On the contrary, they
insure that the species will continue to feel the evolutionary pressure of
such interactions.

The quasi-equilibrium Van Valen (1973) and Rosenzweig (1973b) independently, and for different reasons, proposed that interacting species are locked in an eternal struggle. Each evolves as fast as natural selection allows it. But no species gains and no species loses by that evolution because all species are evolving to counter each other's advances. Van Valen, following Felsenstein (1971), termed this the Red Queen principle because 'It takes all the running you can do merely to stay in the same place' (Lewis Carroll, *Alice Through the Looking-glass*).

Van Valen's argument for Red Queen evolution stems from the fossil record. He thought he observed that taxa have the same probability of extinction regardless of their age. If so, that means they neither senesce nor wax stronger despite much evolution.

I grounded my argument in a theory of predator–victim coevolution. If the rate of evolutionary improvement depends upon the reward for evolutionary improvement, then predators and their victims should have a self-regulated system of coevolutionary rates. If one species temporarily gets ahead of the other, its reward for doing even better declines. But the reward to the other species increases, which makes it catch up. Schaffer and Rosenzweig (1978) used a more realistic model of this argument and found it still worked.

The trouble with both these ideas is that 'all the running you can do' may be none. When that happens, we say the system has reached an Evolutionary Stable Strategy (Maynard Smith and Price, 1973). No individual can change its phenotype for the better. Evolution stops.

I noted the likelihood of ESS's in my 1973 paper (although I did not know the term then). ESS's come about because of the conflicting purposes for which a phenotype needs to be used. If an individual improves its ability to fulfill one of those purposes, the selective pressure on it to improve further diminishes. But, at the same time, the selective pressure to improve a conflicting purpose increases. Thus, phenotypes are a jumble of compromises, of evolutionary deadlocks that stop evolutionary change.

What makes compromise necessary? Different functions of the phenotype correlate with each other producing trade-offs. A bigger dragonfly is not just better able to defend a richer territory. It also loses some ability to use poorer territories.

Many phenotypic properties function in more than one way. These functions, tied together statistically and often mechanically, cause the need to compromise. Thus, they prevent any single function from being done perfectly. But, knowing what stops evolutionary change also teaches us what will start it again.

Key adaptations: beakthroughs to evolutionary progress Vermeij (1973a) was
the first to recognize that natural selection can weaken or break
correlations between phenotypic properties by increasing 'the number of
independent parameters controlling form.' More independent parameters
would mean 'fewer adaptive compromises need to be made, and more
functions can be optimized without detriment to other structures and
functions.' That frees evolution for a new round of progress. Useful
functions that once were incompatible, become compatible.

Versatility is the ability to satisfy various functions with one phenotype
(Vermeij, 1973b). Versatility comes from increasing 'the number of independent parameters controlling form'. Vermeij believes that versatility increases
in evolutionary time. He (Vermeij, 1973b) and I (Rosenzweig *et al.*, 1987;
Rosenzweig and McCord, 1991) have suggested several examples.

- A tree, with its dead support tissue, no longer has to pay so high a
  cost as an herb to be tall and compete for light.
- Zooidal budding of cheilostome bryozoans 'partly decouples the
  outward growth of the colony as a whole from the finite ontogeny
  of individual zooids' (Lidgard, 1986). This allows them to 'raise
  their growing margin above the substrate, overtopping and over-
  growing competitors' limited by intrazooidal budding (Lidgard and
  Jackson, 1989). The ultimate reduction of tradeoff occurs in species
  such as *Schizoporella floridana*. It can overgrow competitors, but it
  also retains the ability to revert to single-layered growth. Single-layered growth maximizes the rate at which it carpets its substrate in
  the absence of competitors (Lidgard, 1985).
- A balanoid barnacle with tubiferous wall plates can grow more
  rapidly in overall bulk than a barnacle with dense walls (Stanley
  and Newman, 1980).
- Gastropods have decoupled their shell's weight from its ability to
  defend them against predators. They grow shell varices (narrow
  shell ridges) that reinforce gastropod vulnerable points without
  adding greatly to overall shell thickness (Bertness and Cunningham,
  1981). Or they grow stout, spiny protuberances that prevent a shell
  from fitting into the gape of a predator (Palmer, 1979).
- Pit vipers have a set of electromagnetic wave receptors in addition
  to their eyes. Because the focal length of an electromagnetic wave is
  tightly coupled to its wavelength, each set of receptors can focus
  sharply on only a small subset of available radiation. Thus, com-

pared with a true viper, a pit viper can be sensitive to a wider spectrum of wavelengths without having blurry vision.

- The bolyerine snakes (endemic to Mauritius) have a complete joint between their anterior and posterior maxilla. This allows them separately to improve the shape of their forward teeth for capturing prey, and that of their rear teeth for swallowing it. They no longer have to compromise on a single shape to be used for both tasks (Frazetta, 1970).
- A marsupial carnivore's molars must all look like carnassials because they will all eventually move into the carnassial position. But a eutherian carnivore has a fixed caranassial tooth, allowing its other molars to evolve into non-carnassial shapes (Werdelin, 1987).
- *Bolitoglossa occidentalis*, a salamander, embodies at least three developmental dissociations that increase its versatility (Alberch and Alberch, 1981). For instance, as its feet grow, they suddenly stop changing shape. Foot size and shape are closely linked in all its congeners. Similarly, it manages to dissociate the growth rates of its phalangeal elements from each other.

Does an increase in versatility support an increase in diversity? Maybe. To prove that, we should have to prove that new clades with higher versatility support higher speciation rates or lower extinction rates. There is no evidence of lower extinction rates. But Van Valen (1984, 1985a, b) and Gilinsky and Bambach (1987) looked at fossil speciation rates and determined that new clades do have higher speciation rates. After some millions of years, those rates fall.

But Rosenzweig and McCord (1991) suggest that the higher speciation rates come about because new clades can refill old niches by competitive speciation. Once the old niches are filled, the speciation rate should settle back. Hence, the equilibrium diversity should not change. So, we really cannot be sure whether increased exploration of niche space adds to diversity.

One case may help. It is the increase in land plant diversity that accompanied the spread of the angiosperms.

Flowers flourish The broad outlines of vascular plant evolution tell of a sequence of dissociations (Haig and Westoby, 1991). When land plants first appeared some 420 Myr ago in the Silurian Period, their gametes were homosporous. Homosporous gametes are spores – made by the diploid stage (sporophyte) – that will turn into male or female gametophytes; but the spores cannot be told apart by size.

Ferns took the next step in evolution. They dissociated male and female gametophyte sizes. Heterosporous ferns produce megaspores that will become female gametophytes, and microspores that will become males. This allows the sporophyte to provision the sexes differently. Sure enough, its megaspores are much larger than its microspores, and the new generation of sporophyte gets most of its nutrition from the sporophyte of the previous one.

But ferns still have a serious constraint. They must first provision their megaspores and then set them free to do their best as gametophytes. They are constrained to giving all their megaspores a standard supply of nutrients because they cannot predict which will get fertilized.

Seed plants break the constraint. They keep their megaspores (now called ovules) in their own bodies while fertilization takes place. Thus, they can wait until after fertilization before committing resources to the fertilized ovule (which is of course the seed). They have dissociated ovule initiation from ovule provisioning. Unsuccessful ovules get aborted or resorbed. Pollinated ones become seeds.

In gymnosperms (pines, firs, spruces, ginkos, junipers, etc.), each seed has to have its own accessory organs (e.g. a stigma to receive pollen). But in angiosperms there is another basic dissociation. Seeds can share accessory organs. So the old rule – one set of accessories for each gymnosperm seed – vanishes in angiosperms. One perianth can produce many seeds or few or even one.

Each of these increases in versatility provoked a biotic replacement. Today, tree-sized lycopods are extinct and tree-sized ferns are few. Even gymnosperms are reduced to a shadow of their former diversities 150 Myr ago. Yet, we do not see an increase in plant diversity for any of these steps except the last.

Angiosperms appeared in the fossil record about 120 Myr ago (early Lower Cretaceous Period: Cronquist, 1982). Gradually over the next 60 Myr, they increased in diversity and come to dominate all other land plants (Lidgard and Crane, 1990). Simultaneously, the diversity of fossil floras increased from about 30 species to about 54 (Knoll, 1986). Because this conclusion comes from analyzing individual macrofloras, it avoids the problem of the 'pull-of-the-recent'. Lidgard and Crane (1990) confirm the increase. They also find it in floras based on pollen fossils. Is this increase related to the key adaptation of having flowers?

Haig and Westoby (1991) believe it is. They suggest a robust model to summarize the fitness (W) contributed by a seed to its parents:

$$W = s/(a + k) \qquad\qquad (10.2)$$

Evolution of Seed Size

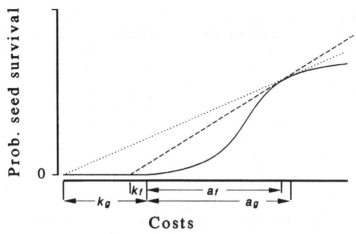

Costs

Figure 10.8. Smaller seeds evolve if a plant can invest less in the accessory costs of each one. The subscript *g* refers to gymnosperms; they have large accessory cost per seed (*k*) because each seed has its own accessory organs. The subscript *f* refers to angiosperms; they have smaller accessory cost per seed because their seeds can share accessory organs. The parameter *a* symbolizes the evolved optimal size of seeds.

The proof is implicit in the graph. Assume both taxa have the same curve of seed size vs seed survival (solid sigmoid curve), and that over larger seed sizes this curve is convex – as argued by Haig and Westoby (1991). Assume that the two curves differ only in *k*. By definition (see text), fitness equals y/x. So, fitness equals the slope of the line connecting a point on the curve to its origin, and optimum *a* lies under the tangent that intersects the origin. Notice that the origins of the two curves (one for *f* and one for *g*) differ because of their different *k*-values. Now find the optimum for gymnosperms (a_g) using the straight dotted line. Holding the point on the sigmoid curve constant, rotate the straight line counter-clockwise until it reaches the origin for angiosperms. (You will have to imagine this yourself as it made the figure too complex.) The line you get is steeper, indicating that the angiosperms have improved upon the fitness of the gymnosperms. But they still haven't reached their optimum because they can achieve an even steeper slope by reducing their seed size. To find their best seed size for this value of *k*, we rotate their line counterclockwise about their origin until it too becomes a tangent (dashed line). However, because their seeds will now be smaller, there can be more per flower. This may further reduce *k* in some clades and lead to further seed size reduction. The graph and the proof are based on an idea of Haig and Westoby (1991).

where s is the probability that a seed survives; a is the direct cost of provisioning the seed (essentially, the seed's size); k is the indirect cost of the seed. Indirect costs include stigma and perianth production, as well as the cost of aborted seeds. Since k is the cost per seed, we get it by measuring the accessory costs and dividing by the number of seeds.

Haig and Westoby try to show why angiosperms can have smaller seeds than gymnosperms. Their argument rests on the fact that the perianth allows the female plant to distribute the cost of making a seed among more than one seed. Perhaps their proof has a weakness, but it is easy to fix (see Figure 10.8). Moreover, the fossil record does show that angiosperms do have smaller seeds than gymnosperms. Some Cretaceous angiosperms had seeds that were smaller by an order of magnitude compared with any previous seeds. (Today, the smallest angiosperm seeds are four orders of magnitude smaller than the smallest gymnosperm seeds, and the largest are an order of magnitude larger. But that could be a sampling-size artifact. There are, after all, so many more species of angiosperms.)

Haig and Westoby believe that species with smaller seeds may have smaller minimum viable population sizes. If so, their extinction rate curve would fall beneath that of larger seeded plants and they would achieve higher diversities.

It is too early to be sure of the connection proposed by Haig and Westoby. However, some patterns suggest its validity. For example, many monocot taxa – such as grasses – have only one seed per flower; these are not very speciose. On the other hand, speciose monocots especially orchids and lilies, have smaller seeds borne many to a fruit. Those of some orchids are incredibly tiny. Even if the Haig and Westoby hypothesis is correct, we still have the mixed result that some increases in versatility were not accompanied by diversity increases. So, perhaps key adaptations sometimes enhance diversity, but they do not always do so. Moreover, when they do, it may be only a coincidence. Angiosperms were a good evolutionary idea regardless of whether they increased plant diversity. They got their place in the sun because they can dissociate the number of seeds from the effort put into accessory organs.

Chapter 11

Other patterns with dynamic roots

Population dynamics and food webs

We begin with the two clear patterns from Chapter 4.

- The trophic level pattern: *diversity declines at higher trophic levels, so much so that some levels entirely lack species.*
- The omnivory pattern: *fewer omnivorous species exist than we expect.*

Ecology has known the first of these patterns for a long time. It was first enunciated by Charles Elton (1927), a founder of modern ecology. He pointed out the limit to the number of trophic levels in animal communities in all sorts of biomes. Although I have not found a place where he explicitly noted that diversity declines as we appproach the top level, it is a trivial deduction from what he did say.

Stuart Pimm and John Lawton discovered the second pattern while investigating a hypothesis to explain all food web patterns. Their hypothesis is called *the dynamical stability hypothesis.* Because the dynamical stability hypothesis underlies their treatment of the trophic level pattern as well as the omnivory pattern, I will begin this chapter by explaining it.

Pimm and Lawton propose that if associations of species deviate from their usual patterns, they become dynamically unstable and simply do not last. Instead, deviant associations lose some of their species and thus change to other associations. They keep changing until they happen on a dynamically stable association. Then they do last and do fit the patterns. Why do unstable associations lose species? Because of the dynamical equations that govern their population sizes. If those equations are not stable enough, then, too often, they lead to extremely low population size. As we know, low population size puts a species at risk of extinction. Recently, Pimm (1991) has reaffirmed this hypothesis in a lucid and far-ranging book.

To test their hypothesis, Pimm and Lawton had to have a crisp definition of dynamical stability. After all, the essence of risk is lack of stability. The literature already provided them with one definition. And they complemented it with a second. Let us now explore both.

Dynamical stability

Qualitative stability Consider a set of interacting species. Suppose there exists a set of population sizes at which all the species have non-zero populations and none of their population sizes are changing. We call this set of sizes an equilibrium.

But not all equilibria are reliable. The test? Move the set a little bit away from equilibrium and see if it returns. If it does return, call it stable. If not, call it unstable. That test is called perturbation analysis. Scientists of many disciplines use it.

Perturbation analysis can be done experimentally. It can even be done in the field. But more much often, we do it with a mathematical analysis of the dynamical equations governing a set of species interactions.

First, we note that each species has a complicated non-linear differential equation governing its population growth. These equations are so complicated that we usually do not know enough even to write them down, let alone to solve them. Fortunately, mathematicians, beginning with the great Liapunov, have given us ways to discover how their solutions behave, even though we cannot solve them.

We remember from calculus that we can approximate all continuous functions, including those that specify population growth rates. The usual formula for approximation is a Taylor series. A Taylor series has a sequence of terms that are various powers of the independent variable(s). A first order Taylor approximation has only the linear term(s) of the Taylor series. So it is a linear equation. A second order series approximates the same function, but has the squared term(s) too. A third order series has its cubic term(s). And so on.

Knowing that we can approximate the dynamical equations as linear equations, we do so. We write a linear differential equation for each species. Its independent variables are the densities of each species. The coefficients of those variables are unknown. Its dependent variable is the growth rate of one of the species.

One of Liapunov's two great theorems teaches us the value of our approximations. It tells us that we can usually learn about the stability of the full, unwritten, non-linear set of equations by analyzing the linear set.

There are exceptions (which he stated explicitly). But if we linearize near the equilibrium, the stability of the non-linear system will be the same as the stability of the simpler linear system. (Linearizing near an equilibrium means using, in the linear differential equations, the set of coefficients that hold true at the equilibrium, whether or not they are true anywhere else.)

So, how can we find out if the linearized system's equilibrium is stable? We build a special equation from the coefficients of the dynamical equations. This equation, called the characteristic equation, has unknowns called eigenvalues. One characteristic equation covers all the species that interact in the community. There are exactly as many eigenvalues as there are species.

Each eigenvalue may have a real part and an imaginary part. Or it may lack one of those. (If it lacks a real part, it constitutes one of Liapunov's exceptions, and we cannot safely analyze it by linearization.) Pimm and Lawton did not concern themselves with the imaginary parts because these do not determine stability. The real parts determine the stability. (However, the imaginary parts do cause oscillations in the populations they govern.)

If any of the real parts exceeds zero, the equilibrium of the whole system is unstable. If all are negative, then the equilibrium is stable. The system's population sizes will return to equilibrium after perturbations that do not carry the system very far away from equilibrium.

Notice the imprecision. We do not know how far is 'very far'. We cannot specify how serious a perturbation the system can resist. That is a cost of linearization. But we can tell if the equilibrium is unable to recover from any perturbation, however small.

Thus, the qualitative concept of stability. An equilibrium is either stable or not stable. It all depends on the sign of the real part of its dominant eigenvalue, λ_d, i.e. the eigenvalue with the largest real part. If that sign is positive, the equilibrium is unstable. If negative, it is stable.

It seems reasonable to call an unstable equilibrium, a 'delicate balance'. Stable equilibria, in contrast, are robust at least to some extent. Together with most ecologists, Pimm and Lawton expect that delicate balances will not survive. Now that may stand the conventional, popular notion on its head, but it is true. Ecologists believe that Nature comprises robust balances. The delicate ones pass quickly from the real world.

Of course, you must not forget the fuzzy, but crucial concept of the perturbation that is not 'very far' from equilibrium. Natural balances may need to be somewhat robust, but they do not have infinite capacity to resist and repair the environmental foolishness we inflict on them. So all ecologists will agree that even robust balances can be made to seem delicate.

Return time, a quantitative measure of stability Pimm and Lawton
recognized that a qualitative measure of stability could not do a complete
job. Perturbations in the real world are too common. Populations at
equilibrium are too unusual. Just because a population might theoretically
return to equilibrium does not mean it will. Thus, once it passes the
qualitative test, we should like to know how stable it is. Is its stability
strong enough to give it a reasonable chance to get back to equilibrium?

As their index of the strength of the equilibrium's stability, they decided
to evaluate the time a system takes to return to that equilibrium. The most
readily available index of return time is already contained in the dominant
eigenvalue. If its real part is close to zero, the system will take many generations to return after a perturbation. If its real part is a large negative number, the system will return quickly after a perturbation.

Pimm and Lawton defined the return time of a system as the absolute
value of the inverse of the real part of its dominant eigenvalue, $1/|\lambda_d|$. Thus
λ_d close to zero means long return time and weak stability. They assume
that a system that takes a long time to get back to equilibrium is less likely
ever to get there, and more likely to suffer an extinction on the way.

Return time is not a perfect concept. Some systems have unstable equilibria and stable trajectories, like a planet orbiting the sun. The planet's equilibrium is near the center of the sun, but it never plunges in. In case we find
such a stable trajectory, we should like to know how close to destruction
the trajectory carries the system, and how strongly the system returns to its
trajectory after it is bumped away. In addition, other systems do not even
have stable trajectories. They exhibit non-linear dynamics, moving around
their equilibria so chaotically that we would have a hard time saying what
we mean by return.

Nevertheless, Pimm and Lawton provide a place to start. If the concepts
of linear stability and return time make accurate predictions about species
diversity patterns, then they will have proved themselves useful. We now
return to the patterns themselves and see whether this is the case.

Why are food chains short?

When I was a graduate student, everybody knew the answer to this question.
'The second law of thermodynamics.' No less. It was among the glories of
ecology. We had a pattern and we were using a core principle of physics to
explain it! We proudly taught it even to non-majors in basic biology.

When Elton (1927) noted that food chains are short, he attributed it to the general decline in total numbers of animals at higher and higher trophic levels. Starting with Lindemann (1942), ecologists observed that this decline in numbers occurs because each trophic level receives more free energy than it transfers to the next. Now that rule really is the second law of thermodynamics in ecological clothing. The second law of thermodynamics holds for all systems, and we rely on physics to establish it in general. So we ecologists need not trouble ourselves to establish it for ecological systems in particular.

The interesting ecological problem comes in applying the second law to species diversity. In the tradition of Elton, Hutchinson (1959) proposed that higher trophic levels have no species because they lack enough energy to support a minimum viable population. How could that be wrong?

So no one bothered to test it.

During the summer of 1978, I visited Israel for the first time. Zvika Abramsky, Dan Baharav and I were walking in the Wilderness of Paran (honest). That desert, worthy of its Biblical mention, makes Arizona look like ... well, The Garden of Eden! All around us was desolation. Shrubs – called locally trees – are scarce enough to get put on maps. We saw a few scorched herbs scattered sparsely about the landscape. Otherwise the place was hard to distinguish from the surface of Mars. Then, about 100 m away, I spotted an insect flying. Rushing over to identify it – to greet it really – I couldn't believe what it turned out to be. It was a robberfly!

What did it live on, we wondered? Here it was, an active predator searching for food in one of the world's legendary wastelands. I doubted that all three of us hunting together could have found enough to keep the robberfly alive, let alone allow it to reproduce.

I saw many other predatory species that day. (It always seems to me that I see more of them in the Negev than have a chance at sustenance.) Ever since, I have had doubts about the thermodynamic explanation for the number of trophic levels.

When Pimm and Lawton (1977) began to suspect this explanation, they resolved to put it to the test by forcing it to make another prediction. They noted that ecosystems lose about 80 to 90% of their free energy as it is transferred from one trophic level to another. Let's suppose that the thermodynamic hypothesis is true. Let's suppose that the next higher trophic level is empty because it lacks enough energy to support a minimum viable population. It follows that if productivity increases an order of magnitude, then the next higher trophic level should appear.

It takes too long to wait for evolution to fill such a trophic level, so we cannot do the experiment. But we can almost do it. The world's biomes vary immensely in productivity – they cover about three orders of magnitude. If the thermodynamic explanation is correct, then biomes with the highest productivity should have two or three more trophic levels than those with the least.

Pimm and Lawton explored the data. Briand and Cohen (1987) have too. But variation in the maximum length of chains does not support the thermodynamic explanation. Most of the world's known food webs have three or four trophic levels (Figures 4.5 and 4.6). Moreover, the richest ones have no stronger tendency to have the most levels. And some of the poorest ones have very long food chains. My favorite case comes from the Namib Desert. It has six trophic levels. Despite its energetic poverty, it is the longest food chain among the terrestrial chains listed by Schoener (1989). There is no correlation between the length of trophic chains and productivity.

Yet, we cannot dismiss the thermodynamic hypothesis entirely. Some evidence favors it. For example, Yodzis (1984) noted that endotherms are so energetically expensive that they must transfer less energy to their potential predators than do ectotherms. If energy flow is important in determining whether a trophic level can exist, then endotherms should support a predator less often than do ectotherms. Moreover, invertebrate ectotherms transfer more of their energy than do vertebrate ectotherms. Thus, the thermodynamic hypothesis predicts a hierarchy with invertebrate ectotherms most likely to support predators and vertebrate endotherms least likely. And that is just what he discovered (Table 11.1).

No one disputes the trophic level of the primary producers (or basal level) of an ecosystem; they are level one. But beyond level one, agreement disappears. Yodzis (1993) examined food chain lengths using his own definition of a species' trophic level: 'unity plus the minimum number of links from the producer level'. Let us call this 'minimum trophic level'. Probably, in real food webs, most energy travels through the shortest trophic pathway, so Yodzis' definition is just as interesting as the more popular: 'maximum number of links.'

Once he defined minimum trophic level, Yodzis (1993) focused on 113 food webs that could be classed as low or high productivity ecosystems. In each, he determined the trophic level(s) of its top consumers. Altogether, these webs had 129 top consumers.

Table 11.2 shows that richer systems do tend to have longer food chains than poorer ones. The result is not statistically significant, however, probab-

Table 11.1. *Proportion of species that support[a] a species at the next higher trophic level*

Group	Ectotherms		Endotherms Vertebrate
	Invertebrate	Vertebrate	
% (N)	20 (119)	11 (57)	7 (27)

Note: [a] By definition, a species 'supports' a consumer species if the consumer eats no other species from that or a lower trophic level (Yodzis, 1984).
Data from Yodzis (1984).

Table 11.2. *Food chain length of top consumers*

Number of trophic levels	Low productivity	High productivity
2	28 (27%)	3 (12%)
3	65 (62%)	16 (67%)
4	12 (11%)	5 (21%)

Adapted from Yodzis (1993).

ly because there are few data and they are dominated by the intermediate class, a class which shows about the same proportion in rich and poor systems.

Chapter 4 supplies more evidence in favor of thermodynamic control. There you will see that Figure 4.7 agrees most spectacularly with the thermodynamic hypothesis. First, a decline in diversity does accompany the decline in energy flow at higher trophic levels. But more impressive is the shape of that decline. It is linear in a semilog space. As you will now see, that is exactly what the hypothesis predicts.

Suppose productivity declines by a standard proportion at each higher trophic level. Then:

$$P_L = c\mu^{(L-1)} \tag{11.1}$$

where P is productivity, c is productivity of the first trophic level, μ is the proportion of productivity transferred to the next higher trophic level and L is trophic level.

Now let diversity, S, respond linearly to P:

$$S_L = mP_L \tag{11.2}$$

Thus,

$$S_L = k\mu^{(L-1)} \tag{11.3}$$

where $k = mc$. And the logarithmic form of that equation is:

$$\log S_L = \log k - \log \mu + L \log \mu \tag{11.4}$$

Let the constant $\phi = \log k - \log \mu$ and we have:

$$\log S_L = \phi + L \log \mu \quad (11.5)$$

And that is the form of Figure 4.7!

Can it really be that simple? Well, no. The slope of the regression in Figure 4.7 is too gentle. It implies a productivity ratio P_{i+1}/P_i of $10^{-0.463}$. In other words, it says that 34.4% of free energy gets passed along between trophic levels. But we know that only about 10 to 20% gets passed along (Figure 11.1). What could be amiss?

Recall that Schoenly *et al.* score each species for only its highest trophic position. The error produced by using maximum trophic levels has the

Insect Food Webs

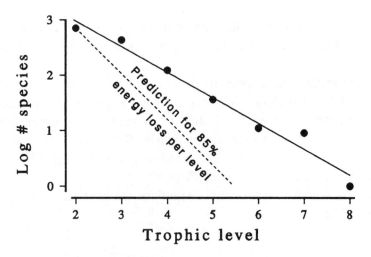

Figure 11.1. Diversity would follow the steeper line if free energy declined at 85% per trophic transfer *and* free energy alone determined the diversity of consumers. The next figure suggests that it is gentler merely because maximum trophic level seriously overestimates the trophic level of the higher level species in a food

effect of gentling the slope of the relationship. Why? Certainly, a species placed in level 2 does take all of its food from level 1. But a species placed in level 7 (say) undoubtedly takes most of its food from levels below 6. So, the higher the trophic score, the more to the right a species gets displaced from its true average trophic level. Would correcting only this problem suffice to make the slope steep enough to fit known rates of energy transfer in ecosystems? Such rates require a slope between −0.7 and −1.

Although we do not have the data for average trophic level, we can determine minimum trophic level. This ought to be very close to the average. Even if it is not, combined with the maximum trophic level, it will bracket the average. So, with the help of my students in Species Diversity (spring 1994), I set out to re-examine the data used by Schoenly *et al.*

We were able to locate almost all the data sets in Schoenly *et al.* However, we included only 36 webs. (They had 61.) In some cases, we did not feel comfortable assigning trophic levels to species. In some cases, our count of species differed substantially. In some cases, we simply could not find as many webs in a paper as they had. But I am sure that the 25 fewer webs would not have mattered much. For one thing, most of the species (896/1321) were in the webs we did reuse. For another, as we examined webs, we added their data to the graph a few at a time; it quickly assumed a slope similar to the one in Figure 11.2 and changed very little as we accumulated new webs to complete the figure.

The new analysis produced a slope of −0.86. Remarkably, that agrees with an energy transfer efficiency of 13.8%, very much like the efficiencies that ecosystem ecologists see in nature. Level 3 provides the only possible exception to the simple thermodynamic hypothesis. Level 3 is roughly half an order of magnitude too diverse for the general trend line. We need more data to be sure of the significance of this exception. But if it is true, it will be sending an interesting message. It will be saying that natural selection chooses phenotypes of primary carnivores that conserve energy better than those of other trophic levels. It will be saying that we have more species of primary carnivores than we might expect from a raw and untested ecosystem.

Oksanen *et al.* (1981, 1994) have also found support for the thermodynamic hypothesis. They study arctic systems, especially systems on a mountain gradient in northernmost Norway. The lowland systems (≤500 m) have three trophic levels. The middle elevations have two. And the extremely poor, sparsely covered 'blockfields' have only plants and an occasional stray ptarmigan. Oksanen (1992) and Oksanen *et al.* (1992) provide more evidence of these conclusions.

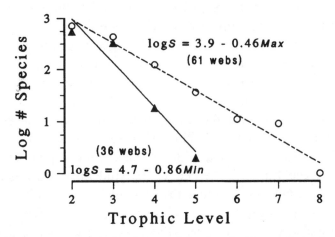

Figure 11.2. Reanalysis of most of the data in Figure 11.1 using minimum trophic levels (triangles and solid line). Now the slope (–0.86) indicates a decline of 86.2% per trophic transfer, which agrees closely with estimates from real ecosystems. (The analysis of Figure 11.1 – open circles and dashed line – appears for comparison.)

Oksanen *et al.* (1994) also review the arctic lowland data often cited as having three trophic levels. In some cases the productivity of these places had been considerably underestimated. For example, preliminary and incomplete data suggested to Pimm that mesic mountain birch forest at Kevo, Finland had a productivity of 125 g/m^2 per year. Data that have since been published for similar sites in Norway reveal a productivity closer to 780 g/m^2 per year. In other cases, predators are present in a system only because they are supported in nearby and much richer marine ecosystems. All in all, the data seem to justify their contention: large inland expanses of truly poor energy flow (20–300 g/m^2 per year) in the Arctic lose trophic level 3 (the carnivores). And polar deserts, such as that on Devon Island, Canada (whose productivity is only 7.4 g/m^2 per year) lose both their carnivores and their herbivores, just as Norwegian mountain blockfields do.

Oksanen and Pimm define 'trophic level' differently (Pimm, 1991). For Oksanen, a trophic level in a biome must satisfy two criteria. It must regulate the population size(s) of its food species in the biome and reproduce successfully there. Thus, something unusual, like short-eared owls – which invade the poor Arctic highlands only to feed on extraordinarily high lemming populations – do not count. But Pimm and Lawton judge matters differently. The owls do appear about every five years, so they count them as a higher trophic level.

Neither definition is wrong. They are designed to reflect different phenomena. That of Oksanen *et al.* is more useful for studying population dynamics and other food web phenomena. But Pimm and Lawton's definition is useful for studying the problem of maximum food chain length.

At first I thought that the reason for the difference between Oksanen's and Pimm's views of the data arose solely from their different definitions of a trophic level. But that cannot be correct. As Oksanen *et al.* (in press) emphasize, the really poor habitats actually do lack one or two trophic levels. They report one poor blockfield where they have trapped patiently for years without finding a single mouse or seeing any sign of any other herbivore except a few rock ptarmigan. Whether or not you wish to count the ptarmigan as a second trophic level (they would not; Pimm and his colleagues might), there are no predators at all. By anyone's definition, the third trophic level is absent from high alpine boulderfields and polar deserts.

Persson *et al.* (1992) also found that the very poorest ecosystems lack a trophic level. They studied food webs in 11 temperate lakes. Those of very low productivity lacked a fourth trophic level (the piscivores), whereas all those of moderate productivity had it.

In sum, we now have evidence to support the thermodynamic hypothesis in the world's poorest and coldest habitats. They have trophic levels in proportion to their productivity. But, what about the rest of the world? It contains habitats with much higher productivities than a mesic mountain birch forest or a moderately productive lake, and yet its food chains are rarely longer than three or four. If productivity is the sole explanation, we should see a response in these habitats too. But we do not. What else could be controlling the number of trophic levels?

Before there was any evidence to support the productivity hypothesis, Pimm and Lawton (1977) proposed an ingenious alternative. Paradoxically, their hypothesis to explain the food-chain pattern lies in population dynamics. They have evidence that the equilibrium points of longer food chains tend to have longer return times. Thus the dynamic hypothesis: *long food chains self-destruct owing to intrinsic dynamical instability.*

Pimm and Lawton (1977) built a computer model of population dynamics in a community of four species. They arranged it so that they could vary the number of trophic levels (Figure 11.3). In one series of tests they used four levels, one species per level. In another, they used three levels with two

Food Webs of Four Species

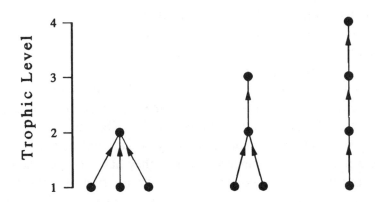

Figure 11.3. In this series of computer simulations, Pimm and
Lawton (1977) varied the number of trophic levels
without changing the number of species or the number of feeding links.

species on the same level. And in the third series they used two levels with
three species on the same level.

Pimm and Lawton ran their computer model over and over. For each
run, the computer selected a set of linear interaction coefficients at random.
But it kept the coefficients within a realistic range of values.

Consider the distribution of return times they got. Two-level chains
rarely had long return times. Four-level chains had return times greater
than 150 in 34% of their runs. On the other hand, long chains rarely had
short return times; fewer than 1% had return times of 5 or less. Finally,
short chains had short return times in 50% of the runs.

Pimm and Lawton also tested model systems with one species per trophic
level. The more levels, the higher the return times. We have already seen
that four-level systems with one species per level had fewer than 1% return
times of 5 or less. But two-species, two-level systems had 70% of their
return times that low.

The picture is consistent. Adding trophic levels weakens the stability of
model community equilibria. You can thus suspect that food chains are
short, not because they run out of free energy, but because longer ones
aren't stable enough.

The dynamic hypothesis did run into one statistical problem. Briand and

Cohen (1987) tried to test it using the set of 113 webs they collected from the literature. They suggest that the hypothesis predicts a correlation between chain length and stability. There was correlation, but they explained it as coming from a third variable (dimensionality: see below).

An interesting problem undermines this test. Pimm and Lawton have predicted that truly unstable systems will not survive. So the ones we see should be a narrow subset of random ones. They have not predicted that the ones we see will all have the same stability. Nor have they predicted that any correlation between chain length and stability will remain among surviving webs. Other web properties also affect stability and could easily override any residual chain-length effect.

I suspect that also accounts for the results of Moore *et al.* (1993). They took interaction coefficients from actual food webs in the soil. Then they simulated the effects of those coefficients on stability. They found that real ecosystems do appear to have sufficient dynamic stability to resist small perturbations. In fact, three-and four-level food chains differed little in stability. Four levels have better quantitative stability than threes, although the reverse characterizes qualitative stability. (Twos outperform both threes and fours in both categories.)

Does this apparent indifference to whether a web has three or four levels mean that the Pimm–Lawton hypothesis is nothing but an artifact of the coefficients they chose for their computer? Probably not. First, we must ask why real coefficients are so restricted. Could it not be that others exist from time to time but have dire dynamic consequences and therefore disappear? Second, we already know that four-level chains are real (and therefore possess the requisite stability). What we need now are some simulations of five- and six-level chains with realistic coefficients. If these turn out to be as stable as threes and fours, then the dynamic hypothesis will indeed have suffered a blow.

Moore *et al.* (1993) made their simulations with another item on their agenda. They wondered if the dynamic hypothesis and the thermodynamic hypothesis are independent of each other. Thus they performed their dynamic simulations at a large variety of simulated productivities.

Moore *et al.* (1993) found that productivity affects both qualitative stability ('feasibility') and return time. The more productive an ecosystem, the more feasible it is, and the shorter its likely return time. So, perhaps, there is no difference between the two hypotheses after all? Yet, two reasons keep me from lumping the hypotheses together.

- First, Moore *et al.* (1993) discover that they simulated productivities partly inside and partly outside the bounds of real ecosystems. Most of those that lie within the bounds of reality show a phenomenon called flat laxity, i.e., there is very little relationship between the dependent and independent variables. So, the correlation between productivity and dynamic stability is strong, but lies mostly in the region of productivities so poor that they are unreal.

   Make no mistake. They are not entirely unreal. In fact, the graph of Moore *et al.* (1993) plateaus somewhere between 100 and 1000 g/m^2 per year. So it could easily agree with the threshold value of about 400–500 g/m^2 per year suggested by the work of Oksanen *et al.*, (1994). Obviously, we need more data to pin down the coefficients and thus the threshold of Moore's conclusion.

- The second reason comes from the limits of the models themselves. They are strictly linear. 'So what?' you may ask. 'That has been true all along, but you never warned us of it before.' Right, but it has not before caused a contradiction. Now, it has. When I introduced the hypothesis that productivity influences stability, I used a non-linear model (Rosenzweig, 1971). I concluded that productivity reduces the chance of stability – precisely the opposite of Moore *et al.* (1993). Which is correct? Both.

Moore *et al.* (1993) focus on the effects of extremely **low** productivity. For instance, you can reduce the carrying capacity of a resource species only so far before their predators won't be able to break even. That is why their result contains a virtual threshold: above a certain productivity, productivity matters little.

On the other hand, I focused on the consequences of **high** productivity. Above some threshold productivity, competition among the individuals of the resource species loses its grip on their population dynamics. It gets replaced by the destabilizing force of intraspecific mutualism. Unfortunately, to detect that shift, you need a non-linear model of dynamics. So, Moore *et al.* (1993) couldn't have found that result. It seems to me that the time has come for students of food webs to graduate to non-linear models.

Meanwhile, two other hypotheses offer explanations for the length of food chains.

1. Three dimensional systems have longer chains than do two dimensional systems (Briand and Cohen, 1987). Three dimensional systems include forests and open oceans. Two dimensional systems include bottom communities, grasslands and reefs. Briand and Cohen found statistical support for this hypothesis in the data.

Unfortunately, further examination of the evidence suggests that three dimensional systems do not have more trophic levels than flat ones. Pimm (*in litt.*) believes that Briand and Cohen's data show a dimensional effect primarily because their three dimensional systems are oceanic, whereas their two dimensional systems are intertidal. The oceanic systems are credited with predatory fish, but the intertidal ones are not. But fish do feed in intertidal systems when they enter them at high tide. So, they should also have been reckoned in the intertidal webs.

Moore *et al.* (1989) also note that predators have not been counted in the intertidal systems. And they point out a second glaring difference in the way the data of the two environments have been treated. In oceanic webs, phytoplankton and zooplankton are separated. In intertidal webs, they are simply listed together as plankton. That difference costs intertidal systems one trophic level compared with oceanic systems.

Without the biases introduced by treating the data differently, there probably would have been no difference between the lengths of two and three dimensional systems. It all shows how cautious you must be in comparing data collected by different people. Briand and Cohen did not introduce the biases themselves. They simply did not notice them. In an enterprise like food-web analysis, we must use data from many investigators. But we must be particularly vigilant lest some systematic difference in techniques or convention between subfields gives us spurious patterns.

2. Systems with greater total energy (i.e. productivity multiplied by area) have longer food chains

Schoener (1989) terms this the 'productive space hypothesis'. It is identical to Wright's species-energy hypothesis (Wright *et al.*, 1993; see Chapter 12), although Wright, to my knowledge, never applied it specifically to the question of food chain length. The idea is that pure energy-flow rate cannot tell us how many individuals an ecosystem can support. For that, we must multiply the rate by the total area over which it applies. Only then we will know whether the system can support a minimum viable population at a high trophic level.

Schoener sees this hypothesis – the energy-area hypothesis – hard at work in the island systems he has studied for so long in the Bahamas. There, large islands have five trophic levels, smaller ones four, still smaller ones three. Tiny islets have no more than three and may lack even those.

In Chapter 8, we learned that island biotas are particularly poor in predator species. Schoener is reminding us of that well-established fact in the context of trophic chain lengths. In addition, he examines the large data base of food webs (Cohen *et al.*, 1990) to look for tests of the energy–area hypothesis. This task requires much more information than is now at hand. Nevertheless, Schoener extracts some reasonable hints: Very small areas do have shorter chains. But longer chains have all sorts of productivity levels.

From these hints I conclude that large area is a necessary feature of long chains, but high productivity is not. Lack of area cuts into the number of sustainable levels on islands and other very small systems.

Perhaps some combination of the thermodynamic hypothesis, the area hypothesis, and the dynamic hypothesis limits the number of trophic levels in all systems. The data suggest that area and productivity limit food chain length only in the smallest or poorest systems. Beyond that threshold point, some other variable takes over and controls the number of levels in richer systems. For now, dynamical stability is the likeliest candidate to be that other variable.

Clearly, we have much left to account for. What happens to dynamical stability if non-linear models, rather than linear ones, get programmed? What happens if realistic coefficients are inserted into five-and six-level models? What distinguishes pelagic webs and gall-forming insect webs from other biomes and gives them such unusually long chains?

And what happens to the relationship between trophic level and the logarithm of diversity if we get good level 1 diversity data and extend Figure 4.7 leftward? Does plant diversity continue the trend found among insects?

In this book, you will not find the answer to any of those questions except the very last. The answer to it is, 'No.' Look for it in the next chapter.

Why are there not more species of omnivores?

Pimm and Lawton (1978) used their computer-model method to examine this question just as they had the previous one. They built a model of species' linear dynamics. Then they programmed the computer to choose coefficients at random, but within a biologically reasonable range. The computer ran each model a thousand times, accumulating information about its stability properties.

The models all had four species. But they varied in number of omnivores. They also varied in the position of the omnivores in the food web. Figure 11.4 depicts these variations. Webs without omnivores grade at Rank 0. Those with one omnivorous link are Rank 1. Those with two are Rank 2.

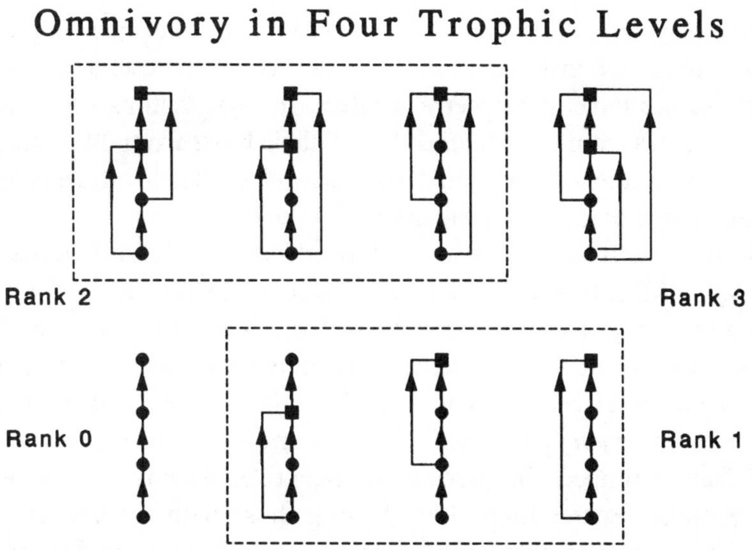

Omnivory in Four Trophic Levels

Figure 11.4. Pimm and Lawton's (1978) model webs. All have four
trophic levels, but they vary in omnivory. Omnivores
appear as squares instead of dots.

Those with three are Rank 3. Rank 3 webs have a species that eats from all
three trophic levels beneath it.

Pimm and Lawton had the computer choose coefficients from three different categories of interaction. These mimicked quite different natural systems and I follow them in using evocative names for the categories. The
names make it easier to understand the flow of their work.

Vertebrate systems: Here, they assumed that predators exert a much
larger effect on their victims than victims do on their predators. Hence, the
predator's coefficient of interaction with its victims comes from the interval
−10 to 0, but the victim's comes from the interval 0 to +0.1. Another way of
putting that: each predator may do a lot of damage to its victims, but each
victim won't help its predator very much. The predator's equilibrium population is much less than its victim's.

Vertebrate/insect systems: Here, the basal trophic level – imagine it to be
a species of tree – can have a great effect on its predator – which you can
think of as an insect. The tree's coefficient comes from the interval 0 to +10,
and the insect's from −0.1 to 0. Similarly, that which eats insects – say birds
– can do a lot of harm to the insect. But it won't be much supported by the
demise of a single victim. The bird's effect comes from the interval −10 to 0,
the insect's effect on the bird from 0 to +0.1.

Parasitoid systems: The plant's effect on its consumer can be great, 0 to +10. An individual consumer is not so noticeable, −0.1 to 0. The parasitoids of the consumer have a symmetrical effect on their victims however. Their coefficient comes from -1 to 0, and that of their hosts from 0 to +1.

In all cases, plants compete amongst themselves. Their intraspecific interaction coefficient comes from the interval −1 to 0.

Unlike the results for food chain length, these results also involve qualitative stability. All four-species chains without omnivores are stable. But the overwhelming majority of those with one or two omnivores are unstable. Moreover, almost all stable systems with omnivores come from parasitoid systems. That led directly to a new prediction: *omnivores ought to be found much more often among parasitoids than among other kinds of predators.*

Then they examined the percentage of stable systems with long return times (i.e. those greater than 100). Among those with omnivores, the systems in which the top carnivore feeds on non-adjacent trophic levels (i.e. levels 3 and 1) were the systems with many long return times. This was true even for the parasitoids. Thus, the dynamic hypothesis makes another new prediction: *where they do occur, omnivores ought rarely to feed on non-adjacent trophic levels.*

We already know that omnivores occur less commonly than we expect (Chapter 4). Is dynamics the correct explanation?

But wait. I've written that backwards. Here is the true history. First came the computer work and the prediction that omnivory should be rare. Then came the study of real webs and the demonstration that it is! Prediction was followed by confirming test. That is the classic way of science.

What is the difference? In the end we have a model producing a deduction, and a fact gleaned from the real world. They match. Why should we care about the order in which they were produced?

We care because any set of facts has an infinite number of explanations. That is one reason science cannot prove, only disprove, theories. In all science, therefore, we take special notice when a theory successfully predicts a phenomenon no one has ever before recorded. Offering an alternative explanation after it is recorded carries much less weight. Let the alternative do some fresh and successful predicting of its own. Then we will respect it too.

But in science, we also dare not be too sure of ourselves. Thus, we gladly take the extra opportunity to check our explanation by testing the additional two predictions made by the computer models. If they also hold true, we should accept dynamical instability as the probable cause of these food web patterns.

Pimm and Lawton (1978) looked at real parasitoid webs and compared them with others. The parasitoid webs averaged 2.5 omnivore species per top predator. But the others averaged only 0.96. The difference is statistically significant. So the first additional prediction is valid.

The second prediction checks too. There were 23 omnivores in 23 food webs. Only one fed on non-adjacent prey. If omnivores had selected their resource trophic levels at random, we would have expected 7.67 species on non-adjacent levels and 15.33 on adjacent levels. The actual data differ significantly from random.

Perhaps you can think of an alternative hypothesis to explain why non-adjacent omnivory occurs so infrequently. Pimm and Lawton did. They suggest the possibility that it may be too difficult to evolve structures and physiologies allowing feeding on both plants and animals. But if this were true, omnivores should most often be top carnivores feeding on both primary carnivores and herbivores. However, the division is virtually even. Eleven of the 23 omnivore species feed on both plants and animals. So this alternate hypothesis must be wrong.

Sprules and Bowerman (1988) report an exception to the rule that omnivory is scarce. They found it to be common in food webs of zooplankton in Canadian glacial lakes. Such lakes have much more omnivory than predicted by the dynamic hypothesis.

This exception deserves further study, but the lure of the dynamical hypothesis has Sprules and Bowerman seeking its explanation in dynamic terms. They suggest that the top invertebrate predator in these systems, *Mysis*, takes so much of its food from low trophic levels that the food chain is effectively a short one. (Short food chains confer stability.) They also suggest that the high incidence of cannibalism in the systems increases their stability. And finally they suggest that what we see as omnivory may not be dynamically so damaging because it is 'life-history omnivory'.

Life-history omnivores are species whose individuals change trophic level as they grow and develop. So, the life stages of life-history omnivores can be decomposed mathematically into separate, non-omnivorous, dynamic equations. Their stability should reflect their separateness at any one time, rather than their omnivory over the course of their life span. Indeed, Pimm and Rice (1987) studied the dynamical consequences of life-history omnivory theoretically. They found that it does not destabilize population interactions. No wonder then, that life-history omnivory is commonplace not only in Canadian lakes, but also in marine food webs.

Detritivores also feed from many trophic levels (Pimm *et al.*, 1991). But this, too, is an exception that tempts us to accept the rule. Detritivores wait to dine until their food is dead. Thus they have no direct dynamical influence on it. No wonder their omnivory cannot destabilize interactive systems.

The dynamic hypothesis has done all we can ask of any hypothesis. It has predicted a new set of patterns that actually do occur among real systems. It is a strong hypothesis that will be difficult to unseat.

Predator–victim ratios

At first, Figures 4.8, 4.9 and 4.11 may not surprise you. Why should that which influences victim diversity differ from that which influences predator diversity?

But Mithen and Lawton (1986) have shown that predator diversity and victim diversity are not merely dancing to the same piper. Instead, they are directly, dynamically coupled. Thus, we may not yet have good descriptions of their relationship, and we may not understand what we do have, but Mithen and Lawton's work teaches us that one day we will.

Mithen and Lawton modeled two-level food webs using the same mathematics as Pimm and Lawton. They set up an imaginary pool of predator and victim species and programmed the computer to select a set at random. This set became the initial community.

Next the species in the community interacted. Some became extinct. Finally a point was reached when all those remaining had a positive equilibrium population size. They called this the first feasible community. If the equilibrium point of this community was locally stable, it passed to the next step. Otherwise the whole set was discarded, and the computer tried again.

Now the computer introduced new species to the feasible community. The dynamic result set the fate of the combination: the new species might survive, become extinct or cause others to become extinct. It could even disrupt the entire combination.

Then a second new species was picked and its impact determined. Then a third, and so on. After a preset number of introductions, the model run was ended. Mithen and Lawton recorded how many predator species and how many victim species existed in the model system at three stages: initially; in the first feasible community; and at the end.

Mithen and Lawton performed three runs of models on the computer (see Table 11.3). In each they completed ten different assemblages. However, each run used a different set of species in the pool of community candidates. They designed the differences to mimic different kinds of bio-

Table 11.3. *Results of Mithen and Lawton's simulations.*

Run No.	Species of predator		Species of victim		Predator–victim ratio	
	Mean	SD	Mean	SD	Mean	SD
1	3.2	0.632	16.7	3.02	0.196	0.039
2	17.7	1.059	21.5	2.22	0.828	0.066
3	2.6	1.075	7.9	2.51	0.329	0.095

From Mithen and Lawton (1986).

logical conditions. For example, run 2 allowed for intraspecific predator mutualism,[1] and 40% of possible food links were actually established (at random) by the computer. In contrast, run 1 allowed no such mutualism and only 10% of the food links were established. (Consult their Table 2 for complete details of parameter ranges.)

Initial communities varied widely and overlapped greatly in predator and victim diversities and in predator–victim ratios. But the interactive differences among the runs eventually prevailed. Each tended toward a characteristic set of diversities and predator–victim ratio (Figure 11.5).

Of course, you must not take as predictions, the precise numbers Mithen and Lawton obtained. Their model systems leave out most of the interactive biology that ecologists like to study. They have no interspecific competition, for example. And only two trophic levels.

But please do notice that even without such links, the diversities and predator–victim ratios of their model systems did not float freely or randomly. They were constrained. They zeroed in on typical values.

Mithen and Lawton performed other computer experiments in which they varied a specific parameter over a wide range of values (e.g. intraspecific predatory competition). These showed that predator–victim ratios could remain virtually constant even though the diversity of final communities varied over more than an order of magnitude.

That tells me that one day we can hope to sort it all out. We should be able to predict predator–victim ratios from interaction coefficients and similar parameters. And we should be able to understand how these parameters work their dynamic consequences. So far, that goal is only a dream.

---

[1] Intraspecific mutualism means that the net per capita reproductive rate increases if the population does.

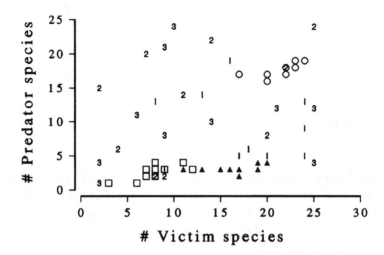

Figure 11.5. Results of Mithen and Lawton's computer experiments indicate that model systems converge on certain values of predator and of victim diversity
depending on the model coefficients. Initial points are
coded by numbers: I = Run 1; 2 = Run 2; 3 = Run 3.
These initial points are scattered fairly uniformly
about the graph. Completed communities: boxes for
Run 1; circles for Run 2; triangles for Run 3. These
points are concentrated in three different and
restricted areas of the same graph. In other words,
each type of community collapses into a small characteristic part of the predator–victim space. Data from
Table 1, Mithen and Lawton (1986).

Polyploidy

The proportion of polyploid species – especially plant species – grows with
latitude (see Figure 2.33). Many have suggested hypotheses to explain this
pattern (see review in Grant, 1971). The most promising started from the
observation that plant taxa vary greatly in their tendency to have polyploids. Those that consist mostly of perennial herbs with vegetative reproduction also make up most of Arctic floras. They also have a high proportion of polyploids. Perhaps the latitudinal gradient in polyploidy merely
reflects a gradient in the importance of various plant families (Gustafsson,

1948)? But this hypothesis failed, as have the others. The gradient shows up even within such plant families (Löve and Löve, 1948).

Let us seek an explanation for the latitudinal pattern by keeping our eye on speciation and extinction rates. We know that polyploidy works much faster than geographical speciation, orders of magnitude faster (three? six? more?). So, we ought to wonder why polyploids do not accumulate and overwhelm non-polyploids altogether.

Perhaps the quickness of polyploidy gets counterbalanced by a similarly high rate of extinction? Such an explanation could work, but I know of no evidence in its favor. Polyploids can be vigorous, aggressive competitors, well suited to their habitats and having large population sizes. No one has suggested they tend to go extinct instantly. In fact, we can best advance this discussion by assuming that polyploids and non-polyploids have the same probability of extinction (other things, such as population size, being equal).

I believe the basis of the answer lies in the autonomous braking system that seems to inhere in polyploidy. The higher the grade of polyploidy, the fewer species have it. We saw an example of this in Figure 5.2. Higher order polyploids (hexaploids, octaploids, etc.) are much rarer than tetraploids. Figure 11.6 shows the same phenomenon for a large sample of the flowering plants of New Zealand. Grant (1982) shows it for angiosperms in general.

So, we made a mistake. The instantaneous rate of a single polyploidy event in the laboratory does not translate into a very rapid overall rate in the field. Instead, we expect that assemblages already rich in polyploids will produce more polyploids very, very slowly.

Polyploidy must brake itself. That means we know how to increase the rate of polyploidy in any assemblage of species: Decrease the proportion that are polyploid. Keep that conclusion handy. I will need to use it at a pivotal point in the following theory.

Suppose we examine a system at $\hat{S}$(steady-state diversity) with a proportion p of polyploids. At $\hat{S}$, the speciation rate from polyploidy (S_p) plus that from non-polyploidy (S_g) exactly offsets the extinction rate. But if $S_g > S_p$, and if species produced by polyploidy have the same extinction rates as those produced geographically, then polyploids will dwindle and vanish. And if $S_g < S_p$, then polyploids will increase and sweep out the non-polyploids. What prevents both of these outcomes? What keeps p at some intermediate level? The self-braking nature of polyploidy does.

If $S_g < S_p$, then as p grows, S_p falls. On the other hand, if $S_g > S_p$, then as p falls, S_p grows. The system moves toward a steady-state value of p at which $S_g = S_p$. This conclusion is mechanical. It does not rely on any biological

New Zealand Angiosperms

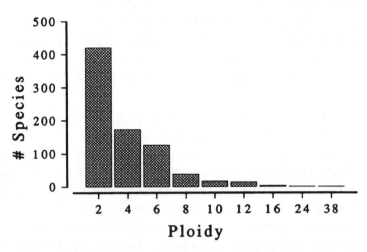

Figure 11.6. Grades of polyploidy among New Zealand flowering
plants. Data from Hair (1966) who found cytological
data for 40.2% of the country's 1977 indigenous
angiosperm species. The two species not included in
the graph are triploid.

property of polyploid species or of the polyploidy process except its self-
braking nature.

Now recall the theory of the latitudinal gradient (Chapter 9). Tropical
assemblages are richer primarily because they cover more area. That gives
them an elevated speciation curve and a lower extinction curve. At $\hat{S}$, the
total rate of speciation equals that of extinction, as at any latitude. But
because of the changes in their rate curves, tropical systems have higher
total rates at equilibrium than do other latitudinal zones (Figure 9.16).

So, the theory of the latitudinal gradient says that $S_g + S_p$ increases
toward the Equator. And $S_g = S_p$ when p is at steady state. Thus S_p also
must increase toward the Equator. How can it? There is one way. Decrease
p. Hence the latitudinal gradient in p.

Again, the result depends only on the self-braking nature of polyploidy.
The rest is pure mechanism. No other biology entered into the theory. The
proportion of polyploids declines as we approach the Equator because the
latitudinal increase in total diversity comes from higher total rates of speciation and extinction. Polyploidy must participate in these higher rates
because of each system's inherent evolutionary dynamics. And – with total

diversity held at steady state – raising the rate of polyploidy requires decreasing its proportion.

Once more our promise to concentrate on rates has paid off. A messy controversy, practically forgotten because of the frustration it caused, melts in the face of one biological fact, long accepted by all parties but never connected with the latitudinal aspect of their work. Higher latitudes have higher proportions of polyploids because high-order polyploids are scarce everywhere.

Disturbance and non-equilibrium systems
Why diversity peaks at intermediate disturbance frequencies

The disturbance pattern exists at relatively small scales of space and time. It involves neither evolution nor immigration from foreign biotic provinces. It begins with a fixed pool of species in a single region. But it takes into account that in any small patch of habitat, the number of species at one instant will not be at equilibrium. Instead, some patches will be growing in diversity while others decline.

The disturbance pattern assumes that species diversities are constantly changing at any locale. But the theory that explains it shares its philosophy and approach with equilibrium theories. It asks, what are the dynamic forces that change diversity at a site? And it compares these forces in size.

The theory of the disturbance pattern has three component processes, two negative and one positive.

- Species may disappear slowly from a patch by competition.
- Or, they may disappear suddenly from a patch because something (a disturbance), like a figurative broom, sweeps them away.
- Against these tides of dynamic destruction, species move into the patch and replenish it.

The result of these dynamic processes is a distribution of diversities among patches in the region. The mean diversity of the distribution and its variance depend upon the frequency of disturbances in the region.

Where disturbances happen often, the average patch accumulates only a few species before the destructive broom returns. So, most such patches are depauperate.

At smaller disturbance rates, more species accumulate before disaster strikes. But disturbance still comes often enough to interrupt the process of competitive exclusion. The average patch is quite diverse.

Where disturbances rarely happen, then competition can usually complete its work. Diversity is lost. The average patch suffering infrequent disturbance will be mature and depauperate.

Now you can fully understand why the small experimental boulders of Sousa (1979) had even more species than natural medium-sized boulders (Figure 2.27). The natural medium boulders must have lain undisturbed for a variety of times. By chance some would have been disturbed recently, some not for a very long time, and some in between. Only those at the intermediate time would have maximal diversities. So the average would be less than the maximum. Meanwhile, the experimental boulders were all sterilized with a blowtorch at the same time in July, 1975. They marched together through the stages of accumulating species. By the time of their censuses 15 months later, they were all simultaneously near the maximum.

At first, the theory of diversity and disturbance in small regions (Levin and Paine, 1974; Paine and Levin, 1981) may appear complex to you. But I believe I have summarized its essence above. In truth, it has elegance and simplicity. Petraitis *et al.* (1989) offer a recent review of this topic, a topic that is one of the success stories of ecological science.

The disturbance pattern emerges from the interplay of two opposing dynamical trends – disturbance and competitive exclusion – operating at similar rates, and therefore similarly influential. Other such clashes between quasi-equal forces should have similar consequences. We can point to at least one example.

Lubchenco (1978) studied the effects of predation and competition on the diversity of algae. These algae grow in intertidal systems on the rocky New England coast. Periwinkle snails, *Littorina littorea*, eat them.

But the snails have their preferences. Chief among them are the tender, green *Enteromorpha* species. Least preferred are the tough perennials like Irish moss, *Chondrus crispus*.

Lubchenco worked with two kinds of systems – tidal pools and emergent surfaces. The latter are alternatively dry and wet as the tide ebbs and flows. But tidal pools occupy depressions in the rocks, and so retain some seawater even at low tide. The biology of these two systems differs considerably.

Although tidal pools get covered by the ocean at every high tide, the snails move between pools very little. That allowed Lubchenco to change the densities of snails in the pools, and create varying experimental predator pressures. Pools with many periwinkle snails had few *Enteromorpha* and many *Chondrus crispus*. You probably expected that from the food preference of the snails. What you could not have predicted happens under low predator pressure. The *Enteromorpha* take over by outcompeting *Chondrus crispus*. In between, with only moderate snail densities, neither predation nor competition can dominate the results. We see many *Enteromorpha* and much *Chondrus crispus*. Also, several ephemeral species of algae get added to the pool. These species would usually be seen only seasonally. Diversity peaks at intermediate predation levels (Figure 11.7).

The emergent surfaces present a contrasting situation. Here competiton and predation work in tandem. The snails still prefer the more tender algae to the tougher perennials. But the perennials are also the competitive winners. With nothing else to bother the algae, you would expect to see nothing but perennials. But something else does intervene to preserve diversity on these surfaces. Waves scour them at times, creating empty patches. Thus, the more wave disturbance, the greater the diversity. Because waves remove the

New England Intertidal

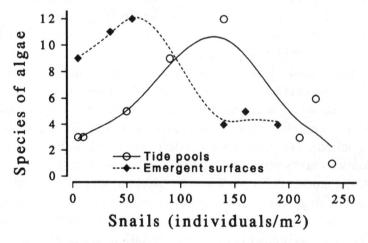

Figure 11.7. Small-scale processes interact in many ways to produce diversity patterns. Competition and predation oppose each other in tidal pools, so that diversity peaks when neither is dominant. But on emergent surfaces in the same area, competition and predation work together to promote a few species of perennial algae. Wave disturbance works against both. The time since a disturbance is inversely proportional to snail density on an emergent surface. Data from Lubchenco (1978). Lowess (locally weighted) regression lines.

snails too, the density of snails is a good inverse index of the time since the last disturbance. Yet, algal colonists arrive so rapidly that they almost obliterate the increasing part of the disturbance pattern (Figure 11.7).

You can see that each of these local diversity patterns will follow its own local circumstances. Yet we can understand them all by paying attention to the rates at which species enter local patches and to the rates at which they disappear by competition, predation or disturbance.

Recently, Caswell and Cohen (1993) produced a pair of models that join the disturbance pattern to species–area curves. The models depend on a fixed species pool, and are thus not meant to handle evolutionary time and space. The world is composed of a large number of patches, all of the same habitat. Species colonize patches, and patches suffer disturbances thus losing all their species. One model allows no competition. The other assumes that all but one species will go extinct owing to competition if disturbance is long enough delayed.

With or without strong competition, the models produce diversities which rise monotonically as area grows. This work suggests a new way to collect and analyze diversity data: census an increasingly large set of similar patches with a similar disturbance regime, and determine whether the set's diversity grows according to the theory.

On the other hand, the results of the models must not be compared to the species–area curves we already have. Elements crucial to known species–area curves do not appear in these models. In particular, they lack both habitat variability and evolutionary processes (i.e. speciation and global extinction). So, even if the models match real data, we will know that the known curves get their shape from other processes.

In fact, the models differ from known curves in several substantive properties. The models predict convex-upward curves that glide to an asymptote (the species pool). The data show curves that are straight or even concave-upward. The models predict considerable variation (about an order of magnitude) in z-values depending on disturbance frequency: the higher the disturbance frequency, the steeper the slope. Real z-values, taken at scales for which disturbance can possibly govern diversity, cluster tightly in the range 0.1–0.2.

But those discrepancies should not cause us to reject the models. They must be tested with new data sets collected with the models especially in mind. We should not re-use sets that incorporate evolutionary events. Nor should we reuse sets in which habitat-absence (rather than disturbance) is the usual reason a species is not found.

Chapter 12

Energy flow and diversity[1]

Many ecologists believe that productivity is one of the most pervasive influences on diversity. But, as I completed this book, I realized that I hardly understood that influence. Yes, diversity exhibits spatial patterns that seem related to productivity. And, as you will see, we understand the pattern that occurs at small spatial scales. We even think we understand a part of the larger-scale pattern. Yet, unlike the other spatial patterns, the productivity pattern remains somewhat mysterious. Not that people have ignored it. They have caused a river of ink to flow in its name. We just aren't sure where the river is headed.

We have two patterns to account for. First, when experimental ecologists increase productivity to small patches of plants, plant diversity declines. Second, as productivity rises on a regional scale ($c.$ 10^6 km^2), animal diversity first increases, then it declines.

Experimental increase of productivity

Correlations help us search for patterns. However, patterns may not reflect causes. They may instead reflect phantom correlations, correlations of one of our variables with another variable, a variable we may not even have thought about, let alone measured. That caution applies to no variable more strongly than to productivity since productivity correlates with many other important ecological variables. So, once we find a productivity pattern, we must investigate it further, preferably by experiment.

Proper control of ecological experiments requires a small scale. So all productivity experiments have been done at small scales. Each comes with a ready-made set of species already provided by evolution. And, by design, each produces small patches of super-rich environment that do not exist naturally anywhere nearby. The species that might be able to live in them may live thousands of kilometers away. Or they may not yet exist. How can

---

[1] Much of this chapter appeared in an earlier edition as Rosenzweig and Abramsky (1993). The preface contains special acknowledgements for it.

diversity not fall? Maybe evolutionary immaturity is all that accounts for the experimental pattern?

Yet, those who do these experiments see a general mechanism at work. Usually, instead of a subset of the plants dying of nitrate burns, or of some other malady brought on by unfamiliar good conditions, the plants that die get overgrown by aggressive competitors.

Tilman (1987) reports the results of systematic experiments to study the effects of nutrient enrichment in various successional stages from new field to woods. Increasing the productivity drives diversity down. In three years, more than 60% of the species disappeared from high nitrogen treatments. He believes 'that nutrient addition makes plots more homogeneous spatially, forcing more species to compete for the same limiting resource.'

Certainly, the natural history survey data taken in the area of Tilman's experiments support his hypothesis (Inouye *et al.*, 1987). The older a field, the more nitrogen and the fewer species it has. Goldberg and Miller (1990) also support Tilman's interpretation.

On the theoretical side, Rosenzweig (1971) and Wollkind (1976) showed that enrichment can destabilize predator–victim interactions. Riebesell (1974) did the same for competition. I still believe that loss of stability most probably accounts for the loss of species in polluted aquatic systems. But I know of no field experiments to test this prediction.

Competitive displacement and community immaturity may combine to explain the experimental pattern in terrestrial plants. Suppose most communities contain a mixture of competitive types. Some are aggressive competitors able to take advantage of richer circumstances, but are badly hurt by suboptimal conditions. And some are subordinate species not badly harmed by poorer conditions and thus dependent on them for their existence. I believe that mixture to be common, and to reflect a common kind of community organization called 'shared preferences' or 'tolerance differences' (Rosenzweig, 1987a, 1991a). The competitively subordinate species tolerate a wider range of habitats.

Natural selection cannot outfit a species for environments that the species never use. So, you would also expect the range of conditions to which the whole set of plants is adapted to reflect the range ordinarily available to them. Hence, when you enrich the system experimentally, you greatly help the aggressors and remove the poorer microenvironments that the subordinates actually depend on.

But if you were to maintain the enrichment for a longer time, say a million years, the plant community's norm would increase. Species would evolve that were able to take even better advantage of the very rich environment you provide. By comparison, today's dominants would be tomorrow's lambs. And diversity might very well rise again.

Maybe you don't agree with that. Maybe you believe that plant biology is too rigid to allow it. Maybe you believe that a rich environment will always be rich, and a poor one always poor. If so, consider this. Using a variety of adaptations, the shrubs growing luxuriantly on Australia's heathlands manage on nutrient concentrations low enough to kill most anything else (Lamont, 1984). Yet, if you supplement their nutrient supply, you do them no favor (Specht, 1981). They do grow faster, but die in as little as half the usual time. Moreover, their seedlings suffer from phosphorus toxicity after fire and usually fail to survive. If they do survive, they are particularly susceptible to attack by root-rotting soil fungi.

A similar combination of interactive forces and immaturity could also produce the loss of species from aquatic systems. Rosenzweig and Schaffer (1978) showed that natural selection, given enough time, would indeed tend to restore the stability of enriched predatory systems.

Consequently, the experimental results now available cast little or no light on patterns at larger scales of time and space. None of these experimental results takes evolution into account, but the evolution of species to take advantage of higher productivity must constitute an important part of the response of a region to higher productivity. Some experiments fail to allow even enough time for succession, although we know how important that can be.

We must not be tempted to extrapolate the results of smaller time scales to larger ones. Huston (1993) provides a worrying example of the results of such extrapolation. It leads – quite erroneously I believe – to the conclusion that intense agricultural use will rarely depress species diversity providing that only free market forces are allowed to control which hectares get cleared and plowed. Try telling that to a conservation officer charged with saving the flora and fauna of Australia's rich wheatbelts.

Before enrichment experiments learn how to compensate for lack of time, their relevance will remain restricted. We should use them solely to understand and predict the short-term consequences of local enrichments. For that purpose, they are ideal.

The unimodal pattern in regions

Theoreticians and empiricists have long agreed that productivity must
affect diversity (e.g. Connell and Orias, 1964; Leigh, 1965; MacArthur and
Pianka, 1966; Pianka, 1966; Rosenzweig, 1971; Brown, 1973; Tappan and
Loeblich, 1973). But they have disagreed about the mechanism that underlies it. They have even disagreed about the direction of the correlation
(Valentine, 1976; Elseth and Baumgardner, 1981). Some – typically those
studying aquatic systems or enriched plant systems – found fewer species at
higher productivities. Others – especially those studying terrestrial vertebrates – found the opposite.

We now know that within regions about the size of small to medium-
sized nations, animal species diversity is often – perhaps usually – a unimodal function of productivity (or some well-accepted index of it like rainfall in arid regions). To remind you of the pattern, here are more examples.
Figure 12.1 comes from benthic megafauna (vertebrates and invertebrates)
in the North Atlantic. Figure 12.2 provides yet another mammal case, this
one from the Gobi Desert of Mongolia. So does Figure 12.3, which tracks

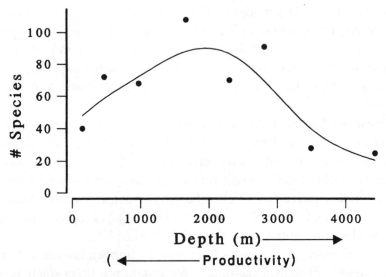

Figure 12.1. Benthic megafauna in the North Atlantic follow the
unimodal productivity pattern. Most species are fish,
echinoderms or decapod crustacea. Depths are the
midrange points of series of samples. Data from
Haedrich *et al.* (1980).

Gobi Desert Rodents

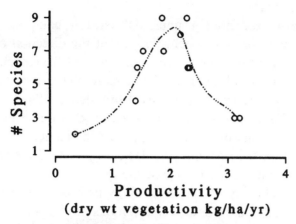

Figure 12.2. Rodents of gravel and rocky plains habitats of the
Gobi Desert peak in diversity at intermediate produc-
tivities. Konstantin Rogovin supplied the data from
Kazantseva (1986) and Rogovin *et al.* (1986).
Productivities are averages of data taken from 1978
to 1984. The regression line is lowess.

African Herbivorous Mammals Larger than 10kg

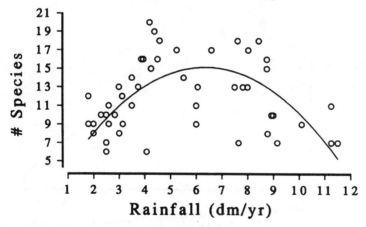

Figure 12.3. Large herbivorous mammal diversity peaks over
intermediate rainfall in African ecosystems.
Herbivores must weigh at least 10 kg to be included.
The systems come from all over Africa. Redrawn
from an idea in Western (1991); data supplied by
David Western.

the number of species of large herbivorous mammals in a wide variety of African ecosystems.

We can easily see how a unimodal pattern could cause confusion. Scientists reached opposite conclusions about the direction of the relationship because they were looking at opposite ends of the camel. Brown (1973, 1975) for example, was looking at the increase phase (over the poor end of the productivity spectrum) (see also Bramlette, 1965; Tappan, 1968; Meserve and Glanz, 1978). Students of eutrophication (e.g. Sawyer, 1966; Whiteside and Harmsworth, 1967; Lipps, 1970; Hessler and Jumars, 1974) usually focused on the rich end (the decrease phase). Take two steps backward, however, and you see the whole hump.

The data of Schoenly *et al.* (1991) allow us a new perspective. It abandons taxonomically based data sets and looks at all species. The intertaxonomic pattern is also unimodal (Figure 12.4). Peak diversity lies in the second trophic level. If species of the first trophic level followed the straight regression line of Figure 4.7, they would be about an order of magnitude more diverse. If they followed the regression slope of Figure 11.2 they would be almost two orders of magnitude more diverse.

Insect Food Webs

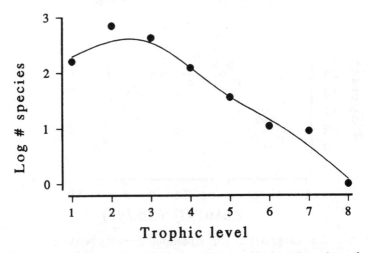

Figure 12.4. Diversity in the first trophic level is less than that of the second. Community food web data of Schoenly *et al.* (1991), but the trend is confirmed by the small number of plant species in the world (relative to insects). Lowess regression.

Perhaps the unimodality is false? Perhaps the one point, from the first trophic level, that produces the unimodality does not reflect the true diversity of primary producers relative to their consumers? After all, Schoenly *et al.* assure us that their animals are much more finely identified than their plants. Many plants and other level 1 species are lumped together. Does that explain the dearth of plant species? I doubt it. Remember – from Chapter 1 – that insects are the Earth's most diverse taxon. They probably have tens of millions of species. Plants have fewer than 250 000 worldwide. So, the diversity of level 1 must be less than that of its consumers. The intertaxonomic productivity pattern is also unimodal.

Knowing what the pattern is, we can begin to progress in explaining it. For convenience, let us address the problem as two separate patterns: the increase phase and the decrease phase.

The increase phase

As productivity rises from very low to moderate levels, diversity also rises. That is the increase phase of the productivity-diversity pattern.

An interesting example of this part of the pattern allows us to factor out the effect of time. That is worth doing because until fairly recently, many of the least productive places were covered by glaciers. Thus, it is possible that their low diversity comes from their immaturity.

Hebert and Hann (1986) amassed the diversities of shallow tundra ponds in 11 regions of the Canadian Arctic. These were all glaciated until about 7000 years ago. Assuming that the number of degree days (above 0 °C) provides a reasonable surrogate for productivity, these regions have diversities of microcrustaceans proportional to productivity (Figure 12.5; $R^2 = 0.54$; $p = 0.006$). Are warmer, richer regions also younger? Is it immaterial that they also happen to be warmer and more productive? Is age the real actor here?

Luckily, Hebert and Hann had a comparable data set available from northern Alaska. This area, unlike the Canadian areas, had not been glaciated during Wisconsin times. Yet, it too shows the increase (the three Alaskan points in Figure 12.5 are insufficient for regression, but they come from 251 different ponds and the trend is clear). True, the Alaskan locations have many more species than the Canadian ones. That reveals the effect of age. But the positive relationship between productivity and diversity characterizes them both.

Actually, the increase phase of the relationship troubles no one. Ecologists who have thought about it, consider it to sit on a solid theoreti-

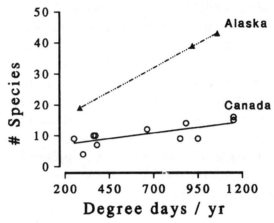

Figure 12.5. Shallow Canadian tundra ponds are only 7000 years
old, but both they and their much older counterparts
in northern Alaska show the increase phase of the
productivity pattern. However, the older system does
have more species for a given productivity. Warmth is
the surrogate for productivity in these systems.
Redrawn from Hebert and Hann (1986). See text for
more details.

cal base. A poor environment supplies too meager a resource supply for its
would-be rarest species, and they become extinct.

Preston (1962a, b) developed the theory behind this hypothesis. He proposed that the abundances of species in a region fit a distribution called the
lognormal (see Chapter 9). The abundance of a species is all its individuals.
So, if the area of a region is small, then the sparsest species of the log-
normal distribution will have insufficient abundance to survive.

Preston used the metaphor of the 'veil line' to describe the effect of rarity. A small area veils the existence of all the species whose total abundance
falls below a critical minimum. The critical minimum is the veil line. Today,
we call the veil line, 'the minimum viable population' (see Chapter 6).

Wright *et al.* (1993) have been extending Preston's theory to the variable
of productivity. They call it 'species-energy theory'. It notes that the species
of an unproductive region will be relatively rare for their abundance rank.
So, the region's veil line should occur at a fairly high abundance rank and
all lower-ranking species will be veiled (i.e. non-existent).

Assume a variety of productivities and biotas in different regions. Assume all start with the same diversity. The scarcest species in the most productive region will be more abundant than in others. Therefore, scarce species of the most productive region will better resist accidental extinction. Diversity will change in all regions until the scarcest species in all regions have similar chances of accidental extinction. Because the pie is larger in a more productive place, it must be sliced into many more pieces before its smallest are about the same size as the smallest in a poorer place. So, richer places have more species.

I do not think Preston's theory is wrong. In fact, I believe Prestonian theory rightly permeates ecological thinking (see Chapters 2, 3, 8, 9 and 10). It does much more than explain the increase phase of the productivity–diversity pattern. If rarity does not raise extinction rates, then the whole foundation of conservation ecology crumbles. If rarity does not raise extinction rates, then we must reinvent the basic dynamic theories of both island (MacArthur and Wilson, 1963) and continental (Rosenzweig, 1975) diversity. If rarity does not raise extinction rates, then we all have a lot of work to do. We will have to rethink a host of ecological processes and applications we've come to rely on. We generally use Frank Preston's theory the way we use aspirin: often, without much thought, and without credit to its inventor.

But, just as we overuse aspirin, sometimes we overuse Preston. Preston intended his theory to deal with the relationship of diversity to species' abundance distributions. Applying it to the productivity–diversity pattern all by itself may be stretching it near its limit. To do it, we must assume that diversity is entirely governed by the ability of the rarest species to survive accidental extinctions. And we must assume that the contribution of the accidental extinction rate dominates all other facets of extinction and speciation. Perhaps my pointing out those assumptions to you, makes you unsure whether you still believe that more productivity ought always to raise diversity. I hope so, because as you learned in Chapter 2, it doesn't.

Yet, I suspect that Preston's theory, as extended by Wright, explains a good part of the productivity pattern. In fact, at very low productivities, the consequences to the extinction rate of having a tiny population may well dominate all other influences on extinction. Diversity will rise as populations are freed from this constraint. Thus, to me, the decrease phase presents the real puzzle: **why, past a certain point, does enhanced productivity tend to reduce the number of species?**

Hypotheses to explain the decrease phase

The literature contains nine different hypotheses to explain the decrease phase. Although losers do emerge from the list of hypotheses, I am not sure whether there are any winners. So, I present you all of them.

To maintain discipline and a parallel format, I treat each hypothesis under three subheadings. First I state it briefly. Then I explain why it might be true. Then I evaluate it. Please understand that this format requires me to play devil's advocate on behalf of several hypotheses. That is, although I do not believe them, I begin by arguing for them as well as I can. But, in the evaluations, I write my own opinions and the reasons for them.

1. Environmental heterogeneity

HYPOTHESIS: Under conditions of extreme low productivity, there is not much habitat or resource heterogeneity. The landscape is uniformly barren. An average location will not sustain any species. As productivity rises, the average variety of micronutrient combinations in fertile sites increases. Alternatively, some fertile spots have more light with sparser nutrients while others have less light with richer nutrients. In either case, plant diversity increases and plant physiognomies diversify, allowing animal diversity to increase also.

Past a certain point, more productivity has the opposite effect. It reduces heterogeneity of micronutrient combinations and habitats. Productivity tends to be spread more evenly within and between years, reducing the variety of viable temporal specializations. Diversity declines.

Notice that this hypothesis explains both the increase and decrease phases of the productivity pattern. It does not require low productivity to cause rarity and thus higher extinction rates. So it predicts the entire hump-shaped pattern with no help from any other hypothesis.

REASONING: The variety of habitats in space and time underlies much of the specialization that supports diversity (Rosenzweig 1987a). Most ecologists would agree that relatively barren areas offer only a few kinds of habitable times and places. The mean habitat is inhospitable, but some unusually favorable times or places cross the line and support niches. Moderately productive areas have excellent mean habitats. But also, their variance encompasses a wealth of different sorts of exploitable niche opportunities. Very productive areas also have excellent mean habitats. But their variance rarely presents significant challenges to life. A productive patch that falls to half its mean productivity from one year to the next is still very productive. Similarly, a patch 0.5 km away with half the productivity is still very productive.

Tilman (1982), using micronutrient combinations as the measure of habitat specialization, argues persuasively for this hypothesis. Recently, Tilman (1987) and Tilman and Pacala (1993) have been exploring a similar model. Newman (1973) noted that as nutrients increase, light becomes more and more a problem for competing plants. This sets up a gradient along which Tilman posits a specialty for each plant species. Regions of poor productivity will include little of the whole gradient and, therefore, few of the plant species that specialize along it. Regions of high productivity will also support few of the species because they include little of the gradient. Most of their sites will cause intense competition for light.

Abrams (1988) developed this model formally. He discovered that it could also lead to a monotonic rise in diversity as productivity grows. But, can the assumptions necessary for monotonicity ever be satisfied? Tilman and Pacala (1993) doubt it. Abrams (personal communication) does not.

Once the plant pattern appears, a similar animal pattern will evolve. Myriads of studies recognize the importance of plant diversity (in physiognomy as well as species) to the maintenance of animal diversity.

EVALUATION: Study after study shows the importance of habitat diversity to species coexistence. All such studies favor this hypothesis. Moreover, if you take a close look at specific cases, you become even more convinced. For example, desert rodents in southeastern Arizona are sitting right on the North American rodent peak. Increase the productivity a bit and their desert becomes a semi-arid grassland. We lose the shrubs and open patches that support so much of the desert's diversity. The grass spreads out and minimizes just those aspects of habitat heterogeneity that many small mammal species depend on (Rosenzweig, 1977a; Lemen and Rosenzweig, 1978; Brown, et al., 1979; Kotler, 1985; Kotler and Brown, 1988). Both Rosenzweig (1973a) and Whitford et al. (1978) showed experimentally that simplifying the structure of the plant community reduces rodent diversity.

Israel's sand-dwelling rodents also seem to fit. Areas with intermediate productivity have patchy ground cover exploitable both by species usually living in denser cover and by those often found where there is little cover (Rosenzweig *et al.*, 1984; Abramsky *et al.*, 1985; Rosenzweig and Abramsky, 1985, 1986).

However, most of the evidence cited by others in favor of this hypothesis deals with the results of short-term experiments. As I have already pointed out, these results do not bear on patterns present in evolutionarily mature associations.

The heterogeneity hypothesis also leaves us a nagging logical question. Is it tautology? Recall that habitat and resource heterogeneity are co-evolved responses of organisms (Chapter 7). We expect that life will subdivide any particular variance into as many niches as natural selection forces it to. In particular, more species means more selection for finer habitat discrimination.

- That is why birds in Puerto Rican rainforest recognize only two foliage levels while birds in Panamanian rainforest recognize four (Figure 7.7) (MacArthur *et al.*, 1966). That is why birds of southwestern Australian islands have far fewer species for any level of foliage diversity than their mainland counterparts (Figure 7.9). And that is why birds of Caribbean islands use a wider variety of habitats when their island has fewer species (Figure 7.10).
- That is why some of the world's richest floras grow on the impoverished soils of southwestern Australia and South Africa (Figure 7.5).
- That is why there is 'such exuberant biological diversity in (the deep sea), an environment apparently lacking in ... habitat complexity' (Gage and May, 1993).
- That is why similar-sized areas of wet tropical forest in different biological provinces have different diversities of plants, of fish and of vertebrate frugivores (Figure 9.1).
- That is why similar-sized areas of similar environments in Australia usually differ substantially in diversity compared to other continents (Morton, 1993).

Where provincial origination and extinction processes yield many species, life recognizes many habitats. Where they yield few species, life recognizes few habitats.

If species are forced to recognize more habitats when there are more species, then we chase our tails to say that the reason there are so many species is that there are so many habitats. We need an independent model. It must start with a habitat continuum. It must show that speciation and extinction rates vary with productivity in such a way that we finish with more species (and thus more recognized habitats) at intermediate productivity levels.

We cannot start with an effect (habitat diversity). Then, notice that the effect correlates closely with its cause (species diversity). And then conclude that the effect is the cause of the cause.

2. Dynamical instability

HYPOTHESIS: More productivity reduces dynamical stability. The loss of dynamical stability increases extinction rates, reducing diversity.

REASONING: I invented this hypothesis in a theory of eutrophication (Rosenzweig, 1971). Higher productivity reduces the negative feedback of competition within species, and increases the positive feedback that predatory control produces (Rosenzweig, 1977b). There is a net loss of dynamical stability at higher productivities.

Wollkind (1976) extended the theory to three-level food chains. Riebesell (1974) extended it to competition between species.

EVALUATION: This hypothesis breaks down when natural selection has enough time to do its job. Rosenzweig and Schaffer (1978) showed that natural selection tends to restore the dynamical stability of enriched systems. That is how some extremely productive biomes like coral reefs and tropical forests can be extraordinarily diverse. Moreover, I cannot explain the intertrophic level pattern with this hypothesis (Figure 12.4). All trophic levels join to produce the dynamics of a food web. We cannot say that the dynamics of a web are stable for consumers but not for their food plants.

Yet, many have reported that diversity does decline after nutrient enrichment. In addition to the plant examples, which I mentioned in connection with the previous hypothesis, there are several aquatic examples (e.g. Swingle, 1946; Yount, 1956; Schindler, 1990). I cannot easily explain all these cases as the result of increasing competition for light, or homogenization of habitat. So perhaps the hypothesis of dynamical instability does apply to some recently enriched environments, especially the aquatic ones like eutrophic lakes. At least the stability hypothesis makes a field-testable prediction that could someday convince us to accept it: enrichment should be accompanied by an increase in oscillatory dynamics and a decline in return times (Pimm, 1982).

3. Changes in ratio of predators to victims

HYPOTHESIS: As productivity increases, predators absorb much more than a proportional share, and reduce the diversity of consumers.

REASONING: Predators can absorb most or all of any increase in standing crop caused by higher productivities (Rosenzweig, 1971, 1972). Moreover, Oksanen *et al.* (1981, 1992, in press) determined theoretically that increased productivity adds controlling levels in a food chain. A new higher trophic level should considerably reduce the standing crops of the species beneath it. Case and Bolger (1991) demonstrated that predators of lizards do reduce total populations of all lizard species on islands. Smaller standing crops should produce higher extinction rates and diminished diversity.

EVALUATION: Predator–victim diversity ratios are a topic of debate (see Chapter 4). Yet all data do agree in one particular. All data show that more victim species are associated with more predators (Pimm, 1991). That contradicts the prediction of the hypothesis. The hypothesis requires that victim diversities decrease in the presence of more predators.

Even if I did not know about the predator–victim ratios, I would distrust the hypothesis. The theory on which it is based depends on the presence of weak interaction coefficients among predator individuals. Individuals that form dominance hierarchies or steal each other's territories don't fit the theory. But such animals (e.g. Texas carnivores) do exhibit the hump-shaped pattern.

Furthermore, a lot of work has demonstrated that predators can add to the sustainable diversity of their victims. Much of this work consists of incontrovertible field experiments done in all sorts of biomes on various taxa (e.g. Summerhayes, 1941; Paine, 1966; Hay, 1985). More recently, theoretical studies have explained how this can happen as apparent competition or competition for predator-free space (Holt, 1977, 1984; Jeffries and Lawton, 1984).

The predator–victim ratio hypothesis fails.

4. Intertaxonomic competition

HYPOTHESIS: Once a critical productivity is reached, a taxon cannot absorb any more. All further increases go to a competing taxon. In fact, the competing taxon takes even more than the increase. It actually reduces the productivity going to the first taxon. So the first taxon declines in diversity.

Notice that this hypothesis claims there is only one relationship between diversity and productivity: The more productivity, the more diversity. The twist is – according to this hypothesis – that higher system productivities sometimes mean lower productivites to some taxa. (The predator–victim ratio hypothesis shares this twist, but otherwise it is too weak to consider further.)

REASONING: Intertaxonomic competition exists. For instance, granivorous rodents do compete with ants (Brown *et al.* 1979a; Davidson *et al.*, 1984). Brown and Davidson (1977) detected a likely suppression of rodent diversity by ants in their east–west productivity transect. Possibly, each type (*bauplan*) of organism competes best at a restricted set of productivities and is largely defeated at others.

EVALUATION: Competitive abilities among species often do differ along a richness gradient (Rosenzweig 1987a, 1991a; Keddy, 1990). Why shouldn't the same be true among higher taxa?

Also, taxa differ in the productivities at which their diversities peak, just as you would expect from this hypothesis. Rodents peak in southeastern Arizona, carnivores in eastern Texas. Various marine taxa (Haedrich *et al.*, 1980; Rex, 1981) peak over very different ocean depths. What makes a place remarkably diverse in one taxon does not always make it remarkably diverse in another.

Nevertheless, this hypothesis needs much more work. By definition, it cannot explain the vertical intertaxonomic pattern (Figure 12.4). It also needs a coherent theoretical treatment to formalize it and enrich its set of predictions. More predictions would make it easier to test. One untested prediction: the broader the taxonomic grouping, the weaker the decrease phase.

Finally, some taxa should exist that do not decline at higher productivities. Where are they? As Tilman and Pacala (1993) point out, we know of no group whose diversity rises monotonically with productivity.

5. Change in competitive structure

HYPOTHESIS: Interference competition prevails at intermediate productivities and adds considerably to the diversity maintainable at them.

Notice that this hypothesis also requires no other to predict the entire hump-shaped pattern.

REASONING: Territoriality appears commonly in asymmetrical competitive systems and can help to promote competitive coexistence in them (e.g. Pimm *et al.*, 1985). But, Brown (1971b) showed that territoriality depends on productivity. Among chipmunks, it first increases and then declines as productivity increases. Brown argues cogently that this pattern makes sense. Productivity should influence territoriality. Poor situations are not worth defending. Rich ones are too costly to defend because they support so many individuals that excluding them would take too much time.

Perhaps species are less diverse in richer places because they cannot therein ameliorate the effects of competition by being territorial. In the terminology of Nicholson (1954), perhaps high productivity forces species from contest competition into scramble competition.

We may be able to extend this reasoning to plants. Perhaps plants in poorer places cannot afford the costs of chemical defense. And perhaps plants in very rich places cannot preserve the areas around themselves for their own seedlings because, if they did, they would encourage too many herbivores.

The plant argument uses herbivory to understand how interference competition could wane at high productivity. The animal argument uses the time cost of active territoriality. Nevertheless, I join them into one hypothesis because they make the same broad prediction: interference competition should peak at intermediate levels of productivity.

EVALUATION: This hypothesis has three problems. They stem from the fact that a rich place has plenty of levels of productivity on which to specialize.

- Interference (especially as exemplified by territoriality) is a well-documented phenomenon in some of the Earth's most productive places (e.g. coral reefs and tropical rainforests). Any successful hypothesis concerning interference will have to predict that where productivity is high, interference should decline, but not very much.
- All species in an ecosystem do not experience its productivity to the same extent. In a richer one, some species specialize on wealth while others can also use the sparser times and places that an environment offers. Even in a region of high productivity, species may specialize on moderate habitats, and so escape the pressure to forgo territoriality. A good example is the bee community of the Santa Catalina Mountains (Schaffer *et al.*, 1979). During each day, honeybees forage first, when nectar supplies are most plentiful. Then come bumblebees, and finally carpenter bees. Another case is the system of pond fish in Michigan (Werner and Hall, 1979). There, the near-shore tangle of aquatic vegetation provides the richest

habitat. All three fish species prefer it, but once fish grow past the tiny stages of their life, only one species uses it much. Arizona hummingbirds give us a third example (Pimm *et al.*, 1985). One species lives exclusively in the rich riparian forest along the canyon bottom. The other two also prefer that habitat, but usually forage in poorer woods, arid slopes or higher elevations.

* Species may indeed stake out a range of habitat richnesses for their niche. But, although they may do so by interference, they need not (Brown 1986, 1989a, b). Various sorts of morphological or physiological adaptations can take the place of interference if that gets to be an impractical strategy. But only interference can reduce diversity. Other means of subdividing a habitat-richness axis add to diversity.

For example, some species of desert rodents forage during the poorer months of the year, or in poorer patches of seeds. Others actually require the richer times and places that all prefer. But among heteromyid species, only the largest kangaroo rats use interspecific territoriality to protect their end of the habitat spectrum (the richest) (Frye, 1983; Brown and Munger, 1985). The niches of the others are determined by their position in a trade-off continuum: the more efficiently a rodent deals with food (once found), the less efficiently it travels in space and/or time to find it. (Hibernation – and torpor in general – provides the efficient way of traveling between times of abundance.) Efficient travelers tend to discover the rich patches first and so **tend** to monopolize them. But, usually because they are larger, efficient travelers are too inefficient at food use to exploit the poorer patches at all (Brown, 1986, 1989a; Kotler and Brown, 1988).

Someone needs to produce a quantitative model predicting the predominance of interference and its effects on diversity. Otherwise, I cannot believe this hypothesis will help us understand the diversity–productivity pattern.

6. Time

HYPOTHESIS: Richer patches have been around a shorter time than poorer patches. They have not reached equilibrium and are producing new species faster than they are losing them. The decrease phase is temporary.

REASONING: Speciation takes time. Considering the upheavals of the Pleistocene, many habitats and taxa may not have reached equilibrium. If the most productive habitats are also the newest or were hardest hit, they should be most depressed below equilibrium.

EVALUATION: I know of no evidence to support the hypothesis. It depends on richer patches being considerably younger than the time it takes evolution to fill them. It also depends on richer patches being considerably younger than poorer patches. Does anyone think this is generally true? Even if it is, are plants younger than their consumers? If not, how does this hypothesis explain Figure 12.4?

The greatest damage to this hypothesis comes from the fossil record. We now know that the unimodal pattern goes back at least to Paleozoic times.

The breakthrough came when Ziegler (1965) noted the good correlation of sediment type and relative ocean depth. The finer the sediment, the deeper the water in which it was deposited. So, sediment type becomes an index of relative productivity. Ziegler and other paleobiologists began to use that correlation to describe ancient environments and their communities.

We now have estimates of invertebrate diversity over depth gradients for several epochs in the Ordovician and the Silurian Periods. All show the hump-shaped pattern. I could find no summary data on diversity in Llandovery time of the Lower Silurian. Yet it, too, shows the pattern (Rosenzweig and Abramsky, 1993).

In Figure 12.6 I plot the pattern in four fossil transects. Were any of these to stand alone, it might not convince you. But the pattern occurs repeatedly. The combined Silurian and Ordovician investigations represent some 75 Myr of fossil history. And each graph incorporates a very large amount of data. For example, each point of the Ludlow series (Watkins, 1979) of six communities (Figure 12.6: early Silurian Period) is the mean diversity per 50 individuals per sample. There are 200 samples and no Ludlow point comprises fewer than 11. The Ordovician bars synthesize 'about 2000 samples collected through about 5 km of strata representing about 200 000 individual identifications' (Lockley, 1983).

How can the time hypothesis explain the pattern's existence and persistence for 75 million years during the Ordovician and Silurian Periods? I mention the time hypothesis, but I also reject it.

7. Disturbance

HYPOTHESIS: Productivity itself is not a cause. It is just a correlate of disturbance rate. So, the productivity–diversity pattern is the disturbance–

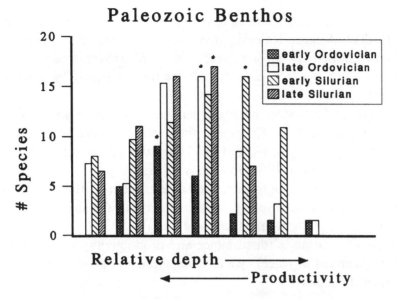

Figure 12.6. Brachiopod-dominated faunas of the Paleozoic Era
show the productivity pattern. The stars indicate the
peak diversity of each period. Ordovician data from
Lockley (1983). Lower Silurian data from Watkins
(1979). Upper Silurian data from Hancock *et al.*
(1974). For more details, see Rosenzweig and
Abramsky (1993).

diversity pattern (Chapters 2, 11). As disturbance rate falls, diversity first
rises then falls (Grime, 1973, 1979; Levin and Paine, 1974; Connell, 1978;
Lubchenco, 1978; Paine and Levin, 1981; Petraitis *et al.*, 1989). Varying
disturbance rates cause the productivity–diversity pattern.

The connection between productivity and disturbance depends on the
system. But regardless of the system, there is a strong connection.

- Terrestrial relationship: the higher the productivity, the less frequent the disturbances.
- Marine relationship: the higher the productivity, the more frequent
  the disturbances.

In a sense, this hypothesis also predicts the entire hump-shaped pattern.
But remember that the disturbance hypothesis itself requires two mechanisms: local extinction from disturbance and local extinction from competition. So it is not inherently simpler than others.

REASONING: On land, as rainfall increases, its coefficient of variation certainly does decline. Rainfall, necessary for actual evapotranspiration, helps set productivity (Rosenzweig 1968). Moreover, even in tropical biomes some ecologists believe that the wettest, warmest habitats are the most stable.

In the sea, shallow water allows violent waves to reach down to the bottom and destroy life on it. The deeper the water, the more protected its benthic inhabitants from storms. But shallow water allows more productivity (see Chapter 2; Sanders, 1968; and many others).

The marine paleoecologist sees the same pattern in the rocks. Mikulic and Watkins (1979) for instance, make it clear that the shallow, productive community is most storm-influenced and unstable.

Why use two variables (disturbance and productivity) to do the work of one? Let's keep disturbance – we have experimental proof of its role – and forget about productivity.

EVALUATION: You should suspect part of the reasoning. Few ecologists accept uncritical, undefined statements about stability any more. Few believe they know how to rank biomes, let alone habitats, as to their stability or freedom from disturbance. Take a walk in a Neotropical lowland rainforest. That popping and crashing you will hear all the time is the sound of falling vegetation creating new open spaces. How is that open space so different from a patch of intertidal substrate newly opened by a violent wave?

All right, maybe it is far too soon to be sure that productivity and disturbance correlate well at middle and higher productivities. But there is no question that they do at lower productivities. From the most extreme deserts to semi-arid grasslands to mesic forests, productivity and lack of disturbance surely go together.

However, the disturbance–diversity pattern comes from a well-understood theory that makes several collateral predictions. As diversity grows from extreme deserts to richer places, do those predictions come true? If it turns out that the richest places really do have the lowest frequencies of disturbance, do those collateral predictions fit the data of tropical mammals or trees?

What are the collateral predictions?

- The species found in the least disturbed patches should be a subset of those in the most diverse patches. No species will be restricted to the least disturbed patches.

- Once it does get disturbed, the recuperation history of one of the least disturbed patches should follow a course much like the pattern of the combined patches. It should begin by accumulating species, reach a diversity like that of a patch with intermediate disturbance, and then decline in diversity owing to loss of species already present. In other words, patches with little disturbance should recapitulate in their own histories the entire diversity–disturbance pattern.

The diversity–productivity graphs themselves offer no information to help us decide if they match the collateral predictions. But I know enough of the details of the mammal patterns to believe that they do not.

Points with low diversity and high productivity do not contain a small subset of the species from peak diversity points. The species lists from east Texas (high productivity) and from lowland rainforests in tropical Australia (high productivity) contain many species not found at all in peak diversity places. This is glaringly so in Texas: only a few species of the rich, Trans-Pecos rodent fauna also live in east Texas. And in east Texas they make up a small proportion of its low diversities.

The fossil data also do not fit this collateral prediction of the disturbance hypothesis. For instance, Mikulic and Watkins (1979) report that all three species of trilobite that lived in the shallowest community (most productive) of the Upper Silurian, lived nowhere else.

The second collateral prediction also fails, at least for the mammals of southern Arizona. There is no apparent historical pattern. Occasionally, I have seen the most species-rich patches devastated by a predator (such as a badger). But soon (less than a year later), the same species that were wiped out, recolonized. And no one has ever seen an Arizona short grass patch (slightly higher productivity, considerably lower diversity) at an 'intermediate stage of history' with lots of the species generally found in mixed desert scrub patches (of highest diversity and lower productivity). An army of students of mammals has sampled so many short grass patches for so many decades that by now someone should have reported such a high diversity assemblage in a short grass patch. Reported one, that is, if they exist. No one has.

The theoretical flaw in the disturbance hypothesis would kill it even without any other problem. The flaw lies in assuming that processes operating at one scale will operate much the same way at all scales. Those who suggest the disturbance hypothesis, forget that its mechanisms operate at very short time scales and very local spatial scales. Species do not evolve to fill empty patches. They come from a pre-existing local pool, and disperse to empty patches.

Despite this, paleobiologists and marine biologists have appealed to the disturbance relationship for explanations of the patterns they find (e.g. Watkins, 1979; Rex, 1981). But Rex *et al.* (1993) have recently made clear that explanations of larger-scale patterns of diversity should not be sought in disturbance regimes. No one knows if the rate of brief, local disturbances like wave scouring, indicates anything about the sorts of disturbances that drive whole species extinct.

Moreover, even if whole species extinction and local extinction correlate closely, the disturbance hypothesis cannot generate the decrease phase in terrestrial regions. On an evolutionary time scale, the higher the rate of extinction, the fewer the species. So, terrestrial locales with high–productivity and low–disturbance should have the most species. They do not.

In an address to the August, 1994 meeting of the Ecological Society of America, Warren Allmon introduced a most promising suggestion for rescuing the disturbance hypothesis as an explanation for the unimodal productivity–diversity curve. Allmon focused on disturbance's effects on speciation rates. In doing so, he has left the domain of the scouring wave and the wildfire. These he has replaced with the sort of climatological and geological disturbances that fragment gene pools and begin the process of geographical speciation.

Allmon notes that where large-scale disturbances are rare, speciation rates ought to be low. On the other hand, if they are too common, then budding species will be interrupted before they achieve taxonomic independence. It is the intermediate disturbance rate, he concludes, that ought to maximize speciation rates. If so, it is quite possible that diversity will peak over intermediate rates of large-scale disturbance. I hope that Allmon's idea will attract a serious modeling effort over the next several years. But even if it turns out to be likely, it may have nothing to do with the productivity pattern. We know that small-scale disturbances correlate with productivity. However, no one has suggested that large-scale disturbances do. If they do not, then the disturbance pattern – even at large scales – will stand apart from the productivity pattern.

In sum, small-scale disturbances cannot explain the productivity pattern, because the disturbance pattern talked about in textbooks exists at much smaller scales of space and time than the productivity pattern. The disturbance pattern depends on a pool of species settling small patches, growing, and being removed by local catastrophes. Patches that are quickly disturbed don't have time to collect a full complement from the pool. Patches that are rarely disturbed allow some of the species to overgrow and eliminate others.

It will take a lot of work before we can replace 'settlement' with 'speciation' and 'local competitive exclusion' with 'extinction'. To succeed, we have to explain how the disturbance hypothesis can account for the decrease phase. On an evolutionary time scale, when extinction-causing disturbances occur at a lower rate, we should always expect more species. The sole hope appears to be that intermediate rates of disturbance may promote the highest rates of speciation and somehow be connected to intermediate productivities.

8. Reduction in the covariance of population densities

HYPOTHESIS: High temporal covariance of population sizes among species leads to higher diversity. As productivity increases, the covariance diminishes. So the decrease phase of the productivity pattern is due to decreasing covariance, not increasing productivity. For example, this covariance would be high if species A tends to have about 185% of its long-term average whenever species B has about 185% of its average; and A tends to have about 30% whenever B has about 30%.

REASONING: Population sizes fluctuate. The covariance statistic of this hypothesis summarizes the tendency for different species to experience above average populations simultaneously, and – at other times – to experience below average populations simultaneously.

Density-dependent optimal foraging theory predicts that individuals of competing species should restrict themselves to their special habitat(s) only when they **and** their competitors (of other species) are similarly common relative to their respective averages (Rosenzweig, 1979, 1987a). When species do restrict themselves to their special habitat(s), they compete minimally. That gives them the best chance to coexist. If their population sizes do have high covariance, then they will usually find themselves similarly common or similarly scarce, and minimizing their competition. On the other hand, when one species is very common and another is very rare, then the common one must use the rare one's special habitat, and they compete intensely (Rosenzweig, 1981; Pimm and Rosenzweig, 1981; Brown and Rosenzweig, 1986). In sum, according to optimal habitat selection, high temporal covariance leads to dissimilar behavior, reduced competition and lower extinction rates; low covariance to similar behavior, increased competition, and higher extinction rates.

In terrestrial biomes, covariance and productivity probably do correlate negatively (Rosenzweig, 1979). In a truly harsh, unproductive place, some master variable (like water availability in deserts) should govern the fate of all (or most) species. A good year for one is likely to be good for all. Once productivities increase, other, more diverse variables should exert more control, thus reducing covariances.

EVALUATION: This mechanism is too restricted. It applies only to unstable environments. It requires species to have true habitat specialties (not shared preferences). And it applies only if individuals cannot sense a patch's quality except by taking resources from it (Brown and Rosenzweig, 1986).

Desert rodents, for example, do not conform to these requirements. They can sense seed quantities in their immediate vicinity (Brown, 1989a) – probably by olfaction. And they do not have true habitat specializations. Some species merely get to the best places first (Brown, 1989a) or are capable of defending them better (Frye, 1983). But all prefer areas with the highest seed abundances. Such a relationship among the niches in a guild is called 'shared preferences' or 'tolerance differences'. Field ecologists discover shared preference relationships more than any other kind of community organization (Rosenzweig, 1991). The hypothesis of covariance reduction can govern none of them.

Another deficiency: the fundamental assumption of this hypothesis has not been tested. No one has good evidence for the connection between productivity and covariance. True, several field experiments do support the isoleg models that make the optimal foraging predictions underlying this hypothesis (Pimm *et al.*, 1985; Rosenzweig, 1986; Abramsky *et al.*, 1990, 1991, 1992, 1994). But only theory says that higher covariance leads to lower extinction rates.

I include this hypothesis because I want to emphasize covariance relationships. But the hypothesis may need so much revision that it becomes unrecognizable before it becomes very useful. Nevertheless, I guess we will need to test a better hypothesis based on covariance before we can settle the question of the productivity pattern. The models of Chesson may supply the improvements (Chesson and Huntly, 1988).

9. Area

HYPOTHESIS: High productivity habitat is scarce compared to intermediate habitat. Small areas harbor few species. The productivity pattern is just the species–area curve on different coordinate axes.

If the productivity of very large patches is distributed with a central tendency (say, normally or log-normally), then this hypothesis also predicts the entire humped pattern. Both rich and poor patches will be relatively scarce and relatively depauperate.

REASONING: Like all variables, productivity should have a central tendency. Deviations in each direction should be less and less probable as they depart from the mean. The rest is just the species–area curve in action.

EVALUATION: Much suggests that the area hypothesis does not account for the productivity pattern. First, only one productivity can represent the most common habitat. So, if area is the answer, all taxa should peak over productivities similar to it. But they don't. Compared to plants, desert rodents in Israel peak at half the productivity. Compared to carnivores, rodents in Texas peak at about one-tenth the productivity (Owen, 1988).

Second, the area hypothesis cannot apply to USA rodents. They peak in the semi-desert and fall to much lower diversities in grasslands. Who will defend the idea that grasslands are relatively scarce in North America compared to semi-deserts?

Finally, and most distressingly, the productivity–diversity pattern remains in data even after analysts take out the unequal-area effects. Abramsky and Rosenzweig (1984) discovered this in their Israel rodent data set. But there is a second example which is truly spectacular.

Every birdwatcher, every fan of natural history television shows, and certainly every ecologist knows that bird species fairly ooze from the lowland tropics. Nobody has ever found another place that comes close. Who would have guessed that higher productivities depress tropical bird diversities?

Yet, Rahbek (personal communication) showed that the highest productivities are associated with lower diversities. He did it by removing the effect of area. Compared with the less productive higher elevations, the lowlands are depauperate! (As you read the following summary of his findings, keep in mind that elevation is a good inverse index of productivity in the wet tropics.)

Rahbek found that, in the Neotropics, the area of lowland far exceeds that of any other elevation. But, in similar-sized areas, the more productive lowlands have fewer bird species than subtropical elevations. For example, a lowland area of 10^5 km^2 has about 526 species, but at subtropical elevations, an area of that size has 855 (Figure 2.4).

The temperate elevation bird species-area curve is like the lowland's: a 10^5 km^2 region at temperate elevation has 461 species. The high elevation curve is the lowest of the four: its 10^5 km^2 region has only 176 species. Thus, from high elevations down to subtropical elevations, the more productivity, the more bird diversity.

But the even greater productivity at low elevations does not add to diversity. It decreases diversity. We see so many more birds in the lowlands merely because the lowlands are so extensive. The tropics would be even richer if we could make them somewhat less productive for several million years.

The literature points out that ecologists often confound area and productivity (Wright, 1983; Turner *et al.*, 1987). But some have tried to separate them (Abramsky and Rosenzweig 1984; Owen 1988; Turner *et al.*, 1988). Rahbek's work teaches us how astonishing and rewarding it is to disentangle them.

The global scale

So far I have avoided the big picture. What is the productivity–diversity relationship amongst biogeographical provinces? Is it monotonically positive? I am not sure.

Wright (1983), realizing that a barren hectare has no species, extended the concept of species-area studies. He created a new variable by multiplying area times productivity. The result is gratifying. Diversity does increase with this variable. Of that there is no doubt.

Doesn't that monotonic relationship contradict the unimodal relationship? No. Wright *et al.* (1993) agree that the pattern at the regional scale is unimodal. The monotonic pattern appears at the global scale.

But Wright's new variable is not productivity. It is a combination of productivity and area. Because of the combination, Wright relinquishes the ability to determine the influence of area and productivity separately.

I am no reductionist, but if a mechanism exists which tells us that one of two variables has a separate and powerful influence on diversity, then I prefer to treat it separately. Area exerts such an influence. It influences allopatric speciation rates and extinction rates. Through that influence, it sets up diversity differences among biogeographic provinces. Through that influence, it produces latitudinal gradients. And, through its influence on extinction rates, it produces patterns of island diversity.

Now you can appreciate why I am unsure of the global relationship of productivity and diversity. Diversity does increase monotonically with Wright's variable. But that result could easily stem from its area component rather than its energy flow component. On a global scale the area component may be so important as to overwhelm and mask the influence of productivity.

Prospects

The connection between productivity and diversity – long thought to be intimate – remains murky. All the nine hypotheses to explain the decrease phase have noteworthy weaknesses. Not a single hypothesis successfully explains the pattern (yet).

The two most attractive hypotheses are covariance of population densities and intertaxonomic competition. However, at present, the covariance hypothesis relies entirely on theory. And even those theories need fuller treatment.

The other strong hypothesis, intertaxonomic competition, fits most of the few facts we have. It predicts great variety from taxon to taxon in the position of the peak diversity on the productivity axis. Certainly, we see this. But the hypothesis of intertaxonomic competition lacks a mechanistic model and is therefore poor in predictions.

The intertaxon hypothesis needs adequate explanation. Why should taxa have optima along a productivity gradient? When that optimum is exceeded, why can't they at least defend the share of the productivity that they have already acquired? And which are the taxa succeeding at the highest productivities? And why are primary producers less diverse than their consumers?

Maybe there will never be a hypothesis that fully explains all known instances of the decline phase. Maybe that hypothesis is a fantasy. Suppose, instead, that the increase phase comes from the relationship of productivity to population size (as most believe it does). Suppose that once a system passes a critical point, further increases in population size bring insignificant returns in reduced extinction rates. Then, beyond that point, the diversity of any taxon may be little more than a balloon waiting for a pin. Any number of environmental changes associated with increased productivity would deflate the diversity.

But do not surrender hope yet. Just because the matter is still perplexing, do not conclude that the unimodal curve has no unified explanation. It fits too many animal taxa. It fits in too many habitats and on too many continents. Something so pervasive ought to have a simple explanation.

Chapter 13

Diversity dynamics: a hierarchical puzzle

My friend, Arthur Shapiro, sanely wary of ecological theory, took a look at the first 12 chapters of this book and pronounced them somewhat unfulfilling. Where is the grand theory that unites everything? Are ecological theoreticians forever doomed to jury-rigging a bit of a theory for this question and another for that? Isn't there a single equation of which all the rest are special cases? Although Art wasn't quite that harsh, that's the essence of his complaint.

As Art himself is aware (Shapiro, 1993), some scientists like to solve puzzles and some to build systems. Puzzle solvers joyfully arrange the bits in their puzzle box until they get a satisfying picture. Then they move to another box, until it too looks like it is finished. Or they fill out paper squares with letters/numbers that satisfy the rules of another sort of puzzle. Or they organize scraps of sheet metal, odd bolts, and snarled springs until they have built a contraption that – pick one – flies, hulls Brazilnuts, or supplies the energy of fusion to people all over the world.

System builders, on the other hand, want a machine into which they can pour the unsorted bits and have them emerge effortlessly as a completed puzzle or gadget. Of course, they will happily settle for a set of device-building rules. Let somebody else actually build the thing! I don't mean to judge. I would thrill to see such a theory in Ecology and I wish all the luck in the world to those who would discover it.

But maybe ecology was invented for puzzle solvers? Maybe ecologists who like to build general systems are pre-maladapted? I have no sure answer for that question, but I am not embarrassed to be a puzzle solver. Besides, ecological puzzles form a special subset of puzzles. Like crossword puzzles or jigsaw puzzles, they are hierarchical.

First, we take bits of data that seem to measure the same sort of phenomenon at various times, or in various places, or among various taxa, or with respect to some other even more abstract property like trophic level.

Then we try to fit them together by looking for patterns that regularize them. Once we have patterns, we invent explanations for them, that is, we invoke processes that can produce them.

But we also continue. Not just to other puzzles, but to the enterprise of fitting the solved puzzles into some larger scheme. An explanation for island diversity may be lovely, but it is also incomplete. We know it is incomplete just as soon as we first read it, no matter how much pleasure we take in that first encounter with a beautiful and elegant explanation for an established pattern. Not every diversity pattern involves islands. And some islands have quite dissimilar diversities despite their equal areas and equal distances from a colonization source. So, we move on to provinces, to latitudes, to trophic levels. It as if we had just pieced together a handsome tulip in a jigsaw puzzle, but had finished only a few square centimeters of the whole. We move on to the rose, and then the lily. And when we have them done, we face the added challenge of connecting them into a larger whole.

In a few important cases, ecological patterns emerged only after their processes had been modeled. Equations for predation and competition (or at least deductive arguments for their consequences) preceded our recognition of oscillatory dynamics, niche relationships or competitive exclusion. But in predation's case, you could argue that the initial data come from the observation that species eat each other; equations merely try to fit all that eating into some regulated framework.

Thus, discovering competition may be the only system-building that ecologists have ever done. Is that why its biggest hurdle was getting people to accept its very existence? Perhaps. But no one claims that **diversity** hid unobserved until someone deduced its existence. Those who investigate diversity are surely solvers of hierarchical puzzles.

The role of differential equations

Albert Einstein overthrew the entire system of physics built by Isaac Newton. Yet, he also idolized Newton. He recognized that Newton had made science possible by giving it a method to separate science from history. Whatever can be expressed as derivatives, as a set of rates, can be understood as a process with rules. That is science. The rest is capricious history.

While it is true that ecologists can overdo their respect for physics by aping it, they cannot overdo their use of Newton's method. In particular, we do use derivatives in the best understood segments of the study of diversity. We model the rates at which new species appear and extant species vanish. That gives us a process that will make predictions.

MacArthur and Wilson (1963, 1967) understood that derivatives matter. They produced a theory which set rates of immigration against rates of extinction on islands. Their theory displaced an anecdotal biogeography which tried merely to discern the sequence of accidents that had led to current diversities on various islands. Just look at what one eminent biogeographer (Zohary, 1962, p. 60) had to say:

> It is indisputable that factors of this (phytogeographical) distribution are largely to be sought in the past history of the flora concerned. De Candolle (1855) went so far as to state in that regard that '*les causes physiques et géographique de nôtre époque ne joue qu'un rôle très secondaire.*'

Ironically, MacArthur and Wilson entered the scene in 1963, the very next year! So much for indisputability.

Differential equations have fostered many successes in understanding diversity. They lie at the heart of the theory that explains the disturbance pattern: local immigration vs catastrophic local extinction. They form the basis of my own theory of provincial diversity: speciation modulated by area vs total extinction modulated by area. They anchor both theories of trophic chain length: the Pimm–Lawton dynamical theory (interactive instability or weak stability of population growth equations), and the Elton–Hutchinson thermodynamic theory (decrease of free energy as it passes through the trophic chain). And here is the most subtle example – it is fitness (a rate of increase) that gets optimized in optimal foraging theory. Optimal foraging theory leads to our understanding of niche separation in space and time, and thus to our explanations of how competitors avoid extinction. So, natural selection itself (based on fitness considerations) is a theory centered on differential equations.

In many cases, we have not yet succeeded in mobilizing differential equations for our explanations. But, precisely those cases find us still in the dark. The declining right side of the productivity pattern is a good example. Although productivity itself is a rate, we know no process that relates it negatively to speciation or extinction rate. I predict that when we find one, we will solve this question too. Until then, our understanding of the left side will have to do: more productivity tends to mean larger populations; larger populations mean lower extinction rates.

Finally, look at our understanding of the latitudinal gradient. Before I added differential equations to the controversy, all we had was a confusing catalogue of contradictory correlations. But once we see how range size influences speciation and extinction rates, Terborgh's three points about the large area of the tropics become a compelling basic explanation of the pattern (Rosenzweig, 1992). Moreover, if, as I suspect, we need to include low productivity to get the full explanation, it will be because low productivity makes too many species rare (i.e. makes species with high extinction rates).

When you think about it, there is no mystery. Origination rate is the combination of immigration and speciation rates. Diversity is the net result of origination and extinction rates. Naturally, any successful theory will have to model those rates. And the explanation of every real pattern will boil down to the influence of the pattern's independent variables on the rates that determine diversity.

A large piece of the puzzle: area effects

Species-area relationships make up a large fragment of the diversity puzzle. They are also the most nearly assembled region of it. We can write a differential equation representing diversity processes at several scales of area:

$$dS/dt = O(S) + I(S) - E(S) \tag{13.1}$$

where $O(S)$ is speciation rate, $I(S)$ is immigration rate, and $E(S)$ is extinction rate.

Now we unpack $I(S)$ into immigration of species already present, $I(S)_p$, and immigration of 'new' species, $I(S)_n$. I put 'new' in quotes because the new species in this term are only locally new. Using the unpacking, we rewrite Equation 13.1:

$$dS/dt = O(S) + I(S)_p + I(S)_n - E(S) \tag{13.2}$$

Although Equation 13.2 applies at all scales of time and space, its terms vary greatly in importance. At small scales, extinction is local and rapid. So is immigration, but the predominating term will be $I(S)_p$. That allows species with average $R_0 < 1.0$ to persist. These are the sink species, the mass effect species. On islands, they disappear because $I(S)_p$ is too low to rescue any species regularly. Immigration is dominated by $I(S)_n$. Extinction also slows, because all species present have average $R_0 = 1.0$. Finally, at even grander scales where immigration is so rare that speciation rate approaches or even exceeds it, we can ignore $I(S)$ altogether. We expect provincial dynamics. In short, each piece of the puzzle was assembled under the aegis of Equation 13.2, but investigators took account only of its dominant terms at the scale they worked.

One day, ecologists will also explain the species-time curve in terms of Equation 13.2. But when they do, they will need only its first term, $O(S)$. They will evaluate $O(S)$ at the steady-state diversity and integrate to reach their answer:

$$S(t) = \int^{t} O(S) dt \qquad (13.3)$$

Equation 13.3 does not mean that if you are studying fossils, only speciation rates matter. Extinction rates may also be important. It all depends on the question. When accumulating species for a species-time curve, we do not erase a species after its extinction. That is why Equation 13.3 includes only speciation. But Labandeira and Sepkoski (1993) wanted to explain a case of high **standing** diversity, the high **standing** diversity of insects. So they imagined just the alternatives I have explained here: speciation rate and extinction rate. (They concluded that insect diversity is high because insect extinction rates are low.)

Future exploration of data for pattern

When science explores a new field, it must do so almost with the blindness of Justice. But once it has learned some lessons about that field, it must not hesitate to use that knowledge in order to acquire more. That is not bias; it is wisdom. It is the hard-won skill of the riverboat pilot navigating around the underwater sand bars of the Mississippi.

So it is with diversity. In 1800, we knew nothing about diversity except that it exists. But now we know that area influences it, and we know a lot about how. Once we know that area plays a dominant role in regulating diversity at some scale of space and time, we must take that role into account first, before we can assess the role of another variable.

What I am saying is that the sun has set on the day of the multiple linear fishing expedition. At least for diversity work, it has. We should quit publishing studies in which (1) a column of diversities is given to a computer along with several columns of other variables, (2) the data get ground through a multiple linear regression (any model), and (3) the equations that emerge are pontificated about in a serious fashion.

Does that mean the end of multiple linear regression work in diversity?

No. There are ways to do it right. For example, before doing the regression that asks questions, you do one or more regressions that incorporate already available answers. By 1978, Wilcox had showed how to do that.

Wilcox (see Chapter 6) wanted to measure the extinction rates of lizards on islands in the Sea of Cortez. But the islands varied in latitude and area. So, he first regressed log S on log A. Then he regressed the deviations of this regression against latitude. (Deviations are also called residuals.) The equation that resulted accounts for both independent variables. It would have been silly for him to ignore them. It would also have been inaccurate.

Once Wilcox had an equation for diversity in terms of both area and latitude, plenty of unexplained variance remained. So, he studied the residuals of this equation to see whether old islands have fewer species than area and latitude predict. They do.

Perhaps you have a statistical package that allows you to force regressions against a subset of variables. If so, force the variables you already know must be accounted for. The rest give you your exploratory regression. If Wilcox had had such a package, he could have forced the regressions of both area and latitude before allowing the rest of the multiple linear regression. We might call this method 'guided multiple linear regression.'

Rahbek's work provides another way to proceed. Instead of working on the deviations of points from a regression line, he studied the differences between regression lines. He calculated four bird species–area curves, each for a different biome; by comparing them, he could tease out the altitudinal (i.e. productivity) influence.

A quasi-experimental style of analysis may also help. For instance, following Simpson (1964) and Wilson (1974), I examined the effects of latitude on mammal diversity by restricting data to equal-area blocks (Rosenzweig, 1992). Turner *et al.* (1987, 1988) have used a similar strategy and followed it with multiple linear regression. This method may be more practical than Rahbek's because his requires so much data. But if you can get the data, his is better. When you have to hold area constant in a mock experiment, you may obscure what could be going on at other scales of area.

The dinosaur's challenges

In the preface, I compared the study of species diversity to a dinosaur that has come alive. I would like to know many things about that dinosaur, but here are the ten at the top of my list.

1. Re-doing the theory of species–area curves Since Preston (1962), we thought we knew why species–area curves are nearly straight in log-log space. We also thought we knew why their slopes should cluster around 0.25. The answer was that species abundance distributions fit a truncated canonical log-normal distribution. The species–area curve could be deduced from that.

Now we know that some of the phenomena 'explained' by the canonical log-normal do not exist. Most important, we know that z-values are not so tightly clustered around 0.25: they vary systematically. The more isolated the island, for example, the steeper its z. The curve among provinces has z-values near unity. We also notice that the theory of the canonical log-normal does not account for the c-values at all. In fact, it never tried to.

The original theory of species–area curves depended on a fixed log-normal distribution getting unveiled as area grows. This may well be appropriate for islands of different size. But I am guessing it is not so suitable for provinces. For them I believe we need a theory that stretches the distribution in the other direction. Let the abundance of the maximally abundant species grow with the area of the province, and keep both shoulders of the bell. I followed the outline of such a model in producing Figure 9.9.

2. Developing the species–time curve Just as we need a working theory for species–area curves, we also need one for species-time curves. But just as important here is the tiny amount of analysis that we have so far accomplished to describe this pattern. I am no less tantalized than Frank Preston himself to dream that ecology will find a powerful ergodic pattern that species follow as they accumulate in space and time.

3. Understanding why diversity declines over high productivities Developing a coherent, well tested hypothesis that explains this anomalous pattern would give me particular satisfaction. It is one of the two phenomena I remain totally puzzled by. We also need to find out whether plant diversities follow the pattern. I hope data are available to answer that question, but I suspect they are not. Too much has been gathered at the inappropriately small scale of 0.1 ha.

4. Determining the role of productivity in latitudinal gradients I strongly believe that low productivity depresses diversity at higher latitudes. Now, we need to prove it.

5. Testing the two major hypotheses of food-web length The thermodynamic hypothesis – *energy runs out at high trophic levels* – and the dynamic hypothesis – *systems get unstable if they include high trophic levels* – are ripe for a discriminating series of simulations. These would involve systems with five and six trophic levels, and systems with some nonlinear governing equations. Perhaps they will already have been finished before this book comes out.

6. Exploring predator–victim ratios What are the patterns? Why?

7. Explaining species flocks This is the other puzzle that frustrates and humbles me. I visited the kwongan itself in 1993 to try absorbing a hypothesis from one of the greatest of the flocks. I saw a flat sandy heath with no obvious excuse for a high speciation rate. Is there something there that keeps extinction rates low?

8. Exploring the effect of absolute environmental variance on habitat diversity Considerable evidence led me to the proposition that absolute environmental variance does not matter. But I don't really know that. I do know that it does not matter as much as we once thought. There are too many depauperate sets of species in normally habitat-rich environments. And too many speciose sets in monotonous ones. So, I stated the hypothesis as starkly as possible to prevent it from getting overlooked: any landscape can be subdivided into any number of habitats; how many depends only on how many species geology and genetics supply it. That becomes a null hypothesis because it presupposes that no amount of environmental variation carries with it any intrinsic habitat heterogeneity at all. Fire away! I am eager to see the evidence that unseats the null.

9. Applying the machinery to measure point diversities To represent point diversities, we can add a constant term to the Arrhenius equation:

$$S = k + cA^z \tag{13.4}$$

Who knows what interesting patterns will turn up as we measure k in different taxa and biomes?

10. Discovering what controls lowland tropical diversity Lowland tropical plots vary considerably in diversity. So far, no one has produced a consistent pattern that could lead us to understand this variation. Suggested candidates include soil nutrients, mycorrhyzae, seasonality (or a lack thereof), and total precipitation. Perhaps there is no consistent answer?

Long live the dinosaur.

Salute

I do not want to err by ending this book with a list of unresolved questions. What we have learned remains satisfying and useful even in the face of what we have not.

We have identified **area** as the primary regulator of species diversity. It works first by affecting speciation and extinction rates: Because species ranges should usually contract as diversity rises, and probably also because their total populations should decline, the interplay of diversity and geography sets up a self-regulating steady state in the number of species.

In response to higher diversities, species coevolve narrower specializations. Each species uses fewer types of resources and fewer habitats, and is active at fewer seasons for fewer hours of the day and during a smaller proportion of years. In restricting itself, each species is surviving by developing and emphasizing its special talents and strengths.

Severe limitation of energy flow in an ecosystem curtails the steady-state diversity. That relaxes the pressure to specialize. Plants and animals recognize fewer habitat types. So do we.

All of that becomes the basis of conservation biology. Preservation requires saving considerable area, and not just because we enjoy giving tigers room to romp. They must have considerable area because they need sufficient population size to survive. And they must also have sufficiently widespread refuges to minimize the risk that all their refuges will vanish accidentally. A small, narrowly–distributed population is an extinction in a queue – an accident waiting its turn for a lighthouse keeper's cat.

Given the quantitative regularities of the geographical signal, we can even estimate what we will leave our great grandchildren. Suppose we save, in its natural state, a random 5% of the area of a biogeographical province.[1] We stand to lose species immediately. And we will lose them not on the basis of the mainland species–area curve, but on the basis of the island curve. For 5% of the area to keep as much as 5% had in the year 1900 (say), it would have to keep its sink species. But it cannot. Where will

---

[1]Few countries have protected as much as 10% (Huston, 1993).

they immigrate from? Thus, we will bequeath the proportion $0.05^{0.25}$ (i.e. 47%) to our descendants.[2]

My calculation implies that it won't matter whether we preserve a single block of 5% of a province or many little blocks that add up to 5%. Yet, for two decades, theoretical conservation biologists have debated which of these strategies will save the most species. They call it the SLOSS controversy: Single Large Or Several Small. I have just opined that SLOSS doesn't matter. Why?

Empirical evidence shows that the diversity and the area of whole archipelagos falls on the same species–area curve as the separate islands that constitute them (Figure 2.11). That, in itself, justifies the claim that SLOSS does not matter to overall diversity. It means that if there were an island as large as the entire archipelago, it would have the same diversity as the cumulative total of the separate islands.

Is Figure 2.11 general? I suspect so, although I would like to see a more formal treatment of the question than that which I have space for here. The argument may look something like the following.

- Assume islands are veiled samples of a single mainland log-normal curve.
- How could a set of islands have more species than a single island of their total area? I do not think they can. You might suggest that they could if they deviate from islandness and develop inter-island endemicity. Then different islands could preserve different ecological vicars.

However, that violates our assumptions. We asked what would happen in a few human generations. And we assumed islands would all sample from the same mainland log-normal distribution. Once we begin to allow our preserves to evolve separately, we have raised the scale and must consider many other processes.

- How could a set of islands have fewer species than a single island of their total area? It could if the rarer species that get unveiled at large areas were rare because they were thinly spread over the whole island. Then, no small island would have a total population sufficient to support them.

But that is not how rare species are distributed. Instead, they are nar-

---

[2] OK, I exaggerate the loss. The peopled areas will keep a few starlings and cockroaches. Maybe we'll leave 48%.

rowly distributed and spotty. (See the recent overview of this topic in Hanski *et al.*, 1993.) So, a little island could, in fact, contain the entire population of a rare species.

Yet, as we scan up the trophic chain, a key change occurs. The commonest species of carnivore **is** likely to be relatively scarce and widespread. So, the SLOSS question may need to be changed. As we subdivide our reserve system into smaller areas, will we lose trophic levels? Do predator–victim ratios decline if we subdivide a large reserve into several small ones? Are the largest, most charismatic species poor candidates for preservation in a subdivided reserve system? Quite possibly all these questions have 'yes' as their answer. If so, at the very least, we shall need to be most watchful of the status of predators, ready quickly to inject propagules into preserves that suffer local extinctions. Eventually, they all will.

When we calculated species losses in an archipelago of preserves, we assumed the areas were randomly chosen. They do not have to be. If we deliberately diversify the habitats in our preserves, we can get them to work harder for us. The species they will preserve have evolved their habitat specializations in a much larger context. Whereas that context may be gone, the specializations are not. Rather than operate blindly, we must carefully study those specializations and the mechanisms that they take advantage of to preserve diversity. Then we should get much better performance from our preserve system.

Not only can we choose those preserves carefully, but knowing why we did so, we can also manage them carefully. If we use the entire area of the preserve system, exchanging propagules as needed to keep the total population of rarer species as large as we can, then we can surely maintain as many species as if we had one large, habitat-rich preserve. Perhaps we can maintain 60 or 70% instead of 47%.

But what about the evolutionary time scale? Will losses increase dramatically in evolutionary time?

If we examine two provinces, one at 100% and one at 5% of some arbitrary size, we know what to expect. The two will fall on a species–area curve with a z of approximately 0.8 to 1.1. Suppose $z = 1$. Then the smaller province will harbor only 5% of the diversity of the larger one (not 47%).

Now suppose we shrink a province to 5% of its former size. Will it lose, in the fullness of time, 95% of its diversity? Lacking management, it will. It will relax to its new equilibrium perhaps in as short a time as *Homo sapiens* and *Canis familiaris* have been mutualists to each other (*c.* 25 000 years). We cannot predict how long it will take, but we have seen enough interprovincial data to know that this secondary loss should be even more dev-astating than the primary loss. However, understanding it, we can at least greatly delay it.

The secondary loss will come because the remaining natural area will suf-fer increased extinction and reduced speciation. But, at first, the species in the preserves will be those that evolved in a much richer context (i.e. before the area reduction). So, they will recognize habitat differences that are finer than those that would coevolve in a new, depauperate system. That lets us delay their extinction. We can do it by carefully preserving these finely dis-tinguished habitats.

Yet, as extinctions take their toll, the remnant of the great natural diver-sity that once covered the Earth, now limited to preserves, will expand its habitat use and obliterate forever some of the finer habitat distinctions. And we will not get them back. Thus, we can but hope that someday soon we learn enough to fend off those extinctions. May this book be a milepost on that journey.

References

Abbott, I. (1974). Numbers of plant insect and land bird species on nineteen remote islands in the Southern Hemisphere. *Biological Journal of the Linnaean Society* **6**: 143–52.

Abbott, I. (1977). Species richness, turnover and equilibrium in insular floras near Perth, Western Australia. *Australian Journal of Ecology* **1**: 275–80.

Abbott, I. (1978). Factors determining the number of land bird species on islands around south-western Australia. *Oecologia* **33**: 221–33.

Abbott, I. and Black, R. (1980). Changes in species composition of floras on islets near Perth, Western Australia. *Journal of Biogeography* **7**: 399–410.

Abbott, I. and Black, R. (1987). Diversity of terrestrial invertebrates on islets: interrelationships among floristics, vegetation, microhabitats and sampling effort. In *Readings in Australian Geography*, ed. A. Conacher, pp. 476–81. Perth: Institute of Australian Geographers (WA branch) and Dept. of Geography, University of Western Australia.

Abrams, P.A. (1983). The theory of limiting similarity. *Annual Review of Ecology and Systematics* **14**: 359–76.

Abrams, P.A. (1988). Resource productivity – consumer species diversity: simple models of competition in spatially heterogeneous environments. *Ecology* **69**: 1418–33.

Abramsky, Z. (1978). Small mammal community ecology: changes in species diversity in response to manipulated productivity. *Oecologia* **34**: 113–23.

Abramsky, Z., Brand, S. and Rosenzweig, M.L. (1985). Geographical ecology of gerbelline rodents in the sand dune habitats of Israel. *Journal of Biogeography* **12**: 363–72.

Abramsky, Z., Ovadia, O. and Rosenzweig, M.L. (1994). The shape of a *Gerbillus pyramidum* (Rodentia: Gerbillinae) isocline: an experimental field study. *Oikos* **69**: 318–26.

Abramsky, Z. and Rosenzweig, M.L. (1984). Tilman's predicted productivity–diversity relationship shown by desert rodents. *Nature* **309**: 150–1.

Abramsky, Z., Rosenzweig, M.L., Pinshow, B., Brown, J.S., Kotler, B. and Mitchell, W.A. (1990). Habitat selection: an experimental field test with two gerbil species. *Ecology* **71**: 2358–69.

Abramsky, Z., Rosenzweig, M.L. and Pinshow, B. (1991). The shape of a gerbil isocline: an experimental field study using principles of optimal habitat selection. *Ecology* **72**: 329–40.

Abramsky, Z., Rosenzweig, M.L. and **Subach, A.** (1992). The shape of a gerbil iso-cline: an experimental field study. *Oikos* **63**: 193–9.

Adams, D. (1985). *So Long, and Thanks for All the Fish*. New York: Harmony Books.

Adamson, R.S. (1927). The plant communities of Table Mountain. *Journal of Ecology* **15**: 278–309.

Adler, G.H. (1992). Endemism in birds of tropical Pacific islands. *Evolutionary Ecology* **6**: 296–306.

Alberch, P. and **Alberch, J.** (1981). Heterochronic mechanisms of morphological diversification and evolutionary change in the neotropical salamander, *Bolitoglossa occidentalis* (Amphibia: Plethodontidae). *Journal of Morphology* **167**: 249–64.

Allègre, C. (1988). *The Behavior of the Earth: continental and seafloor mobility*. Cambridge, Mass: Harvard University Press.

Allmon W.D., Rosenberg, G., Portell, R.W. and **Schindler, K.S.** (1993). Diversity of Atlantic coastal plain mollusks since the Pliocene. *Science* **260**: 1626–9.

Anderson, J.M. (1978). Inter- and intra-habitat relationships between woodland Cryptostigmata species diversity and the diversity of soil and litter micro-habitats. *Oecologia* **32**: 341–8.

Anderson, S. and **Koopman, K.F.** (1981). Does interspecific competition limit the size of ranges of species? *American Museum Novitates* **2716**: 1–10.

Arnold, S.J. (1972). Species densities of predators and their prey. *American Naturalist* **106**: 220–36.

Arrhenius, O. (1921). Species and area. *Journal of Ecology* **9**: 95–9.

Audubon, J.J. (1831). *Ornithological Biographies*, Vol. 1. Edinburgh.

Audubon, J.J. (1843). *The Birds of America*, Vol. 5. Reprinted 1967. New York: Dover.

Audubon, J.J. (1957). Letter of 1834 to John Bachman. In *The Bird Biographies of John James Audubon*, ed. A. Ford, pp. vii–viii. New York: Macmillan.

Bambach, R.K. (1977). Species richness in marine benthic habitats through the Phanerozoic. *Paleobiology* **3**: 152–67.

Barel, C.D.N., Dorit, P., Greenwood, P.H., Fryer, G., Hughes, N. and **Jackson, P.B.N.** (1985). Destruction of fisheries in Africa's lakes. *Nature* **315**: 19–20.

Barr, T.C. (1967). Observations on the ecology of caves. *American Naturalist* **101**: 475–92.

Bartlett, M.S. (1957). Measles periodicity and community size. *Journal of the Royal Statistical Society, Series A* **120**: 48–60.

Bazzaz, F.A. (1975). Plant species diversity in old-field successional ecosystems in southern Illinois. *Ecology* **56**: 485–8.

Begon, M., Harper, J.L. and **Townsend, C.R.** (1990). *Ecology of Individuals, Populations and Communities*, 2nd edn. Boston: Blackwell Scientific.

Benson, R.H. (1979). In search of lost oceans: a paradox in discovery. In *Historical Biogeography*, ed. J. Gray and A. Boucot, pp. 379–89. Corvallis: Oregon State University Press.

Bernstein, T.M. (1971). *Miss Thistlebottom's Hobgoblins: the careful writer's guide* *to the taboos, bugbears and outmoded rules of English usage.* Farrar, New York: Straus and Giroux.

Bertness, M.D. and **Cunningham, C.** (1981). Crab shell-crushing predation and gastropod architectural defense. *Journal of Experimental Marine Biology and Ecology* **50**: 213–30.

Beschel, R.E. and **Webber, P.J.** (1963). Bemerkungen zur log–normalen struktur der vegetation. In *Festschrift Helmut Gams*, ed. H. Pitschmann and H. Reisigl, pp. 9–22. *Berichte des Naturwissenschaftlich–Medizinischen Vereins in Innsbruck* **53**: Band 1959–63. Innsbruck: Universitätsverlag Wagner.

Best, A.E.G. (1950). Records of light traps, 1947–48. *Entomology Gazette* **1**: 228–9.

Birks, H.J.B. (1980). British trees and insects: a test of the time hypothesis over the last 13 000 years. *American Naturalist* **115**: 600–5.

Björkman, O. (1981). Responses to different quantum flux densities. In *Physiological Plant Ecology I: Responses to the Physical Environment.* ed. O.L. Lange, P.S. Nobel, C.B. Osmond and H. Ziegler, pp. 57–107. Berlin: Springer Verlag.

Björkman, O. and **Ludlow, M.M.** (1972). Characterization of the light climate on the floor of a Queensland rainforest. *Carnegie Institution of Washington Yearbook* **71**: 85–94.

Björkman, O., Ludlow, M.M. and **Morrow, P.A.** (1972). Photosynthetic performance of two rainforest species in their native habitat and analysis of their gas exchange. *Carnegie Institution of Washington Yearbook* **71**: 94–102.

Black, F.L. (1966). Measles endemicity in insular populations: critical community size and its evolutionary implication. *Journal of Theoretical Biology* **11**: 207–11.

Blackburn, T.M., Lawton, J.H. and **Pimm, S.L.** (1993). Non-metabolic explanations for the relationship between body size and animal abundance. *Journal of Animal Ecology* **62**: 694–702.

Blair, W.F. (1950). Ecological factors in the speciation of *Peromyscus. Evolution* **4**: 253–75.

Bock, C.E. and **Ricklefs, R.E.** (1983). Range size and local abundance of some North American songbirds: a positive correlation. *American Naturalist* **122**: 295–9.

Boecklen, W.J. and **Simberloff, D.** (1986). Area-based extinction models in conservation. In *Dynamics of Extinction*, ed. D.K. Elliott, pp. 247–76. New York: John Wiley.

Boecklen, W.J. and **Spellenberg, R.** (1990). Structure of herbivore communities in two oak (*Quercus* spp.) hybrid zones. *Oecologia* **85**: 92–100.

Bond, W.J. and **Goldblatt, P.** (1984). Plants of the Cape Flora. A descriptive catalogue. *Journal of South African Botany*, Supplementary Vol. **13**: 1–455.

Bonython, C.W. (1955). The filling and drying-up. In *Lake Eyre, South Australia; the Great Flooding of 1949–50*, pp. 27–36 & 74. Adelaide: Royal Geographical Society of Australasia.

Boss, K.J. (1978). On the evolution of gastropods in ancient lakes. In *Pulmonates*, Vol. 2A. *Systematics, evolution and ecology*, ed. V. Fretter and J. Peake, pp. 385–428. London: Academic Press.

Boström, U. and **Nilsson. S.G.** (1983). Latitudinal gradients and local variations in species richness and structure of bird communities on raised peat-bogs in Sweden. *Ornis Scandinavica* **14**: 213–26.

Boswell, M.T. and **Patil, G.P.** (1971). Chance mechanisms generating the logarithmic series distribution used in the analysis of number of species and individuals. In *Statistical Ecology*, Vol. 3. ed. G.P. Patil, E.C. Pielou and W.E. Waters, pp. 99–130. University Park, PA: Pennsylvania State University Press.

Boucot, A.J. (1979). Community evolution and rates of cladogenesis. In *Evolutionary Biology*, Vol. 11, ed. M.K. Hecht, W.C. Steere and B. Wallace, pp. 545–636 & 647–55. New York: Plenum Press.

Boucot, A.J. (1983). Area-dependent-richness hypotheses and rates of parasite/pest evolution. *American Naturalist* **121**: 294–300.

Bovbjerg, R.V. (1970). Ecological isolation and competitive exclusion in two crayfish (*Orconectes virilis* and *Orconectes immunis*). *Ecology* **51**: 225–36.

Bowers, J.H., Baker, R.J. and **Smith, M.H.** (1973). Chromosomal, electrophoretic and breeding studies of selected populations of deer mice (*Peromyscus maniculatus*) and black-eared mice (*P. melanotis*). *Evolution* **27**: 378–86.

Bramlette, M.N. (1965). Massive extinctions in biota at the end of Mesozoic time. *Science* **148**: 1696–9.

Bretsky, P.W. and **Bretsky, S.W.** (1976). The maintenance of evolutionary equilibrium in Late Ordovician benthic marine invertebrate faunas. *Lethaia* **9**: 223–33.

Briand, F. and **Cohen, J.E.** (1987). Environmental correlates of food chain length. *Science* **238**: 956–60.

Brichard, P. (1978). *Fishes of Lake Tanganyika*. Neptune City, NJ: TFH Publications.

Brooks, J.L. (1950). Speciation in ancient lakes. *Quarterly Review of Biology* **25**: 30–60.

Brower, L.P., Brower, J.V.Z. and **Corvino, J.M.** (1967). Plant poisons in a terrestrial food chain. *Proceedings of the National Academy of Sciences USA* **57**: 893–8.

Brown, W.L. Jr (1957). Centrifugal speciation. *Quarterly Review of Biology* **32**: 247–77.

Brown, J.H. (1971a). Mammals on mountaintops: nonequilibrium insular biogeography. *American Naturalist* **105**: 467–78.

Brown, J.H. (1971b). Mechanisms of competitive exclusion between two species of chipmunks. *Ecology* **52**: 305–11.

Brown, J.H. (1973). Species diversity of seed-eating desert rodents in sand dune habitats. *Ecology* **54**: 775–87.

Brown, J.H. (1975). Geographical ecology of desert rodents. *Ecology and Evolution of Communities*, ed. M.L. Cody and J.M. Diamond, pp. 315–41. Cambridge, MA: Belknap Press of Harvard University Press.

Brown, J.H. (1984). On the relationship between abundance and distribution of species. *American Naturalist* **124**: 225–79.

Brown, J.H. and **Davidson, D.W.** (1977). Competition between seed-eating rodents and ants in desert ecosystems. *Science* **196**: 880–2.

Brown, J.H., Davidson, D.W. and **Reichman, O.J.** (1979a). An experimental study of competition betweeen seed-eating desert rodents and ants. *American Zoology* **19**: 1129–43.

Brown, J.H. and **Kodric–Brown, A.** (1977). Turnover rates in insular biogeography: effect of immigration on extinction. *Ecology* **58**: 445–9.

Brown, J.H. and **Munger, J.C.** (1985). Experimental manipulation of a desert rodent community: food addition and species removal. *Ecology* **66**: 1545–63.

Brown, J.H. and **Nicoletto, P.F.** (1991). Spatial scaling of species composition: body masses of North American land mammals. *American Naturalist* **138**: 1478–1512.

Brown, J.H., Reichman, O.J. and **Davidson, D.W.** (1979). Granivory in desert ecosystems. *Annual Reveiw of Ecology and Systematics* **10**: 201–27.

Brown, J.S. (1986). Coexistence on a resource whose abundance varies: a test with desert rodents. Ph.D. dissertation, University of Arizona.

Brown, J.S. (1988). Patch use as an indicator of habitat preference, predation risk, and competition. *Behavioral Ecology and Sociobiology* **22**: 37–47.

Brown, J.S. (1989a). Desert rodent community structure: a test of four mechanisms of coexistence. *Ecology Monographs* **59**: 1–20.

Brown, J.S. (1989)b. Coexistence on a seasonal resource. *American Naturalist* **133**: 168–82.

Brown, J.S. (1990). Habitat selection as an evolutionary game. *Evolution* **44**: 732–46.

Brown, J.S. and **Pavlovic, N.B.** (1992). Evolution in heterogeneous environments: effects of migration on habitat specialization. *Evolutionary Ecology* **6**: 360–382.

Brown, J.S. and **Rosenzweig, M.L.** (1986). Habitat selection in slowly regenerating environments. *Journal of Theoretical Biology* **123**: 151–71.

Burnham, C.R., Rutter, P.A. and **French, D.W.** (1986). Breeding blight resistant chestnuts. *Plant Breeding Review* **4**: 347–97.

Burnham, K.P. and **Overton, W.S.** (1979). Robust estimation of population size when capture probabilities vary among animals. *Ecology* **60**: 927–36.

Burrows, C.J. (1990). *Processes of Vegetation Change.* London: Unwin Hyman.

Bush, A.O. Aho, J.M. and **Kennedy, C.R.** (1990). Ecological versus phylogenetic determinants of helminth parasite community richness. *Evolutionary Ecology* **4**: 1–20.

Bush, G.L. (1969). Sympatric host race formation and speciation in frugivorous flies of the genus *Rhagoletis* (Diptera, Tephritidae). *Evolution* **23**: 237–251.

Bush, G.L. and **Howard, D.J.** (1986). Allopatric and non-allopatric speciation; assumptions and evidence. In *Evolutionary Processes and Theory*, ed. S. Karlin and E. Nevo, pp. 411–38. New York: Academic Press.

Carlton, J.T., Vermeij, G.J., Lindberg, D.R., Carlton, D.A. and **Dudley, E.C.** (1991). The first historical extinction of a marine invertebrate in an ocean basin: the demise of the eelgrass limpet *Lottia alveus. Biological Bulletin* **180**: 72–80.

Carr, G.D. (1987). Beggar's ticks and tarweeds: masters of adaptive radiation. *Trends in Ecology and Evolution* **2**: 192–5.

Carson, H.L. and Kaneshiro, K.Y. (1976). *Drosophila* of Hawaii: Systematics and ecological genetics. *Annual Review of Ecology and Systematics* **7**: 311–45.

Case, T.J. (1983). Niche overlap and the assembly of island lizard communities. *Oikos* **41**: 427–33.

Case, T.J. and Bolger, D.T. (1991). The role of introduced species in shaping the distribution of island reptiles. *Evolutionary Ecology* **5**: 272–90.

Caswell, H. (1976). Community structure: a neutral model analysis. *Ecological Monographs* **46**: 327–54.

Caswell, H. and Cohen, J.E. (1993). Local and regional regulation of species–area relations: a patch occupancy model. In *Species Diversity in Ecological Communities: historical and geographical perspectives*, ed. R. Ricklefs and D. Schluter, pp. 99–107. Chicago: University of Chicago Press.

Charnov, E.L. (1979). Simultaneous hermaphroditism and sexual selection. *Proceedings of the National Academy of Sciences USA* **76**: 2480–4.

Charnov, E.L. and Bull, J.J. (1977). When is sex environmentally determined? *Nature* **266**: 828–30.

Chesson, P. and Huntly, N. (1988). Community consequences of life history traits in a variable environment. *Annales Zool. Fennici* **25**: 5–16.

Clark, C.W. and Rosenzweig, M.L. (1994). Extinction and colonization processes: parameter estimates from sporadic surveys. *American Naturalist* **143**: 583–96.

Clark, T.W., Warnecke, R.M. and George, G.G. (1990). Management and conservation of small populations. In *Management and Conservation of Small Populations*, ed. T.W. Clark and J.H. Seebeck, pp. 1–18. Chicago: Chicago Zoological Society.

Cody, M.L. (1975). Towards a theory of continental diversities: bird distribution over mediterranean habitat gradients. In *Ecology and Evolution of Communities*, ed. M.L. Cody and J.M. Diamond, pp. 214–57. Cambridge, Mass: Belknap Press of Harvard University Press.

Cody, M.L. (1993). Bird diversity components within and between habitats in Australia. In, *Species Diversity in Ecological Communities: historical and geographical perspectives*, ed. R. Ricklefs and D. Schluter, pp. 147–58. Chicago: University of Chicago Press.

Cohen, A.S. (1992). Criteria for developing viable underwater natural reserves in Lake Tanganyika. *Mitteilungen Internat. Verein. Limnol.* **23**: 109–16.

Cohen, A.S. and Johnston, M.R. (1987). Speciation in brooding and poorly dispersing lacustrine organisms. *Palaios* **2**: 426–35.

Cohen, J.E. (1976). Irreproducible results and the breeding of pigs (or nondegenerate limit random variables in biology). *Bioscience* **26**: 391–4.

Cohen, J.E. (1977). Ratio of prey to predators in community food webs. *Nature* **270**: 165–7.

Cohen, J.E., Briand, F., Newman, C.M. and Palka, Z.J. (1990). *Community Food Webs; Data and theory*. Berlin: Springer-Verlag.

Coleman, B.D., Mares, M.A., Willig, M.R. and Hsieh, Y. (1982). Randomness, area and species-richness. *Ecology* **63**: 1121–33.

Collins, N.M. (1989). Termites. In, *Ecosystems of the world, Vol. 14B. Tropical rain forest ecosystems; Biogeographical and ecological studies*, ed. H. Lieth and M.J.A. Werger, pp. 455–71. Amsterdam: Elsevier.

Colwell, R.K. (1973). Competition and coexistence in a simple tropical community. *American Naturalist* **107**: 737–60.

Colwell, R.K. (1985). Community biology and sexual selection: lessons from hummingbird flower mites. In *Ecological Communities*, ed. T. Case and J.M. Diamond, pp. 406–24. New York: Harper and Row.

Colwell, R.K. and Coddington, J.A. (1994). Estimating terrestrial biodiversity through extrapolation. *Philosophical Transactions of the Royal Society, London* B **345**: 101–18.

Colwell, R.K. and Winkler, D.W. (1984). A null model for null models in biogeography. In *Ecological Communities: conceptual issues and the evidence*, ed. D.R. Strong Jr, D. Simberloff, L.G. Abele and A.B. Thistle, pp. 344–39. Princeton, NJ: Princeton University Press.

Compton, S.G., Lawton, J.H. and Rashbrook, V.K. (1989). Regional diversity, local community structure, and vacant niches: the herbivorous insects of bracken in South Africa. *Ecological Entomology* **14**: 365–73.

Connell, J.H. (1961). The influence of interspecific competition and other factors on the distribution of the barnacle *Chthamalus stellatus*. *Ecology* **42**: 710–23.

Connell, J.H. (1978). Diversity in tropical forests and coral reefs. *Science* **199**: 1302–10.

Connell, J.H. (1983.) On the prevalence and relative importance of interspecific competition: evidence from field experiments. *American Naturalist* **122**: 661–96.

Connell, J.H. and Orias, E. (1964). The ecological regulation of species diversity. *American Naturalist* **98**: 399–414.

Connor, E.F. and McCoy, E.D. (1979). The statistics and biology of the species–area relationship. *American Naturalist* **113**: 791–833.

Connor, E.F. and Simberloff, D. (1979). The assembly of species communities: chance or competition? *Ecology* **60**: 1132–40.

Cook, R.E. (1969). Variation in species density in North American birds. *Systematic Zoology* **18**: 63–84.

Coope, G.R. (1987). The response of late Quaternary insect communities to sudden climatic changes. In *Organization of Communities Past and Present*, ed. J.H.R. Gee and P.S. Giller, pp. 421–38. Oxford: Blackwell Scientific.

Cowling, R.M., Gibbs Russell, G.E., Hoffman, M.T. and Hilton-Taylor, C. (1989). Patterns of plant species diversity in southern Africa. In *Biotic Diversity in Southern Africa: concepts and conservation*, ed. B.J.Huntley, pp. 19–50. Cape Town: Oxford University Press.

Cowling, R.M., Holmes, P.M. and Rebelo, A.G. (1992.) Plant diversity and endemism. In *The Ecology of Fynbos: nutrients, fire and diversity*, ed. R.M. Cowling, pp. 62–112. Cape Town: Oxford University Press.

Cox, G.W. and Ricklefs, R.E. (1977). Species diversity, ecological release, and community structure in Caribbean landbird faunas. *Oikos* **29**: 60–6.

Crane, P.R. and Lidgard, S. (1989). Angiosperm diversification and paleolatitudinal gradients in cretaceous floristic diversity. *Science* **246**: 675–8.

Cronquist, A. (1982). Magnoliophyta. In *Synopsis and Classification of Living Organisms*, Vol. 1, ed. S.P. Parker, pp. 357–487. New York: McGraw-Hill.

Crowell, K.L. (1973). Experimental zoogeography: introductions of mice to small islands. *American Naturalist* **107**: 535–58.

Crowell, K.L. (1986). A comparison of relict versus equilibrium models for insular mammals of the Gulf of Maine. *Biological Journal of the Linnaean Society* **28**: 37–64.

Culver, D., Holsinger, J.R. and **Baroody, R.** (1973). Toward a predictive cave biogeography: the Greenbriar Valley as a case study. *Evolution* **27**: 689–95.

Currie, D.J. and **Paquin, V.** (1987). Large-scale biogeographical patterns of species richness of trees. *Nature* **329**: 326–7.

Darlington, P.J. (1957). *Zoogeography*. New York: John Wiley.

Davidson, D.W., Inouye, R.S. and **Brown, J.H.** (1984). Granivory in a desert ecosystem: experimental evidence for indirect facilitation of ants by rodents. *Ecology* **65**: 1780–86.

Davidsson, (1946). *Acta Naturalia Icelandica* **1(4)**: 1–20.

Davis, R. and **Dunford, C.** (1987). An example of contemporary colonization of montane islands by small, non-flying mammals in the American Southwest. *American Naturalist* **129**: 398–406.

de Kroon, H. and **Schieving, F.** (1991). Resource allocation patterns as a function of clonal morphology: a general model applied to a foraging clonal plant. *Journal of Ecology* **79**: 519–30.

Dial, K.P. and **Marzluff, J.M.** (1988). Are the smallest organisms the most diverse? *Ecology* **69**: 1620–4.

Diamond, J.M. (1972). Biogeographic kinetics: Estimation of relaxation times for avifaunas of southwest Pacific islands. *Proceedings of the National Academy of Sciences USA* **69**: 3199–203.

Diamond, J.M. (1974). Colonization of exploded volcanic islands by birds: the supertramp strategy. *Science* **184**: 803–6.

Diamond, J.M. (1975). Assembly of species communities. In *Ecology and Evolution of Communities*, ed. M.L. Cody and J.M. Diamond, pp. 342–444. Cambridge, Mass: Belknap Press of Harvard University Press.

Diamond, J.M. (1978). Niche shifts and the rediscovery of interspecific competition. *American Scientist* **66**: 322–31.

Diamond, J.M. (1984). 'Normal' extinctions of isolated populations. In *Extinctions*, ed. M.H. Nitecki, pp. 191–246. Chicago: University of Chicago Press.

Diamond, J.M. and **May, R.M.** (1977). Species turnover on islands: dependence on census interval. *Science* **197**: 266–70.

Dony, J.G. (1963). The expectation of plant records from prescribed areas. *Watsonia* **5**: 377–85.

Duellman, W.E. (1990). Herpetofaunas in tropical rainforests: comparative composition, history, and resource use. In *Four Neotropical Rainforests*, ed. A.H. Gentry, pp. 455–505. New Haven, Conn: Yale University Press.

Echelle A. and **Kornfield, I.** (ed.) (1984). *Evolution of Fish Species Flocks*, Orono: University of Maine Press.

Edwards, W.R. and **Eberhardt, L.L.** (1967). Estimating cottontail abundance from live trapping data. *Journal of Wildlife Management* **31**: 87–96.

Eggeling, W.J. (1947). Observations on the ecology of the Budongo rain forest, Uganda. *Journal of Ecology* **34**: 20–87.

Ehrendorfer, F. (1980). Polyploidy and distribution. In *Polyploidy; Biological Relevance*, ed. W.H. Lewis, pp. 103–44. New York: Plenum Press.

Elseth, G.D. and **Baumgardner, K.D.** (1981). *Population Biology*. New York: D. Van Nostrand.

Elton, C. (1927). *Animal Ecology*. New York: Macmillan.

Endler, J.A. (1977). *Geographic Variation, Speciation and Clines*. Princeton, NJ: Princeton University Press.

Erwin, T.L. (1982). Tropical forests: their richness in Coleoptera and other arthropod species. *Coleopterists' Bulletin* **36**: 74–75.

Falla, R.A., Sibson, R.B. and **Turbott, E.G.** (1970). *A Field Guide to the Birds Of New Zealand and Outlying Islands*, 2nd edn. London: Collins.

Felsenstein, J. (1971). On the biological significance of the cost of gene substitution. *American Naturalist* **105**: 1–11.

Felsenstein, J. (1981). Skepticism towards Santa Rosalia, or why are there so few kinds of animals? *Evolution* **35**: 124–38.

Fenner, M. (1985). *Seed Ecology*. London: Chapman and Hall.

Findley, J.S. and **Findley, M.T.** (1985). A search for pattern in butterfly fish communities. *American Naturalist* **126**: 800–16.

Findley, J.S. and **Wilson, D.E.** (1983). Are bats rare in tropical Africa? *Biotropica* **15**: 299–303.

Fischer, A.G. (1961). Latitudinal variations in organic diversity. *American Scientist* **49**: 50–74.

Fischer, A.G. (1984). The two Phanerozoic supercycles. In *Catastrophes and Earth History: the new uniformitarianism*, ed. W.A. Berggren and J.A. Van Couvering, pp. 129–50. Princeton, NJ: Princeton University Press

Fisher, R.A. (1958). *The Genetical Theory of Natural Selection*, 2nd revised edn. New York: Dover.

Fisher, R.A., Corbet, A.S. and **Williams, C.B.** (1943). The relation between the number of species and the number of individuals in a random sample of an animal population. *Journal Animal Ecology* **12**: 42–58.

Fleming, T.H., Breitwisch, R. and **Whitesides, G.H.** (1987). Patterns of tropical vertebrate frugivore diversity. *Annual Review of Ecology and Systematics* **18**: 91–109.

Flesch, R. (1974). *The Art of Readable Writing* (revised edn). New York: Harper & Row.

Flessa, K.W. (1975). Area, continental drift and mammalian diversity. *Paleobiology* **1**: 189–94.

Flessa, K.W. and **Imbrie, J.** (1973). Evolutionary pulsations: evidence from Phanerozoic diversity patterns. In *Implications of Continental Drift to the Earth Sciences*, Vol. 1, ed. D.H. Tarling and S.K. Runcorn, pp. 247–85. London: Academic Press.

Flux, J.E.C. (1993). Relative effect of cats, myxomatosis, traditional control, or competitors in removing rabbits from islands. *New Zealand Journal of Zoology* **20**: 13–18.

Flux, J.E.C. and **Fullagar, P.J.** (1992). World distribution of the rabbit *Oryctolagus cuniculus* on islands. *Mammal Review* **22**: 151–205.

Foster, M.W. (1974). Recent Antarctic and Subantarctic Brachiopods. *Antarctic Research Series*, Vol. 21. Washington, DC: American Geophysical Union.

Fox, B.J. (1983). Mammal species diversity in Australian heathlands: the importance of pyric succession and habitat diversity. In *Mediterranean-Type Ecosystems: the role of nutrients*. ed. F.J. Kruger, D.T. Mitchell and J.U.M. Jarvis, pp. 473–89. Berlin: Springer-Verlag.

Frazetta, T.H. (1970). From hopeful monsters to bolyerine snakes? *American Naturalist* **104**: 55–72.

Freas, K.E. and **Kemp, P.R.** (1983). Some relationships between environmental reliability and seed dormancy in desert annual plants. *Journal of Ecology* **71**: 211–17.

Freed, L.A., **Conant, S.** and **Fleischer, R.C.** (1987). Evolutionary ecology and radiation of Hawaiian passerine birds. *Trends in Ecology and Evolution* **2**: 196–203.

Freemark, K.E. and **Merriam, H.G.** (1986). Importance of area and habitat heterogeneity to bird assemblages in temperate forest fragments. *Biological Conservation* **36**: 115–41.

Fretwell, S.D. and **Lucas, H.L. Jr** (1970). On territorial behavior and other factors influencing habitat distribution in birds. *Acta Biotheoretica* **14**: 16–36.

Frey, J.K. (1993). Modes of peripheral isolate formation and speciation. *Systematic Biology* **42**: 373–81.

Frey, J.K. (1994). Testing among modes of allopatric speciation: a hypothetico-deductive approach. Ph.D. dissertation, University of New Mexico.

Frumkin, R. and **Pinshow, B.** (1983). Notes on the breeding ecology and distribution of the sooty falcon, *Falco concolor*, in Israel. *Ibis* **125**: 251–9.

Frye, R.J. (1983). Experimental field evidence of interspecific aggression between two species of kangaroo rats (*Dipodomys*). *Oecologia* **59**: 74–8.

Fryer, G. and **Iles, T.D.** (1972). *The Cichlid Fishes of the Great Lakes of Africa: their biology and evolution*. Edinburgh: Oliver and Boyd.

Futuyma, D.J. (1979). *Evolutionary Biology*. Sunderland, Mass: Sinauer Associates.

Gage, J.D. and **May, R.M.** (1993). A dip into the deep seas. *Nature* **365**: 609–10.

Gaines, S.D. and **Lubchenco, J.** (1982). A unified approach to marine plant–herbivore interactions. II. Biogeography. *Annual Review of Ecology and Systematics* **13**: 111–38.

Gaston, K.J. (1991). The magnitude of global insect species richness. *Conservation Biology* **5**: 283–96.

Geldenhuys, C.J. and **MacDevette, D.R.** (1989). Conservation status of coastal and montane evergreen forest. In *Biotic Diversity in Southern Africa: concepts and conservation*, ed. B.J. Huntley, pp. 224–38. Cape Town: Oxford University Press.

Gentry, A.H. (1988a). Changes in plant community diversity and floristic composition on environmental and geographical gradients. *Annals of the Missouri Botanical Garden* **75**: 1–34.

Gentry, A.H. (1988b). Tree species richness of upper Amazonian forests. *Proceedings of the National Academy of Sciences USA* **85**: 156–9.

Gibbons, J.R.H. (1979). A model for sympatric speciation in *Megarhyssa* (Hymenoptera: Ichneumonidae): competitive speciation. *American Naturalist* **114**: 719–741.

Gilinsky, N.L. and **Bambach, R.K.** (1987). Asymmetrical patterns of origination and extinction in higher taxa. *Paleobiology* **13**: 427–445.

Gilpin, M.E. and **Soulé, M.E.** (1986). Minimum viable populations: the processes of species extinctions. In *Conservation Biology: the science of scarcity and diversity*, ed. M.E. Soulé, pp. 13–34. Sunderland, Mass: Sinauer Associates.

Gleason, H.A. (1922). On the relation between species and area. *Ecology* **3**: 158–62.

Goldberg, D.E. and **Miller, T.E.** (1990). Effects of different resource additions on species diversity in an annual plant community. *Ecology* **71**: 213–25.

Goldstein, E.L. (1975). Island biogeography of ants. *Evolution* **29**: 750–62.

Goodman, D. (1987). The demography of chance extinction. In *Viable Populations for Conservation*, ed. M.E. Soulé, pp. 11–34. Cambridge: Cambridge University Press.

Gorman, M.L. (1975). Habitats of the land-birds of Viti Levu, Fiji Islands. *Ibis* **117**: 152–61.

Gorman, M.L. (1979). *Island Ecology*. London: Chapman and Hall.

Goulden, C.E. (1969). Temporal changes in diversity. In *Diversity and Stability of Ecological Systems. Brookhaven Symposia in Biology*, No. 22, pp. 96–102.

Gowers, E. (1977). *The Complete Plain Words* (rev. edn). Harmondsworth, UK: Penguin Books.

Gradstein, S.R. and **Pocs, T.** (1989). Bryophytes. In *Ecosystems of the World, Vol. 14B. Tropical rain forest ecosystems; biogeographical and ecological studies*, ed. H. Lieth and M.J.A. Werger, pp. 311–25. Amsterdam: Elsevier Scientific.

Grant, V. (1971). *Plant Speciation*. New York: Columbia University Press.

Grant, V. (1982). Periodicities in the chromosome numbers of the angiosperms. *Botanical Gazette* **143**: 379–89.

Greenbaum, I.F., Baker, R.J. and **Ramsey, P.R.** (1978). Chromosomal evolution and the mode of speciation in three species of *Peromyscus*. *Evolution* **32**: 646–54.

Greenwood, P.H. (1982). *The Haplochromine Fishes of the East African Lakes*. London: British Museum of Natural History.

Grimaldi, D.A. (1990). A phylogenetic, revised classification of genera in the Drosophilidae (Diptera). *Bulletin of the American Museum of Natural History* **197**: 139P.

Grime, J.P. (1973). Control of species density in herbaceous vegetation. *Journal of Environmental Management* **1**: 151–67.

Grime, J.P. (1979). *Plant Strategies and Vegetation*. Chichester: John Wiley.

Groves, R.H. and **Hobbs, R.J.** (1992). Patterns of plant functional responses and landscape heterogeneity. In *Biodiversity of Mediterranean Ecosystems in Australia*, ed. R.J. Hobbs, pp. 47–60. Chipping Norton, NSW: Surrey Beatty & Sons.

Gustafsson, Å. (1948). Polyploidy, life form and vegetative reproduction. *Hereditas* **34**: 1–22.

Haedrich, R.L., Rowe, G.T. and **Polloni, P.T.** (1980). The megabenthic fauna in the deep sea south of New England, USA. *Marine Biology* **57**: 165–179.

Hagerup, O. (1932). Über polyploidie in beziehung zu klima, ökologie und phylogenie: chromosomenzahlen aus Timbuktu. *Hereditas* **16**: 19–40.

Haig, D. and **Westoby, M.** (1991). Seed size, pollination costs and angiosperm success. *Evolutionary Ecology* **5**: 231–47.

Haila, Y. (1983). Land birds on northern islands: a sampling metaphor for insular colonization. *Oikos* **41**: 334–51.

Haila, Y., Jarvinen, S. and **Kuusela, S.** (1983). Colonization of islands by land birds: prevalence functions in a Finnish archipelago. *Journal of Biogeography* **10**: 499–531.

Hair, J.B. (1966). Biosystematics of the New Zealand flora 1945–64. *New Zealand Journal of Botany* **4**: 559–95.

Haldane, J.B.S. (1932). *The Causes of Evolution*. London: Longmans Green.

Hamilton, T.H., Rubinoff, I., Barth, R.H. Jr and **Bush, G.L.** (1963). Species abundance: natural regulation of insular variation. *Science* **142**: 1575–7.

Hammond, P. (1992). Species inventory. In *Global Biodiversity: status of the Earth's living resources*, ed. B. Groombridge, pp. 17–39. London: Chapman and Hall.

Hancock, N.J., Hurst, J.M. and **Fursich, F.T.** (1974). The depths inhabited by Silurian brachiopod communities. *Journal of the Geological Society of London* **130**: 151–6.

Hanelt, P. (1966). Polyploidie-frequenz und geographische verbrietung bei höheren pflanzen. *Biologische Rundschau* **4**(4): 183–96.

Hansen, T.A. (1978). Larval dispersal and species longevity in Lower Tertiary gastropods. *Science* **199**: 885–6.

Hansen, T.A. (1980). Influence of larval dispersal and geographic distribution on species longevity in neogastropods. *Paleobiology* **6**: 193–207.

Hansen, T.A. (1988). Early Tertiary radiation of marine molluscs and the long-term effects of the Cretaceous–Tertiary extinction. *Paleobiology* **14**: 37–51.

Hanski, I. (1982). Dynamics of regional distribution: the core and satellite species hypothesis. *Oikos* **38**: 210–21.

Hanski, I., Kouki, J. and **Halkka, A.** (1993). Three explanations of the positive relationship between distribution and abundance of species. In *Species Diversity in Ecological Communities: historical and geographical perspectives*, ed. R. Ricklefs and D. Schluter, pp. 108–16. Chicago: University of Chicago Press.

Hardin, G. (1960). The competitive exclusion principle. *Science* **131**: 1292–7.

Harman, W.N. (1972). Benthic substrates: their effect on fresh-water mollusca. *Ecology* **53**: 271–7.

Harner, R.F. and **Harper, K.T.** (1976). The role of area, heterogeneity, and favorability in plant species diversity of pinyon–juniper ecosystems. *Ecology* **57**: 1254–63.

Hart, D.D. and **Horwitz, R.J.** (1991). Habitat diversity and the species–area relationship: alternative models and tests. In *Habitat Structure: the physical* *arrangement of objects in space*, ed. S.S. Bell, E.D. McCoy and H.R. Mushinsky, pp. 47–68. London: Chapman and Hall.

Hawksworth, D.L. (1991). The fungal dimension of biodiversity: magnitude, significance and conservation. *Mycological Research* **95**: 641–55.

Hay, M. (1985). Spatial patterns of herbivore impact and their importance in maintaining algal species richness. *Proceedings of the Fifth International Coral Reef Congress (Tahiti)* **4**: 29–34.

Heaney, L.R. and **Rickart, E.A.** (1990). Correlations of clades and clines: geographic, elevational, and phylogenetic distribution patterns among Philippine mammals. In *Vertebrates in the Tropics*, ed. G. Peters and R. Hutterer, pp. 321–32. Bonn: Museum Alexander Koenig.

Hebert, P.D.N. (1982). Competition in zooplankton communities. *Annales Zool. Fennici* **19**: 349–56.

Hebert, P.D.N. and **Emery, C.J.** (1990). The adaptive significance of cuticular pigmentation in *Daphnia*. *Functional Ecology* **4**: 703–10.

Hebert, P.D.N. and **Hann, B.J.** (1986). Patterns in the composition of arctic tundra pond microcrustacean communities. *Canadian Journal of Fisheries and Aquatic Science* **43**: 1416–25.

Hessler, R.R. and **Jumars, P.A.** (1974). Abyssal community analysis from replicate box cores in the central North Pacific. *Deep Sea Research* **21**: 185–209.

Hodkinson, I.D. and **Casson, D.** (1991). A lesser predilection for bugs: Hemiptera (Insecta) diversity in tropical forests. *Biological Journal of the Linnean Society* **43**: 101–9.

Holdaway, R.N. (1989). New Zealand's pre-human avifauna and its vulnerability. *New Zealand Journal of Ecology* **12**: 11–25.

Holloway, J.D. (1977). *The Lepidoptera of Norfolk Island, their Biogeography and Ecology*. The Hague: Junk.

Holt, R.D. (1977). Predation, apparent competition and the structure of prey communities. *Theoretical Population Biology* **12**: 197–229.

Holt, R.D. (1984). Spatial heterogeneity, indirect interactions, and the coexistence of prey species. *American Naturalist* **124**: 377–406.

Holt, R.D. (1993). Ecology at the mesoscale: the influence of regional processes on local comunities. In *Species Diversity in Ecological Communities: historical and geographical perspectives*, ed. R. Ricklefs and D. Schluter, pp. 77–88. Chicago: University of Chicago Press.

Hopper, S.D. (1979). Biogeographical aspects of speciation in the southwest Australian flora. *Annual Review of Ecology and Systematics* **10**: 399–422.

Hopper, S.D. (1992). Patterns of plant diversity at the population and species levels in south-west Australian Mediterranean ecosystems. In *Biodiversity of Mediterranean Ecosystems in Australia*, ed. R.J.Hobbs, pp. 27–46. Chipping Norton, NSW: Surrey Beatty & Sons.

Houssard, C.J., Escarr, J. and **Romane, F.** (1980). Development of species diversity in some Mediterranean plant communities. *Vegetatio* **43**: 59–72.

Hubbell, S.P. and **Foster, R.B.** (1986). Biology, chance, and history and the structure of tropical rain forest tree communities. In *Community Ecology*, ed. J. Diamond and T.J. Case, pp. 314–29. New York: Harper and Row.

Huffaker, C.B. (1958). Experimental studies on predation: dispersion factors and predator–prey oscillations. *Hilgardia* **27**: 343–83.

Hurlbert, S.H. (1971). The nonconcept of species diversity: a critique and alternative parameters. *Ecology* **52**: 577–86.

Huston, M. (1979). A general hypothesis of species diversity. *American Naturalist* **113**: 81–101.

Huston, M. (1993). Biological diversity, soils, and economics. *Science* **262**: 1676–80.

Hutchinson, G.E. (1959). Homage to Santa Rosalia, or why are there so many kinds of animals? *American Naturalist* **93**: 145–59.

Hutchinson, G.E. and **MacArthur, R.H.** (1959). A theoretical ecological model of size distributions among species of animals. *American Naturalist* **93**: 117–25.

Inouye, R.S., Huntly, N.J., Tilman, D., Tester, J.R., Stilwell, M. and **Zinnel, K.C.** (1987). Old-field succession on a Minnesota sand plain. *Ecology* **68**: 12–26.

Jablonski, D. (1982). Evolutionary rates and modes in Late Cretaceous gastropods: role of larval ecology. *Proceedings of the Third North American Paleontological Convention* **1**: 1–5.

Jablonski, D. (1984). Keeping time with mass extinctions. *Paleobiology* **10**: 139–45.

Jablonski, D. (1986). Background and mass extinctions: the alternation of macroevolutionary regimes. *Science* **231**: 129–33.

Jablonski, D. (1991). Extinctions: a paleontological perspective. *Science* **253**: 754–7.

Jablonski, D. and **Lutz, R.A.** (1980). Larval shell morphology: ecology and paleoecological applications. In *Skeletal Growth of Aquatic Organisms*, ed. D.C. Rhoads and R.A. Lutz, pp. 323–77. New York: Plenum Press.

Jablonski, D. and **Valentine, J.W.** (1981). On-shore–off-shore gradients in Recent eastern Pacific shelf faunas and their paleobiogeographic significance. In *Evolution Today: Proceedings of the 2nd International Congress Sytematics of Ecology and Biology*, ed. G.G.E. Scudder and J.L. Reveal, pp. 441–53. Pittsburgh, PA: Carnegie-Mellon University.

Jablonski, D. and **Valentine, J.W.** (1990). From regional to total geographic ranges: testing the relationship in recent bivalves. *Paleobiology* **16**: 126–42.

Jackson, J.B.C. (1974). Biogeographic consequences of eurytopy and stenotopy among marine bivalves and their evolutionary significance. *American Naturalist* **108**: 541–60.

Jackson, R.C. (1976). Evolution and systematic significance of polyploidy. *Annual Review of Ecology and Systematics* **7**: 209–34.

Janzen, D.H. (1967). Why mountain passes are higher in the tropics. *American Naturalist* **101**: 233–49.

Janzen, D.H., Ataroff, D.M., Farinas, M., Reyes, S., Rincon, N., Soler, A., Soriano, P. and **Vera, M.** (1976). Changes in the arthropod community along an elevational transect in the Venezuelan Andes. *Biotropica* **8**: 193–203.

Jeanne R.L. (1979). A latitudinal gradient in rates of ant predation. *Ecology* **60**: 1211–24.

Jeffries, M.J. and **Lawton, J.H.** (1984). Enemy-free space and the structure of ecological communities. *Biological Journal of the Linnean Society* **23**: 269–86.

Jeffries, M.J. and **Lawton, J.H.** (1985). Predator–prey ratios in communities of frreshwater invertebrates: the role of enemy free space. *Freshwater Biology* **15**: 105–12.

Johnson, A.W., Parker, J.G. and **Reese, G.** (1965). Polyploidy, distribution, and environment. In *The Quaternary of the United States*, ed. H.E. Wright Jr and D.G. Frey, pp. 497–507. Princeton, NJ: Princeton University Press.

Johnson, M.P., Mason, L.G. and **Raven, P.H.** (1968). Ecological parameters and plant species diversity. *American Naturalist* **102**: 297–306.

Johnson, M.P. and **Simberloff, D.S.** (1974). Environmental determinants of island species numbers on the British Isles. *Journal of Biogeography* **1**: 149–54.

Johnson, P.A., Hoppenstaedt, F.C., Smith, J.J. and **Bush, G.L.** (1994). Conditions for sympatric speciation: a diploid model incorporating habitat fidelity and non-habitat assortative mating. *Evolutionary Ecology* (in press).

Jones, J.S. (1982). St Patrick and the bacteria. *Nature* **296**: 113–14.

Kadmon, R. and **Shmida, A.** (1990). Spatiotemporal demographic processes in plant populations: an approach and a case study. *American Naturalist* **135**: 382–97.

Kaneshiro, K.Y. and **Boake, C.R.B.** (1987). Sexual selection and speciation: issues raised by Hawaiian *Drosophila*. *Trends in Ecology and Evolution* **2**: 207–12.

Kauffman, E.G. and **Fagerstrom, J.A.** (1993). The Phanerozoic evolution of reef diversity. In *Species Diversity in Ecological Communities: historical and geographical perspectives*, ed. R. Ricklefs and D. Schluter, pp. 315–29. Chicago: University of Chicago Press.

Kazantseva, T.I. (1986). Distribution and dynamics of productivity of aboveground phytomass. In *Deserts of Trans-Altai Gobi*, ed. V.E. Sokolov and P.D. Gunin, pp. 106–13. Moscow: Nauka (in Russian).

Keddy, P.A. (1981). Experimental demography of the sand-dune annual, *Cakile edentula*, growing along an environmental gradient in Nova Scotia. *Journal of Ecology* **69**: 615–30.

Keddy, P.A. (1990). Competitive hierarchies and centrifugal organization in plant communities. In *Perspectives in Plant Competition*, ed. J. Grace and D. Tilman, pp. 265–90. New York: Academic Press.

Kelly, B.J., Wilson, J.B. and **Mark, A.F.** (1989). Causes of the species–area relation: a study of islands in Lake Manapouri, New Zealand. *Journal of Ecology* **77**: 1021–8.

Kelly, C. (1990). Plant foraging: a marginal value model and coiling response in *Cuscuta subinclusa*. *Ecology* **71**: 1916–25.

Kenagy, G.J. (1972). Saltbush leaves: excision of hyper-saline tissue by a kangaroo rat. *Science* **178**: 1094–6.

Kennedy, C.E.J. and **Southwood, T.R.E.** (1984). The number of species of insects associated with British trees: a re-analysis. *Journal of Animal Ecology* **53**: 455–78.

Kerr, R.A. (1991). Dinosaurs and friends snuffed out? *Science* **251**: 160–2.

Key, K.H.L. (1968). The concept of stasipatric speciation. *Systematic Zoology* **17**: 14–22.

Khozov, M. (1963). *Lake Baikal and Its Life: Monographiae Biologicae*, Vol. 11. The Hague: Junk.

Kiester, A.R. (1971). Species density of North American amphibians and reptiles. *Systematic Zoology* **20**: 127–37.

Kirchner, T. (1977). The effects of resource enrichment on the diversity of plants and arthropods in a shortgrass prairie. *Ecology* **58**: 1334–44.

Kitchener, D.J., Chapman, A., Dell, J., Muir, B.G. and **Palmer, M.** (1980a). Lizard assemblage and reserve size and structure in the Western Australian wheatbelt – some implications for conservation. *Biological Conservation* **17**: 25–62.

Kitchener, D.J., Chapman, A., Muir, B.G. and **Palmer, M.** (1980b). The conservation value for mammals of reserves in the Western Australian wheatbelt. *Biological Conservation* **18**: 179–207.

Kitchener, D.J., Dell, J., Muir, B.G. and **Palmer, M.** (1982). Birds in Western Australian wheatbelt reserves – implications for conservation. *Biological Conservation* **22**: 127–63.

Kivilaan, A. and **Bandurski, R.S.** (1981). The one-hundred year period for Dr. Beal's seed viability experiment. *American Journal of Botany* **68**: 1290–2.

Knaben, G. (1961). Cyto-ecologic problems in Norwegian flora groups. Distribution and significance of polyploidy. *Hereditas* **47**: 451–79.

Knoll, A.H. (1984). Patterns of extinction in the fossil record of vascular plants. In *Extinctions*, ed. M.H. Nitecki, pp. 21–68. Chicago: University of Chicago Press.

Knoll, A.H. (1986). Patterns of change in plant communities through geologic time. In *Community Ecology*, ed. J. Diamond and T.J. Case, pp. 126–41. New York: Harper and Row.

Kochmer, J.P. and **Wagner, R.H.** (1988). Why are there so many kinds of passerine birds? Because they are small. A reply to Raikow. *Systematic Zoology* **37**: 68–9.

Koller, D. (1955). The regulation of germination in seeds. *Bulletin of the Research Council of Israel* **5D**: 85–108.

Koller, D. (1956). Germination regulating mechanisms in some desert seeds III. *Calligonum comosum* L'Her. *Ecology* **37**: 430–3.

Koller, D. and **Negbi, M.** (1959). The regulation of germination in *Oryzopsis miliacea*. *Ecology* **40**: 20–36.

Koller, D., Sachs, M. and **Negbi, M.** (1964). Germination-regulating mechanisms in some desert seeds. VIII. *Artemisia monosperma*. *Plant and Cell Physiology* **5**: 85–100.

Kolmogoroff, A.N. (1936). Sulla teoria di Volterra della lotta per l'esistenza. *Giorn. Instituto Ital. Attuari* **7**: 74–80. (Available in English as pp. 1923–40 in F.M. Scudo and J.R. Ziegler (ed.) (1978). *The Golden Age of Theoretical Ecology*, Lecture Notes in Biomathematics No. 22. Springer, Berlin).

Kondrashov, A.S. (1983a). Multilocus model of sympatric speciation. I. One character. *Theoretical Population Biology* **24**: 121–35.

Kondrashov, A.S. (1983b). Multilocus model of sympatric speciation. II. Two characters. *Theoretical Population Biology* **24**: 136–44.

Kotler, B.P. (1985). Microhabitat utilization in desert rodents: a comparison of two methods of measurement. *Journal of Mammalogy* **66**: 374–8.

Kotler, B.P. and **Brown, J.S.** (1988). Environmental heterogeneity and the coexistence of desert rodents. *Annual Review of Ecology and Systematics* **19**: 281–307.

Kotler, B.P., Brown, J.S. and **Hasson, O.** (1991). Owl predation on gerbils: the role of body size, illumination, and habitat structure on rates of predation. *Ecology* **72**: 2249–61.

Kotler, B.P., Brown, J.S., Slotow, R.H., Goodfriend, W. and **Strauss, M.** (1993). The influence of snakes on the foraging behavior of gerbils. *Oikos* **67**: 309–16.

Labandeira, C.C. and **Sepkoski J.J. Jr** (1993). Insect diversity in the fossil record, *Science* **261**: 310–15.

Lack, D.L. (1969). The number of bird species on islands. *Bird Study* **16**: 193–209.

Lack, D. (1970). Island birds. *Biotropica* **2**: 29–31.

Lack, D. (1976). *Island Biology, Illustrated by the Land Birds of Jamaica*. Oxford: Blackwell Scientific.

Lack, D. and **Southern, H.N.** (1949). Birds on Tenerife. *Ibis* **91**: 607–26.

Lamont, B.B. (1984). Specialized modes of nutrition. In *Kwongan: Plant Life of the Sandplain*, ed. J.S. Pate and J.S. Beard, pp. 126–45. Perth: University of Western Australia Press.

Lamont, B.B. (1992). Functional interactions within plants – the contribution of keystone and other species to biological diversity. In *Biodiversity of Mediterranean Ecosystems in Australia*, ed. R.J. Hobbs, pp. 95–127. Chipping Norton, NSW: Surrey Beatty & Sons.

Lamont, B.B., Downes, S. and **Fox, J.E.D.** (1977). Importance–value curves and diversity indices applied to a species-rich heathland in Western Australia. *Nature* **265**: 438–41.

Lamont, B.B., Enright, N.J. and **Bergl, S.M.** (1989). Coexistence and competitive exclusion of *Banksia hookeriana* in the presence of congeneric seedlings along a topographic gradient. *Oikos* **56**: 39–42.

Lande, R. and **Barrowclough, G.F.** (1987). Effective population size, genetic variation and their use in population management. In *Viable Populations for Conservation*, ed. M.E. Soulé, pp. 86–123. Cambridge: Cambridge University Press.

Lawton, J.H. (1984). Non-competitive populations, non-convergent communities, and vacant niches: the herbivores of bracken. In *Ecological Communities: Conceptual Issues and the Evidence*, ed. D.R. Strong, D.S. Simberloff, L.G. Abele and A.B. Thistle, pp. 67–100. Princeton, NJ: Princeton University Press.

Lawton, J.H. (1991). Species richness, population abundances, and body sizes in insect communities: tropical versus temperate comparisons. In *Plant–Animal Interactions: evolutionary ecology in tropical and temperate regions*, ed. P.W. Price, T.M. Lewinsohn, G.W. Fernandes and W.W. Benson, pp. 71–89. New York: John Wiley.

Lawton, J.H., Lewinsohn, T.M. and **Compton, S.G.** (1993). Patterns of diversity for the insect herbivores on bracken. In *Species Diversity in Ecological Communities: historical and geographical perspectives*, ed. R. Ricklefs and D. Schluter, pp. 178–84. Chicago: University of Chicago Press.

Leigh, E.G. Jr (1965). On the relationship between productivity, biomass, diversity and stability of a community. *Proceedings of the National Academy of Sciences USA* **53**: 777–83.

Leigh, E.G. Jr (1981). The average lifetime of a population in a varying environment. *Journal of Theoretical Biology* **90**: 213–39.

Leigh, E.G., Jr, Rand, A.S. and **Windsor, D.M.** (ed.) (1982). *The Ecology of a Tropical Forest: seasonal rhythms and long-term changes.* Washington, DC: Smithsonian Institution Press.

Lemen, C.A. and **Rosenzweig, M.L.** (1978). Microhabitat selection in two species of heteromyid rodents. *Oecologia* **33**: 127–35.

Levin, S.A. and **Paine, R.T.** (1974). Disturbance, patch formation, and community structure. *Proceedings of the National Academy of Sciences USA* **71**: 2744–7.

Levins, R. (1966). The strategy of model building in population biology. *American Scientist* **54**: 421–31.

Levins, R. and **Heatwole**, H. (1973). Biogeography of the Puerto Rican Bank: introduction of species onto Palominitos Island. *Ecology* **54**: 1056–64.

Lidgard, S. (1985). Zooid and colony growth in encrusting cheilostome bryozoans. *Palaeontology* **28**: 255–91.

Lidgard, S. (1986). Ontogeny in animal colonies: A persistent trend in the bryozoan fossil record. *Science* **232**: 230–2.

Lidgard, S. and **Crane, P.R.** (1990). Angiosperm diversification and Cretaceous floristic trends: a comparison of palynofloras and leaf macrofloras. *Paleobiology* **16**: 77–93.

Lidgard, S. and **Jackson, J.B.C.** (1989). Growth in encrusting cheilostome bryozoans: I. Evolutionary trends. *Paleobiology* **15**: 255–82.

Lindemann, R.L. (1942). The trophic–dynamic aspect of ecology. *Ecology* **23**: 399–418.

Lindsey, C.C. (1966). Body sizes of poikilotherm vertebrates at different latitudes. *Evolution* **20**: 456–65.

Lipps, J.H. (1970). Evolution in the pelagic realm. *Geological Society of America, Abstracts with Programs,* **2**: 607–8.

Lloyd, M. and **R.J. Ghelardi** (1964). A table for calculating the 'equitability' component of species diversity. *Journal of Animal Ecology* **33**: 217–25.

Lockley, M.G. (1983). A review of brachiopod dominated palaeocommunities from the type Ordovician. *Palaeontology* **26**: 111–45.

Lockwood, J.L., Moulton, M.P. and **Anderson, S.K.** (1993). Morphological assortment and the assembly of communities of introduced passeriforms on oceanic islands: Tahiti versus Oahu. *American Naturalist* **141**: 398–408.

Lockwood, J.L. and **Moulton, M.P.** (1994). Ecomorphological pattern in Bermuda birds: the influence of competition and implications for nature preserves. *Evolutionary Ecology.* **8**: 53–60

Lomolino, M.V. (1984). Mammalian island biogeography: effects of area, isolation and vagility. *Oecologia* **61**: 376–82.

Lomolino, M.V. (1989). Interpretations and comparisons of constants in the species–area relationship: an additional caution. *American Naturalist* **133**: 277–80.

Lomolino, M.V. (1993). Winter filtering, immigrant selection and species composition of insular mammals of Lake Huron. *Ecography* **16**: 24–30.

Lomolino, M.V. (1994) Species richness of mammals inhabiting nearshore archipelagoes: area, isolation and immigration filters. *Journal of Mammalogy* **75**: 39–49.

Lonsdale, W.M. (1988). Predicting the amount of litterfall in forests of the world. *Annals of Botany* **61**: 319–24.

Löve, A. (1953). Subarctic polyploidy. *Hereditas* **39**: 113–24.

Löve, A. and **Löve, D.** (1943). The significance in the distribution of diploids and polyploids. *Hereditas* **29**: 145–63.

Löve, A. and **Löve, D.** (1948). Chromosome numbers of northern plant species. *Department of Agriculture Report* **B3**: 1–131. Institute of Applied Science, Iceland University, Reykjavik.

Löve, A. and **Löve, D.** (1957). Arctic polyploidy. *Proceedings of the Genetics Society of Canada* **2**: 23–27.

Lubchenco, J. (1978). Plant species diversity in a marine intertidal community: importance of herbivore food preference and algal competitive abilities. *American Naturalist* **112**: 23–39.

Lyell, C. (1833). *Principles of Geology*, Vol. 3. London: John Murray.

MacArthur, R.H. (1958). Population ecology of some warblers of Northeastern coniferous forests. *Ecology* **39**: 599–619.

MacArthur, R.H. (1964). Environmental factors affecting bird species diversity. *American Naturalist* **98**: 387–97.

MacArthur, R.H. and **Levins, R.** (1967). The limiting similarity, convergence and divergence of coexisting species. *American Naturalist* **101**: 377–85.

MacArthur, R.H. and **Pianka, E.R.** (1966). On the optimal use of a patchy environment. *American Naturalist* **100**: 603–9.

MacArthur, R.H., Recher, H.F. and **Cody, M.L.** (1966). On the relation between habitat selection and species diversity. *American Naturalist* **100**: 319–32.

MacArthur, R.H. and **Wilson, E.O.** (1963). An equilibrium theory of insular zoogeography. *Evolution* **17**: 373–87.

MacArthur, R.H. and **Wilson, E.O.** (1967). *The Theory of Island Biogeography*. Princeton, NJ: Princeton University Press.

McCabe, T.T. and **Blanchard, B.D.** (1950). *Three Species of Peromyscus*. Santa Barbara, Calif: Rood Assoc.

McCune, A.R. (1987). Lakes as laboratories of evolution: endemic fishes and environmental cyclicity. *Palaios* **2**: 446–54.

McGowan, J.A. and **Walker, P.W.** (1993). Pelagic diversity patterns. In *Species Diversity in Ecological Communities: historical and geographical perspectives*, ed. R. Ricklefs and D. Schluter, pp. 203–14. Chicago: University of Chicago Press.

McGuinness, K.A. (1984). Equations and explanations in the study of species–area curves. *Biological Reviews* **59**: 423–40.

McLay, C.L. (1978a). Comparative observations on the ecology of four species of ostracods living in a temporary freshwater puddle. *Canadian Journal of Zoology* **56**: 663–75.

McLay, C.L. (1978b). Population biology of *Cyprinotus carolinensis* and *Herpetocypris reptans* (Crustacea, Ostracoda). *Canadian Journal of Zoology* **56**: 1170–9.

McLay, C.L. (1978c). Competition, coexistence, and survival: a computer simulation study of ostracods living in a temporary puddle. *Canadian Journal of Zoology* **56**: 1744–58.

Magurran, A.E. (1988). *Ecological Diversity and its Measurement.* Princeton, NJ: Princeton University Press.

Maly, E.J. and **Doolittle, W.L.** (1977). Effects of island area and habitat on Bahamian land and freshwater snail distribution. *American Midland Naturalist* **97**: 59–67.

Marchant, N. (1991). The vascular flora of South Western Australia. *Association of Societies for Growing Australian Plants, 16th Biennial Conference*, pp. 16–18. Perth.

Mares, M.A. and **Ojeda, R.A.** (1982). Patterns of diversity and adaptation in South American hystricognath rodents. *Special Publication of the Pymatuning Laboratory of Ecology* **6**: 393–432.

Marlier, G. (1973). Limnology of the Congo and Amazon Rivers. In *Tropical Forest Ecosystems in Africa and South America: a comparative review*, ed. B.J. Meggars, E.S. Ayensu and W.D. Duckworth, pp. 223–38. Washington, DC: Smithsonian Institution Press.

Martin, A.P. and **Palumbi, S.R.** (1993). Body size, metabolic rate, generation time, and the molecular clock. *Proceedings of the National Academy of Sciences USA* **90**: 4087–91.

Martin, P.S. (1984). Prehistoric overkill: the global model. In *Quaternary extinctions: a prehistoric revolution*, ed. P.S. Martin and R. Klein, pp. 354–403. Tucson: University of Arizona Press.

Marzluff, J.M. and **Dial, K.P.** (1991). Life history correlates of taxonomic diversity. *Ecology* **72**: 428–39.

May, R.M. (1975). Patterns of species abundance and diversity. In *Ecology and Evolution of Communities*, ed. M.L. Cody and J.M. Diamond, pp. 81–120. Cambridge, Mass: Belknap Press of Harvard University Press.

May, R.M. (1978). Dynamics and diversity of insect faunas. In *Diversity of Insect Faunas*, ed. L.A. Mound and N. Waloff, pp. 188–204. Oxford: Blackwell Scientific.

May, R.M. (1990). How many species? *Philosophical Transactions of the Royal Society of London B* **330**: 293–304.

May, R.M. and **MacArthur, R.H.** (1972). Niche overlap as a function of environmental variability. *Proceedings of the National Academy of Sciences USA* **69**: 1109–13.

Maynard Smith, J. (1966). Sympatric speciation. *American Naturalist* **100**: 637–50.

Maynard Smith, J. and **Price, G.R.** (1973). The logic of animal conflict. *Nature* **246**: 15–18.

Mayr, E. (1941). The origin and the history of the bird fauna of Polynesia. *Proceedings of the Sixth Pacific Science Congress*, **4**: 197–216. (A revision is in Mayr, E. 1976. *Evolution and the Diversity of Life*, pp. 601–17. Belknap Press of Harvard University Press, Cambridge, Mass.)

Mayr, E. (1954). Change of genetic environment and evolution. In *Evolution as a Process*, ed. J.S. Huxley, A.C. Hardy and E.B. Ford, pp. 157–80. London: Allen and Unwin.

Merkel, H.W. (1906). A deadly fungus on the American chestnut. *New York Zoological Society Annual Report* **10**: 97–103.

Meserve, P.L. and **Glanz, W.E.** (1978). Geographical ecology of small mammals in the northern Chilean arid zone. *Journal of Biogeography* **5**: 135–48.

Meyer, A. (1991). Phylogenetic relationships and evolutionary processes in East African cichlid fishes. *Trends in Ecology and Evolution* **8**: 279–84.

Meyer, A., Kocher, T.D., Basasibwaki, P. and **Wilson, A.C.** (1990). Monophyletic origin of Lake Victoria cichlid fishes suggested by mitochondrial DNA sequences. *Nature* **347**: 550–55.

Michel, A.E., Cohen, A.S., West, K., Johnston, M.R. and **Kat, P.W.** (1992). Large African lakes as natural laboatories for evolution: examples from the endemic gastropod fauna of Lake Tanganyika. *Mitteilungen Internat. Verein. Limnol.* **23**: 85–99.

Mikulic, D.G. and **Watkins, R.** (1981). Trilobite ecology in the Ludlow Series of the Welsh Borderland.In *Communities of the Past*, ed. Gray, J., A.J. Boucot and W.B.N. Berry, p. 101–17. Stroudsburg, PA: Hutchinson Ross.

Miller, A. and **Sepkoski, J.J. Jr** (1988). Modeling bivalve diversification: the effect of interaction on a macroevolutionary system. *Paleobiology* **14**: 364–9.

Miller, D.J. (1989). Introductions and extinction of fish in the African great lakes. *Trends in Ecology and Evolution* **4**: 56–9.

Mitchell, W.A., Abramsky, Z., Kotler, B.P., Pinshow, B. and **Brown, J.S.** (1990). The effect of competition on foraging activity in desert rodents: theory and experiments. *Ecology* **71**: 844–54.

Mitchell, W.A. and **Valone, T.J.** (1990). The optimization research program: studying adaptations by their function. *Quarterly Review of Biology* **65**: 43–52.

Mithen, S.J. and **Lawton, J.H.** (1986). Food–web models that generate constant predator–prey ratios. *Oecologia* **69**: 542–50.

Moore, J.C., Walter, D.E. and **Hunt, H.W.** (1989). Habitat compartmentation and environmental correlates to food–chain length. *Science* **243**: 238–9.

Moore, J.C., deRuiter, P.C. and **Hunt, H.W.** (1993). Influence of productivity on the stability of real and model ecosystems. *Science* **261**: 906–8.

Morse, D.R., Stork, N.E. and **Lawton, J.H.** (1988). Species number, species abundance and body–length relationships of arboreal beetles in Bornean lowland rain forest trees. *Ecological Entomology* **13**: 25–37.

Morton, S.R. (1993). Determinants of diversity in animal communities of arid Australia. In *Species Diversity in Ecological Communities: historical and geographical perspectives*, ed. R. Ricklefs and D. Schluter, pp. 159–69. Chicago: University of Chicago Press.

Mott, J.J. (1972). Germination studies on some annual species from an arid region region of western Australia. *Journal of Ecology* **60**: 293–304.

Mott, K. (1994). A functional morphological approach to feeding by dabbling ducks. MSc. thesis, Dept. Zoology, University of Guelph, Ontario.

Moulton, M.P. and **Pimm, S.L.** (1987). Morphological assortment in introduced Hawaiian passerines. *Evolutionary Ecology* **1**: 113–24.

Mueller–Dombois D. (1987). Forest dynamics in Hawaii. *Trends in Ecology and Evolution* **2**: 216–20.

Muhlenberg, M., Liepold, D., Mader, H.J. and **Steinhauer, B.** (1977). Island ecology of arthropods. I. Diversity, niches, and resources on some Seychelles Islands. *Oecologia* **29**: 117–34.

Mulkey, S.S. (1986). Photosynthetic acclimation and water-use efficiency of three species of understory herbaceous bamboo (Gramineae) in Panama. *Oecologia* **70**: 514–19.

Naveh, Z. and **Whittaker, R.H.** (1979). Structural and floristic diversity of shrublands and woodlands in northern Israel and other Mediterranean areas. *Vegetatio* **41**: 171–90.

Negre, R. (1953). Discussion of Went's contribution. p. 239 (in French). In M. Balaban (ed.), *Desert Research Proceedings, Special Publication No. 2*. Jerusalem: Research Council of Israel.

Nei, M. and **Roychoudhury, A.K.** (1974). Sampling variances of heterozygosity and genetic distance. *Genetics* **76**: 379–90.

Nelson, J.S. (1984). *Fishes of the World*, 2nd edn. New York: Wiley–Interscience.

Newman, E.I. (1973). Competition and diversity in herbaceous vegetation. *Nature* **244**: 310–11.

Nichols, J.D. (1992). Capture–recapture models. *Bioscience* **42**: 94–102.

Nichols, J.D. and **Pollock, K.H.** (1983). Estimating taxonomic diversity, extinction rates, and speciation rates from fossil data using capture–recapture models. *Paleobiology* **9**: 150–63.

Nicholson, A.J. (1954). An outline of the dynamics of animal populations. *Australian Journal of Zoology* **2**: 9–65.

Nicholson, S.A. and **Monk, C.D.** (1974). Plant species diversity in old-field succession on the Georgia Piedmont. *Ecology* **55**: 1075–85.

Nilsson, S.G., Bengtsson, J. and **Ås, S.** (1988). Habitat diversity or area *per se*? Species richness of woody plants, carabid beetles and land snails on islands. *Journal of Animal Ecology* **57**: 685–704.

Nudds, T.D. and **Bowlby, J.N.** (1984). Predator–prey size relationships in North American dabbling ducks. *Canadian Journal of Zoology* **62**: 2002–8.

Nudds, T.D., Sjöberg, K. and **Lundberg, P.** (1994). Ecomorphological relationships among Palearctic dabbling ducks on Baltic coastal wetlands and a comparison with the Nearctic. *Oikos* **69**: 295–303.

Odum, S. (1965). Germination of ancient seeds: floristic observations and experiments with archeologically dated soil samples. *Dan. Bot. Ark.* **24**: 1–70.

Oksanen, L. (1992). Evolution of exploitation ecosystems I. Predation, foraging ecology and population dynamics in herbivores. *Evolutionary Ecology* **6**: 15–33.

Oksanen, L., Fretwell, S.D., Arruda, J. and **Niemelä, P.** (1981). Exploitation ecosystems in gradients of primary productivity. *American Naturalist* **118**: 240–61.

Oksanen, L., Oksanen, T., Ekerholm, P., Moen, J., Lundberg, P., Bondestad,

L., **Schneider, M., Aruoja, V.** and **Armulik, T.** (1994). Structure and dynamics of arctic–subarctic grazing webs in relation to primary productivity. In *Food Webs: integration of patterns and dynamics*, ed. G.A. Polis and K. Winemiller. London: Chapman and Hall.

Oksanen, T., Oksanen, L. and **Gyllenberg, M.** (1992). Exploitation ecosystems in heterogeneous habitat complexes II: impact of small-scale heterogeneity on predator–prey dynamics. *Evolutionary Ecology* **6**: 383–98.

Opler, P.A. (1974). Oaks as evolutionary islands for leaf-mining insects. *American Scientist* **62**: 67–73.

Osman, R.W. (1977). The establishment and development of a marine epifaunal community. *Ecological Monographs* **47**: 37–63.

Osmond, C.B., Björkman, O. and **Anderson, D.J.** (1980). *Physiological Processes in Plant Ecology: towards a synthesis with Atriplex.* Berlin: Springer-Verlag.

Owen, J.G. (1988). On productivity as a predictor of rodent and carnivore diversity. *Ecology* **69**: 1161–5.

Paillet, F.L. and **Rutter, P.A.** (1989). Replacement of native oak and hickory tree species by the introduced American chestnut (*Castanea dentata*) in southwestern Wisconsin. *Canadian Journal of Botany* **67**: 3457–69.

Paine, R. and **Levin, S.** (1981). Intertidal landscapes: disturbance and the dynamics of pattern. *Ecological Monographs* **51**: 145–78.

Paine, R.T. (1966). Food web complexity and species diversity. *American Naturalist* **100**: 65–75.

Palmer, A.R. (1979). Fish predation and evolution of gastropod shell sculpture: experimental and geographic evidence. *Evolution* **33**: 697–713.

Park, T. (1962). Beetles, competition and populations. *Science* **138**: 1369–75.

Parker, S.P. (1982). *Synopsis and Classification of Living Organisms.* New York: McGraw–Hill.

Parsons, R.F. and **Cameron, D.G.** (1974). Maximum plant species diversity in terrestrial communities. *Biotropica* **6**: 202–3.

Patalas, K. (1990). Diversity of the zooplankton communities in Canadian lakes as a function of climate. *Verh. Internat. Verein. Limnol.* **24**: 360–8.

Paterniani, E. (1969). Selection for reproductive isolation between two populations of maize, *Zea mays* L. *Evolution* **23**: 534–47.

Patrick, R.A. (1963). The structure of diatom communities under varying ecological conditions. *Transactions of the New York Academy of Sciences* **108**: 359–65.

Pearson, D.L. and **Mury, E.J.** (1979). Character divergence and convergence among tiger beetles (Coleoptera: Cicindelidae). *Ecology* **60**: 557–66.

Pearson, T.H. and **Rosenberg, R.** (1978). Macrobenthic succession in relation to organic enrichment and pollution of the marine environment. *Oceanography and Marine Biology Annual Review* **16**: 229–311.

Persson, L., Diehl, S., Johansson, L., Anderson, G. and **Hamrin, S.F.** (1992). Trophic interactions in temperate lake ecosystems: a test of food chain theory. *American Naturalist* **140**: 59–84.

Petraitis, P.S., Latham, R.E. and **Niesenbaum, R.A.** (1989). The maintenance of species diversity by disturbance. *Quarterly Review of Biology* **64**: 393–418.

Pianka, E.R. (1966). Latitudinal gradients in species diversity: a review of concepts. *American Naturalist* **100**: 33–46.

Pianka, E.R. (1967). On lizard species diversity: North American flatland deserts. *Ecology* **48**: 333–50.

Pianka, E.R. (1986). *Ecology and Natural History of Desert Lizards: analyses of the ecological niche and community structure*. Princeton, NJ: Princeton University Press.

Pidgeon, I.M. and **Ashby, E.** (1940). Studies in applied ecology, I. A statistical analysis of regeneration following protection from grazing. *Proceedings of the Linnean Society New South Wales* **65**: 123–143.

Pielou, E.C. (1974). *Population and Community Ecology: Principles and Methods*. New York: Gordon and Breach Science.

Pimentel, D., Nagel, W.P. and **Madden, J.L.** (1963). Space–time structure of the environment and the survival of parasite–host systems. *American Naturalist* **97**: 141–67.

Pimm, S.L. (1979). Sympatric speciation: a simulation model. *Biological Journal of the Linnean Society* **11**: 131–9.

Pimm, S.L. (1982). *Food Webs*. London: Chapman and Hall.

Pimm, S.L. (1987). The snake that ate Guam. *Trends in Ecology and Evolution* **2**: 293–5.

Pimm, S.L. (1991). *The Balance of Nature? Ecological issues in the conservation of species and communities*. Chicago: University of Chicago Press.

Pimm, S.L. (1993). Life on an intermittent edge. *Trends in Ecology and Evolution* **8**: 45–6.

Pimm, S.L., Jones, H.L. and **Diamond, J.** (1988). On the risk of extinction. *American Naturalist* **132**: 757–85.

Pimm, S.L. and **Lawton, J.H.** (1977). The number of trophic levels in ecological communities. *Nature* **268**: 329–31.

Pimm, S.L. and **Lawton, J.H.** (1978). On feeding on more than one trophic level. *Nature* **275**: 542–4.

Pimm, S.L., Lawton, J.H. and **Cohen, J.E.** (1991). Food web patterns and their consequences. *Nature* **350**: 669–74.

Pimm, S.L. and **Rice. J.A.** (1987). The dynamics of multispecies, multi-life-stage models of aquatic food webs. *Theoretical Population Biology* **32**: 303–25.

Pimm, S.L. and **Rosenzweig, M.L.** (1981). Competitors and habitat use. *Oikos* **7**: 1–6.

Pimm, S.L., Rosenzweig, M.L. and **Mitchell, W.** (1985). Competition and food selection: field tests of a theory. *Ecology* **66**: 798–807.

Pollock, K.H. (1982). A capture–recapture design robust to unequal probability of capture. *Journal of Wildlife Management* **46**: 752–7.

Prance, G.T. (1977). Floristic inventory of the tropics: where do we stand? *Annals of the Missouri Botanical Garden* **64**: 659–84.

Preston, F.W. (1948). The commonness, and rarity, of species. *Ecology* **29**: 254–83.

Preston, F.W. (1960). Time and space and the variation of species. *Ecology* **41**: 785–90.

Preston, F.W. (1962a). The canonical distribution of commonness and rarity. *Ecology* **43**: 185–215.

Preston, F.W. (1962b). The canonical distribution of commonness and rarity. *Ecology* **43**: 410–32.

Preston, F.W. (1979). The invisible birds. *Ecology* **60**: 451–4.

Preston, F.W. (1980). Noncanonical distributions of commonness and rarity. *Ecology* **61**: 88–97.

Proctor, J., Anderson, J.M., Chai, P. and **Vallack, H.W.** (1983). Ecological studies in four contrasting lowland rainforests in Gunung Mulu National Park, Sarawak. I. Forest environment, structure and floristics. *Journal of Ecology* **71**: 237–60.

Pulliam, H.R. (1988). Sources, sinks and population regulation. *American Naturalist* **132**: 652–61.

Pulliam, H.R. and **Danielson, B.J.** (1991). Sources, sinks, and habitat selection: a landscape perspective on population dynamics. *American Naturalist* **137**: S50–S66.

Quinn, S.L., Wilson, J.B. and **Mark, A.F.** (1987). The island biogeography of Lake Manapouri, New Zealand. *Journal of Biogeography* **14**: 569–81.

Ralph, C.J. (1985). Habitat association patterns of forest and steppe birds of northern Patagonia, Argentina. *Condor* **87**: 471–83.

Raup, D.M. (1976a). Species diversity in the Phanerozoic: a tabulation. *Paleobiology* **2**: 279–88.

Raup, D.M. (1976b). Species diversity in the Phanerozoic: an interpretation. *Paleobiology* **2**: 289–97.

Raup, D.M. (1989). The case for extraterrestrial causes of extinction. *Philosophical Transactions of the Royal Society of London, Series B* **325**: 421–35.

Raup, D.M. (1992). Large-body impact and extinction in the Phanerozoic. *Paleobiology* **18**: 80–8.

Recer, G.M., Blanckenhorn, W.U., Newman, J.A., Tuttle, E.M., Withiam, M.L. and **Caraco, T.** (1987). Temporal resource variability and the habitat-matching rule. *Evolutionary Ecology* **1**: 363–78.

Recher, H.F. (1969). Bird species diversity and habitat diversity in Australia and North America. *American Naturalist* **103**: 75–80.

Reed, T.M. (1987). Island birds and isolation: Lack revisited. *Biological Journal of the Linnaean Society* **30**: 25–9.

Rex, M.A. (1981). Community structure in the deep sea benthos. *Annual Review of Ecology and Systematics* **12**: 331–53.

Rex, M.A., Stuart, C.T., Hessler, R.R., Allen, J.A., Sanders, H.L. and **Wilson, G.D.F.** (1993). Global-scale latitudinal patterns of species diversity in the deep-sea benthos. *Nature* **365**: 636–9.

Rexstad, E. and **Burnham, K.** (1992). *User's Guide for Interactive Program CAPTURE.* Colorado Cooperative Fish and Wildlife Unit, Colorado State University, Fort Collins, Colo.

Rhoades, D.F. (1985). Offensive–defensive interactions between herbivores and plants: their relevance in herbivore population dynamics and ecological theory. *American Naturalist* **125**: 205–38.

Rice, B. (1984). No evidence for divergence between Australia and elsewhere in plant species richness at tenth-ha scale. *Proceedings of the Ecological Society of Australia* **14**: 99–101.

Rice, B. and Westoby, M. (1983). Plant species richness at the 0.1 hectare scale in Australian vegetation compared to other continents. *Vegetatio* **52**: 129–40.

Rice, W.R. (1984). Disruptive selection on habitat preference and the evolution of reproductive isolation: a simulation study. *Evolution* **38**: 1251–60.

Rice, W.R. (1985). Disruptive selection on habitat preference and the evolution of reproductive isolation: an exploratory experiment. *Evolution* **39**: 645–56.

Rice, W.R. (1987). Speciation via habitat specialization: the evolution of reproductive isolation as a correlated character. *Evolutionary Ecology* **1**: 301–15.

Rice, W.R. and Salt, G.W. (1988). Speciation via disruptive selection on habitat preference: experimental evidence. *American Naturalist* **131**: 911–17.

Richards, P.W. (1969). Speciation in the tropical rain forest and the concept of the niche. *Biological Journal of the Linnaean Society* **1**: 149–53.

Richards, P.W. (1973). Africa, the 'Odd Man Out'. In *Tropical Forest Ecosystems in Africa and South America: a comparative review*, ed. B.J. Meggers, E.S. Ayensu and W.D. Duckworth, pp. 21–6. Washington, DC: Smithsonian Institution Press.

Richter–Dyn, N. and Goel, N.S. (1972). On the extinction of a colonizing species. *Theoretical Population Biology* **3**: 406–33.

Ricklefs, R.E. (1977). Island biology illustrated by the land birds of Jamaica, a review. *Auk* **94**: 794–7.

Riebesell, J.F. (1974). Paradox of enrichment in competitive systems. *Ecology* **55**: 183–7.

Riebesell, J.F. (1982). Arctic–alpine plants on mountaintops: agreement with island biogeography theory. *American Naturalist* **119**: 657–74.

Rigby, C. and Lawton, J.H. (1981). Species–area relationships of arthropods on host plants: herbivores on bracken. *Journal of Biogeography* **8**: 125–33.

Roane, M.K., Griffin, G.J. and Elkins, J.R. (1986). *Chestnut Blight, Other Endothia Diseases, and the Genus Endothia*. St Paul, Minn: American Phytopathological Society.

Rohde, K. (1992). Latitudinal gradients in species diversity: the search for the primary cause. *Oikos* **65**: 514–27.

Rogovin, K.A., Kulikov, V.F., Surov A.V. and Vasilieva, N.Y. (1986). Small mammals. In *Deserts of Trans–Altai Gobi*, ed. V.E. Sokolov and P.D. Gunin, pp. 122–31. Moscow: Nauka (in Russian).

Romer, A.S. (1949). Time series and trends in animal evolution. In *Genetics, Paleontology and Evolution*, ed. G.L. Jepson, E. Mayr and G.G. Simpson, pp. 103–21. Princeton, NJ: Princeton University Press.

Rosenzweig, M.L. (1966). Community structure in sympatric Carnivora. *Journal of Mammalogy* **47**: 602–12.

Rosenzweig, M.L. (1968). Net primary productivity of terrestrial environments: predictions from climatological data. *American Naturalist* **102**: 67–84.

Rosenzweig, M.L. (1971). Paradox of enrichment: destabilization of exploitation ecosystems in ecological time. *Science* **171**: 385–7.

Rosenzweig, M.L. (1972). Stability of enriched aquatic ecosystems. *Science* **175**: 564–5.

Rosenzweig, M.L. (1973a). Habitat selection experiments with a pair of coexisting heteromyid rodent species. *Ecology* **54**: 111–17.

Rosenzweig, M.L. (1973b). Evolution of the predator isocline. *Evolution* **27**: 89–94.

Rosenzweig, M.L. (1974). On the evolution of habitat selection. *Proceedings of the First International Congress of Ecology*, pp. 401–4.

Rosenzweig, M.L. (1975). On continental steady states of species diversity. In *The Ecology of Species Communities*, ed. M.L. Cody and J.M. Diamond, pp. 121–40. Cambridge, Mass: Belknap Press of Harvard University Press.

Rosenzweig, M.L. (1977a). Coexistence and diversity in heteromyid rodents. In *Evolutionary Ecology*, ed. B. Stonehouse and C. Perrins, pp. 89–99. London: Macmillan.

Rosenzweig, M.L. (1977b). Aspects of biological exploitation. *Quarterly Review of Biology* **52**: 371–80.

Rosenzweig, M.L. (1978a). Competitive speciation. *Biological Journal of the Linnean Society* **10**: 275–89.

Rosenzweig, M.L. (1978b). Geographical speciation: on range size and the probability of isolate formation. In *Proceedings of the Washington State University Conference on Biomathematics and Biostatistics*, ed. D. Wollkind, pp. 172–94. Pullman, Wash: Washington State University.

Rosenzweig, M.L. (1979). Optimal habitat selection in two–species competitive systems. In *Population Ecology, Fortschr. Zool.* **25**. ed. U. Halbach and J. Jacobs, pp. 283–93. Stuttgart: Gustav Fischer.

Rosenzweig, M.L. (1981). A theory of habitat selection. *Ecology* **62**: 327–35.

Rosenzweig, M.L. (1986). Hummingbird isolegs in an experimental system. *Behavioral Ecology and Sociobiology* **19**: 313–22.

Rosenzweig, M.L. (1987a). Community organization from the point of view of habitat selectors. In *Organization of Communities Past and Present*, ed. J.H.R. Gee and P.S. Giller, pp. 469–90. Oxford: Blackwell Scientific.

Rosenzweig, M.L. (1987b). Habitat selection as a source of biological diversity. *Evolutionary Ecology* **1**: 315–30.

Rosenzweig, M.L. (1989). Habitat selection, community organization, and small mammal studies. In *Patterns in the Structure of Mammalian Communities*, ed. D.W. Morris, B.J. Fox and Z. Abramsky, pp. 5–21. Lubbock, Tex: Texas Technical University Press.

Rosenzweig, M.L. (1991a). Habitat selection and population interactions: the search for mechanism. *American Naturalist* **137**: S5–S6.

Rosenzweig, M.L. (1991b). Ecological uniqueness and loss of species; Commentary. In *The Preservation and Valuation of Biological Resources*. ed. G. Orians, G.M. Brown Jr, W.E. Kunin and J.E. Swierzbinski, pp. 188–98. Seattle: University of Washington Press.

Rosenzweig, M.L. (1992). Species diversity gradients: we know more and less than we thought. *Journal of Mammalogy* **73**: 715–30.

Rosenzweig, M.L. and Abramsky, Z. (1985). Detecting density–dependent habitat selection. *American Naturalist* **126**: 405–17.

Rosenzweig, M.L. and Abramsky, Z. (1986). Centrifugal community organization. *Oikos* **47**: 339–48.

Rosenzweig, M.L. and Abramsky, Z. (1993). How are diversity and productivity related? In *Species Diversity in Ecological Communities: historical and geographical perspectives*, ed. R. Ricklefs and D. Schluter, pp. 52–65. Chicago: University of Chicago Press.

Rosenzweig, M.L., Abramsky, Z. and Brand, S. (1984). Estimating species interactions in heterogeneous environments. *Oikos* **43**: 329–40.

Rosenzweig, M.L., Brown, J.S. and Vincent, T.L. (1987). Red queens and ESS: the coevolution of evolutionary rates. *Evolutionary Ecology* **1**: 59–94.

Rosenzweig, M.L. and Clark, C.W. (1994). Island extinction rates from regular censuses. *Conservation Biology* **8**: 491–4.

Rosenzweig, M.L. and Duek, J.L. (1979). Species diversity and turnover in an Ordovician marine invertebrate assemblage. In *Contemporary Quantitative Ecology and Related Ecometrics*, ed. G.P. Patil and M.L. Rosenzweig, pp. 109–19. Fairland, Md: International Co-operative Publishing House.

Rosenzweig, M.L. and MacArthur, R.H. (1963). Graphical representation and stability conditions of predator–prey interactions. *American Naturalist* **97**: 209–23.

Rosenzweig, M.L. and McCord, R.D. (1991). Incumbent replacement: evidence for long-term evolutionary progress. *Paleobiology* **17**: 23–7.

Rosenzweig, M.L. and Schaffer, W.M. (1978). Homage to the Red Queen II: Coevolutionary response to enrichment of exploitation ecosystems. *Theoretical Population Biology* **9**: 158–63.

Rosenzweig, M.L. and Taylor, J.A. (1980). Speciation and diversity in Ordovician invertebrates: filling niches quickly and carefully. *Oikos* **35**: 236–43.

Rosenzweig, M.L. and Vetault, S. (1992). Calculating speciation and extinction rates in fossil clades. *Evolutionary Ecology* **6**: 90–3.

Rosenzweig, M.L. and Winakur, J. (1969). Population ecology of desert rodent communities: habitats and environmental complexity. *Ecology* **50**: 558–72.

Rydin, H. and Borgegård, S.O. (1988). Plant species richness on islands over a century of primary succession: Lake Hjälmaren. *Ecology* **69**: 916–27.

Saenger, P., Moverley, J. and Stephenson, W. (1988). Seasonal and longer term patterns in the macrobenthos versus benthic stability in a subtropical estuary. In *The Ecology of Australia's Wet Tropics; Proceedings of a symposium held at the University of Queensland, Brisbane August 25–27, 1986; Proceedings of the Ecological Society of Australia, Vol. 15*, ed. R.L. Kitching, pp. 229–37. Chipping Norton, NSW: Surrey Beatty & Sons.

Salzman, A.G. (1985). Habitat selection in a clonal plant. *Science* **228**: 603–4.

Sanders, H.L. (1968). Benthic marine diversity: a comparative study. *American Naturalist* **102**: 243–82.

Savidge, J.A. (1987). Extinction of an island forest avifauna by an introduced snake. *Ecology* **68**: 660–8.

Sawyer, C.N. (1966). Basic concepts of eutrophication. *Journal of Water Pollution Federation* **38**: 737–44.

Schaffer, W.M. (1974). Optimal reproductive effort in fluctuating environments. *American Naturalist* **108**: 783–90.

Schaffer, W.M. (1985). Order and chaos in ecological systems. *Ecology* **66**: 93–106.

Schaffer, W.M., Jensen, D.B., Hobbs, D.E., Gurevitch, J., Todd, J.R. and Schaffer, M.V. (1979). Competition, foraging energetics and the cost of sociality in three species of bees. *Ecology* **60**: 976–87.

Schaffer, W.M. and Rosenzweig, M.L. (1978). Homage to the Red Queen I. Coevolution of predators and their victims. *Theoretical Population Biology* **9**: 135–57.

Scharloo, W. (1971). Reproductive isolation by disruptive selection: Did it occur? *American Naturalist* **105**: 83–6.

Scheiner, S.M. and Rey-Benayas, J.M. (1994). Global patterns of plant diversity. *Evolutionary Ecology* 8:331–47.

Schindler, D.W. (1990). Experimental perturbations of whole lakes as tests of hypotheses concerning ecosystem structure and function. *Oikos* **57**: 25–41.

Schluter, D. and Ricklefs, R.E. (1993). Convergence and the regional component of species diversity. In *Species Diversity in Ecological Communities: historical and geographical perspectives*, ed. R. Ricklefs and D. Schluter, pp. 230–40. Chicago: University of Chicago Press.

Schoener, A. and Schoener, T.W. (1981). The dynamics of the species–area relation in marine fouling systems: 1. Biological correlates of changes in the species–area slope. *American Naturalist* **118**: 339–60.

Schoener, T.W. (1976). The species–area relation within archipelagoes: models and evidence from island land birds. *Proceedings of the XVI International Ornithological Congress*: 629–42.

Schoener, T.W. (1983). Field experiments on interspecific competition. *American Naturalist* **122**: 240–85.

Schoener, T.W. (1986). Patterns in terrestrial vertebrate versus arthropod communities: do systematic differences in regularity exist? In *Community Ecology*, ed. J. Diamond and T.J. Case, pp. 556–86. New York: Harper & Row.

Schoener, T.W. (1989). Food webs from the small to the large. *Ecology* **70**: 1559–89.

Schoener, T.W. and Spiller, D.A. (1987). High population persistence in a system with high turnover. *Nature* **330**: 474–7.

Schoener, T.W. and Spiller, D.A. (1992). Is extinction rate related to temporal variability in population size? An empirical answer for orb spiders. *American Naturalist* **139**: 1176–1207.

Schoenly, K., Beaver, R.A. and Heumier, T.A. (1991). On the trophic relations of insects: a food–web approach. *American Naturalist* **137**: 597–638.

Schopf, T.J.M. (1970). Taxonomic diversity gradients of ectoprocts and bivalves and their geologic implications. *Geological Society of America Bulletin* **81**: 3765–8.

Schopf, T.J.M. (1979). The role of biogeographic provinces in regulating marine-faunal diversity through geologic time. In *Historical Biogeography, Plate Tectonics, and the Changing Environment*, ed. J. Gray and A.J. Boucot, pp. 449–57. Corvallis: Oregon State University Press.

Schorger, A.W. (1955). *The Passenger Pigeon: its natural history and extinction,* Madison: University of Wisconsin.

Schroder, G. and **Rosenzweig, M.L.** (1975). Perturbation analysis of competition and overlap in habitat utilization between *Dipodomys ordii* and *Dipodomys merriami. Oecologia* **19**: 9–28.

Sepkoski, J.J. Jr (1978). A kinetic model of Phanerozoic taxonomic diversity I. Analysis of marine orders. *Paleobiology* **4**: 223–51.

Sepkoski, J.J. Jr (1984). A kinetic model of Phanerozoic taxonomic diversity. III. Post–Paleozoic families and mass extinctions. *Paleobiology* **10**: 246–67.

Sepkoski, J.J. Jr (1989). Periodicity in extinction and the problem of catastrophism in the history of life. *Journal of Geological Society of London* **146**: 7–19.

Shaffer, M.L. (1981). Minimum population sizes for species conservation. *BioScience* **31**: 131–4.

Shaffer, M. (1987). Minimum viable populations: coping with uncertainty. In *Viable Populations for Conservation,* ed. M.E. Soulé, pp. 69–86. Cambridge: Cambridge University Press.

Shapiro, A.M. (1993). Haldane, Marxism, and the conduct of research. *Quarterly Review of Biology* **68**: 69–77.

Shelly, T.E. (1984). Comparative foraging behavior of Neotropical robber flies (Diptera: Asilidae). *Oecologia* **62**: 188–95.

Shmida, A. (1984). Whittaker's plant diversity sampling method. *Israel Journal of Botany* **33**: 41–6.

Shmida, A. and **Ellner, S.** (1984). Coexistence of plant species with similar niches. *Vegetatio* **58**: 29–55.

Shmida, A. and **Whittaker, R.H.** (1981). Pattern and biological microsite effects in two shrub communities, southern California. *Ecology* **62**: 234–51.

Shmida, A. and **Wilson, M.V.** (1985). Biological determinants of species diversity. *Journal of Biogeography* **12**: 1–20.

Silvertown, J. (1980). The dynamics of a grassland ecosystem: Botanical equilibrium in the park grass experiment. *Journal of Applied Ecology* **17**: 491–504.

Simberloff, D.S. (1974). Permo–Triassic extinctions: effects of area on biotic equilibrium. *Journal of Geology* **82**: 267–74.

Simberloff, D.S. (1976a). Species turnover and equilibrium island biogeography. *Science* **194**: 572–8.

Simberloff, D.S. (1976b). Experimental zoogeography of islands: effects of island size. *Ecology* **57**: 629–48.

Simberloff, D.S. and **Wilson, E.O.** (1969). Experimental zoogoegraphy of islands. Defaunation and monitoring techniques. *Ecology* **50**: 267–78.

Simon, C. (1987). Hawaiian evolutionary biology: an introduction. *Trends in Ecology and Evolution* **2**: 175–8.

Simpson, E.H. (1949). Measurement of diversity. *Nature* **163**: 688.

Simpson, G.G. (1950). History of the fauna of Latin America. *American Scientist* **38**: 361–89.

Simpson, G.G. (1953). *The Major Features of Evolution,* New York: Columbia University Press.

Simpson, G.G. (1964). Species density of North American recent mammals. *Systematic Zoology* **13**: 57–73.

Slade, A.J. and **Hutchings, M.J.** (1987). Clonal integration and plasticity in foraging behaviour in *Glechoma hederacea*. *Journal of Ecology* **75**: 1023–36.

Slatkin, M. (1970). Selection and polygenic characters. *Proceedings of the National Academy of Sciences USA* **66**: 87–93.

Slobodkin, L.B. (1965). On the present incompleteness of mathematical ecology. *American Scientist* **53**: 347–57.

Slobodkin, L.B. and **Rapoport, A.** (1974). An optimal strategy of evolution. *Quarterly Review of Biology* **49**: 181–200.

Smith, G.R. (1987). Fish speciation in a western North American Pliocene rift lake. *Palaios* **2**: 436–45.

Solem, A. (1984). A world model of land snail diversity and abundance. In *World-Wide Snails*, ed. A. Solem and A.C. Van Bruggen, pp. 6–22. Leiden: E.J. Brill/Dr. W. Backhuys.

Soriano, A. (1953). Estudios sobre germinación, I. *Rev. Investig. Agricult.* **7**: 315–40.

Somero, G.N. (1978). Temperature adaptation of enzymes: biological optimization through structure–function compromises. *Annual Review of Ecology and Systematics* **9**: 1–29.

Soulé, M.E. (1980). Thresholds for survival: maintaining fitness and evolutionary potential. In *Conservation Biology: an evolutionary–ecological perspective*, ed, M.E. Soulé and B.A. Wilcox, pp. 151–70. Sunderland, Mass: Sinauer Associates.

Sousa, W.P. (1979). Disturbance in marine intertidal boulder fields: the nonequilibrium maintenance of species diversity. *Ecology* **60**: 1225–39.

Southwood, T.R.E. (1961). The number of species of insect associated with various trees. *Journal of Animal Ecology* **30**: 1–8.

Specht, R.L. (1981). Ecophysiological principles determining the biogeography of major vegetation formations in Australia. In *Ecological Biogeography of Australia, Vol. 1*, ed. A. Keast, pp. 301–33. The Hague: Junk.

Specht, R.L. (1988). Origin and evolution of terrestrial plant communities in the wet–dry tropics of Australia. In *The Ecology of Australia's Wet Tropics*, ed. R.L. Kitching. *Proceedings of the Ecological Society of Australia* **15**: 19–30.

Spira, T.P. and **Wagner, L.K.** (1983). Viability of seeds up to 211 years old extracted from adobe brick buildings of California and northern Mexico. *American Journal of Botany* **70**: 303–7.

Sprules, W.G. and **Bowerman, J.E.** (1988). Omnivory and food chain length in zooplankton food webs. *Ecology* **69**: 418–26.

Stanley, S.M. (1975). A theory of evolution above the species level. *Proceedings of the National Academy of Sciences USA* **72**: 646–50.

Stanley, S.M. (1979). *Macroevolution*. San Francisco: W. H. Freeman.

Stanley, S.M. and **Newman, W.A.** (1980). Competitive exclusion in evolutionary time: the case of the acorn barnacles. *Paleobiology* **6**: 173–83.

Stanton, N.L. (1979). Patterns of species diversity in temperate and tropical litter mites. *Ecology* **60**: 295–304.

Steadman, D.W. (1993). Biogeography of Tongan birds before and after human impact. *Proceedings of the National Academy of Sciences USA* **90**: 818–22.

Steadman, D.W. and **Zarrielo, M.C.** (1987). Two new species of parrots (Aves: Psittacidae) from archeological sites in the Marquesas Islands. *Proceedings of the Biological Society of Washington* **100**: 518–28.

Stebbins, L. (1950). *Variation and Evolution in Plants*, New York: Columbia University Press.

Stehli, F.G., Douglas, R.G. and **Newell, N.D.** (1969). Generation and maintenance of gradients in taxonomic diversity. *Science* **164**: 947–9.

Stevens, G.C. (1989). The latitudinal gradient in geographical range: how so many species coexist in the tropics. *American Naturalist* **133**: 240–56.

Stone, E.C. and **Juhren, G.** (1951). The effect of fire on the germination of *Rhus ovata* Wats. *American Journal of Botany* **38**: 368–72.

Storer, R.W. (1966). Sexual dimorphism and food habits in three North American accipiters. *Auk* **83**: 423–36.

Stork, N.E. (1988). Insect diversity: facts, fiction and speculation. *Biological Journal of the Linnean Society* **35**: 321–37.

Strong, D.R. (1974). The insects of British trees: community equilibration in ecological time. *Annals of the Missouri Botanical Garden* **61**: 692–701.

Sugihara, G. (1980). Minimal community structure: an explanation of species abundance patterns. *American Naturalist* **116**: 770–87.

Summerhayes, V.S. (1941). The effect of voles (*Microtus agrestis*) on vegetation. *Journal of Ecology* **29**: 14–48.

Sutherland, W.J. and **Stillman, R.A.** (1988). The foraging tactics of plants. *Oikos* **52**: 239–44.

Swingle, H.S. (1946). Experiments with combinations of largemouth black bass, bluegills and minnows in ponds. *Transactions of the American Fisheries Society* **76**: 46–62.

Tappan, H. (1968). Primary production: isotopes, extinctions and the atmosphere. *Palaeogeography, Palaeoclimatology, Palaeoecology.* **4**: 187–210.

Tappan, H. and **Loeblich, A.R.** (1973). Evolution of the oceanic plankton. *Earth Science Rev.* **9**: 207–40.

Tauber, C.A. and **Tauber, M.J.** (1977). Sympatric speciation based on allelic changes at three loci: evidence from natural populations in two habitats. *Science* **197**: 1298–9.

Tauber, C.A. and **Tauber, M.J.** (1987). Food specificity in predaceous insects: a comparative ecophysiological and genetic study. *Evolutionary Ecology* **1**: 175–86.

Taylor, L.R., Kempton, R.A. and **Woiwod, I.P.** (1976). Diversity statistics and the log–series model. *Journal of Animal Ecology* **45**: 255–72.

Terborgh, J. (1973). On the notion of favorableness in plant ecology. *American Naturalist* **107**: 481–501.

Terborgh, J. (1977). Bird species diversity on an Andean elevational gradient. *Ecology* **58**: 1007–19.

Terborgh, J., Robinson, S.K., Parker III, T.A., Munn, C.A. and **Pierpont, N.** (1990).

Structure and organization of an an Amazonian forest bird community. *Ecological Monographs* **60**: 213–38.

Thoday, J.M. (1972). Disruptive selection. *Proceedings of the Royal Society London, Series B* **182**: 109–43.

Thoday, J.M. and Gibson, J.B. (1962). Isolation by disruptive selection. *Nature* **193**: 1164–6.

Thomas, W.W. and de Carvalho, A.M. (1993). Estudo fitossociologico de Serra Grande, Uruçuca, Bahia, Brasil. *XLIV Congresso Nacional de Botânica, São Luis, 24–30 de Janeiro de 1993, Resumos* **1**: 224. Sociedade Botânica do Brasil, Universidade Federal de Maranhão.

Tilman, D. (1982). *Resource Competition and Community Structure*, Princeton, NJ: Princeton University Press.

Tilman, D. (1987). Secondary succession and the pattern of plant dominance along experimental nitrogen gradients. *Ecological Monographs* **57**: 189–214.

Tilman, D. (1988). *Plant strategies and the Dynamics and Structure of Plant Communities*. Princeton, NJ: Princeton University.

Tilman, D. and Pacala, S. (1993). The maintenance of species richness in plant communities. In *Species Diversity in Ecological Communities: historical and geographical perspectives*, ed. R. Ricklefs and D. Schluter, pp. 13–25. Chicago: University of Chicago Press.

Toft, C.A. and Schoener, T.W. (1983). Abundance and diversity of orb spiders at 106 Bahamian islands: biogeography at an intermediate trophic level. *Oikos* **41**: 411–26.

Tolkamp, C.R. (1993). Filter-feeding efficiencies of dabbling ducks (*Anas* spp.) in relation to microhabitat use and lamellar spacing. MSc. thesis, Ontario: University of Guelph.

Tonn, W.M. and Magnuson, J.J. (1982). Patterns in the species composition and richness of fish assemblages in northern Wisconsin lakes. *Ecology* **63**: 1149–60.

Tracy, C.R. and George, T.L. (1992). On the determinants of extinction. *American Naturalist* **139**: 102–22.

Tryon, R. (1989). Pteridophytes. In *Ecosystems of the World, Vol. 14B. Tropical Rain Forest Ecosystems: biogeographical and ecological studies*, ed. H. Lieth and M.J.A. Werger, pp. 327–338. Amsterdam: Elsevier Scientific.

Turner, J.R.G., Gatehouse, C.M. and Corey, C.A. (1987). Does solar energy control organic diversity? Butterflies, moths and the British climate. *Oikos* **48**: 195–205.

Turner, J.R.G., Lennon, J.L. and Lawrenson, J.A. (1988). British bird species distributions and the energy theory. *Nature* **335**: 539–41.

Ugland, K.I. and Gray, J.S. (1982). Lognormal distributions and the concept of community equilibrium. *Oikos* **39**: 171–178.

Usher, M.B. (1979). Changes in the species–area relation of higher plants on nature reserves. *Journal of Applied Ecology* **16**: 213–5.

Utida, S. (1957). Population fluctuation, an experimental and theoretical approach. *Cold Spring Harbor Symposia on Quantitative Biology* **22**: 139–51.

Valentine, J.W. (1971). Plate tectonics and shallow marine diversity and endemism, an actualistic model. *Systematic Zoology* **20**: 253–64.

Valentine, J.W. (1973). *Evolutionary Paleoecology of the Marine Biosphere*, Englewood Cliffs, NJ: Prentice–Hall.

Valentine, J.W. (1976). Genetic strategies of adaptation. In *Molecular Evolution*. ed. F.J. Ayala, pp. 78–94. Sunderland, Mass: Sinauer Associates.

Valentine, J.W., Foin, T.C. and Peart, D. (1978). A provincial model of Phanerozoic marine diversity. *Paleobiology* **4**: 55–66.

Valentine, J.W. and Jablonski, D. (1991). Biotic effects of sea level change: the Pleistocene test. *Journal of Geophysical Research* **96**: 6873–8.

Valentine, J.W., Tiffney, B.H. and Sepkoski, Jr J.J. (1991). Evolutionary dynamics of plants and animals: a comparative approach. *Palaios* **6**: 81–8.

Van Valen, L. (1973). Body size and numbers of plants and animals. *Evolution* **27**: 27–35.

Van Valen, L. (1984). A resetting of Phanerozoic evolution. *Nature* **307**: 50–2.

Van Valen, L. (1985a). How constant is extinction? *Evolutionary Theory* **7**: 93–106.

Van Valen, L. (1985b). A theory of origination and extinction. *Evolutionary Theory* **7**: 133–42.

Van Valkenburgh, B. and Janis, C.M. (1993). Historical diversity patterns in North American large herbivores and carnivores. In *Species Diversity in Ecological Communities: historical and geographical perspectives*, ed. R. Ricklefs and D. Schluter, pp. 330–40. Chicago: University of Chicago Press.

Vartanyan, S.L., Garutt, V.E. and Sher, A.V. (1993). Holocene dwarf mammoths from Wrangel Island in the Siberian Arctic. *Nature* **362**: 337–40.

Vaughan, R.E. and Wiehe, P.O. (1941). Studies in the vegetation of Mauritius. III. *Journal of Ecology* **29**: 127–60.

Venable, D.L. (1989). Modeling the evolutionary ecology of seed banks. In *Ecology of Soil Seed Banks*, ed. M.A. Leck, V.T. Parker and R.C. Simpson, pp. 67–87. San Diego, Calif: Academic Press.

Vermeij, G.J. (1973a). Biological versatility and earth history. *Proceedings of the National Academy of Sciences USA* **70**: 1936–8.

Vermeij, G.J. (1973b). Adaptation, versatility and evolution. *Systematic Zoology* **22**: 466–77.

Vorontsov, N.N. and Lyapunova, E.A. (1984). Explosive chromosomal speciation in seismic active regions. *Chromosomes Today* **8**: 279–94.

Vrba, E.S. (1987). Ecology in relation to speciation rates: some case histories of Miocene–Recent mammal clades. *Evolutionary Ecology* **1**: 283–300.

Vuilleumier, F. (1970). Insular biogeography in continental regions. I. The northern Andes of South America. *American Naturalist* **104**: 373–88.

Vuilleumier, F. (1972). Bird species diversity in Patagonia (temperate South America). *American Naturalist* **106**: 266–71.

Vuilleumier, F. (1973). Insular biogeography in continental regions. II. Cave faunas from Tessin, southern Switzerland. *Systematic Zoology* **22**: 64–76.

Vuilleumier, F. and Simberloff, D. (1980). Ecology versus history as determinants of patchy and insular distributions in high Andean birds. *Evolutionary Biology* **12**: 235–379.

Wace, N.M. (1961). The vegetation of Gough Island. *Ecological Monographs* **31**: 337–67.

Walsh, J.B. (1995). How often do duplicated genes evolve new functions? *Genetics* (in press).

Watkins, R. (1979). Benthic community organization in the Ludlow Series of the Welsh Borderland. *Bulletin of the British Museum (Natural History) Geology* **31**: 175–280.

Watkins, R. and **Boucot, A.J.** (1978). Temporal pattern of species diversity among some Silurodevonian brachiopods. In *Evolutionary Biology*, 11, ed. M.K. Hecht, W.C. Steere and B. Wallace, pp. 636–47. New York: Plenum Press.

Watkinson, A.R. (1988). On the growth and reproductive schedules of plants: a modular viewpoint. *Acta Oecologica/Oecologia Plantarum* **9**: 67–81.

Watson, G.E. (1964). Ecology and evolution of passerine birds on the islands of the Aegean Sea. Ph.D. dissertation, Yale University (Diss. microfilm 65–1956).

Webb, S.D. (1969). Extinction–origination equilibria in late Cenozoic land mammals of North America. *Evolution* **23**: 688–702.

Webb, S.D. (1984). On two kinds of rapid faunal turnover. In *Catastrophes and Earth History: the new uniformitarianism*, ed. W.A. Berggren and J.A. Van Couvering, pp. 417–36. Princeton, NJ: Princeton University Press.

Weider, L.J. and **Hebert, P.D.N.** (1987). Ecological and physiological differentiation among low-arctic clones of *Daphnia pulex*. *Ecology* **68**: 188–98.

Went, F.W. (1953). The effects of rain and temperature on plant distribution in the desert. In *Desert Research Proceedings, Special Publication No. 2*, ed. M. Balaban, pp. 230–7. Jerusalem: Research Council of Israel.

Went, F.W. (1957). Experimental control of plant growth: with special reference to the Earhart Plant Research Laboratory at the California Institute of Technology. *Chronica Botanica*, Vol. 17. Waltham, Mass: Chronica Botanica Co.

Werdelin, L. (1987). Jaw geometry and molar morphology in marsupial carnivores: analysis of a constraint and its macroevolutionary consequences. *Paleobiology* **13**: 342–50.

Werner, E.E. and **Hall, D.J.** (1979). Foraging efficiency and habitat switching in competing sunfishes. *Ecology* **60**: 256–64.

Western, D. (1991). Climatic change and biodiversity. In *A Change in the Weather: African perspectives on climatic change*, ed. S.H. Ominde and C.Juma, pp. 87–96. Nairobi: African Centre for Technology Studies Press.

Westman, W.E. (1983). Island biogeography: studies on the xeric shrublands of the inner Channel Islands, California. *Journal of Biogeography* **8**: 421–25.

White, M.J.D. (1978). *Modes of Speciation*, San Francisco: W.H. Freeman.

Whiteside, M.C. and **Harmsworth, R.V.** (1967). Species diversity in chydorid (Cladocera) communities. *Ecology* **48**: 664–7.

Whitford, W.G., Dick–Peddie, S., Walters, D. and **Ludwig, J.** (1978). Effects of shrub defoliation on grass cover and rodent species in a Chihuahuan desert ecosystem. *Journal of Arid Environments* **1**: 237–42.

Whitham,T.G., Morrow, P.A. and **Potts, B.M.** (1994). Plant hybrid zones as centers of biodiversity: the herbivore community of two endemic Tasmanian eucalypts. *Oecologia* (in press).

Whitmore, T.C. (1990). *An Introduction to Tropical Rain Forests*, Oxford: Clarendon Press.

Whittaker, R.H. (1970). *Communities and Ecosystems*, London: Macmillan.

Whittaker, R.H. (1972). Evolution and measurement of species diversity. *Taxon* **21**: 213–51.

Wilcox, B.A. (1978). Supersaturated island faunas: A species–age relationship for lizards on post–pleistocene land–bridge islands. *Science* **199**: 996–8.

Wilcox, B.A. (1980). Insular ecology and conservation. In *Conservation Biology*, ed, M.E. Soulé and B.A. Wilcox, pp. 95–117. Sunderland, Mass: Sinauer Associates.

Williams, A.B. (1936). The composition and dynamics of a beech–maple climax community. *Ecological Monographs* **6**: 318–408.

Williams, C.B. (1943). Area and the number of species. *Nature* **152**: 264–7.

Williams, C.B. (1964). *Patterns in the Balance of Nature.* London: Academic Press.

Williamson, M.H. (1981). *Island Populations.* Oxford: Oxford University Press.

Williamson, M.H. (1983). The land-bird community of Skokholm: ordination and turnovers. *Oikos* **41**: 378–84.

Williamson, M.H. and **Lawton, J.H.** (1991). Fractal geometry of ecological habitats. In *Habitat Structure; The physical arrangement of objects in space*, ed. S.S. Bell, E.D. McCoy and H.R. Mushinsky, pp. 69–86. London: Chapman and Hall.

Willis, E.O. and **Oniki, Y.** (1978). Birds and army ants. *Annual Review of Ecology and Systematics* **9**: 243–63.

Wilson, C.C. and **Hebert, P.D.N.** (1992). The maintenance of taxon diversity in an asexual assemblage: an experimental analysis. *Ecology* **73**: 1462–72.

Wilson, C.C. and **Hebert, P.D.N.** (1993). Impact of copepod predation on distribution patterns of *Daphnia pulex* clones. *Limnology and Oceanography* **38**: 1304–10.

Wilson, E.O. (1961). The nature of the taxon cycle in the Melanesian ant fauna. *American Naturalist* **95**: 169–93.

Wilson, J.W. III. (1972). Analytical Zoogeography of North American Mammals. Ph.D dissertation, University of Chicago.

Wilson, J.W. III. (1974). Analytical zoogeography of North American mammals. *Evolution* **28**: 124–40.

Winterbourn, M.J. (1987). The arthropod fauna of bracken (*Pteridium aquilinum*) on the Port Hills, South Island, New Zealand. *New Zealand Entomologist* **10**: 99–104.

Wolda, H. (1980). Seasonality of tropical insects. I. Leafhoppers (Homoptera) in Las Cumbres, Panama. *Journal of Animal Ecology* **49**: 277–90.

Wolda, H. (1982). Seasonality of Homoptera on Barro Colorado Island. In *The Ecology of a Tropical Forest: seasonal rhythms and long-term changes*, ed. E.G. Leigh, Jr, A.S. Rand and D.M. Windsor, pp. 319–30. Washington, DC: Smithsonian Institutional Press.

Wollkind, D.J. (1976). Exploitation in three trophic levels: an extension allowing intraspecies carnivore interaction. *American Naturalist* **110**: 431–47.

Wright, D.H. (1983). Species–energy theory: an extension of species–area theory. *Oikos* **41**: 496–506.

Wright, D.H., Currie, D.J. and **Maurer, B.A.** (1993). Energy supply and patterns of species richness on local and regional scales. In *Species Diversity in Ecological Communities: historical and geographical perspectives*, ed. R. Ricklefs and D. Schluter, pp. 66–74. Chicago: University of Chicago Press.

Wright, S. (1931). Evolution in Mendelian populations. *Genetics* **16**: 97–159.

Wright, S.J. (1981). Intra-archipelago vertebrate distributions: the slope of the species–area relation. *American Naturalist* **118**: 726–48.

Wright, S.J. (1985). How isolation affects rates of turnover of species on islands. *Oikos* **44**: 331–40.

Wu, R.S.S. (1982). Periodic defaunation and recovery in a subtropical epibenthic community, in relation to organic pollution. *Journal of Experimental Marine Biology and Ecology* **64**: 253–69.

Wunderle, J.M. Jr (1985). An ecological comparison of the avifaunas of Grenada and Tobago, West Indies. *Wilson Bulletin* **97**: 356–65.

Yodzis, P. (1984). Energy flow and the vertical structure of real ecosystems. *Oecologia* **65**: 86–8.

Yodzis, P. (1989). *Introduction to Theoretical Ecology*. New York: Harper and Row.

Yodzis, P. (1993). Environment and trophodiversity. In *Species Diversity in Ecological Communities: historical and geographical perspectives*, ed. R. Ricklefs and D. Schluter, pp. 26–38. Chicago: University of Chicago Press.

Yount, J.L. (1956). Factors that control species numbers in Silver Springs, Florida. *Limnology and Oceanography* **1**: 286–95.

Yule, G.U. (1944). *The Statistical Study of Literary Vocabulary*. Cambridge: Cambridge University Press.

Ziegler, A.M. (1965). Silurian marine communities and their environmental significance. *Nature* **207**: 270–2.

Zohary, M. (1962). *Plant Life in Palestine*, New York: Ronald Press.

Zon, R. (1904). Chestnut in southern Maryland. *Forest Service Bulletin* No. 53. Washington, DC: US Department of Agriculture.

Index

Artamus, white-breasted woodswallow, 185
Artemisia monosperma, 172
artifacts
    habitat diversity, 307–10
    sampling, 191
Asilidae, robberflies, 155
Atlantic Ocean
    biomes, 288
    megafaunas, 348
    molluscs, 292
    ostracodes, 58
Atriplex, 97–8, 154–5
Audubon, J.J.
    on passenger pigeon, 122–3
    on writing, *quoted, ii*
Australia
    Broken Hill, NSW, species–area curves, 33
    equal-area samples, 291
    Green Island, 245
    heathlands, nutrient enrichment, 347
    islands
        birds, 184, 356
        plants, 245, 250–2
        species–area curves, 15
    Lake Eyre, brine shrimps, 174
    mammals, 204–6
    Norfolk Island flora, 278
    Queensland, rainforest understory plants, 155
    South-Western Botanical Province kwongan,
        29, 176, 187
    Tasmania, eucalypts, 47–8
    tropical aquatic species, seasonality, 71–2
    turtles, 192
    Western Australia
        birds, 184
        islands, plant extinctions and immigration,
            250–2
        kwongan, 29
        wheatbelt, 204–9, 347
Azores
    birds, 234
    ferns, 235–6

Bahamas
    birds, 235
    energy–area hypothesis, 331–2
    orb-web spiders, 129
    snails, 217
    spider predation, 233
Balanus balanoides, barnacle, 152
bamboo
    Pharus latifolius, 153–4
    Streptochaeta sodiroana, 153–4
Banksia hookeriana, 187
barnacle
    Balanus balanoides, 152
    Chthamalus stellatus, 152
    disturbance experiment, 37–8
barriers, *see* geographical speciation
Barro Colorado Island, Panama, ants, 119–20

bats
    North America, 293
    North and Central America, 26
    species–area curves and z-values, 264–5
bees, Santa Catalina mountains, 360
beetles, 89
    Bornean tropics, 74
    Lake Mälaren, 226
    St Helena, 215
    total numbers, 1–3
benthos, *see* marine benthos
beta diversity, 33
biogeographical provinces, 191–2
biological province, defined, 212, 264
biomass, and productivity, 44–5
biotas, types, *see* patterns
biotic revolutions, 110
birch forest, Finland, 326
birds
    chaparral, compared, 16
    Darwin's finches, 89
    habitat and species diversity, 2, 35
    hummingbirds, 235, 361
    islands
        extinction rates, 139–40
        off Panama, 255–7
        see also named islands and archipelagos
    of:
        Äland, Finland, 218–24
        Azores and Madeiras, 234–5
        Bahamas, 235
        Britain, 69, 139, 294
        Guam, 231–2
        Hawaii, 230
        lowland tropics, 369
        Neotropics, species–area curves, 13, 14
        New Guinea, 185
        Ohio, 64, 69, 71
        Pacific archipelagos, 240–1
        Panama, 180–1
        Patagonia, 182–3
        Pennsylvania, species–area curve, 23
        Peru, 32
        Sweden, 193–5
        tropical rainforests, 356
        West Indies, 15
    Páramo, species–area curve, 20
    passenger pigeon, 122–3, 125–6
    seasonality, 69–72
blue palo verde, *Cercidium*, 172, 173–4
body size, 73–7
    and optimal foraging, 302
    trade-off principle, 155
Boiga irregularis, brown snake of Guam, 231–3
Bolitoglossa, salamander, 313
Borneo
    beetles, 74
    species diversity, 2–3
brachiopods
    Paleozoic, 59